Communications in Computer and Information Science   1576

More information about this series at https://link.springer.com/bookseries/7899

KC Santosh · Ravindra Hegadi ·
Umapada Pal (Eds.)

Recent Trends in Image Processing and Pattern Recognition

4th International Conference, RTIP2R 2021
Msida, Malta, December 8–10, 2021
Revised Selected Papers

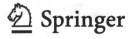

Editors
KC Santosh (iD)
University of South Dakota
Vermillion, SD, USA

Ravindra Hegadi
Central University of Karnataka
Gulbarga, India

Umapada Pal (iD)
Indian Statistical Institute
Kolkata, India

ISSN 1865-0929   ISSN 1865-0937 (electronic)
Communications in Computer and Information Science
ISBN 978-3-031-07004-4   ISBN 978-3-031-07005-1 (eBook)
https://doi.org/10.1007/978-3-031-07005-1

This Springer imprint is published by the registered company Springer Nature Switzerland AG
The registered company address is: Gewerbestrasse 11, 6330 Cham, Switzerland

Preface

It is our great pleasure to introduce this collection of research papers in Springer's Communication in Computer and Information Science (CCIS) series from the fourth International Conference on Recent Trends in Image Processing and Pattern Recognition (RTIP2R 2021). Initially we aimed to hold RTIP2R 2021 in-person at the University of Malta, Malta, during December 8–10, 2021, in collaboration with the 2AI: Applied Artificial Intelligence Research Lab, University of South Dakota (USA), and the Central University of Karnataka (India). Due to the unprecedented impact of COVID-19 and related travel restrictions, the RTIP2R 2021 team decided to hold the event virtually, making it possible for authors, scholars, and academicians to present their research studies online, with an average audience size of 40–50 per day.

As announced in the call for papers, RTIP2R 2021 attracted current and/or recent research on image processing, pattern recognition, and computer vision with several different applications, such as document understanding, biometrics, medical imaging, and image analysis in agriculture. Altogether, we received 84 submissions and selected 36 papers for conference presentations. For publication, unlike in the past, the conference chairs decided not include no-show papers as well as those papers that were not revised in accordance with the chairs' reports. Taking this into account, the conference chairs decided to move forward with 33 papers for publication. As a result, the acceptance rate for this volume is 39.29%. On average, each paper selected for conference presentation received at least three reviews with the exception of the few submissions that had desk rejections.

In brief, the event was a great platform bringing together research scientists, academics, and industry practitioners. We categorized the papers into five different tracks: a) Healthcare: medical imaging and informatics; b) Computer vision and pattern recognition; c) Document analysis and recognition; d) Signal processing and machine learning; and e) Satellite imaging and remote sensing.

The conference was full of innovative ideas, and we are grateful to the following keynote speakers for their insightful talks: Sally McClean (Ulster University, UK), Ajith Abraham (Machine Intelligence Research Labs, USA), Neeraj Kumar (Thapar Institute of Engineering & Technology, India), and Girijesh Prasad (Ulster University, UK). We would like to thank everyone who contributed to the success of RTIP2R 2021.

January 2022

KC Santosh
Ravindra Hegadi
Umapada Pal

Organization

Honorary Chairs

Carl James Debono University of Malta, Malta
Sally McClean Ulster University, UK
Oge Marques Florida Atlantic University, USA
Linlin Shen Shenzhen University, China
Umapada Pal Indian Statistical Institute, India

General Chairs

Lalit Garg University of Malta, Malta
KC Santosh University of South Dakota, USA

Program Chairs

Ravindra Hegadi Central University of Karnataka, India
Hubert Cecotti California State University, Fresno, USA
M.-R. Bouguelia Halmstad University, Sweden
Vitoantonio Bevilacqua Polytechnic University of Bari, Italy
Mickael Coustaty La Rochelle University, France
Robertas Damasevicius Kaunas University of Technology, Lithuania
Ram Bilas Pachori IIT, Indore, India
Nilanjan Dey JIS University, India

Workshop Chairs

Hanan Salam New York University Abu Dhabi, UAE
Rajesh Kumar Institute of Forensic Science, India
Nibaran Das Jadavpur University, India

Special Track Chairs

Loveleen Gaur Amity University, India
Fernando Ortiz-Rodriguez Universidad Autonoma de Tamaulipas, Mexico

Publication Chairs

Mufti Mahmud   Nottingham Trent University, UK
Karm Veer Arya   ABV-IIITM, Gwalior, India

Local Chairs

Michel Camilleri   University of Malta, Malta
Peter Xuereb   University of Malta, Malta
Emeka Chukwu   University of Malta, Malta
Sameer Kumar Jasra   University of Malta, Malta

Conference Treasurer

Ravindra Hegadi   Central University of Karnataka, India

Publicity Chairs

Sameer Antani   National Library of Medicine, USA
Valentina Emilia Balas   Aurel Vlaicu University of Arad, Romania
Giancarlo Fortino   Università della Calabria, Italy
Szilard Vajda   Central Washington State University, USA
Justin Smith   Saint Luke's Health System, USA
Sema Candemir   Ohio State University, USA
Shivaramakrishnan Rajaraman   National Library of Medicine, USA
Sanju Tiwari   Universidad Autonoma de Tamaulipas, Mexico
Mamoun Alazab   Charles Darwin University, Australia
Laurent Wendling   Université Paris Cité, France
Xianqing Mao   University of Luxembourg, Luxembourg
Virach Sornlertlamvanich   Musashino University, Japan
Thanaruk Theeramunkong   SIIT, Thammasat University, Thailand
Patrice Boursier   International Medical University, Malaysia
Satish K Singh   IIIT Allahabad, India
Kaushik Roy   West Bengal State University, India
M. A. Jabbar   Vardhaman College of Engineering, India
Geetha A. Kiran   Malnad College of Engineering, India

Technical Program Committee

Haroon Lone   University of South Dakota, USA
Anabik Pal   National Institutes of Health, USA
Saïd Mahmoudi   University of Mons, Belgium
Gaurav Garg   Ulster University, UK

Sunil Aryal	Deakin University, Australia
Alice Othmani	University of Paris Est-Creteil, France
Sandeep Gupta	Università degli Studi di Trento, Italy
Himadri Mukherjee	New York University Abu Dhabi, UAE
Ameni Boumaiza	Hamad Bin Khalifa University, Qatar
Deepak Garg	Bennett University, India
Oubbati Omar Sami	University of Laghouat, Algeria
Nilanjan Dey	JIS University, India
Kaushik Roy	West Bengal State University, India
Mallikarjun Hangarge	Karnatak Arts, Science and Commerce College, Bidar, India
Debnath Bhattacharya	KL University, India
Thippa Reddy Gadekallu	Vellore Institute of Technology, India
Vijay Prakash	Thapar Institute of Engineering & Technology, Patiala, India
Tarun K. Sharma	Shobhit University, India
Robert Splinter	University of North Carolina at Charlotte, USA, and Advanced BioInformatics, Malta
Vedika Gupta	Bharati Vidyapeeth's College of Engineering, India
K. B. Ramesh	RV College of Engineering, India
Ayush Goyal	Texas A & M University Kingsville, Texas
Ghanapriya Singh	NIT, Uttarakhand, India
Hari Prabhat Gupta	IIT BHU, India
Iyyakutti Iyappan	IIT Indore, India
Jose E. Medina Pagola	Universidad de las Ciencias Informaticas, Cuba
Jose Ruiz Shulcloper	Universidad de las Ciencias Informaticas, Cuba
Millie Pant	IIT Roorkee, India
Nandana Mihindukulasooriya	IBM, USA
Onur Dogan	Izmir Bakircay University, Turkey
Piyush Joshi	University of Birmingham, UK
Ravinder M.	IGDTUW, India
Rudresh Dwivedi	Pandit Deendayal Petroleum University, India
Sailesh Iyer	Rai University, India
Sanjeevi Kumar Padmanaban	Aalborg University, Esbjer, Denmark
Shikha Mehta	JIIT Noida, India
Surya Prakash Agnihotri	IIT Indore, India
Shishir Shandilya	VIT Bhopal University, India
Syed Sadaf Ali	IIT Indore, India
Yusniel Hidalgo Delgado	Universidad de las Ciencias Informaticas, Cuba

Contents

Document Analysis and Recognition

Signal Processing and Machine Learning

Satellite Imaging and Remote Sensing

Healthcare: Medical Imaging and Informatics

Cleaning Highly Unbalanced Multisource Image Dataset for Quality Control in Cervical Precancer Screening

Zhiyun Xue[1](✉), Peng Guo[1], Sandeep Angara[1], Anabik Pal[1], Jose Jeronimo[2], Kanan T. Desai[2], Olusegun K. Ajenifuja[3], Clement A. Adepiti[3], Silvia D. Sanjose[2], Mark Schiffman[2], and Sameer Antani[1]

[1] National Library of Medicine, Bethesda, MD 20894, USA
zhiyun.xue@nih.gov
[2] National Cancer Institute, Rockville, MD 20850, USA
[3] Obafemi Awolowo University, Ile Ife, Nigeria

Abstract. Automated visual evaluation (AVE) of uterine cervix images is a deep learning algorithm that aims to improve cervical pre-cancer screening in low or medium resource regions (LMRR). Image quality control is an important pre-step in the development and use of AVE. In our work, we use data retrospectively collected from different sources/providers for analysis. In addition to good images, the datasets include low-quality images, green-filter images, and post Lugol's iodine images. The latter two are uncommon in VIA (visual inspection with acetic acid) and should be removed along with low-quality images. In this paper, we apply and compare two state-of-the-art deep learning networks to filter out those two types of cervix images after cervix detection. One of the deep learning networks is Deep-SAD, a semi-supervised anomaly detection network, while the other is ResNeSt, an improved variant of the ResNet classification network. Specifically, we study and evaluate the algorithms on a highly unbalanced large dataset consisting of four subsets from different geographic regions acquired with different imaging device types. We also examine the cross-dataset performance of the algorithms. Both networks can achieve high performance (accuracy above 97% and F1 score above 94%) on the test set.

Keywords: Cervical cancer · Deep learning · Highly unbalanced dataset · Cross-dataset evaluation · Anomaly detection · Acetowhitening · Green-filter · Lugol's iodine

1 Introduction

Cervical cancer affects a significant majority of the developing world where access to clinical care is limited. Having an effective screening program in those regions would reduce the incidence and mortality of cervical cancer significantly. VIA (visual inspection with acetic acid) is a screening method often used in low resource settings. It is

KC Santosh et al. (Eds.): RTIP2R 2021, CCIS 1576, pp. 3–13, 2022.
https://doi.org/10.1007/978-3-031-07005-1_1

an inexpensive alternative to Pap smear and colposcopy test which are methods requiring significantly higher medical resources with respect to personnel, infrastructure, and devices. In VIA, the cervix before and after the application of a diluted (3–5%) acetic acid is examined by health care practitioners with the naked eye. Based on the visual evaluation results, eligible positive patients can be treated in the same visit with ablation to reduce the loss to follow-up often encountered in low resource regions. While being simple, affordable, and able to provide immediate result and treatment, VIA, which relies on subjective visual evaluation, has moderate sensitivity, specificity, and inter-observer reproducibility [1]. We have recently proposed Automated Visual Evaluation (AVE) using deep learning techniques as an adjunct or a complementary screening method to improve VIA performance [2–4]. AVE has demonstrated promising results on both a large longitudinal population-based dataset of cervigrams (captured using a now-obsolete cerviscope) collected in Guanacaste Costa Rica [2] and a small dataset of images taken by a smartphone enhanced device from several countries [3]. A pilot study has also demonstrated the promise of using deep learning to aid the decision-making process on whether to ablate or not among VIA positives [5]. These results have emboldened a large multi-organizational study initiated and led by the National Cancer Institute (NCI), aiming to improve VIA using automatic computerized algorithms on smartphones or a low-cost specialized handheld device. Due to the adverse impact of COVID-19 on acquiring new data from field studies and the desire of accumulating a large dataset as fast as possible, we have focused on collecting retrospective data from different sources around the world (mainly colposcopy clinics). A side effect of acquiring such retrospective collection is that the data can be of poor visual quality and varied based on the local clinical protocols. Given the huge number of images being processed in the future, automatic handling, in particular, is of high interest. Our studies have aimed to address these using machine learning techniques for image quality control as well as data cleaning in these retrospectively collected datasets. We have developed new algorithms to filter out non-cervix images and blurry images [6, 7]. In this paper, we present our work on separating green-filtered and Lugol's iodine cervix images from regular color cervix images taken before or after the application of acetic acid under a white-light illumination.

Cervical cancer is caused by persistent infection from certain high-risk types of HPV (Human Papillomavirus). One main key component in VIA as well as in colposcopy is to observe the color change of the epithelium of the cervix after the weak acetic acid application, a reaction termed as acetowhitening, as HPV infected abnormal tissues may appear more whitish than the neighboring normal squamous epithelium of the cervix. Based on the extent of this reaction (e.g. density, quickness, opacity, thickness), and other visual characteristics, such as vascular patterns, health care providers may assess and grade the severity of the disease. A green filter is commonly used in colposcopy to enhance the visualization of cervical tissue vessels, making suspicious patterns easier to recognize. These green filtered images can be captured by using a green light source, physically attaching a green filter to the camera lens, or created digitally by color manipulation algorithms [8]. Lugol's iodine is another contrast agent applied with the aim of helping identify the lesions overlooked when using acetic acid. Precancerous or cancerous lesions may have different reactions to the iodine solution and may appear in different shades of brown stain from normal tissues, for example, abnormal tissues could appear to be thick mustard yellow or saffron-colored while normal epithelium tissues would show brown or black color [9]. Figure 1 shows examples of regular, green-filtered, and Lugol's iodine cervix images respectively.

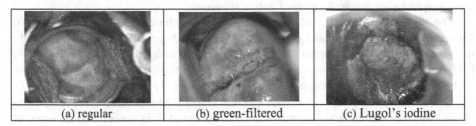

| (a) regular | (b) green-filtered | (c) Lugol's iodine |

Fig. 1. Examples of regular, green-filtered, and Lugol's iodine cervix images. (Color figure online)

Although green filter and iodine solution are not usually used in VIA, it is a common practice to use them in colposcopy examinations for visual evaluation of cervix. Therefore, the multi-source datasets we have obtained also contain these two types of images (we call them both non-regular cervix images) and they need to be filtered out. It may appear that these three types of images have distinguished color difference and would be easy to separate, however, there exists a large variance within each type across datasets and there are some images whose color differences across types are subtle and are difficult to differentiate. Further, there is significant variation in the saturation of the green filter which is sometimes also digitally applied as a post-acquisition step. In addition to the goal of automatic cleaning of retrospectively collected data, we want to design the experiments to analyze and study the issues of learning from highly unbalanced dataset and cross dataset/device variance, two main challenges many applications in medical domain face. To the best of our knowledge, this is the first work aiming to investigate these topics for uterine cervix images. The insights gained from this work would help us on applying similar machine learning techniques to other more challenging tasks in AVE.

2 Image Data

We aim to investigate two main issues using these retrospective image datasets: 1) training a model using highly unbalanced data; and 2) examining the model performance across datasets. To this end, in our experiments, we use four datasets which we call the **China dataset**, the **Nigeria dataset**, the **MobileODT dataset** and the **Peru dataset** which were collected from different geographic regions by different providers with different imaging devices. The images within each dataset or across datasets have a large appearance variance with respect to not only cervix or disease related factors (such as woman's age, parity, and cervix anatomy and condition) but also non-cervix or non-disease related factors (such as illumination, focus, specular reflection, presence of clinical instruments, embedded pixel (or graphic) text, imaging device, and variable zoom and angle).

The **China dataset** is a public dataset shared by the authors of [10] on IEEE Dataport. It contains cervix images of 475 patients collected from July 2013 to February 2017 at the First Affiliated Hospital of Science and Technology of China. There are seven images for each subject: one image of pre acetic acid application, four post acetic acid application images taken at different times, one image taken using a green filter, and one image photographed after the application of iodine solution.

The **Nigeria dataset** was collected at the colposcopy clinic of the Obafemi Awolowo University Teaching Hospitals Complex (OAUTHC) in Nigeria by a recent NCI study designed to evaluate the ultimate strategy of AVE triage with self-sampled HPV typing [11]. For each participating woman, multiple images of the cervix were captured using each of the following three image capture devices in order: 1) cellphone, 2) MobileODT EVA, and 3) colposcope mounted with a DSLR camera. MobileODT EVA is a smartphone enhanced device which contains a cross-polarized light source and an external magnifying lens. The images were taken at least one minute after the application of the acetic acid. The data used in this work is the one collected from December 2018 to November 2019. There are no green-filtered images or images with iodine application in this dataset.

In [3], we used a dataset provided by MobileODT to assess whether a deep learning AVE algorithm could perform well on smartphone images. The images were collected from various countries/regions in the world by different providers using MobileODT EVA devices. Each woman had only a single visit, but there were images of varying numbers taken during that visit. The dataset was reviewed for visual quality and images with acceptable/good quality were then annotated by a group of gynecologic oncologists at Rutgers University. The images used in this work are from a subset of the final dataset used to train and evaluate the AVE classifier in [3]. Similar to the Nigeria dataset, this **MobileODT dataset** has no green-filtered images and Lugol's iodine images.

The **Peru dataset** consists of images selected by the collaborating gynecologists in Peru for some of the teaching/training classes on colposcopic visual impression to residents or students. These images were originally collected from the Peruvian Cancer Institute with three different colposcopes. Most of these images have lesions, polyps, or any other important features/characteristics suitable for teaching. Each patient in this dataset has a varied number of images. In addition to acetowhitening images, some patients may have green-filtered images and/or Lugol's iodine images. Some example images in the four datasets are shown in Fig. 2.

3   Method

As mentioned before, among these four datasets the Nigeria and MobileODT datasets have no iodine and green-filtered images, and only the China and Peru datasets contain such images. To investigate deep networks on high data imbalance and cross-dataset performance, in our experiments, we use China, Nigeria, and MobileODT datasets to train and validate the model and use Peru dataset to test the model. We also set up the problem as separating white light images taken pre or post acetic acid application (named as "regular" images) from green-filtered images and iodine applied images (named as "non-regular" images), that is, a two-class problem ("regular" vs "non-regular"), since the latter two types of images ("non-regular" images) are usually not used in VIA.

As mentioned previously, there is a large variety in images across datasets and within each dataset. In some images, such as Fig. 2(b), there is a significant area outside the cervix region. We have previously developed a cervix detector using RetinaNet [12]. The cervix detector was trained with a dataset other than the images used in this study. Some examples of cervix detection results are shown in Fig. 3.

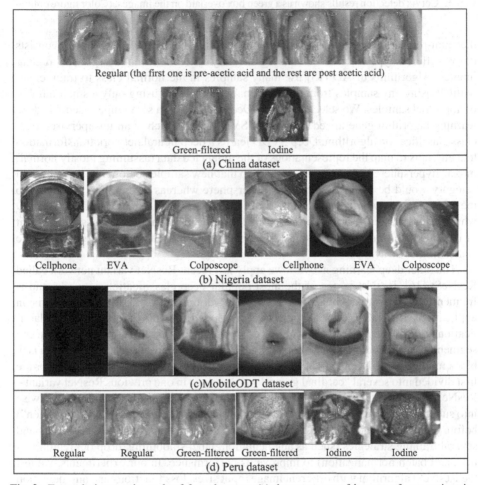

Regular (the first one is pre-acetic acid and the rest are post acetic acid)

Green-filtered   Iodine
(a) China dataset

Cellphone   EVA   Colposcope   Cellphone   EVA   Colposcope
(b) Nigeria dataset

(c)MobileODT dataset

Regular   Regular   Green-filtered   Green-filtered   Iodine   Iodine
(d) Peru dataset

Fig. 2. Example images in each of four datasets: (a) the sequence of images of one patient in China dataset; (b) images of one patient taken by three devices in Nigeria dataset; (c) images in MobileODT dataset collected from multiple providers in the world; and (d) images of three types in Peru dataset.

Next, we classify the extracted cervix regions into two categories: (a) regular and (b) non-regular images. To this end, we apply and compare two types of deep learning networks. One was designed for anomaly detection (AD), the task of identifying unusual or rare data samples that are significantly different from the majority of data. Our application fits the AD scenario naturally as there are a lot more regular images ("normal")

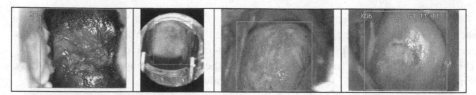

Fig. 3. Cervix detection results shown as a green box overlaid on the images. (Color figure online)

than non-regular images ("abnormal") in our dataset and the non-regular images consists of two different types each of which is significantly different from the large set of regular images. Algorithms of AD [13] use many samples in the normal class to train, either without using any samples from the abnormal class or with using only a small number of abnormal samples. We select and apply Deep SAD [14], a semi-supervised AD deep learning algorithm generalized from Deep SVDD [15] which is an unsupervised one-class classification algorithm. Deep SVDD learns a deep neural network transformation that attempts to map the representations of the unlabeled data (assuming mostly normal) into a "hypersphere" of minimum volume, so that new samples belonging to the normal category would be mapped within this hypersphere whereas the samples belonging to the other category would be mapped outside. Deep SAD is an extension of Deep SVDD which includes a new loss term representing the influence of the additional small amount of labelled data to make the distance of labelled abnormal samples to the hypersphere center further away.

The other deep learning network we apply is a recent ResNet variant network called ResNeSt [16]. ResNet is one of the most popular deep classification networks and is frequently used as a backbone/base network in various networks for computer vision applications. ResNeSt is a variant of ResNet developed with aim of improving the classification performance of ResNet as well as downstream tasks such as object detection and segmentation with comparable computation cost. ResNeSt proposed and included a new block module named "split attention" block. Specifically, in each block, feature maps are first divided into several "cardinal groups", as was done in one previous ResNet variant – ResNeXt [17]. Then, the feature maps in each cardinal group are separated channel-wise into subgroups ("splits"). The features across subgroup splits are combined ("attention") before being concatenated for all the groups. ResNeSt also applies network tweaks and several training strategies (such as augmentation, label smoothing, drop out regularization, and batch normalization) to improve its performance. In our experiments, we test the ResNeSt algorithm with different image input sizes, loss functions and augmentation methods.

4 Experiments and Discussions

As stated previously, four datasets are used for the task of non-regular cervix image filtering. Among them, the China and Peru datasets contain non-regular cervix images, respectively, while the Nigeria and MobileODT datasets contain regular cervix images only. The training set consists of the Nigeria dataset and a part of the China dataset (the original China training set used by the authors for disease abnormality classification

Table 1. Number of patients in the training/validation/test set

Splits	Dataset	Patients
Train	China	427
	Nigeria	988
Validation	China	48
	MobileODT	418
Test	Peru	79

Table 2. Number of training images

Regular		Non-regular	
China (acetowhite)	1895	China (green)	380
Nigeria (cellphone)	8402	China (iodine)	380
Nigeria (EVA)	4815		
Nigeria (colposcope)	5634		
Total: 20746		Total: 760	

Table 3. Number of validation images

Regular		Non-regular	
China (acetowhite)	240	China (green)	48
MobileODT	812	China (iodine)	48
Total: 1052		Total: 96	

Table 4. Number of test images

Regular		Non-regular	
Peru (acetowhite)	307	Peru (green)	58
		Peru (iodine)	43
Total: 307		Total: 101	

in [10]). The validation set consists of the MobileODT dataset and the remainder of the China dataset. The test set consists of the Peru dataset. Table 1 lists the number of patients in each dataset in the training, validation, and test set, respectively. Tables 2, 3 and 4 list the number of corresponding images in both classes in the training, validation, and test sets, respectively. As shown in Table 2, the ratio between the number of regular and non-regular images in the training set is $20746:760 \approx 27.3$, which is relatively high. The images across datasets have varied sizes. All of them are resized to the same size before inputting to the networks.

For Deep SAD, we adopt the same network architecture used in [14] as the starting point, specifically, the LeNet type CNN for CIFAR-10 in [14] which consists of three modules of $32 \times (5 \times 5)$-filters, $64 \times (5 \times 5)$-filters, and $128 \times (5 \times 5)$-filters, followed by a final dense layer of 128 units. The inverse squared norm loss function is used. For training, the weights are initialized using pretrained autoencoder. The batch size is 4. Adam optimizer with a learning rate of 10^{-4} and weight decay regularization with value $0.5e-6$ are used. The number of epochs is set as 150. Figure 4 shows the box plot of the output scores (radius to the hypersphere center) of the images in the validation set, and Fig. 5 shows images with high scores and low scores and regular images with high scores after sorting, respectively. Based on the results on the validation set, the threshold for the radius to the hypersphere center is set to be 10. Even though the input image size is small (32×32), the model obtains high classification performance on the

Table 5. Confusion matrix for Deep SAD on the test set

Peru → GT	Non-regular	Regular
Non-regular	94	0
Regular	7	307

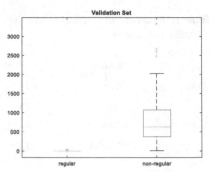

Fig. 4. DeepSAD output scores on val. Set

test set, achieving sensitivity (recall) 93.1%, specificity 100%, precision 100%, F1 score 96.4%, and accuracy 98.3%, with the cropped cervix images (Non-regular is the positive class). Table 5 lists the corresponding confusion matrix. Figure 6 shows several images misclassified by Deep SAD. They are green-filtered images but are classified as regular images. These images have only a very subtle greenish tone and are hard to distinguish visually unless compared with the regular images from the same patient. Please note, there are some images in the dataset that were zoomed in by the providers to see the region-of-interest when taking the photos and the original images only cover part of the cervix (not due to the failure of cervix detection).

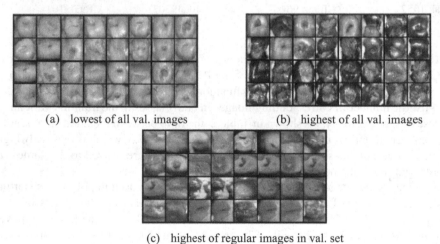

(a)   lowest of all val. images   (b)   highest of all val. images

(c)   highest of regular images in val. set

Fig. 5. Images in the validation set with DeepSAD low/high scores

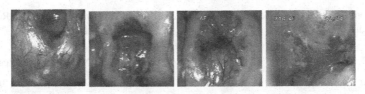

Fig. 6. Misclassified images by DeepSAD (Color figure online)

For ResNeSt (specifically, ResNeSt50), we first use the same image size as the one for Deep SAD: 32×32. The model is initialized with weights from ImageNet pretrained model. The augmentation methods are random resized crop, random rotation, random horizontal flip and center crop. The loss function is binary cross entropy weighted by the class weight (the total sample size divided by (two times the number of regular/non-regular images)). The optimizer is Adam ($\beta_1 = 0.9$, $\beta_2 = 0.999$) with a learning rate of 5×10^{-4}. The batch size is 256. The model is trained for 100 epochs and the one with the highest performance on validation set is selected. We also train a model with input images of larger size: 224×224. For this model, all the above parameters remain the same except the batch size is 64. The performance metrics of all the models on the test set are listed in Table 6. For image size 32×32, the performance of ResNeSt model is significantly lower than that of Deep SAD. After increasing the input image size to 224×224, the performance (e.g., sensitivity) improves considerably and the F1 score improves to 0.948 from 0.764. The confusion matrix of the ResNeSt models for input size 32×32 and 224×224 are given in Tables 7 and 8, respectively. We also extract the features from the average pooling layer of the ResNeSt models and plot the t-SNE of those features with ground truth labels. As shown in Figs. 7 and 8, the ResNeSt (224×224) model features in the two categories are separated much better than those from ResNeSt (32×32) model.

Table 6. Performance of models

	Sens./recall	Spec.	Prec.	F1	Acc.
ResNeSt, 32×32	0.624	0.997	0.984	0.764	0.904
ResNeSt, 224×224	0.901	1.000	1.000	0.948	0.976
Deep SAD, 32×32	0.931	1.000	1.000	0.964	0.981

Table 7. Confusion matrix for ResNeSt (32 × 32) on the test set

Peru → GT	Non-regular	Regular
Non-regular	63	1
Regular	38	306

Table 8. Confusion matrix for ResNeSt (224 × 224) on the test set

Peru → GT	Non-regular	Regular
Non-regular	91	0
Regular	10	307

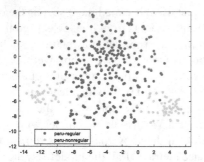

Fig. 7. The t-SNE plot of ResNeSt (32 × 32) features (GT labels)

Fig. 8. The t-SNE plot of ResNeSt (224 × 224) features (GT labels)

5   Conclusion and Future Work

In this paper, we present an approach to filter out two non-regular types of images seldomly used in VIA screening of cervical cancer: green-filtered images and iodine-applied images. We are interested in studying data imbalance issue and cross-dataset generalization capacity besides the goal of cleaning retrospectively collected data. To achieve this, we use a combination of several datasets that contain images obtained from four different sources. In the combined dataset, there is large variation with respect to imaging device, patient demography, image quality, illumination source, and existence of clinical obstruction. In addition, there is high imbalance between the number of regular and non-regular images in the combined dataset. To evaluate the model's performance and robustness across multiple datasets, we use images from different sources to train and test in the experiments. We first use an object detection network to identify cervix region. For classification, we apply and compare two types of state-of-the-art deep learning networks: 1) Deep SAD, a semi-supervised anomaly detection network; and 2) ResNeSt, a variant of ResNet. Options such as input image size and loss weighting are compared. High performance can be achieved by both networks (F1 score above 94%). Future work includes testing the model on more datasets, developing a customized Deep SAD network for larger image input size, and removal of other unusable images such as post-treatment cryotherapy images and poor-quality regular images.

Acknowledgement. This research was supported by the Intramural Research Programs of the National Library of Medicine (NLM) and the National Cancer Institute (NCI), both part of the National Institutes of Health.

References

1. Jeronimo, J., Schiffman, M.: Colposcopy at a crossroads. Am. J. Obstet. Gynecol. **195**, 349–353 (2006)
2. Hu, L., et al.: An observational study of deep learning and automated evaluation of cervical images for cancer screening. J. Natl. Cancer Inst. **111**, 923–932 (2019)
3. Xue, Z., et al.: A demonstration of automated visual evaluation of cervical images taken with a smartphone camera. Int. J. Cancer **147**, 2416–2423 (2020)
4. Pal, A., et al.: Deep metric learning for cervical image classification. IEEE Access **9**, 53266–53275 (2021). https://doi.org/10.1109/ACCESS.2021.3069346
5. Guo, P., et al.: Network visualization and pyramidal feature comparison for ablative treatability classification using digitized cervix images. J. Clin. Med. **10**(5), 953 (2021). https://doi.org/10.3390/jcm10050953
6. Guo, P., et al.: Ensemble deep learning for cervix image selection toward improving reliability in automated cervical precancer screening. Diagnostics (Basel, Switz.) **10**(7), 451 (2020). https://doi.org/10.3390/diagnostics10070451
7. Guo, P., Xue, Z., Long, L.R., Antani, S.: Deep learning for assessing image focus for automated cervical cancer screening. In: Proceedings of the IEEE International Conference on Biomedical and Health Informatics, Chicago, IL, USA, 19–22 May 2019 (2019)
8. Digiovanni, S.L., Guaragnella, C., Rizzi, M., Falagario, M.: Healthcare system: a digital green filter for smart health early cervical cancer diagnosis. In: IEEE 2nd International Forum on Research and Technologies for Society and Industry Leveraging a better tomorrow (RTSI), Bologna, Italy, pp. 1–6 (2016). https://doi.org/10.1109/RTSI.2016.7740564
9. Sellors, J.W., Sankaranarayanan, R. (eds.): An introduction to colposcopy: indications for colposcopy, instrumentation, principles and documentation of results. Colposcopy and treatment of cervical intraepithelial neoplasia: a beginners' manual. https://screening.iarc.fr/colpochap.php?lang=1&chap=4
10. Yue, Z., et al.: Automatic CIN grades prediction of sequential cervigram image using LSTM with multistate CNN features. IEEE J. Biomed. Health Inform. **24**(3), 844–854 (2020). https://doi.org/10.1109/JBHI.2019.2922682
11. Desai, K.T., et al.: Design and feasibility of a novel program of cervical screening in Nigeria: self-sampled HPV testing paired with visual triage. Infect. Agents Cancer **15**, 60 (2020). https://doi.org/10.1186/s13027-020-00324-5
12. Lin, T., Goyal, P., Girshick, R., He, K., Dollár, P.: Focal loss for dense object detection. In: 2017 IEEE International Conference on Computer Vision (ICCV), Venice, Italy, pp. 2999–3007 (2017). https://doi.org/10.1109/ICCV.2017.324
13. Chalapathy, R., Chawla, S.: Deep learning for anomaly detection: a survey. https://arxiv.org/abs/1901.03407
14. Ruff, L., et al.: Deep semi-supervised anomaly detection. In: The International Conference on Learning Representations (ICLR) (2020)
15. Ruff, L., et al.: Deep one-class classification. In: Proceedings of the 35th International Conference on Machine Learning, PMLR, vol. 80, pp. 4393–4402 (2018)
16. Zhang, H., et al.: ResNeSt: split-attention networks. https://arxiv.org/abs/2004.08955
17. Xie, S., Girshick, R., Dollár, P., Tu, Z., He, K.: Aggregated residual transformations for deep neural networks. https://arxiv.org/abs/1611.05431

Detection of Male Fertility Using AI-Driven Tools

Debasmita Ghosh Roy[1]([✉]) and P. A. Alvi[2]

[1] School of Automation, Banasthali Vidyapith, Banasthali 304022, Rajasthan, India
sarkar11debasmita@gmail.com
[2] Department of Physics, Banasthali Vidyapith, Banasthali 304022, Rajasthan, India

Abstract. In the last few decades, the nation has been experiencing a low fertility rate due to fast changes in human lifestyle over a short period. Many lifestyle factors, such as liquor consumption, physical latency, cigarette smoking, caffeine intake, and others, can adversely affect on reproductive performance. These factors are associated with sperm quality, which is a pivotal key feature to identify male fertility status. In this experiment, three different feature selection methods have been applied to assess the uppermost features which are deeply connected with seminal quality. The final dataset contains three lifestyle features of hundred males under 18 to 36 years of age, having normal and altered output labels. Four artificial intelligence methods such as logistics regression, support vector machine, decision tree, and k-nearest neighbor are utilized to identify the male reproductive state. Finally, K-nearest neighbor algorithm has excelled in male fertility prognosis with 90% efficacy, and the receiver operating characteristic value is 0.85.

Keywords: Male fertility · AI tools · Feature selection · Receiver Operating Characteristic (ROC)

1 Introduction

The decline of the fertility rate is a trending phenomenon around the globe. According to World Health Organization (WHO), 60–80 million couples have impacted the ill effects of infertility issues. The idea is untrue that the fertility rate is declining due to female factors where male fertility is well past. Documented evidence indicated that male fertility factors played a harmful role in deteriorating fertility rate worldwide. Recently, about 50% of infertility cases have been identified with male characteristics, mainly due to a spermatogenesis failure [19], which is developed by lifestyle pattern and environmental exposure [9]. The association of these two factors is directly connected to male seminal quality leading to the impaired male reproductive system. Many publications reported that exposure to sedentary lifestyles and work culture could negatively affect seminal parameters. Improper lifestyle gave rise to testicular dysgenesis syndrome problems with various underlying disorders such as hypospadias, cryptorchidism, and testicular cancer [23]. Besides, semen motility and concentration

© Springer Nature Switzerland AG 2022
KC Santosh et al. (Eds.): RTIP2R 2021, CCIS 1576, pp. 14–25, 2022.
https://doi.org/10.1007/978-3-031-07005-1_2

worsen by age, and erectile dysfunction has been observed in men who intake more alcohol and tobacco [11]. The rise-in scrotal temperature was discovered in men with a hot bath, sauna user, febrile illness, and tight jockey shorts and suspensories that adversely affected men's testicular function [5]. Beyond that fact, male children can also get involved by wearing plastic-lined diapers that may increase the scrotal temperature, which may be the reason for delayed conception in the future. These factors are modifiable, which provide a significant chance for ignoring infertility among males if corrected at the proper time. Thus, it is crucial to understand which factors are the utmost for identifying male fertility status. The relationship between lifestyle factors and a decrease in seminal quality should be a significant concern. The changing lifestyle patterns can prevent infertility and help a couple to achieve a better quality of life. As a result, there is a possibility of increasing the chances of conception by reducing the male fertility-related problem. Moreover, improper lifestyle and environmental factors play a vital role in natality, and its consequences on the upcoming human populace make a significant public health issue in this century. Hence, preservation of fertility has become a challenging task day by day as well as awareness is of much importance in young adults and adolescents, which enhances human civilization.

In this modern era, the medical facility is becoming more frequent and costly due to laboratory testing, a primary step for disease diagnosis. Insignificant testing expenses increase the financial and psychological burden among general people. In that situation, the AI-based computational model helps clinicians to identify the disease and understand the relevant test requirement to reduce unwanted medical expenses [8]. Besides this, the patient and physician can be motivated to utilize this technology to move from theoretical to clinical reality. This concept can be used to manage the actual clinical situation like fewer hospital visits, reduced patient admission rate, control long term health hazards, reduction of mortality rate, reduced psychological and financial burden, saving time, and increased efficacy in the test results.

Many researchers put their effort to diagnose human fertility using AI. However, lifestyle factors are considered a significant manifestation of identifying the male seminal quality. The changes of lifestyle factors can often be affected in seminal profile in the form of normal and altered. Our prime objective is to figure out the best and complimenting features. These specially selected features will help the underlying classifier to produce a clinical decision to distinguish between normal and altered semen quality.

Our aim to implement optimal features set for male fertility and classification scenario was of three-fold: i) improve the prediction performance of the underlying classifier, ii) provide an optimal feature set to describe seminal quality such as normal and altered ones, and iii) give a straight comparison of our outcomes with the previous studies where the same dataset was used. In addition to the prime goal to figure out the optimal feature set providing high classification efficacy, our second goal was to select a fast and well-performing classifier like naïve bayes [3]. Such a model is able to define the decision to differentiate between male fertility status relying only on features. Hence, feature selection will also make an overall lesser processing time due to the fact that only a reduced number of features is to be extracted and utilized in the classification process.

In this article, we have proposed an intelligent system that is capable to detect male fertility status using only feature selection and AI techniques. The rest of the article is framed as follows: "Related works" provides a brief idea of state of the art, "Methods" discusses the methods in use - including detailing of dataset, features selection, and classification. "Experiments" give a brief explanation of the used optimal feature set, the evaluation protocols, and different outcomes. Finally, a compact summary highlighting the strength of our article is provided in "Conclusion".

2   Related Works

The study in [3] has recently analyzed seminal quality using ensemble learning techniques such as bagged decision tree, logistic regression, gaussian naïve bayes with an accuracy of 88%, 84%, and 88%, respectively. In [16] deep learning method has been applied for the classification of human sperm with 94.1% accuracy. A fuzzy radial basis function has been used to estimate the semen quality in [2] with 90% accuracy. The study performed in [6] was for predicting fertility quality using an artificial neural network approach with training, testing accuracy of 1.521×10^{-1} and 1.31×10^{-1}, respectively. In [21], a hybrid fuzzy clustering approach has been proposed to diagnose male fertility and compare the performance using four techniques such as logistic regression, naïve bayes, neural network, and fuzzy C-means with ROC values of 0.76, 0.77, 0.34, and 0.73, respectively. The study performed in [12] male fertility prediction using supervised and unsupervised learning methods using three classification techniques such as decision tree, support vector machine, bayesian, and k-nearest neighbor with an accuracy of 100%, 100%, 98.4%, and 100%, respectively. A comparative analysis has been done in [15], using classification, clustering, and regression techniques where support vector machine is used for regression, naïve bayes for classification, and K means for clustering. In [1], the seminal quality prediction has been performed using multilayer layer perception, genetic algorithm, decision tree, support vector machine, and naïve bayes, and obtained accuracy is 93.86%, 83.82%, 80.88%, and 73.10%. In [20], a comparative analysis has been performed using naïve bayes and artificial neural network algorithms to predict seminal quality where both classifiers obtain 97% efficacy. In [17], different data mining techniques such as multi-layer perceptron, support vector machine, support vector machine with particle swarm optimization, naïve bayes -kernel have been used to predict male fertility. The accuracy obtained from the above-mentioned classifiers are 92%, 91%, 94%, and 89%, respectively. Data pre-processing techniques such as support vector machine, evolutionary logistic regression, support vector machine with particle swarm optimization, correlation, principal component analysis, T-test, and chi test have been used to identify the feature importance with output label. In [7], an artificial neural network has been used to determine sperm concentration and sperm mobility with an accuracy of 90% and 82%, respectively.

In our literature review, an in-depth analysis has not been performed on feature reduction techniques for predicting male fertility using lifestyle factors. All researchers used nine features, and there is no clear idea about which features can primarily impact male fertility. Hence, a clear understanding of the features and their combination is necessary to provide a well-defined model design for future use of male fertility detection.

3   Methods

In this section, we discuss the different processing steps of the model: starting with feature detailing, feature selection, and finally the classification techniques which give the male fertility status that either belongs to a normal or an altered class.

3.1   Features Detailing

The fertility dataset has been taken from UCI machine learning repository and we have used it in this study [22]. One hundred male volunteers were involved, with ages between 18 to 36 years. Their semen samples were analyzed according to WHO's criteria set by 2010. The dataset comprises of nine input variables and an output variable classified into two classes assigned as normal and altered. The dataset seems to be imbalance with 88 normal and 12 altered instances. The features detailing is listed in Table 1.

Table 1. Male fertility dataset [22]

Feature number	Input features	Values
F1	Season	Winter, spring, summer, fall
F2	Age	18–36 years
F3	Childish disease	Yes, no
F4	Accident	Yes, no
F5	Surgery	Yes, no
F6	High fever	Less than three months ago, more than three month ago, No
F7	Alcohol consumption	Several times a day, every day, several times a week, once a week, hardly ever or never
F8	Smoking habit	Never, occasional, daily
F9	Sitting hours	0–16 hours
Output	Class label	Normal, altered

3.2   Feature Selection

Feature selection is one of the prime assessment space for the usage of AI and ML. This method is used for feature subset evaluation and creates the best subset of a dataset without losing the data information, which improves the prediction accuracy of designed predictive models. To fulfill our aim, we first consider wrapper-type feature selection methods such as logistic regression-recursive feature elimination. Secondly, ensemble random forest and support vector machine were used for finding the feature importance depending on their weightage value.

3.3   Feature Selection

Classification techniques are used to classify each feature in a dataset into one of the predetermined sets of classes. A model or classifier is developed to determine class label attributes in the task of data analysis. The main objective of classification is to accurately predict the output class for each case in input features and predict the disease's risk. The most accessible type of classification problem is a two-class classification, mainly used in the health care industry. Various classification algorithms use different methods to identify the relationship between the input label and the target label. These associations can be briefly described in a model that can be applied to a distinct dataset where the class label is unknown. Decision Tree, Support Vector Machine, Logistic Regression, K-Nearest Neighbor are the most widely used algorithms for Classification problem [13,18,24].

1. Support Vector Machine (SVM).
It is a learning method for two-class classification problems and has been shown to perform well in multiple biological analysis areas. A classification has been performed by figuring out the hyperplane that maximizes the boundary between the data points [25]. Different mathematical functions, such as linear, polynomial, and RBF have been utilized to develop a computational intelligence model. This expanded model helps to solve various medical health issues like cancer, cardiac risk, diabetes prediction, etc. In this study, the SVM algorithm has been used to predict male fertility status with the output class label indicated by −1 for altered and +1 for regular. A given set of training data samples is,

$$D = \{(x_1, y_1), (x_2, y_2), \ldots\ldots(x_n, y_n)\} \tag{1}$$

where $x_i \in R^n$ and $y_i \in \{1, -1\}$

The main objective to figure out the best hyperplane which can accurately divide D. The hyperplane can be expressed by,

$$\omega \cdot \varphi(x) + b = 0 \tag{2}$$

where, the weight vector is $\omega \in H$ and bias term is $b \in R$. $\varphi{:}R^n \to H$ means mapping the data D to a higher dimensional feature space. The final optimized problem SVM solves to fit the best parameters given that,

$$y_i \left[\omega \cdot \varphi(x_i) + b \right] \geq 1, \quad \forall x_i \text{ is } \min \left(\frac{||\omega||^2}{2} \right) \tag{3}$$

For each vector x_i such that, x_i belongs to class 1, then

$$\omega \cdot \varphi(x_i) + b \geq 1 \tag{4}$$

x_i belongs to -1, then

$$\omega \cdot \varphi(x_i) + b \leq -1 \tag{5}$$

x_i belongs to decision boundary, then

$$\omega \cdot \varphi(x_i) + b = 0 \tag{6}$$

2. Decision Tree (DT).
DT is the most popular classification tool widely used in clinical industry because decision plays an effective role in diagnosis procedure. The algorithm is generally presented in a tree structure that can provide an extensive representation of features independence with the best feature at each node in the tree. This node can help in separating the training set object in the finest way, comparing with each features' values [14]. The output is displayed in the leaf node by splitting the node based on concept of entropy.

$$\textbf{Entropy} = -p_{(+)}log_2 p_{(+)} - p_{(-)}log_2 p_{(-)} \tag{7}$$

where, $p_{(+)}, p_{(-)}$ are positive and negative samples present in training data samples. The algorithm steps are as follows:

Algorithm 1: Decision Tree algorithm

Input : D sample training dataset-attributes with a output class label
for ∀ *Attributes* **do**
    for *Individual sample* **do**
        | Execute the DT algorithm.
    end
    Identify the attribute space $a_1, a_2, a_3, \ldots, a_x$ of the dataset UCI.
end
Obtain the total number of leaf nodes $l_1, l_2, l_3, \ldots, l_n$ with its constraints.
Split the dataset D into $d_1, d_2, d_3, \ldots, d_n$ depends on the leaf nodes constraints.
Output : Partition dataset $d_1, d_2, d_3, \ldots, d_n$

---

3. Logistic Regression (LR).
It is a widely used data mining technique for binary classification, where the target variable is categorical [10]. The concept behind this algorithm is to minimize the cost function $C(\emptyset)$ defined as,

$$C(\emptyset) = -\frac{1}{m}(\sum_{i=1}^{m} y^{(i)}\log(h_{\emptyset}\left(x^{(i)}\right) + \left(1 - y^{(i)}\right)\log\left(1 - h_{\emptyset}\left(x^{(i)}\right)\right)) \tag{8}$$

where, $\emptyset$ is a matrix of weight vectors and $x^{(i)}$ is the feature vector of each data sample. $y^{(i)}$ is a binary vector assigned by either 0 (altered seminal quality) or 1 (normal seminal quality) for each data samples. For preventing the overfitting regularization factor is ω has been used. $h_{\emptyset}(x)$ is defined as the sigmoid function which is,

$$h_{\emptyset}(x) = \frac{1}{1 + e^{-(\emptyset.x)}} \tag{9}$$

here, $\emptyset.x$ identifying the dot product of weight vector $\emptyset$ and the feature vectors x, the exponential function is denoted by e.

To minimized the cost function gradient decent technique has been utilized and weight vector upgradation is required in every step. In this study, we need to compute the derivative of cost function with respect to weight vectors.

$$\emptyset_j = \emptyset_j - \beta\frac{\partial(C(\emptyset))}{\partial\emptyset_j} \tag{10}$$

where β is the step size in gradient decent algorithm. The derivative of the cost function with respect to weight vectors is,

$$\frac{1}{m}\sum_{i=1}^{m}(h_{\emptyset}(x^{(i)}) - y^{(i)})x_j^{(i)} \tag{11}$$

Continually improving the weight vectors will result in the minimization of cost function.

4. K-Nearest Neighbor (KNN).
It is a non-parametric supervised learning method that makes predictions directly from the data samples. Predictions are made for new data samples by searching through the entire training set for the K most similar data samples and summarize the target variable for those K instances. For regression, this might be the mean output variable, and in classification, this might be the mode of class value [4]. Distance measurement is required to determine which of K instances in the training data samples are close to new input. The Euclidean distance measurement technique is used for real-time data samples which are defined as D,

$$D(x, x_i) = \sqrt{\sum(x_j - x_{ij})^2} \tag{12}$$

where, x is new data samples fact, existing fact (x_i) across all input features j. Assume, (X_i, Y_i) where $i = 1, 2, 3, \ldots, n$ number of data sample facts. X_i

and Y_i represents the feature values and target classes for X_i for each i. $Y_i \in \{1, 2, 3, \ldots, n\}$ for all values of i. Let, x be a point for which label is unknown,
The algorithms steps are as follows:

1. Evaluate $D(x, x_i)$, where D represents the distance between the focuses.
2. Organize the determined n Euclidean distances in non-decreasing order.
3. K should be a positive value and choose the initial K distances from this sorted list.
4. Figure out those K facts relating towards these K distances.
5. let, K_i defines the number of facts having a place with i^{th} class among K points that is $K \geq 0$.
6. If $K_i > K_j \forall\ i \neq j$ at that point place x in class i.

3.4   The Workflow of Proposed Model

An optimal feature set is used for the classification of male fertility status. This dataset, which has no missing values, can be classified into training and testing data. The four classification techniques are applied, and the efficacy of prediction of an individual classifier is compared. The classifier with optimal efficacy is utilized for prediction. The flow of the work process is depicted in Fig. 1.

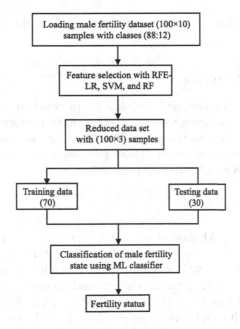

Fig. 1. Workflow of the proposed model

4   Experiments

This section provides a detailed explanation of the optimal feature set that has been used for the evaluation protocol considered for the experiments. Finally, the comparison has been made for the selection of the best classifier along with optimal accuracy.

4.1   Data

For the feature selection, each feature importance score was recorded, and after that, the top three features were carried out. Among them, some features are common according to their ranking, and we have selected the standard features (see Table 2). Finally, we used the common features such as F1, F4, F7, and created a reduced dataset that is further used to classify male fertility status.

Table 2. Reduced dataset

Methods	Features number	Values
Ensemble random forest	F9, F2, F1	0.20, 0.18, 0.13
Recursive feature elimination with logistic regression	F1, F4, F7	True =1, rest are false
Support vector machine	F7, F4, F6	0.7, 0.37, 0.18

4.2   Evaluation Protocols

For the evaluation of the designed model, a proper evaluation process was considered. Accuracy was selected to estimate the model performance. In addition, the ROC curve also gives us the possibility to adjust our classification threshold for the aim of our application. These two key indicators are necessary to understand the behavior of underlying classifiers.

4.3   Results

Accuracy and ROC of AI models with different data set were recorded (see Table 3). From the initial run, it looks like SVM and KNN performed good with the original dataset (86% accuracy) and the ROC value are 0.58 and 0.6, respectively. Secondly, KNN provides the optimal accuracy and ROC value with a reduced feature set when $k = 10$. In the SVM classifier RBF kernel trick, the C value is used as a 0.1 and gamma estimation of 10. The accuracy is achieved with a 70 : 30 ratio of the train and test split dataset, respectively. In order to identify our proposed model performance, we compare some of existing models' performance where the same data set was used (see Table 4).

Table 3. Comparison of accuracy with different dataset

Classification Techniques	Original dataset		Reduced dataset	
	Accuracy (%)	ROC	Accuracy (%)	ROC
LR	80	0.649	86	0.911
SVM	86	0.582	90	0.750
DT	76	0.606	80	0.911
K-NN	86	0.606	90	0.857

Table 4. Comparison with previous studies that used the same dataset to distinguish between normal and altered semen quality of male

Reference (year)	No. of features	Accuracy (%)
[3] (2020)	9	88
[2] (2018)	9	90
[1] (2015)	9	93.86
[7] (2013)	9	82
Our model	3	90

5 Conclusion

In this article, we presented an intelligent model which can detect the normal or altered seminal profile of males. This model can be used as a clinical decision-making system for the prediction of male fertility and it may help to create general awareness among male society. Additionally, these three trigger features can be used to set the conditions for semen donors. In previous studies, nine features were considered for the prediction of male fertility status and classification accuracy differs in every case. In this experiment, we have used only three features and a classification accuracy of 90% is achieved by KNN. Besides this, the ROC value of 0.857 proved that our intelligent model performance is good compared to other models where the same data set was utilized. However, direct comparison with previous studies is meaningless because they used nine attributes and the maximum classification accuracy was 93.86% [1]. Considering the result involving the features selection, the classification accuracy score is higher than other models [2,3,7]. Also, these three features could lead to an increase in the model performance and help to understand the deep-rooted connection with male reproductive biology. This proposed model can be examined on a large dataset to illustrate its accuracy strength in the upcoming time.

References

1. Bidgoli, A.A., Komleh, H.E., Mousavirad, S.J.: Seminal quality prediction using optimized artificial neural network with genetic algorithm. In: 2015 9th International Conference on Electrical and Electronics Engineering (ELECO), pp. 695–699. IEEE (2015)
2. Candemir, C.: Estimating the semen quality from life-style using fuzzy radial basis functions. Int. J. Mach. Learn. Comput. **8**(1), 44–8 (2018)
3. Dash, S.R., Ray, R.: Predicting seminal quality and its dependence on life style factors through ensemble learning. Int. J. E-Health Med. Commun. (IJEHMC) **11**(2), 78–95 (2020)
4. Dey, N., Ashour, A.S., Borra, S.: Classification in BioApps: Automation of Decision Making, vol. 26. Springer, Cham (2017). https://doi.org/10.1007/978-3-319-65981-7
5. Durairajanayagam, D.: Lifestyle causes of male infertility. Arab. J. Urol. **16**(1), 10–20 (2018)
6. Engy, E., Ali, E., Sally, E.G.: An optimized artificial neural network approach based on sperm whale optimization algorithm for predicting fertility quality. Stud Inf. Control **27**(3), 349–358 (2018)
7. Girela, J.L., Gil, D., Johnsson, M., Gomez-Torres, M.J., De Juan, J.: Semen parameters can be predicted from environmental factors and lifestyle using artificial intelligence methods. Biol. Reprod. **88**(4), 99–1 (2013)
8. Hamet, P., Tremblay, J.: Artificial intelligence in medicine. Metabolism **69**, S36–S40 (2017)
9. Kumar, S., Murarka, S., Mishra, V., Gautam, A.: Environmental and lifestyle factors in deterioration of male reproductive health. Indian J. Med. Res. **140**(Suppl 1), S29 (2014)
10. Kurt, I., Ture, M., Kurum, A.T.: Comparing performances of logistic regression, classification and regression tree, and neural networks for predicting coronary artery disease. Expert Syst. Appl. **34**(1), 366–374 (2008)
11. Mathur, P.P., D'cruz, S.C.: The effect of environmental contaminants on testicular function. Asian J. Androl. **13**(4), 585 (2011)
12. Mendoza-Palechor, F.E., Ariza-Colpas, P.P., Sepulveda-Ojeda, J.A., De-la Hoz-Manotas, A., Piñeres Melo, M.: Fertility analysis method based on supervised and unsupervised data mining techniques. Int. J. Appl. Eng. **11**, 10374–10379 (2016)
13. Nath, S.S., Mishra, G., Kar, J., Chakraborty, S., Dey, N.: A survey of image classification methods and techniques. In: 2014 International conference on control, instrumentation, communication and computational technologies (ICCICCT), pp. 554–557. IEEE (2014)
14. Podgorelec, V., Kokol, P., Stiglic, B., Rozman, I.: Decision trees: an overview and their use in medicine. J. Med. Syst. **26**(5), 445–463 (2002). https://doi.org/10.1023/A:1016409317640
15. Rhemimet, A., Raghay, S., Bencharef, O.: Comparative analysis of classification, clustering and regression techniques to explore men's fertility. In: El Oualkadi, A., Choubani, F., El Moussati, A. (eds.) Proceedings of the Mediterranean Conference on Information and Communication Technologies 2015. LNEE, vol. 380, pp. 455–462. Springer, Cham (2016). https://doi.org/10.1007/978-3-319-30301-7_48
16. Riordon, J., McCallum, C., Sinton, D.: Deep learning for the classification of human sperm. Comput. Biol. Med. **111**, 103342 (2019)

17. Sahoo, A.J., Kumar, Y.: Seminal quality prediction using data mining methods. Technol. Health Care **22**(4), 531–545 (2014)
18. Sharma, K., Virmani, J.: A decision support system for classification of normal and medical renal disease using ultrasound images: a decision support system for medical renal diseases. Int. J. Ambient Comput. Intell. (IJACI) **8**(2), 52–69 (2017)
19. Sharpe, R.M.: Environmental/lifestyle effects on spermatogenesis. Philos. Trans. R. Soc. B: Biol. Sci. **365**(1546), 1697–1712 (2010)
20. Simfukwe, M., Kunda, D., Chembe, C.: Comparing Naive Bayes method and artificial neural network for semen quality categorization. Int. J. Innovative Sci. Eng. Technol. **2**(7), 689–694 (2015)
21. Soltanzadeh, S., Zarandi, M.H.F., Astanjin, M.B.: A hybrid fuzzy clustering approach for fertile and unfertile analysis. In: 2016 Annual Conference of the North American Fuzzy Information Processing Society (NAFIPS), pp. 1–6. IEEE (2016)
22. UCI: Fertility data set. https://archive.ics.uci.edu/ml/datasets/Fertility. Accessed 11 Feb 2021
23. Virtanen, H., Rajpert-De Meyts, E., Main, K., Skakkebaek, N., Toppari, J.: Testicular dysgenesis syndrome and the development and occurrence of male reproductive disorders. Toxicol. Appl. Pharmacol. **207**(2), 501–505 (2005)
24. Wang, Y., et al.: Morphological segmentation analysis and texture-based support vector machines classification on mice liver fibrosis microscopic images. Curr. Bioinform. **14**(4), 282–294 (2019)
25. Zemmal, N., Azizi, N., Dey, N., Sellami, M.: Adaptive semi supervised support vector machine semi supervised learning with features cooperation for breast cancer classification. J. Med. Imaging Health Inf. **6**(1), 53–62 (2016)

An Empirical Study of Vision Transformers for Cervical Precancer Detection

Sandeep Angara$^{(\boxtimes)}$, Peng Guo, Zhiyun Xue, and Sameer Antani

National Library of Medicine, Bethesda, MD 20894, USA
sandeep.angara@nih.gov

Abstract. Cervical precancer is a direct precursor to invasive cervical cancer and a prime target for ablative therapy. This paper presents an empirical study of Vision Transformers (ViT) for cervical precancer classification, an extended study of our previous work using data derived from two studies conducted by the U.S. National Cancer Institute. In this study, we show that ViT can significantly outperform the current state-of-art methods. We also examine data augmentation techniques that help reduce noise that can interfere in precancer detection, such as specular reflection. We achieve 84% accuracy on the test set outperforming the existing works based on the same dataset. Apart from the performance gains, we observe the learned features focus on cervical regions of anatomical significance. Through these experiments, we demonstrate that ViT attains excellent results compared to the current state-of-the-art methods in classifying cervical images for cervical precancer screening.

Keywords: Vision Transformers (ViT) · Cervical cancer · Transfer learning

1 Introduction

Cervical cancer is the fourth most common cancer in women worldwide [1]. It is caused by persistent infection with one of about 15 genotypes of carcinogenic human papillomavirus (HPV). Due to inadequate screening in low-resource settings, cancer is often detected at its late stages, which is very difficult to cure or may require aggressive cervical excision and result in poor quality of life. Early detection of cervical cancer helps in reducing the mortality rate. Visual Inspection with Acetic acid (VIA), one of the commonly screening modalities in low resource regions, is inexpensive and straightforward. However, visual triage is difficult for human observers, and it often results in inadequate performance [2]. The other screening programs, cervical cytology (Pap tests) and colposcopy, require infrastructure and sufficiently trained personnel and are used in high or medium-resource regions. The process of VIA requires applying 3–5% diluted acetic acid to a speculum-exposed cervix by a health care provider. The whitening of the cervical tissue is suggestive of HPV infection, and texture, edge, and vasculature of and around the whitened regions could be indicators of cervical precancer. Sample cerviscopic images of the cervix with acetic acid are shown in Fig. 1.

KC Santosh et al. (Eds.): RTIP2R 2021, CCIS 1576, pp. 26–32, 2022.
https://doi.org/10.1007/978-3-031-07005-1_3

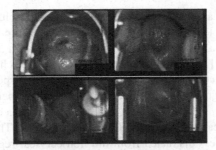

Fig. 1. Examples of cerviscopic cervix images

Convolutional neural networks (CNN's) have become an important tool in today's AI applications. In classification tasks, typical CNN architectures stack multiple convolutional layers together (with nonlinear activations) [3–5] to learn spatial relations for final classifications. Convolution operation can capture only local information but having the capability to abstract and retain information from a large neighborhood boosts the performance in vision tasks [6]. Recently proposed Vision Transformers (ViT) achieve comparable results to CNNs on image classification, object detection, image segmentation, etc. [7]. Moreover, ViT can learn long-range dependencies, which makes transformers an attractive alternative tool to CNNs.

Inspired by the significant success of vision transformers in various computer vision tasks [6], we use ViT with several data augmentation techniques to improve the performance of cervical precancer classification and alleviate the specular reflection issue frequently encountered in cervical images. We also address how long-range dependency learning with transformers can help focus on the cervix region without requiring localization using a detector network and cropping.

2 Related Work

Several deep learning algorithms have been proposed for cervical precancer detection and demonstrated good performance. In the early stage of this research [8], Faster R-CNN [9] algorithm has been used to detect the cervix region and simultaneously predict the case probability. The model was trained on 2000 annotated images using transfer learning with ImageNet weights. The dataset was collected during a National Cancer Institute (NCI) prospective epidemiologic study in the Guanacaste region of Costa Rica. Later the feasibility of automated visual evaluation with cervix images captured using a specialized handheld device was investigated [10]. Both Faster R-CNN and RetinaNet were applied in [10]. Besides using localization and classification based on a single network, [11] developed a customized architecture based using Feature Pyramid Network as the backbone. The last feature layer was built by upsampling and concatenating specific pre-trained feature pyramid layers, followed by a Global Average Pooling (GAP) layer. A fully connected layer for classification was made on top of the GAP layer. The features combined from various layers improved the performance and model explainability compared to related work. BF-CNN combing two-state images [12] has been proposed to fuse images applied with acetic acid and iodine solution, boosting performance. Semi-supervised learning using ResNeSt50 architecture has been used in [13] to leverage unlabeled data, outperformed the model trained with transfer learning based on ImageNet weights. In [13], various augmentation techniques have been suggested to reduce the impact of specular reflection, vaginal walls, metal speculum, shadows, etc. The proposed image augmentation techniques improved the performance and model interpretability. However, the images were first cropped using a cervix region detector trained on the Costa Rica Vaccine Trial (CVT) dataset [14]. The cropping helps the classification model be less distracted from the non-cervical region and focus on the cervix region. In the current work, we omit the step of cervix region detection and use the original images as the input to the ViT classification network.

3 Experiments

3.1 Data Preparation

The dataset was acquired from two NCI studies: One was the Atypical Squamous Cells of Undetermined Significance/Low-grade Squamous Intraepithelial Lesion (ASCUS/LSIL) Triage Study (ALTS), and the other is the Guanacaste Natural History Study (NHS). ALTS [15] was a multicenter, randomized clinical trial designed to evaluate three alternate methods of management: intermediate colposcopy, cytologic follow-up, and triage by human papillomavirus (HPV) DNA testing. This study was conducted in the United States and designed to determine the optimal management plan for low-grade cervical abnormalities. The data was collected from non-pregnant women 18+ years old with no prior hysterectomy or ablative therapy to the cervix. NHS data was collected from the Costa Rica population-based Cancer Registry [16, 17]. The NHS study was designed to understand the natural history of HPV and cervical cancer. It was also conducted to provide the effectiveness of new screening and management tools. In both ALTS and NHS studies, a cerviscope was used to capture the picture of the cervix region after the application of acetic acid. Digitized images were then obtained using scanners and were compressed for storage. Images in ALTS and NHS datasets were manually reviewed to ensure the cervix region was visible in the image. The image may also contain other anatomy or medical devices, e.g., the vaginal wall, external genitalia, metal speculum, swabs, etc., as shown in Fig. 1. Several medical experts in medical screening and epidemiology annotated the images into two classes: Controls and Cases. In our experiments, the images were resized with a shorter edge to 800 pixels and maintain the aspect ratio. The number of images in each class in training, validation, and test set is provided in Table 1, respectively.

3.2 Architecture

In this experiment, we use a ViT "Base" variant [6]. The transformer splits the image into patches and then flattens the patches. The flattened patches with positional embeddings are passed as input sequences to the standard transformer encoder. The transformer encoder consists of alternating layers of multiple self-attention heads and MLP blocks. The only modification is discarding the prediction head (MLP head) and attaching a linear layer with N units, where N is the number of classes.

Table 1. Number of images in training/validation/test set

	Controls	Cases
Training set	1645	843
Validation set	359	182
Test set	230	115

3.3 Training Setup

We train ViT-Base with a 16×16 input patch size. We train the models using SGD optimizer with a learning rate of 0.003 and also using mixed precision. All the models are trained for 2500 steps with a batch size of 512, with cosine learning rate decay. We first finetune the model loaded with ImageNet21k on our dataset using random crop and normalization augmentation techniques. After qualitative and quantitative analysis, we find the trained model is impacted by specular reflection. To make the model robust to the noise [13], we then finetune the model with the following augmentation techniques (using the "Albumentations" library [18]).

- Resize the image to 400-by-400
- Crop a random part of 384-by-384 in the image
- Randomly apply Shift, Scale, Rotate to the image
- Scale hue, saturation, gamma, blur, and brightness
- Apply PCA noise [19] with a coefficient sampled from a normal distribution N (0, 0.1)
- Normalize RGB channels by subtracting mean = (0.5, 0.5, 0.5) and dividing by standard deviation = (0.5, 0.5, 0.5).

In addition, we apply the random sun flares and random fog augmentation techniques used to reduce specular reflections [13].

4 Results and Discussions

Our experiments show that vision transformers trained using transfer learning improve performance significantly compared to the work on the same dataset [13]. Quantitative results are presented in Table 2. The accuracy of the test dataset is improved from 82.0% to 84.0% using the ViT-Base model, and AUC is boosted from 0.87 to 0.91. Figure 2 shows the Precision-Recall curve and ROC curve on the test set, respectively.

We have trained a ViT-Base architecture with augmentation techniques and training setup methods described in Sect. 3. The visualization heatmaps in Fig. 3 demonstrate that the model trained with our suggested augmentation techniques helps reduce specular reflection. The model also concentrates on the cervix region for the final prediction with less impact from unrelated objects like swabs, metal speculum, pubic hair, etc. Unlike our previous work [13], we do not crop the cervix region first and then pass it to the classifier network. As indicated by the attention maps in Fig. 3, the ViT classifier learns to

Table 2. Performance comparison with the work on the same dataset

Model	Method	Image size	Average AUC score	Accuracy
ResNest50 (previous work) [13]	Semi-supervised learning	800 × 800	0.87	82.0%
ViT-Base (16 × 16 patch)	Transfer learning	384 × 384	**0.91**	**84.0%**

concentrate on the cervix region. The underlying self-attention component in the vision transformer helps learn long-range dependencies and integrate the information globally across the image, which makes the network potentially learn rich, high-level features. While the vision transformer achieves better performance, as shown in Fig. 4, the model still distracts from noise in some samples.

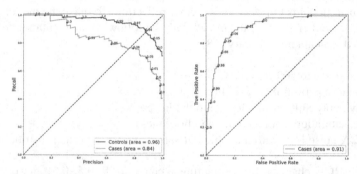

Fig. 2. Precision-Recall and ROC curves on the test dataset

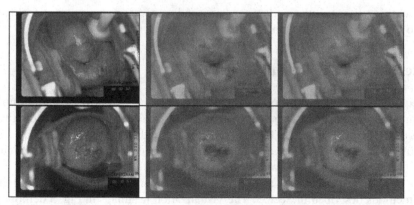

Fig. 3. Images in the first column are input images. Second column images are from the model ViT-Base 16 × 16 model trained with resize and normalization techniques. Heatmaps in the third column represent the model trained with suggested augmentation techniques.

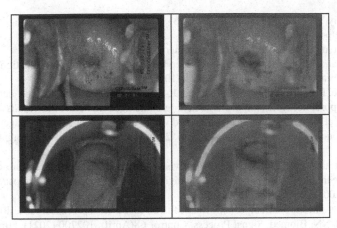

Fig. 4. Heatmaps where the model focuses on text and other noises in the image.

5 Conclusion and Future Work

In this work, we have explored the application of vision transformers with various augmentation techniques. By finetuning the model pre-trained on ImageNet21k on the cervix images, vision transformers improve the efficiency and effectiveness of precancer detection. In addition, the trained model concentrates on the cervix region without using any cervix detector. Future work includes training with higher-resolution images, exploring self-supervised learning, and experimenting with new data augmentation techniques.

Acknowledgment. This work was supported by the Intramural Research Program of the National Library of Medicine, part of the National Institutes of Health. Data used in this research was by agreement between the National Library of Medicine and the National Cancer Institute (NCI). We are grateful to Dr. Mark Schiffman and his team at the NCI for feedback on our findings.

References

1. Schiff, M., et al.: Seminar Human papillomavirus and cervical cancer. https://doi.org/10.1016/S0140-6736(07)61416-0
2. Belinson, J.L., Pretorius, R.G., Permanente, K., Xinfeng Qu, C.: Cervical screening by pap test and visual inspection enabling same-day biopsy in low-resource, high-risk communities (2019). http://journals.lww.com/greenjournal
3. He, K., Zhang, X., Ren, S., Sun, J.: Deep residual learning for image recognition. In: Proceedings of the IEEE Computer Society Conference on Computer Vision and Pattern Recognition, December 2016, vol. 2016-December, pp. 770–778 (2016). https://doi.org/10.1109/CVPR.2016.90
4. Krizhevsky, A., Sutskever, I., Hinton, G.E.: ImageNet classification with deep convolutional neural networks. http://code.google.com/p/cuda-convnet/. Accessed 25 Feb 2021
5. Tan, M., Le, Q.V.: EfficientNet: rethinking model scaling for convolutional neural networks. In: 36th International Conference on Machine Learning, ICML 2019, vol. 2019-June, pp. 10691–10700 (2019). http://arxiv.org/abs/1905.11946. Accessed 25 Feb 2021

6. Dosovitskiy, A., et al.: An image is worth 16×16 words: transformers for image recognition at scale. https://github.com/

7. Han, K., et al.: A survey on visual transformer (2022)

8. Hu, L., et al.: An observational study of deep learning and automated evaluation of cervical images for cancer screening. https://doi.org/10.1093/jnci/djy225

9. Ren, S., He, K., Girshick, R., Sun, J.: Faster R-CNN: towards real-time object detection with region proposal networks. http://image-net.org/challenges/LSVRC/2015/results

10. Xue, Z., et al.: A demonstration of automated visual evaluation of cervical images taken with a smartphone camera. Int. J. Cancer **147**(9), 2416–2423 (2020). https://doi.org/10.1002/ijc.33029

11. Guo, P., et al.: Clinical medicine network visualization and pyramidal feature comparison for ablative treatability classification using digitized cervix images (2021). https://doi.org/10.3390/jcm10050953

12. Yan, L., et al.: Multi state colposcopy image fusion for cervical precancerous lesion diagnosis using BF-CNN. Biomed. Signal Process. Control **68**(April), 102700 (2021). https://doi.org/10.1016/j.bspc.2021.102700

13. Angara, S., Guo, P., Xue, Z., Antani, S.: Semi-supervised learning for cervical precancer detection, pp. 202–206 (2021). https://doi.org/10.1109/CBMS52027.2021.00072

14. Guo, P., Xue, Z., Rodney Long, L., Antani, S.: Cross-dataset evaluation of deep learning networks for uterine cervix segmentation. Diagnostics **10**(1), 44 (2020). https://doi.org/10.3390/diagnostics10010044

15. Schiffman, M., Adrianza, M.E.: ASCUS-LSIL Triage Study Design, Methods and Characteristics of Trial Participants (2000)

16. Rodr Iguez, A.C., et al.: Cervical cancer incidence after screening with HPV, cytology, and visual methods: 18-Year follow-up of the Guanacaste cohort. https://doi.org/10.1002/ijc.30614

17. Herrero, R., et al.: Design and methods of a population-based natural history study of cervical neoplasia in a rural province of Costa Rica: the Guanacaste Project 1 (1997)

18. Buslaev, A., Iglovikov, V.I., Khvedchenya, E., Parinov, A., Druzhinin, M., Kalinin, A.A.: Albumentations: fast and flexible image augmentations. Inf. **11**(2), 125 (2020). https://doi.org/10.3390/info11020125

19. Krizhevsky, A., Sutskever, I., Hinton, G.E.: ImageNet Classification with Deep Convolutional Neural Networks. http://code.google.com/p/cuda-convnet/. Accessed 28 Feb 2021

CheXNet for the Evidence of Covid-19 Using 2.3K Positive Chest X-rays

KC Santosh[✉][iD] and Supriti Ghosh[✉]

2AI: Applied Artificial Intelligence Research Lab, Computer Science,
University of South Dakota, Vermillion, SD 57069, USA
santosh.kc@usd.edu, supriti.ghosh@coyotes.usd.edu

Abstract. CheXNet is not a surprise for Deep Learning (DL) community as it was primarily designed for radiologist-level pneumonia detection in Chest X-rays (CXRs). In this paper, we study CheXNet to analyze CXRs to detect the evidence of Covid-19. On a dataset of size
$4,600$ CXRs ($2,300$ Covid-19 positive cases and $2,300$ non-Covid cases
(Healthy and Pneumonia cases)) and with k(=5) fold cross-validation
technique, we achieve the following performance scores: accuracy of 0.98,
AUC of 0.99, specificity of 0.98 and sensitivity of 0.99. On such a large
dataset, our results can be compared with state-of-the-art results.

Keywords: Deep learning · CheXNet · Covid-19 · Chest X-ray

1 Introduction

Coronavirus (recognized as Covid-19) is a contagious infection that is caused concern by SARS-CoV-2 [1]. According to the World Health Organization (WHO),
the disease was originally found in Wuhan, China, in 2019 and has subsequently
spread over the world, concluding in the Coronavirus outbreak of 2019–2021 [2].
Individuals are primarily infected by the virus via respiratory droplets. SARS-
CoV-2 continues to infect individuals around the world, with over 209.83 million infections and 4.4 million deaths reported one year and eight months after
its discovery (as of August 2021) [3]. Researchers have proven that the virus
can survive on surfaces that have been contacted by an infected person(s). The
spread rate of Coronavirus is high by the end of March 2020 [3]. Also, due
to unprecedented events, no prediction models are accurate as of now [4]. The
polymerase chain reaction (PCR) is the standard method for diagnosing and
detecting Covid-19 patients. SARS-CoV-2 RNA can be detected in respiratory
specimens using nasopharyngeal or oropharyngeal swabs. The PCR technique
takes a long time and needs a lot of resources considering its high accuracy
and sensitivity. As a result, given the virus's extraordinary global transmission
and the disease's rapid progression through a patient's body, a faster screening
method for Covid-19 outbreaks is necessary [5]. Radiography techniques such as

Authors Credit Statement. Authors contributed equally to the paper.

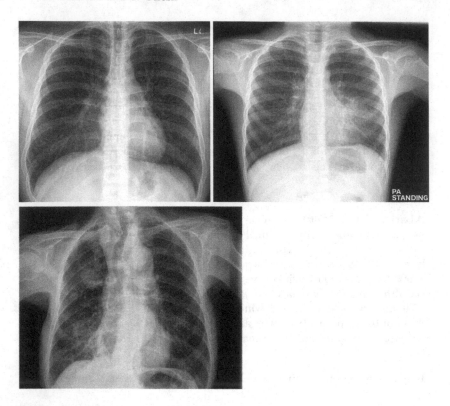

Fig. 1. Chest X-ray image data: Healthy (top-left), Pneumonia (top-right), and Covid-19 positive (bottom-left).

CXRs have been suggested as an alternative to the standard PCR approach for Covid-19 screening. Ground-Glass Opacity patches and consolidation in chest x-rays are the common signs of Covid-19 infection [6–8]. In Fig. 1, we have provided few samples of CXR images to better understand and visualization. Furthermore, researchers in [5] have offered a detailed understanding of the increase in radiographic clues in Covid-19 confirmed cases on a statistical basis as well as the chronological phases of the disease's progression in the body of the host. Authors of [9] have also discussed on the size of dataset that is required to develop robust Covid-19 imaging tools/techniques. For all these reasons, AI-driven tools must be implemented globally for mass screening.

As X-ray imaging equipment are more common and less expensive than CT scan systems, analyzing CXR is a better/wise idea. To name a few, previous studies discovered that CXRs are more effective at detecting lung problems [7,10–14]. For years, deep learning has a rich state-of-the-art literature in computer vision. Medical imaging informatics is no exception [15]. Considering Covid-19 pandemic, in [10], authors stated the importance of active-learning framework to develop cross-population train/test machine learning models that take multitudinal/multimodal data into account. However, for multimodal learning and representation, due to data availability issue, computing scientists do not have enough opportunity. Deep learning models were proposed by the authors in [16] to differentiate Covid-19 cases from Pneumonia as well as healthy cases. In [16], another study offered a CNN-tailored model based on residual connections with 80% positive predictive value. Authors in [17] established the utilization of ResNet50, Inception-ResNet V2, and InceptionNet V3 to detect Covid-19 positive cases. Marques et al. [18] performed a binary classification and a multi-classification across Covid-19, pneumonia, and healthy cases. They used CNN and EfficientNet with a 10 fold cross-validation. In the perspective of Covid-19, similar studies have been presented in [19] that takes transfer learning into account. In [20], authored attempted to employ one deep CNN network to train/test two different image modalities: CXR and CT scan. In [21], authors have designed a deep CNN model, Truncated Inception Net to analyze Covid-19 cases. To categorize pneumonia bacterial, pneumonia virus, normal, and Covid-19 positive cases, Loey et al. [22] employed GoogleNet, ResNet18, and AlexNet DNN models. Using a DarkNet model [23], authors performed a binary classification (healthy and Covid-19) against a multi-class classification (healthy, Covid-19, and Pneumonia). They reported accuracies of 98.08% and 87.02% for binary and multi-class classification, respectively on a dataset of $1,127$ CXRs.

In this paper, we apply deep learning model (CheXNet) to screen Covid-19 using CXRs. CheXNet is not a surprise for DL community as it was primarily designed for radiologist-level pneumonia detection in CXRs. Our study is solely experimental on a dataset of size $8,214$ CXRs, where $2,358$ of them are Covid-19 positive. Instead of reinventing the wheel, we primarily explore how well ChexNet performed on Covid-19 CXRs.

The remainder of the paper is organized as follows. In Sect. 2, we describe dataset we use in our experiments. Then we explain ChexNet implementation in Sect. 3. Experimental results are provided in Sect. 4. It includes evaluation protocol and performance metrics in Sect. 4.1 and analysis of the results in Sect. 4.2. Comparison study is provided in Sect. 4.3. Section 5 concludes the paper.

2   Chest X-ray Dataset

We collected a number of CXR benchmark sets that are publicly available. As there exists no single dataset available for both Covid-19 and non-Covid-19 cases, we considered three different sources to collect Covid-19 dataset and another source to collect healthy and pneumonia dataset:

1. Healthy dataset [24]: It contains $1,583$ CXR images. The dataset was collected from retrospective cohorts of children patients aged one to five years old at Guangzhou Women and Children's Medical Center in Guangzhou. The patients' CXR imaging was done as part of their normal medical care. To analyze CXR images, all CXRs were first reviewed for quality control, with any scans that were low quality or unreadable being removed. After that, the diagnoses for the photographs were rated by two experts before being approved for use in the AI system. A third expert evaluated the evaluation set to make sure there were no grading problems.

Table 1. Dataset summary

Cases	Dataset (size)	Avg Image size
Healthy	1,583	1.35 MB
Pneumonia	4,273	439 KB
Covid-19	2,358	3.31 MB
Total	8,214	1.7 MB

2. Pneumonia dataset [24]: As before, we collected pneumonia CXR images from the exact same source. They were chosen from retrospective cohorts of children patients aged one to five years old at Guangzhou Women and Children's Medical Center in Guangzhou. All CXR imaging was done as part of the patients' regular medical treatment.
3. Covid-19 dataset[1,2,3]: Covid-19 dataset is formed using three different publicly available sources (Radiological Society of North America, Qatar University and University of Dhaka). It is constituted of 2,358 Covid-19 positive CXRs.

In total, there are 8,214 CXRs available (see Table 1). Following Table 1, in order to prepare a balanced dataset for our experiment, we used 4,600 CXRs in total, where 2,300 of them were Covid-19 positive cases and remaining 2,300 were non-Covid-19 cases (Healthy: 1,583 + Pneumonia: 717).

3   CheXNet and Implementation

Pre-trained model CheXNet is typically a 121-layer Dense Convolutional Neural Network (D-CNN), which is called ChexNet, and it is developed on the CXR 14 dataset (Huang et al., 2016) [25]. P. Rajpurkar et al. [26] trained CheXNet on the Chest X-ray14 dataset (Wang et al., 2017) [27], which contains 112,120 frontal-view CXRs that have been individually classified with up to 14 different thoracic illnesses, including pneumonia. To execute the optimization of such deep network flexibility, authors [26] have leveraged dense connections [25] and batch normalization. It can be stimulating for radiologists to detect pneumonia in CXRs as pneumonia might appear unclear, overlap with other diagnoses, and resemble a variety of other innocuous abnormalities. DenseNets increase the information flow and slope through to the network, enabling deep neural networks development tractable. Further, they implemented sigmoid non-linearity after replacing the ultimate fully connected layer. Weights from a model pre-trained on ImageNet are used to initialize the network's weights (Deng et al.,

---

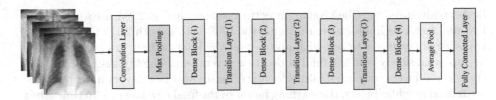

Fig. 2. CheXNet architecture

Table 2. Layers used in pre-trained model CheXNet

Layers	Output size	CheXNet
Convolution layer	112 × 112	7 × 7 conv, stride 2
Pooling	56 × 56	3 × 3 max pool, stride 2
Dense block (1)	56 × 56	$\begin{bmatrix} 1 \times 1 \ conv \\ 3 \times 3 \ conv \end{bmatrix} \times 6$
Transition layer (1)	56 × 56	1 × 1 conv
	28 × 28	2 × 2 average pool, stride 2
Dense block (2)	28 × 28	$\begin{bmatrix} 1 \times 1 \ conv \\ 3 \times 3 \ conv \end{bmatrix} \times 12$
Transition layer (2)	28 × 28	1 × 1 conv
	14 × 14	2 × 2 average pool, stride 2
Dense block (3)	14 × 14	$\begin{bmatrix} 1 \times 1 \ conv \\ 3 \times 3 \ conv \end{bmatrix} \times 24$
Transition layer (3)	14 × 14	1 × 1 conv
	7 × 7	2 × 2 average pool, stride 2
Dense block (4)	7 × 7	$\begin{bmatrix} 1 \times 1 \ conv \\ 3 \times 3 \ conv \end{bmatrix} \times 16$
Classification layer	1 × 1	7 × 7 global average pool
		1000D fully-connected softmax

2009) [28]. Adam is used to train the network from start to finish with conventional parameters (0.9 and 0.999). Authors used 16-piece mini-batches to train the model [25]. Also, authors selected the model with the minimum possible validation loss using an initial learning rate of 0.001 that was decayed by a factor of 10 [25].

In our implementation, we use a regular CNN, where an input image is processed through the network to generate an output predicted label as illustrated in Fig. 2. Each convolutional layer (CL), except the first (which receives the input image), takes the output of the previous CL and produces an output feature map, which is then passed to the next CL. There are L direct connections between each layer and its subsequent layer for all possible layers. CheXNet contains 121 learnable layers: $(6 + 12 + 24 + 16) \times 2 = 116$ layers in the dense blocks and 5 layers from first CL, last fully connected layer (FCL), and three transition layers (TL). For a better understanding, CheXNet architecture is shown in Fig. 2. We use a composite learning factor technique after replacing the 1000-D FCL with 2-D FCL: the early transferred layers are frozen with no update, the intermediate transferred layers are updated slowly, and the final added new layers learn quickly. As intermediate transferred layers have pre-trained weights/biases and new layers have random-initialized weights/biases, the learning factor of the final new layers is 10 times that of middle transferred layers. From Table 2, we can comprehend that the CheXNet model starts with a CL with 7×7 kernel size and stride 2 and a 3×3 max-pooling layer (MPL) with stride 2 and continues with a series of dense block and TLs and closes with a global average pool layer and a FCL. Each CL corresponds to the sequence batch normalization rectified linear unit (ReLU) convolution.

4 Experimental Results

4.1 Evaluation Protocol and Performance Metrics

In our experiments, we follow k(=5) fold cross-validation technique. To measure the performance, the following evaluation metrics are used: Accuracy (ACC), Sensitivity (SEN), Sepecificity (SPEC), and Area under the ROC curve (AUC). They are computed as follows:

- ACC $= (t_p + t_n)/(t_p + t_n + f_p + f_n)$,
- SEN $= t_p/(t_p + f_n)$, and
- SPEC $= t_n/(t_n + f_p)$,

where t_p, f_p, t_n, and f_n are the total number of true positives, false positives, true negatives and false negatives, respectively.

4.2 Results Analysis

Following the evaluation protocol and performance metrics in the preceding section, we summarize the findings of the experiment of ChexNet in Table 3. We emphasize that we provide performance scores obtained from k(=5) fold cross-validation train/test scheme. Results from each fold are reported, and their scores are aggregated in the form of mean ± standard deviation i.e., $\mu \pm \sigma$. Standard deviation helps us understand how consistently/sparsely the results are produced. Using CheXNet on a dataset of size 4,600 images, we achieved the following scores: 0.99 ± 0.008 AUC, 98.45 ± 0.011 ACC, 0.98 ± 0.013 SPEC and 0.99 ± 0.007 SEN. As we observe that the deviation (for all metrics: AUC, ACC, SPEC and SEN) is too small, we confirm that the proposed model is adequate to detect Covid-19 positive images.

4.3 Comparative Study

Since the outbreak of Covid-19, multiple studies have been proposed or announced that use CXRs to distinguish Covid-19 positive cases [9]. Deep learn-ing models require fairly large dataset, and they may not work as planned in

Table 3. Results (CheXNet): AUC, ACC (in %), SPEC, and SEN

CheXNet	AUC	ACC	SPEC	SEN
Fold-1	0.98	97.91	0.97	0.99
Fold-2	0.99	98.87	0.99	0.99
Fold-3	0.98	96.94	0.97	0.98
Fold-4	0.99	98.87	0.99	0.99
Fold-5	1.0	99.68	1.0	1.0
Min	0.98	96.94	0.97	0.98
Max	1.0	99.68	1.0	1.0
$\mu \pm \sigma$	0.99 ± 0.008	98.45 ± 0.011	0.98 ± 0.013	0.99 ± 0.007

Table 4. Comparison: AUC, ACC (in %), SPEC, and SEN of CheXNet, DenseNet169, ResNet50 and VggNet16

$\mu \pm \sigma$	AUC	ACC	SPEC	SEN
CheXNet	0.99 ± 0.008	98.45 ± 0.011	0.98 ± 0.013	0.99 ± 0.007
DenseNet169	0.98 ± 0.005	98.13 ± 0.008	0.99 ± 0.008	0.98 ± 0.008
ResNet50	0.59 ± 0.022	59.18 ± 0.020	0.59 ± 0.022	0.59 ± 0.022
VggNet16	0.59 ± 0.024	58.92 ± 0.025	0.59 ± 0.024	0.59 ± 0.024

the beginning of year 2020, when we did not have that much of clinically annotated dataset. In [9], authors discuss on the use of dataset, technicalities and
corresponding performance scores. Since dataset size has been increased over
time, fair comparison is merely possible, according to authors. Therefore, in our
study, we carried out other popular pre-trained models: DenseNet169, ResNet50
and VggNet16 for a performance comparison. We followed exact same evaluation protocol and metrics as discussed before. Table 4 shows comparative study
among popular deep learning models. Of all, RestNet50 and VggNet16 did not
perform well. In contrast, DenseNet169 performed close to ChexNet.

5   Conclusion and Future Work

As CheXNet was primarily designed to detect radiologist-level pneumonia in
Chest X-rays (CXRs), in this paper, we have employed CheXNet for evidence
of Covid-19. On a dataset of size $4,600$ CXRs ($2,300$ Covid-19 positive cases
and $2,300$ non-Covid cases) and with k(=5) fold cross-validation technique, we
have achieved the following performance scores: accuracy of 0.98, AUC of 0.99,
specificity of 0.98 and sensitivity of 0.99. Considering other deep learning models, CheXNet performed consistently better. To the best of our knowledge, till
this date, we reported results on the largest possible CXR dataset for Covid-19
screening.

Our immediate plan is to extend our work that follows active-learning framework using multitudinal or multimodal data [10]. It also encourages us to pursue cross-population train or test models with a larger dataset. With this, we will also work on how other infectious diseases (TB and Pneumonia, to name a few) can be considered [29].

References

1. World health organization (2020) naming the coronavirus disease (Covid-19) and the virus that causes it. https://www.who.int/emergencies/diseases/novel-coronavirus-2019/technical-guidance/naming-the-coronavirus-disease-%28covid-2019%29-and-the-virus-that-causes-it
2. Hui, D.S., et al.: The continuing 2019-nCoV epidemic threat of novel coronaviruses to global health-the latest 2019 novel coronavirus outbreak in Wuhan, China. Int. J. Infect. Dis. **91**, 264–266 (2020)
3. World health organization (2020) coronavirus disease (Covid-2019) situation reports. https://www.who.int/emergencies/diseases/novel-coronavirus-2019/situation-reports
4. Santosh, K.C.: COVID-19 prediction models and unexploited data. J. Med. Syst. **44**(9), 170 (2020)
5. Li, M., et al.: Coronavirus disease (Covid-19): spectrum of CT findings and temporal progression of the disease. Acad. Radiol. **27**(5), 603–608 (2020)
6. Kong, W., Agarwal, P.P.: Chest imaging appearance of Covid-19 infection. Radiol.: Cardiothorac. Imaging **2**(1), e200028 (2020)
7. Huang, C., et al.: Clinical features of patients infected with 2019 novel coronavirus in Wuhan, China. Lancet **395**(10223), 497–506 (2020)
8. Ng, M.-Y., et al.: Imaging profile of the Covid-19 infection: radiologic findings and literature review. Radiol.: Cardiothorac. Imaging **2**(1), e200034 (2020)
9. Santosh, K.C., Ghosh, S.: Covid-19 imaging tools: how big data is big? J. Med. Syst. **45**(7), 1–8 (2021)
10. Santosh, K.C.: AI-driven tools for coronavirus outbreak: need of active learning and cross-population train/test models on multitudinal/multimodal data. J. Med. Syst. **44**(5), 1–5 (2020)
11. Santosh, K.C., Vajda, S., Antani, S., Thoma, G.R.: Edge map analysis in chest X-rays for automatic pulmonary abnormality screening. Int. J. Comput. Assist. Radiol. Surg. **11**(9), 1637–1646 (2016)
12. Karargyris, A., et al.: Combination of texture and shape features to detect pulmonary abnormalities in digital chest X-rays. Int. J. Comput. Assist. Radiol. Surg. **11**(1), 99–106 (2016)
13. Vajda, S., et al.: Feature selection for automatic tuberculosis screening in frontal chest radiographs. J. Med. Syst. **42**(8), 1–11 (2018)
14. Santosh, K.C., Antani, S.: Automated chest X-ray screening: can lung region symmetry help detect pulmonary abnormalities? IEEE Trans. Med. Imaging **37**(5), 1168–1177 (2017)
15. Kang, M., Gurbani, S.S., Kempker, J.A.: The published scientific literature on Covid-19: an analysis of pubmed abstracts. J. Med. Syst. **45**(1), 1–2 (2021)
16. Wang, L., Lin, Z.Q., Wong, A.: Covid-net: a tailored deep convolutional neural network design for detection of Covid-19 cases from chest X-ray images. Sci. Rep. **10**(1), 1–12 (2020)

17. Narin, A., Kaya, C., Pamuk, Z.: Automatic detection of coronavirus disease (Covid-19) using X-ray images and deep convolutional neural networks. Pattern Anal. Appl. **24**, 1–14 (2021)
18. Marques, G., Agarwal, D., de la Torre Díez, I.: Automated medical diagnosis of Covid-19 through efficientnet convolutional neural network. Appl. Soft Comput. **96**, 106691 (2020)
19. Apostolopoulos, I.D., Mpesiana, T.A.: Covid-19: automatic detection from X-ray images utilizing transfer learning with convolutional neural networks. Phys. Eng. Sci. Med. **43**(2), 635–640 (2020)
20. Mukherjee, H., Ghosh, S., Dhar, A., Obaidullah, S.M., Santosh, K.C., Roy, K.: Deep neural network to detect Covid-19: one architecture for both CT scans and chest X-rays. Appl. Intell. **51**, 1–13 (2020)
21. Das, D., Santosh, K.C., Pal, U.: Truncated inception net: Covid-19 outbreak screening using chest X-rays. Phys. Eng. Sci. Med. **43**(3), 915–925 (2020)
22. Loey, M., Manogaran, G., Khalifa, N.E.M.: A deep transfer learning model with classical data augmentation and CGAN to detect Covid-19 from chest CT radiography digital images. Neural Comput. Appl. 1–13 (2020)
23. Ozturk, T., Talo, M., Yildirim, E.A., Baloglu, U.B., Yildirim, O., Acharya, U.R.: Automated detection of Covid-19 cases using deep neural networks with X-ray images. Comput. Biol. Med. 103792 (2020)
24. Kermany, D., Zhang, K., Goldbaum, M., et al.: Labeled optical coherence tomography (OCT) and chest X-ray images for classification. Mendeley Data **2**(2) (2018)
25. Huang, G., Liu, Z., Van Der Maaten, L., Weinberger, K.Q.: Densely connected convolutional networks. In: Proceedings of the IEEE Conference on Computer Vision and Pattern Recognition, pp. 4700–4708 (2017)
26. Rajpurkar, P., et al.: ChexNet: radiologist-level pneumonia detection on chest X-rays with deep learning. arXiv preprint arXiv:1711.05225 (2017)
27. Wang, X., Peng, Y., Lu, L., Lu, Z., Bagheri, M., Summers, R.M.: ChestX-ray8: hospital-scale chest X-ray database and benchmarks on weakly-supervised classification and localization of common thorax diseases. In: Proceedings of the IEEE Conference on Computer Vision and Pattern Recognition, pp. 2097–2106 (2017)
28. Deng, J., Dong, W., Socher, R., Li, L.-J., Li, K., Fei-Fei, L.: ImageNet: a large-scale hierarchical image database. In: 2009 IEEE Conference on Computer Vision and Pattern Recognition, pp. 248–255. IEEE (2009)
29. Mahbub, M.K., Biswas, M., Gaur, L., Alenezi, F., Santosh, K.C.: Deep features to detect pulmonary abnormalities in chest X-rays due to infectious diseaseX: Covid-19, pneumonia, and tuberculosis. Inf. Sci. **592**, 389–401 (2022)

An Enhanced Deep Convolution Neural Network Model to Diagnose Alzheimer's Disease Using Brain Magnetic Resonance Imaging

Milon Biswas$^{(\boxtimes)}$ ⓘ, Md. Kawsher Mahbub ⓘ, and Md. Abdul Mozid Miah

Bangladesh University of Business and Technology, Dhaka, Bangladesh
milon@ieee.org

Abstract. Alzheimer's disease (AD) is a brain ailment that is irreversible and has an initial warning sign, such as memory cognitive functioning loss. The precise and early diagnosis of AD is exceedingly vital for patient care. The study proposed a deep convolutional neural network (CNN) model for diagnosing AD state using brain magnetic resonance imaging (MRI). The authors' concentrated on a binary classification decision for brain MRI and observed better results compared to the other state-of-the-art studies, with an accuracy of 0.9938, sensitivity 0.9890, specificity 0.9974, precision 0.9970 and F1 score of 0.9932. The experiment was conducted on a 4800 image dataset (Kaggle) using Google collaboratory GPU, Keras library with TensorFlow backend.

Keywords: Alzheimer's disease · Neurological disorder · MRI · Medical imaging · Deep learning

1 Introduction

The illness of AD is a degenerative brain disease triggered by nerve cell damage in the brain [1]. The patient faces difficulty performing day-to-day tasks, with initial signs of memory loss, problems in language, and different cognitive processes. Researchers notably observed that AD is a prevalent cause of dementia and ultimately leads to mortality, a particular focus of study. According to the Alzheimer's Association, AD is the sixth leading reason for mortality in the United States. A survey [2] reveals that 131.5 million individuals (mostly elderly with more than 65 years of age) are at greater risk of dementia globally. The primary cause of AD is the degeneration of the hippocampal region, a component of the brain comprising the ability to think, memory and falls. AD and healthy brain imagery illustrated in Fig. 1 leads to a decline in memory and language powers.

Research on comprehensive review for detection of AD and dementia stages on MRI images applying DL techniques and the significance of DL in medical imaging has been emphasized [4,5]. The artificial intelligence (AI) umbrella

© Springer Nature Switzerland AG 2022
KC Santosh et al. (Eds.): RTIP2R 2021, CCIS 1576, pp. 42–52, 2022.
https://doi.org/10.1007/978-3-031-07005-1_5

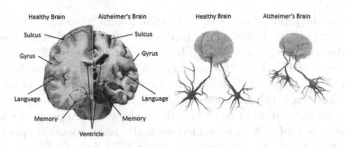

Fig. 1. Cross-sectional brain for visualising the difference between healthy brain and Alzheimer's [3]

encompasses abundant algorithms and methods, e.g. genetic algorithm, that have multiple applications in day to day life. The authors of these books [6, 7] have provided a intellectual study about medical imaging. Biswas et al. [8, 9] has presented a study about neurological disorder and provided an XAI explanation. A neurabooks 1 of tprovide alctual hese netwointelrk that employs many parameters and layers are defined as "deep learning". The authors [10] pre-trained ResNet-18 on ImageNet dataset with convolutional neural network (CNN). The sequence-based models employed were the temporal convolution network (TCN) and several recurrent neural networks (RNN). For AD detection, numerous intense sequence-based models and structures were developed and compared. Several deep learning models, comprising 2D, 3D, CNN, and RNN, have been constructed in previous studies by researchers. Each MRI scan is divided into 2D slices to utilise a 2D CNN on 3D mrin volumes, disregards the link between 2D image slices in MRI volume with a 96.88% precision, a 100% sensitivity and a 94.12% specificity. Many basic network designs are included such as CNNs, which are essentially an extensive space-based CNN employing shared weights [11]. RNNs can leverage their internal state to process input sequences in comparison to neural feedforward networks. The RNNs aims at identifying sequences, for example, a speech signal or the text. Authors of [12] used Alzheimer's disease neuroimaging initiative (ADNI) database magnetic resonance imaging (MRI) and created a computer-aided diagnosis (CAD) system. AD affects the hippocampus and cerebrum, mainly in the gray matter of the cerebrum and retrieves the gray matter area of the brain, multi-modality diagnostic technique based on deep learning is proposed [13] to extract significant traits for these modest variations. The authors of [14] discussed the segmentation of improved AD classification along with segmentation techniques, state-of-the-art methods and comparative findings. Another study [15] proposed a technique to generate maps of disease with a high-resolution range from local brain architecture to a multi-layered perception of individual Alzheimer's risk for an accurate diagnosis.

For multimodal input, the ADNI, Australian imaging biomarkers and lifestyle study of Ageing(AIBL), Framingham heart and the national Alzheimer's coordinating centre (NACC) datasets each had a mean range of 0.996, 0.974, 0.876 and 0.954, respectively. Here the authors [16] demonstrated, utilising ADNI, that deep models surpass shallow models, for example, support vector machine (SVM), decision trees, random forests and neighbouring k-stone neighbours. A sub-study of the heinz nixdorf recall (HNR) study with 120 persons and a baseline model accuracy of 76% is examined with the recommended approach [17]. A 12-layer CNN model was provided with brain MRI data to diagnose AD with 97.75% accuracy using [18] binary classification and data. Other classifications, such as the stroke diagnosis, the brain-predicted age, attention deficit hyperactivity disorder classes (ADHD), used DL techniques for identifying classification using MRI. Few researchers altered the 3D-CNN model for AD diagnostics [19]., Shaik and Ram [20] attempted to extract gray matter from the human brain and to classify it using CNN. The technique given was used for clinical valuation, and a precision of 90.47 was obtained. Hamed et al. [21] presented a technique that gave high accuracy in categorisation with 94.54% accuracy. A wide variety of diseases, such as diabetic retinopathy, cancer or Alzheimer's, are highly promised for clinical decision-making support and DL has been a success for said diseases. DL outperforms low learning for single data modalities such as images, EHRs, and SNP's. Haque et al. [29] utilised previously built models for diagnosing Alzheimer. To detect mild, demented and normal Alzheimer control patients using MRI images, Santosh et al. [30] developed the AlzNet deeper learning model [31].

This research has included Kaggle's dataset comprising very mild demented images and non-demented images for testing the proposed model and the classification of individuals with AD. For the training of MRI imaging data, CNNs is used. After the networks are trained for data modality, authors utilise the validation set to validate the model. Afterwards, the model is accessed using test data to measure the performance outcome. Despite improved clinical decision support, the performance using various data types, lack of well-defined techniques for assessing profound models is a fundamental obstacle for widespread adoption of DL model adoption for the clinical decision-making process. The authors identified this challenge and proposed an improved DL method to discover the key factors influencing choice rapidly. The significant contribution of this study in forecasting the AD stage is highlighted below:

- Proposed a deep CNN model to identify MRI malignancy of Alzheimer.
- Proposed improved DL technique to extract high-performance characteristics.
- The proposed model's results are superior to the contemporary state of the art.

The remaining sections of the papers are as follows: Sect. 2 contains a proposed methodology of deep CNN to detect AD, Sect. 3 discusses the details experiments, and Sect. 4 concludes the paper with future recommendations.

2 Proposed Methodology

Figure 2 demonstrates the proposed deep CNN model including dataset, preprocessing setps, traning and testing steps and lastly the result.

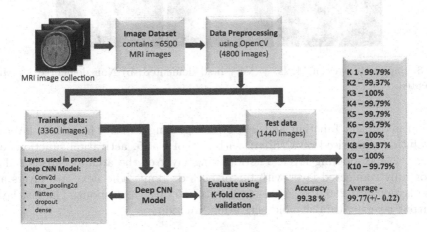

Fig. 2. Proposed deep CNN model for AD detection

2.1 Data Pre-processing

Data preprocessing is a method for the mining of raw data utilized for the usable
and effective formatting of raw data. Data are cleaned, transformed and reduced
in three phases for preprocessing the original data collection. In this work, the
pre-processing of MRI images is performed using OpenCV. The dataset from
Kaggle comprised ~6500 images split into four classes for training and testing.
The experiment is conducted on 4800 JPEG images from two classes of the
selected dataset. The size of images is 8-bit, 96 dpi, and 176 × 208 pixels, which
is scaled to 224 × 224 pixels using OpenCV to match the input dimension of the
proposed deep CNN. The images are converted from RGB to greyscale using
OpenCV following scaling. Figure 3 illustrates a few instances of images.

2.2 Deep CNN: Architecture and Implementation

The model depicted in Fig. 4 comprises an ensemble of blocks, each with multiple
layers performing essential activities such as conv2d, maxpooling2d, activation,
flatten, dropout dense. The architecture of the proposed model has been demonstrated in Fig. 4 with the first layer as the input layer, with input shape (224,
224, 1) and strides 2. The second layer is a convolution layer with 8 filters with
the size of 3 × 3 supported by relu activation function and a 2 × 2 max-pooling
layer. The third layer of convolution comprises of 16 filters, with 3 × 3, followed

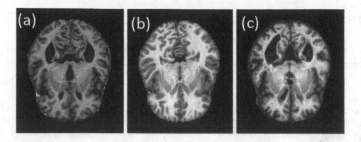

Fig. 3. Sample images of MRIs: a) Very mild demented, b) Non demented, c) Mild demented

by relu activation function and 2 × 2 max-pooling layer. The fourth layer of convolution comprised of 32 filters with size of 5 × 5, activation function relu and 2 × 2 max pooling layer. The following layer of the architecture is a flatten or fully connected layer with 0.5 or 50% dropout. The next two layers are dense layers with 256 and 128 neurons with 0.5 or 50% dropout. The last layer is output layers with a sigmoid activation function.

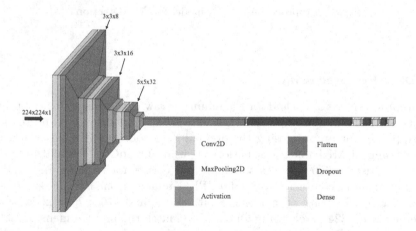

Fig. 4. Proposed deep CNN learning model for AD detection including filter number

Table 1 states the proposed model specification for all the layers of proposed deep CNN along with each layer output shape and layer learning parameters.

Table 1. Number of learning parameter of proposed architecture for 224×224 image

Layer (type)	Output shape	Parameters
conv2d (Conv2D)	(None, 112, 112, 8)	80
max_pooling2d (MaxPooling2)	(None, 56, 56, 8)	0
conv2d_1 (Conv2D)	(None, 54, 54, 16)	1168
max_pooling2d_1 (MaxPooling2	(None, 27, 27, 16)	0
conv2d_2 (Conv2D)	(None, 23, 23, 32)	12832
max_pooling2d_2 (MaxPooling2)	(None, 11, 11, 32)	0
flatten (Flatten)	(None, 3872)	0
dropout (Dropout)	(None, 3872)	0
dense (Dense)	(None, 256)	991488
dropout_1 (Dropout)	(None, 256)	0
dense_1 (Dense)	(None, 128)	32896
dropout_2 (Dropout)	(None, 128)	0
dense_2 (Dense)	(None, 1)	129
Total parameters		1,038,593

2.3 Hyper Parameters in Deep CNN

Recently the biomedical field has shown tremendous developments for gathering multimodal data from several areas. The data is in three general categories (i.e. pictures, signals, and sequences) with enormous quantities and complex characters. The mining of such a tremendous amount of data is a significant challenge and demands advanced machine learning algorithms. The DL techniques provide the solution for handling this challenge by enabling the data to be broken into manageable chunks and automatically extracting features from images. Due to the black-box nature of these DL algorithms and underlying dense network structure, the outcomes' logic is difficult to decode. Consecutively, the model's performance can be monitored and enhanced by altering parameters called loss function, optimizers, layers, drop out, and epochs. The loss function guides and informs the optimizer about the correct path. Optimizers use weighting to shape and create the model as accurately as viable. The dropout technique prevents system overriding by purposefully killing neurons; it is done with a specific probability and is often aimed for a 0.5 probability reduction. The network regularisation is handled by increasing the size of the training synthetically. The model's accuracy may be enhanced by altering the number of layers and instances.

3 Experiments

3.1 Dataset

The dataset utilised for this study is obtained from Kaggle [27] (4 classes of images). It comprises 2240 very light demented samples, 2560 non-cutting samples and 896 mild demented sample images, and 64 moderately demented images. The study uses two classes of images out of 4 classes, with one extremely mild, demented class. The dataset was further split into training and testing with 3360 training images and 1440 test images.

3.2 Validation Protocol and Evaluation Metrics

The 10-fold cross-validation used in this study trains and tests the data set to validate the dataset D1. The 10-fold cross-validation works in subsets of 10 each. Thus, ten separate sub-sets of data are generated. The assessed architecture trained for nine (1–9) sub-set before testing the 10th subset (see Table 2).

Table 2. 10 fold cross-validation accuracy rate (percentage) dataset

Dataset	K1	K2	K3	K4	K5	K6	K7	K8	K9	K10	Average
D1	99.79	99.37	100.0	99.79	99.79	99.79	100.0	99.37	100.0	99.79	99.77($\pm$0.22)

3.3 Results and Discussion

The study utilised two classes of images (2560 and 2240) from Kaggle for training, validation and testing. The experiment was carried out on an HP Intel Corei5 laptop with 4 GB RAM, and Google Collaboratory GPU was used to train the model. The Keras library is used to implement the suggested model, which has a Tensorflow backend. Relu activation is used to test for each CNN neuron. The loss function is binary cross-entropy with 32 batch size. The optimizer used is adam, and the dense activation function used is sigmoid. For 200 epochs, the network is trained. The output is a classification between Alzheimer's patients and non-Alzheimer's patients. The proposed deep CNN model's results are shown in Table 3.

Table 3. Performance of proposed deep CNN

Dataset	Optimizer	Training accuracy	Training loss	Validation accuracy	Validation loss
D1 [27]	Adam	0.9927	0.0182	0.9940	0.0150

For both the training and validation sets, performance is measured in terms of accuracy and loss. The loss provides a highly accurate indication of the model's fit. Figure 5 illustrates the accuracy versus epoch and loss versus epoch graphs for training and validation sets. The training set indicates the training accuracy attained is 99.27%, and the training and validation loss was virtually zero. It also demonstrates the progression of the model during its training phase. The

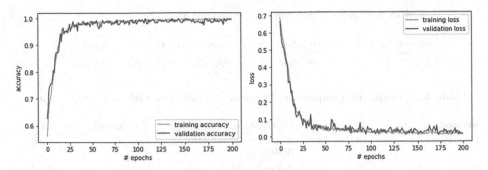

Fig. 5. Training and validation accuracy & loss of proposed deep CNN model for every epoch

validation set, on the other hand, provides a measure of the model's quality. The attained validation accuracy is 99.40%, which indicates that the model can envisage data detection with 99.40% accuracy.

The confusion matrix illustrates the precise versus non-precise predictions spread across each class and occurrence. A receiver operating characteristic curve (ROC) is a graphical representation that depicts the model's performance. The proposed model achieved the highest AUC score possible, indicating that superior results for high-quality separation. To further provide particulars about the performance of confusion matrices, a ROC curve is shown in Fig. 6 for test images.

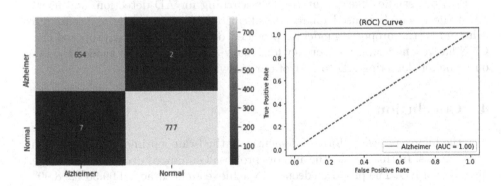

Fig. 6. Confusion matrix and ROC curve of proposed deep CNN model

A classification report is used to assess the accuracy of a classification algorithm's predictions. The classification reports in Table 4 provide the essential classification metrics such as precision, recall, and f1-score.

The Table 5, clearly indicates the superior performance of proposed with 99.38% accuracy as compared to the previous studies by [15, 18, 24–26]. The proposed model has attained superior results as compared to different state of the art.

Table 4. Results of applying the proposed algorithm on test set

Dataset	Accuracy	AUC	Sensitivity	Specificity	Precision	F1-Score
D1 [27]	99.38%	1.00	98.94%	99.74%	99.70%	99.32%

Table 5. Performance comparison of proposed framework with other approaches

Approach	Technique	Classification	Modalities	Accuracy(%)	Dataset
Kang et al. [13]	DL	2 class (EMCI/NC)	MRI	94.2	ADNI
Qiu et al. [15]	DL	2 class NC/AD	MRI	83.40	ADNI
Venugopalan et al. [16]	DL + RF	3 class(AD, MCI CN)	MRI	88.02	ADNI
Pelka et al. [17]	LSTM + RNN	2 class (AD/NC)	MRI + PET	90.00	ADNI
Hussain et al. [18]	CNN	2 class (AD/NC)	MRI	97.75	OASIS
Kundaram et al. [23]	DCNN	3 class (AD/NC/MCI)	MRI	98.57	ADNI
Ruoxuan et al. [24]	MLP-RNN	2 class (AD/NC)	MRI	89.69	ADNI
Shi et al. [25]	SAE & SVM	4 class (AD/ncMCI/ cMCI/NC)	MRI+PET	0.53 ± 0.47 with SAE 0.47 ± 0.18	ADNI
Liu et al. [26]	DCNN + RNN	3 class (AD/MCI/NC)	FDG + PET	91.2–AD vs NC, 89.9–MCI vs NC	ADNI
Haque et al. [29]	DNN + SVM	2 class (AD/NC)	MRI	95.21	
Proposed deep CNN	deep CNN	2 class (AD/NC)	MRI	99.38	Kaggle

Previous studies likewise utilise deep learning for AD detection, and nearly all of the researchers used binary classification; however, superior accuracy is achieved by the proposed model for provided datasets. Thus, the proposed deep CNN has reached superior accuracy for binary classification and yielded the best outcome for detecting AD to best of our knowledge.

4   Conclusion

AD, the highly prevalent form of dementia, is the brain's primary cause of memory ailments. In this article, the authors proposed enhanced deep CNN for better diagnosis of AD. The proposed deep CNN achieve an accuracy of 99.38%, 98.90% sensitivity, 99.74% specificity, 99.70% precision and 99.32% F1 score. The model correctly identified 654 images out of 656 real Alzheimer images, with only seven misidentifications. Hence, the proposed classifier obtained the highest AUC score of 1.00, indicating the best deep CNN for high-class separation. The results may be further improved with high computing machines, which was the limitation of the study. Researchers may replicate the analysis for different applications and on large datasets with high configuration computational power in the future.

References

1. Alzheimer's Association: 2018 Alzheimer's disease facts and figures. Alzheimer's Dementia **14**(3), 367–429 (2018)
2. Prince, M.J., Wimo, A., Guerchet, M.M., Ali, G.C., Wu, Y.T., Prina, M.: World Alzheimer Report 2015-The Global Impact of Dementia: an analysis of prevalence, incidence, cost and trends (2015)
3. The difference between a healthy brain and a brain affected by Alzheimer's. https://www.brightfocus.org/. Accessed 7 July 2021
4. Altinkaya, E., Polat, K., Barakli, B.: Detection of Alzheimer's disease and dementia states based on deep learning from MRI images: a comprehensive review. J. Inst. Electron. Comput. **1**(1), 39–53 (2020)
5. Ghosh, S., Bandyopadhyay, A., Sahay, S., Ghosh, R., Kundu, I., Santosh, K.C.: Colorectal histology tumor detection using ensemble deep neural network. Eng. Appl. Artif. Intell. **100**, 104202 (2021)
6. Santosh, K.C., Das, N., Ghosh, S.: Deep Learning Models for Medical Imaging. Elsevier (2021)
7. Santosh, K.C., Gaur, L.: Artificial Intelligence and Machine Learning in Public Healthcare. Springer, Heidelberg (2021)
8. Biswas, M., Kaiser, M.S., Mahmud, M., Al Mamun, S., Hossain, M.S., Rahman, M.A.: An XAI based autism detection: the context behind the detection. In: Mahmud, M., Kaiser, M.S., Vassanelli, S., Dai, Q., Zhong, N. (eds.) BI 2021. LNCS (LNAI), vol. 12960, pp. 448–459. Springer, Cham (2021). https://doi.org/10.1007/978-3-030-86993-9_40
9. Biswas, M., et al.: Indoor navigation support system for patients with neurodegenerative diseases. In: Mahmud, M., Kaiser, M.S., Vassanelli, S., Dai, Q., Zhong, N. (eds.) BI 2021. LNCS (LNAI), vol. 12960, pp. 411–422. Springer, Cham (2021). https://doi.org/10.1007/978-3-030-86993-9_37
10. Ebrahimi, A., Luo, S., Chiong, R., Alzheimer's Disease Neuroimaging Initiative: Deep sequence modelling for Alzheimer's disease detection using MRI. Comput. Biol. Med. **134**, 104537 (2021). https://doi.org/10.1016/j.compbiomed.2021.104537
11. Alom, M.Z., et al.: A state-of-the-art survey on deep learning theory and architectures. Electronics **8**(3), 292 (2019)
12. Raghavaiah, P., Varadarajan, S.: A CAD system design to Diagnosize Alzheimers disease from MRI brain images using optimal deep neural network. Multimed. Tools Appl. **80**(17), 26411–26428 (2021). https://doi.org/10.1007/s11042-021-10928-7
13. Kang, L., Jiang, J., Huang, J., Zhang, T.: Identifying early mild cognitive impairment by multi-modality MRI-based deep learning. Front. Aging Neurosci. **12**, 206 (2020)
14. Yamanakkanavar, N., Choi, J.Y., Lee, B.: MRI segmentation and classification of human brain using deep learning for diagnosis of Alzheimer's disease: a survey. Sensors **20**(11), 3243 (2020)
15. Qiu, S., et al.: Development and validation of an interpretable deep learning framework for Alzheimer's disease classification. Brain **143**(6), 1920–1933 (2020)
16. Venugopalan, J., Tong, L., Hassanzadeh, H.R., Wang, M.D.: Multimodal deep learning models for early detection of Alzheimer's disease stage. Sci. Rep. **11**(1), 1–13 (2021)
17. Pelka, O., et al.: Sociodemographic data and APOE-4 augmentation for MRI-based detection of amnestic mild cognitive impairment using deep learning systems. PLoS ONE **15**(9), e0236868 (2020)

18. Hussain, E., Hasan, M., Hassan, S.Z., Azmi, T.H., Rahman, M.A., Parvez, M.Z.: Deep learning based binary classification for Alzheimer's disease detection using brain MRI images. In: 2020 15th IEEE Conference on Industrial Electronics and Applications (ICIEA), pp. 1115–1120. IEEE, November 2020
19. Hosseini-Asl, E., Keynton, R., El-Baz, A.: Alzheimer's disease diagnostics by adaptation of 3D convolutional network. In: 2016 IEEE International Conference on Image Processing (ICIP), pp. 126–130. IEEE, September 2016
20. Basheera, S., Ram, M.S.S.: Convolution neural network-based Alzheimer's disease classification using hybrid enhanced independent component analysis based segmented gray matter of T2 weighted magnetic resonance imaging with clinical valuation. Alzheimer's Dementia Transl. Res. Clin. Interv. **5**, 974–986 (2019)
21. Taheri Gorji, H., Kaabouch, N.: A deep learning approach for diagnosis of mild cognitive impairment based on MRI images. Brain Sci. **9**(9), 217 (2019)
22. Suk, H.I., Lee, S.W., Shen, D.: Deep sparse multi-task learning for feature selection in Alzheimer's disease diagnosis. Brain Struct. Funct. **221**(5), 2569–2587 (2016)
23. Kundaram, S.S., Pathak, K.C.: Deep learning-based Alzheimer disease detection. In: Nath, V., Mandal, J.K. (eds.) Proceedings of the Fourth International Conference on Microelectronics, Computing and Communication Systems. LNEE, vol. 673, pp. 587–597. Springer, Singapore (2021). https://doi.org/10.1007/978-981-15-5546-6_50
24. Cui, R., Liu, M., Li, G.: Longitudinal analysis for Alzheimer's disease diagnosis using RNN. In: 2018 IEEE 15th International Symposium on Biomedical Imaging (ISBI 2018), pp. 1398–1401. IEEE, April 2018
25. Shi, J., Zheng, X., Li, Y., Zhang, Q., Ying, S.: Multimodal neuroimaging feature learning with multimodal stacked deep polynomial networks for diagnosis of Alzheimer's disease. IEEE J. Biomed. Health Inform. **22**(1), 173–183 (2017)
26. Liu, M., Cheng, D., Yan, W., Initiative, A.D.N.: Classification of Alzheimer's disease by combination of convolutional and recurrent neural networks using FDG-PET images. Front. Neuroinform. **12**, 35 (2018)
27. https://www.kaggle.com/tourist55/alzheimers-dataset-4-class-of-images Accessed 5 July 2021
28. Li, H., Habes, M., Wolk, D.A., Fan, Y., Initiative, A.D.N.: A deep learning model for early prediction of Alzheimer's disease dementia based on hippocampal magnetic resonance imaging data. Alzheimer's Dementia **15**(8), 1059–1070 (2019)
29. Haque, S.: A deep learning model in the detection of Alzheimer disease. Turkish J. Comput. Math. Educ. (TURCOMAT) **12**(10), 4013–4022 (2021)
30. Santosh, K.C., et al. (eds.): Medical Imaging: Artificial Intelligence, Image Recognition, and Machine Learning Techniques. CRC Press (2019)
31. Ruikar, D.D., Sawat, D.D., Santosh, K.C.: A systematic review of 3D imaging in biomedical applications. Med. Imaging 154–181 (2019)

Automatic Knee Osteoarthritis Stages Identification

Dattatray I. Navale[1], Darshan D. Ruikar[2(✉)], Dattatray D. Sawat[3],
Parshuram M. Kamble[4], Kavita V. Houde[4], and Ravindra S. Hegadi[4]

[1] N B Navale Sinhgad College of Engineering,
Kegaon-Solapur 413255, Maharashtra, India
[2] School of Computer Science, MIT World Peace University,
Pune 411038, India
ddruikar@sus.ac.in
[3] School of Computational Sciences, P.A.H. Solapur University, Solapur 413255,
Maharashtra, India
[4] School of Computer Science, Central University of Karnataka,
Kadaganchi 585367, Karnataka, India

Abstract. Osteoarthritis (OA) is a type of chronic bone joint disorder. Patients may suffer from heavy pain while performing day to day activities. By confirming the description of the Osteoarthritis Initiative (OAI) nowadays, not only older but also younger people are also suffering from knee OA. The early diagnosis and prognosis of OA are necessary to reduce the pains. Manual detection and accurate severity level identification from an X-ray image is a complicated and requires experienced knowledgeable person. Radiographer and expert orthopedic surgeons spend a lot of time to decide the exact OA grade. To reduce expert's effects and to predict exact OA severity grade we have developed a deep neural network (DNN) based Computer-aided detection (CAD) system for knee OA classification which precisely identifies the severity level.

The proposed CAD system works in stages. Initially, an innovative column sum-based histogram modeling function is devised to separate the left and right knee from X-ray image. Later DNN-based five-class classification is applied to identify the severity grade. To achieve this, we have developed our own convolutional neural network named OACnet (Osteoarthritis classification network) which follows Kellgren & Lawrence (K&L) knee OA grading system. On OAI database (9,492 knee X-ray images of various severity grades) our system yields 81.41% result.

Keywords: Osteoarthritis · K&L grading system · NIH-OAI · X-ray image · Expert system · Computer aided diagnosis (CAD) · ROI detection · Deep neural network · Classification

© Springer Nature Switzerland AG 2022
KC Santosh et al. (Eds.): RTIP2R 2021, CCIS 1576, pp. 53–60, 2022.
https://doi.org/10.1007/978-3-031-07005-1_6

1 Introduction

OA shows a disproportion occurred in the continuous process of cartilage destruction and regeneration [1,2]. In OA affected bone joints cartilage destruction is more than reconstruction. Over the period the cartilage (cushion between the bones at joints) will be lost completely. It results in inflexibility, swelling in joint and bone rubbing. Patients suffering from OA feel a lot of pain while doing daytoday activities. OA commonly occurs at the knee, hip, neck, lower back and small joints in hands. Out of all the possibility of knee OA is more. The knee is a prominent weight-bearing joint. In OA affected knee, the space in the knee joint is almost lost. Bones come much nearer that tends to rub of bones on each other. The spur is more and the presence of articular cartilage is also sparse. This results in severe pain while performing everyday activities. So early detection and recovery of knee OA are important.

Early diagnosis of knee OA is important for proper treatments. The experts recommend for radio-graphic scanning of the desired portion (knee joint region). Predicting exact severity level from radio-graphic image is laborious job. A lot of experience and practice are required to decide on specific grading and to perform an accurate diagnosis. To minimize the load on radiographers and medical practitioners, the Deep neural network (DNN) based CAD system is proposed in this paper. The proposed system performs a five-class classification based on Kellgren & Lawrence (K&L) knee OA severity grading system. To achieve promising results we have developed our own convolutional neural network-based architecture OACnet (Osteoarthritis classification network).

2 Literature Review

According to the literature, localization of region of interest (ROI), and knee OA severity prediction (classification) are the general steps to develop CAD for automatic knee OA severity prediction. The CAD system development for automatic knee OA severity identification from X-ray has been proposed as an classification problem.

Patient-specific medical images (X-ray) is the primary requirement of the CAD development for knee OA severity prediction. By confirming literature most of the research attempted to use local databases for experimentation. Nowadays researchers are using the Osteoarthritis initiative (OAI) database to conduct experiments.

ROI localization methods can be divided into manual, semi-automatic, and automatic methods. The manual method is expert-driven and can be used to create templates (ground truth) [3]. Semiautomatic methods (level set and active contour, for instance) expect few user interventions in terms of threshold value, or initial bounding box from the user to start the segmentation process. The third type i.e. fully automatic methods do not expect any sort of user intervention to localize ROI. A neural network-based ROI localization method is proposed in [4]. A fully convolution neural network is trained to localize ROI automatically.

The main aim of feature selection is to represent pathological parameters (joint space distance, bone spur, etc.) precisely. In many literature researcher extracted handcrafted features such as statistical features [5], edge curvature features [6] and textural GLCM (gray level co-occurrence matrix) features [7] to classify input X-ray images to correct class according to severity level. These features are limited in number and have limited power to represent all pathological parameters. To overcome this limitation nowadays researchers are using deep features to perform classification. Deep feature learning methods themselves learn and extract effective features from row input data [8].

In the last step (i.e. knee OA severity prediction) different classifiers are applied to identify correct class of input image. Support vector machine (SVM) [5], feed forward neural network [6,9], and deep convolution neural networks (CNN) based classification methods are adapted to predict severity grade of input X-ray image. The methods proposed in [5] demonstrated 80% and 86.7% accuracy for the healthy and affected images respectively. The method proposed in [10] shows 92% classification accuracy for three class classification, whereas methods discussed in [11] demonstrates 66.71% accuracy for five-class classification.

In the literature, most of the research attempts categorize the images in two classes: normal and OA affected. Only a few research attempts are present which results in five-class categorization. However, the classification accuracy of five class classification is not promising. So in the near future, several successful research attempts must be made to increase the classification results. The DNN-based classification would be better alternatives to improve classification accuracy.

3   Methodology

This section provides a detailed description of the proposed methodology devised to develop a CAD system for knee OA classification from knee X-ray images.

3.1   Data Acquisition

To promote the research, in the field of knee OA classification system, well-organized knee X-ray image database named Osteoarthritis Initiative (OAI) is made available by the National Institute of Health (NIH). The proposed system uses the OAI database for the experimentation. The OAI database contains 4,746 X-ray images.

3.2   Left and Right Knee Segmentation

Figure 1 (a) shows the input X-ray image contains both left and right knee. Before further processing, the input image must be separated into two portions. To achieve this, initially, the input gray-scale image is converted to a binary image. The image-specific threshold value is obtained by applying Otsu's

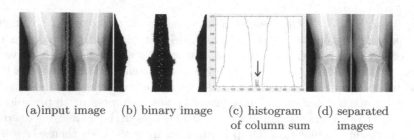

(a)input image   (b) binary image   (c) histogram   (d) separated
                                        of column sum   images

Fig. 1. Left and right knee segmentation process

Algorithm 1. ColumnHist(*BMP*)

Require: *BMI // Binary Map Image* Input BMI.
Ensure: *histogram vector of knee image*
 1: [*colmn, row*]:=size(*BMI*);
 2: for i:=1 to *colmn* do
 3: sumCol[i]:=sum(:,i)
 4: end for
 5: plot (*sumCol*)

---

method. Later column sum is calculated for each column, Algorithm 1 is devised
to compute the column sum.

The histogram is plotted for the calculated sum. The left and right knee
segmentation process is illustrated in Fig. 1. The input X-ray image and equivalent binary image is shown in Fig. 1 (a) and (b) respectively. The histogram of
the column sum are illustrated in Fig. 1 (c). By observing the histogram, it is
clear that there is a valley near the middle of the image. The lowest point of
the valley represents the boundary between the left and right knee. Algorithm 2
is devised to separate left and right knee from input X-ray image. Figure 1 (d)
shows the separated knee images. After the left and right knee segmentation size
of the database becomes double having 9,492 knee images. Further, these images
are segregated into five classes based on severity level. This segregation is done
by consulting expert radiographers and orthopedic physicians. Normal, minor,
mild, moderate, and severe are the labels of five classes.

3.3 ROI Detection

A simple block-based ROI detection method is implemented to extract knee joint
region from input image, illustrated in Algorithm 2. In this method input image
(Fig. 2 (a)) is divided into three equal rows (Fig. 2 (b)) and only middle part is
considered for the further experimentation.

3.4 DNN-Based Classification System

After successful application of preprocessing methods and ROI extraction, next
step is classification. The main aim of this work is to develop a DNN-based classi-

Algorithm 2. KneeSeg(*Image,sumCol*)

Require: *Image* and *sumCol* // Input gray scale Image and histogram vector.
Ensure: *LKnee* and *Rknee* image
1: Length:=size(sumCol)
2: for i=5 to Length do // skip first 5 colmns
3: if (sumCol[i]==0) then
4: ROI=i
5: end if
6: end for
7: LKnee[:]=I[:,start:ROI]
8: RKnee[:]=I[:,ROI:end]

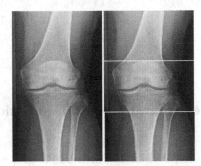

(a)input image   (b) image divided into
                       blocks of rows

Fig. 2. ROI localization process

fication system. The DNN-based architecture OACnet (Osteoarthritis network), especially for knee OA severity classification problems.

OACnet is lightweight than other DNN-based counterpart architecture which are enlisted above. The complexity of the proposed architecture is reduced by limiting the number of convolution layers followed by the fully connected layers at the end. There are 11,75,08,864 parameters in OACnet. In addition to this, our architecture expects input size 112 × 112 pixels whereas rest of the counterpart architectures expect input size much higher than 112 × 112. The main reason behind limiting the layers is that the other DNN-based architectures considered here suffering from over-fitting due to bigger architecture. Such bigger architectures are not needed at least for knee OA severity classification problems.

The proposed model comprises of four blocks of convolution layers followed by max-pooling layers. The activation maps produced by the seventh convolution layer consist of promising features with finer details that are supplied to a fully connected convolution layer having 4096 neurons. At last output of fully connected layers is feed to the softmax layer for five class severity classification. The Table 1 describes the architecture of OACnet in detail.

Table 1. OACnet (Osteoarthritis network) architecture

Layer		Feature map	Output size	Kernel size	Stride
Input	Image	1	112×112	–	–
1	$2 \times$ Convolution	128	$112 \times 112 \times 128$	3×3	1
	Max Pooling	128	$56 \times 56 \times 128$	3×3	2
3	$3 \times$ Convolution	256	$56 \times 56 \times 256$	3×3	1
	Max Pooling	256	$28 \times 28 \times 256$	3×3	2
5	$3 \times$ Convolution	512	$28 \times 28 \times 512$	3×3	1
	Max Pooling	512	$14 \times 14 \times 512$	3×3	2
7	$2 \times$ Convolution	512	$14 \times 14 \times 512$	3×3	1
	Max Pooling	512	$7 \times 7 \times 512$	3×3	2
9	FC	–	4096	–	
Output	SoftMax	–	5	–	

4   Experimental Setup and Result Discussion

For the experimentation machine having windows 10 operating system with i7 processor, 8 GB memory, and Nvidia GeForce 940M graphical processing unit (GPU) is used. Python 3, TensorFlow 1.12, compute unified data architecture (CUDA) 10.0, and CUDNN 7.4 is used for DNN-based implementation. The DNN training parameters, such as batch size, learning rate, and epoch, are set to 16, 0.001, and 20 respectively.

Among the database 50% (4,746) images were used for training, 30% (2,848) images were used for validation, whereas rest 20% (1,898) were kept for testing in both the approaches. Out of 4,746 images, 520 are of grade 0 (normal), 547 are of grade 1 (minor), 726 are of grade 2 (mild), 1255 are of grade 3 (moderate) and 1698 are of grade 4 (severe).

The confusion matrix of training of the proposed OACnet for true label OA images and predicted results are shown in Table 3. Four evaluation parameters, precision, recall, classification accuracy and mean square error (MSE) per grade are considered for the evaluation and are tabulated in Table 2. The overall accuracy (average of per class accuracy) of the DNN-based method it is 81.41%.

Table 2. Precision, recall, accuracy and MSE per severity grade

Grade	0	1	2	3	4	Avg
Precision	0.93	0.81	0.65	0.76	0.89	0.81
Recall	0.95	0.83	0.76	0.72	0.84	0.83
Accuracy	83.52	84.56	89.12	80.25	81.25	83.74
MSE	16.48	15.44	10.88	19.75	18.75	16.26

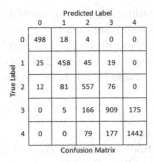

Predicted Label

		0	1	2	3	4
	0	498	18	4	0	0
	1	25	458	45	19	0
True Label 2	2	12	81	557	76	0
	3	0	5	166	909	175
	4	0	0	79	177	1442

Confusion Matrix

Fig. 3. Confusion matrix of OACnet training

4.1 Comparison of OACnet with Other DNN-Based Models

In addition to comparison with conventional NN the performance of OAC-net is compared with other DNN-based architectures such as densenet121, densenet169, densenet201, inceptionv3, resnet153 and vgg16. The evaluation parameters precision, recall and F1 score are calculated for the comparison. The detailed comparison is tabulated in Table 3. Among all the DNN-based architectures, proposed OACnet shows highest precision. Since knee OA classification does not require heavy architecture (i.e. architectures with higher number of parameters), the proposed OACnet best fits for the said task.

Table 3. Performance compassion of various DNN model

Network	Precision	Recall	F1
densenet121	0.67	0.87	0.75
densenet169	0.39	0.45	0.41
densenet201	0.52	0.54	0.52
inceptionv3	0.75	0.72	0.73
resnet153	0.75	0.78	0.76
Vgg16	0.76	0.68	0.71
'OACnet'	**0.81**	**0.83**	**0.82**

5 Conclusion

Development of CADe system for automatic knee OA severity prediction is the drastic need for healthcare society (at least in rural areas where there is less availability of expert radiologists and orthopedic surgeons). The CADe system will help radiologists and orthopedic experts for the right diagnosis and decide on the optimal recovery plan. By confirming the results of the conducted experiments, it is observed that the DNN-based classification system is a better alternative to solve the OA severity classification problem. The developed DNN-based OACnet architecture shows 81.41% overall accuracy. The introduction of the statistical layer would be one of the solutions to improve the overall accuracy.

References

1. Brandt, K.D., Dieppe, P., Radin, E.L.: Etiopathogenesis of osteoarthritis. Rheum. Dis. Clin. North Am. **34**(3), 531–559 (2008)
2. Felson, D.T., Anderson, J.J., Naimark, A., Walker, A.M., Meenan, R.F.: Obesity and knee osteoarthritis: the Framingham study. Ann. Internal Med. **109**(1), 18–24 (1988)
3. Stammberger, T., Eckstein, F., Michaelis, M., Englmeier, K.-H., Reiser, M.: Inter-observer reproducibility of quantitative cartilage measurements: comparison of b-spline snakes and manual segmentation. Magn. Reson. Imaging **17**(7), 1033–1042 (1999)
4. Antony, J., McGuinness, K., Moran, K., O'Connor, N.E.: Automatic detection of knee joints and quantification of knee osteoarthritis severity using convolutional neural networks. In: Perner, P. (ed.) MLDM 2017. LNCS (LNAI), vol. 10358, pp. 376–390. Springer, Cham (2017). https://doi.org/10.1007/978-3-319-62416-7_27
5. Navale, D.I., Hegadi, R.S., Mendgudli, N.: Block based texture analysis approach for knee osteoarthritis identification using SVM. In: 2015 IEEE International WIE Conference on Electrical and Computer Engineering (WIECON-ECE), pp. 338–341. IEEE (2015)
6. Hegadi, R.S., Navale, D.I., Pawar, T.D., Ruikar, D.D.: Osteoarthritis detection and classification from knee X-ray images based on artificial neural network. In: Santosh, K.C., Hegadi, R.S. (eds.) RTIP2R 2018. CCIS, vol. 1036, pp. 97–105. Springer, Singapore (2019). https://doi.org/10.1007/978-981-13-9184-2_8
7. Hegadi, R.S., Navale, D.I., Pawar, T.D., Ruikar, D.D.: Multi feature-based classification of osteoarthritis in knee joint X-ray images. In: Medical Imaging: Artificial Intelligence, Image Recognition, and Machine Learning Techniques, p. 75 (2019)
8. Suresha, S., Kidziński, L., Halilaj, E., Gold, G.E., Delp, S.L.: Automated staging of knee osteoarthritis severity using deep neural networks. Osteoarthritis Cartilage **26**, S441 (2018)
9. Kamble, P.M., Hegadi, R.S.: Comparative study of handwritten Marathi characters recognition based on KNN and SVM classifier. In: Santosh, K.C., Hangarge, M., Bevilacqua, V., Negi, A. (eds.) RTIP2R 2016. CCIS, vol. 709, pp. 93–101. Springer, Singapore (2017). https://doi.org/10.1007/978-981-10-4859-3_9
10. Kawathekar, P.P., Karande, K.J.: Use of textural and statistical features for analyzing severity of radio-graphic osteoarthritis of knee joint. In: 2015 International Conference on Information Processing (ICIP), pp. 1–4. IEEE (2015)
11. Tiulpin, A., Thevenot, J., Rahtu, E., Lehenkari, P., Saarakkala, S.: Automatic knee osteoarthritis diagnosis from plain radiographs: a deep learning-based approach. Sci. Rep. **8**(1), 1727 (2018)

Stacked Dark COVID-Net: A Multi-class Multi-label Classification Approach for Diagnosing COVID-19 Using Chest X-Ray Images

H. Anila Glory⊙, S. Meghana, J. S. Kesav Kumar, and V. S. Shankar Sriram(✉) ⊙

Centre for Information Super Highway (CISH), School of Computing, SASTRA Deemed University, Thanjavur, Tamil Nadu 613401, India
sriram@it.sastra.edu

Abstract. Most challenging yet, the need of the hour is accurate diagnosis of COVID-19, as the Coronavirus cases are increasing drastically day-by-day. Ceaseless efforts by the researchers and innovators have led to the development of several diagnostic models based on Deep Learning for effective diagnosis of COVID-19. However, the Deep Learning techniques that have been developed so far, fail to address major challenges such as overfitting, stability, computation overhead due to the usage of the massive volume of parameters and problems associated with the multi-class classification. Also in the medical perspective, researchers often suffer to identify the infinitesimal difference that exists in the radiographic images among the several lung diseases which makes the decision-making process difficult. Thus, to curb the crisis and to provide promising solutions & expertise for accurate diagnosis, this paper presents a novel lightweight multi-class multi-label COVID-19 detection model to assist physicians with greater ease to fight against this pandemic situation. Radiographic images are pre-processed using Contrast Limited Adaptive Histogram Equalization (CLAHE) and classified using novel Stacked Dark COVID-Net. The proposed model is validated using chest X-ray images and the results confirm the efficacy of the proposed model in terms of classification accuracy, sensitivity, specificity and stability.

Keywords: COVID-19 · CLAHE · Deep learning · ConvNets · DarkNet · Meta-learner

1 Introduction

COVID-19 (Corona Virus Disease), threatening people lives as it spreads exponentially over 213 countries and territories of which more than 4,161,409 deaths have been reported worldwide and 194,105,873 confirmed cases so far [1]. COVID-19 is formerly termed as 2019 novel coronavirus or 2019-nCoV and the virus is referred to SARS-CoV-2 [2]. Owing to zoonotic nature, coronavirus is easily transmitted from animals to human beings which leads to this pandemic state [3]. The most common clinical symptoms include fever, tiredness, sore throat, headache, dry cough, sneezing and facing

© Springer Nature Switzerland AG 2022
KC Santosh et al. (Eds.): RTIP2R 2021, CCIS 1576, pp. 61–75, 2022.
https://doi.org/10.1007/978-3-031-07005-1_7

difficulty while breathing [4]. Predominantly Reverse Transcription–Polymerase Chain Reaction (RT-PCR), quantitative RT-PCR (qRT-PCR) and Enzyme-Linked Immunosorbent Assays (ELISAs) are used for Coronavirus diagnosis [5]. However, these diagnostic methods are comparatively expensive and time-consuming. Moreover, medical imaging techniques such as Computed Tomography (CT) and X-ray plays a vital role in the effective diagnosis of COVID-19 [6, 7]. Researchers believe that these medical images can detect COVID-19 even before the symptoms begin [8].

Limited expert clinicians and swift spread of COVID-19 necessitated automated diagnosis which increases the interest of researchers in developing programmed diagnostic tools based on Deep Learning techniques using Chest X-ray images. Automated diagnosis eliminates the shortcomings like high cost, waiting time and dearth of test kits. In common, COVID-19 detection is viewed as a classification problem which differentiates normal and COVID-19 infected chest X-ray images [9]. Hence, for developing an accurate diagnostic tool, Deep Learning (DL)-based Convolutional Neural Networks (CNN) and its variants are proven successful and widely used, for diagnosing the abnormalities in medical images: solitary cysts discrimination, carcinoma nuclei grading, choroid segmentation, vibrational spectroscopic data analysis, etc. as it convoluted across the image which eventually reduces the number of parameters and neurons of the neural network. However, overfitting, problems related to multi-class classification, determining the network topology & hyperparameters, computation overhead due to the usage of the massive volume of parameters etc. are the major challenges as it deteriorates the generalization ability, stability and convergence rate of the learning model. In the same way from a therapeutic perception, the major drawback of chest X-ray image is it fails to perceive the early stages of COVID-19 and differentiate various lung diseases, as they lack to detect ground-glass opacity (GGO) of human lungs [10].

To address the aforementioned setbacks and to perform accurate diagnosis, this work put forth an improved deep convolutional neural network (Stacked Dark COVID-Net) which employs Contrast Limited Adaptive Histogram Equalization (CLAHE) for preprocessing the radiographic images and Layered DarkNets for effective classification. To the best of the authors' knowledge, the proposed model is unique which can perform multi-class multi-label classification of this kind. The highlights of this work are as follows.

1. CLAHE is applied to improve the lucidity of chest x-ray images and to identify GGO in human lungs without deteriorating the information
2. Stacked Dark COVID-Net is proposed for accurate diagnosis which performs multi-class multi-label classification
3. The proposed model is validated using X-ray images collected from various repositories and the results confirm the predominance of the proposed model over the existing models in terms of sensitivity, specificity, classification accuracy & stability and the ablation study is performed.

The rest of the article is structured as follows: Sect. 2 briefly exposes the recent deep learning practices for COVID-19 detection along with its impact. Section 3 confers the necessitude and the intuition behind the proposed Stacked Dark COVID-Net.

Section 4 portrays the experimentation procedure with essential validations for showing the predominance of Stacked Dark COVID-Net. Section 5 concludes the work with future vision.

2 Literature Review

In recent times, deep learning models are extensively used for diagnosing lung abnormalities using radiographic images. In 2019, Ilyas Sirazitdinov et al. proposed a deep convolutional neural network ensemble (RetinaNet and Mask R-CNN) for detecting pneumonia using chest X-ray images [11]. Hamed Behzadi-khormouji et al. developed deep learning-based ChestNet to detect consolidation on Chest X-ray images and compared with popular Deep Convolutional Neural Networks like DenseNet121 & VGG16. Abhir Bhandary et al. proposed Modified AlexNet (MAN) to identify the lung abnormality using Chest X-ray and CT images. The performance of AlexNet is improved using Principal Component Analysis fusion by identifying the principal features from the feature set [12]. Jaiswal et al. proposed a pneumonia identification model based on Mask-RCNN using chest X-rays. The base network is pre-trained using COCO (Common Objects in Context) weights and post-processing is performed for bounding boxes from manifold architectures [13]. Though the deep architectures are employed, the performance is still improved by applying appropriate pre-processing or post-processing techniques. Thus, it is worthy to mention that, prior to classification the images have to be pre-processed to enhance the contrast and to remove the histogram difference and confounding variables of images [14].

Similarly, for detecting the novel coronavirus infection deep learning models using Chest X-ray or CT images are employed [15, 16]. Several variants of deep learning algorithms are applied for COVID-19 detection using CT images [17–19]. Though CT images produce high-quality images than X-rays, CT scan is expensive and it is not certainly available in rural areas & small hospitals. Hence, to handle this pandemic plight X-rays are more appropriate than CT images. Some of the current deep learning-based COVID-19 detection techniques are discussed as follows: Hemdan et al. proposed COVIDX-Net using X-ray images which comprises seven CNN models [20]. Linda Wang et al. developed a deep learning framework: COVID-Net using chest X-rays, which discriminates normal, non-COVID pneumonia, and COVID-19 classes [21]. Ioannis et al. proposed deep convolutional neural networks by adopting transfer learning for COVID-19 detection using X-ray images [22]. Ali Narin et al. employed three different ConvNets without feature engineering for diagnosing COVID-19 using chest X-ray images of 50 COVID-19 patients with 98% accuracy [23]. Sethy and Behera coupled ResNet50 & SVM for COVID-19 detection using chest X-ray images and achieves better performance [24]. Joaquim et al. proposed an approach for analysing the COVID-19 using chest X-rays [25]. Authors have performed a thorough study by considering diverse pathological situations on the initial stages of known lung diseases, as COVID-19 and viral pneumonia have a similar pathological impact. Tulin Ozturk et al. developed an automated COVID-19 detection model based on DarkNet using X-ray images [3]. The proposed Dark COVID-Net contains seventeen Convolutional layers which is computationally expensive and time-consuming. It struggles to learn steadily and it may suffer due to overfitting, vanishing & exploding gradient problem. Also, the authors performed 5-fold cross-validation which is not appropriate for Deep Convolutional Neural Networks since it increases the computation manifold as the parameters involved in the deep architectures are very high.

Thus, to design a deep learning model by utilizing the advantages of DarkNet, this paper presents a novel Stacked Dark COVID-Net to perform multi-class multi-label classification for the effective and precise diagnosis of COVID-19 using chest X-ray images.

3   Proposed Methodology

This section confers the deep insight into the proposed Multi-class Multi-label classification model. In this work, X-ray images are pre-processed using Contrast Limited Adaptive Histogram Equalization (CLAHE) which is fed as an input to the proposed deep learning model. The novel deep learning model is structured using Layered Dark-Nets (LDN) and the LDNs are stacked together which results in Multi-class Multi-label classification model. The workflow and detailed interpretation of the proposed model is as follows:

3.1   Image Processing

To enhance the contrast factor, Contrast Limited Adaptive Histogram Equalization (CLAHE) is introduced, which is an improvement of Adaptive Histogram Equalization (AHE) [26]. The major objectives of this enhancement are, it prevents the over-amplification of noise and minimizes the edge-shadowing effect of AHE. The other significant advantages of CLAHE are, (i) it introduces significant adjustments in the pixel grey intensities and (ii) it remove artifacts which makes the decision making process difficult [27]. Thus in this work, CLAHE is applied as it eases the process of making decisions and improves the performance of the proposed deep learning model.

CLAHE working is as follows: (i) clip limit is initialized, which plays a vital role to perform contrast limiting as it normalizes the values between 0 and 1 (ii) image is divided into small regions, termed as tiles and if necessary, perform proper padding before splitting it into tiles and set the number of bins of the histogram (iii) each tile is processed using transformation function so that the contrast is improved thereby the plotted histogram matches the distribution parameter of the histogram specified and (iv) finally, the neighbouring tiles are pooled with bilinear interpolation thus eliminating artificially induced margins [28]. By applying CLAHE, the lucidity of a chest x-ray image is improved which provides possible sensitivity towards GGO detection. The pre-processed images using CLAHE are resized to 256×256 pixel image and fed as an input to the respective LDNs (Fig. 1).

3.2   Layered DarkNet (LDN)

The advent of deep architectures and its prevailing features revolutionized automation and made its mark in the diversified research areas [1, 2]. One among them is ConvNet

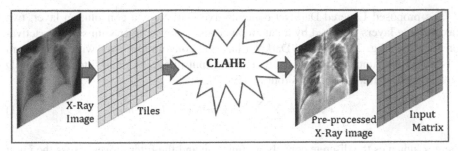

Fig. 1. Image pre-processing: CLAHE

as the name specifies, ConvNet performs a mathematical operation called convolution. A window slides over the image accomplishing convolving function and the window is termed as filter or kernel. In general, ConvNet contains a convolutional layer: extracts significant features from the image using kernels, a pooling layer: reduces the dimensionality of the image by dropping the pixels and a fully connected layer: classifies the output label of the image.

Developing a deep architecture from the scratch is chaotic, thus a well-known and technically accepted model can be used to construct the proposed model. By this rational approach, in this work DarkNet-19 (YOLO – You Only Look Once) architecture is preferred as an initial point, as it is successfully implemented for real-time object recognition.

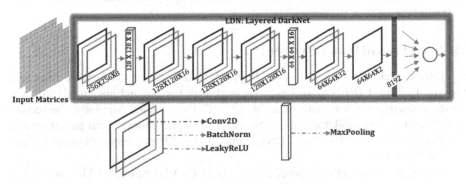

Fig. 2. Layered DarkNet

In the proposed model, the number of layers is reduced thereby reducing the computational overhead and the hyperparameters are adjusted which contribute towards a better performance. A quick insight of DarkNet-19 is as follows: it consists of 19 DarkNets and 5 max-pooling layers with the varying kernel sizes, numbers and stride values [29]. Similarly, DarkCovidNet is implemented effectively for COVID-19 detection with 17 DarkNets and 5 max-pooling layers [3].

The proposed Layered DarkNet contains five DarkNets, a convolution layer, two Max pooling layers followed by a flatten layer and a dense layer with softmax activation function (Fig. 2). A typical DarkNet has one convolution layer with BatchNorm and LeakyRelu functions successively. For an input image (X) and filter (F), the 2D convolving function is defined as follows (Eq. 1).

$$(X * F)_{i,j} = \sum_{l} \sum_{m} F(l, m) X(i - l, j - m) \tag{1}$$

where $*$ indicates the discrete convolving function and the filter moves across the input matrix. Batch Normalization is applied to standardise the inputs as it reduces the training time and increases the stability of the learning model. Leaky ReLU (Eq. 2) is used as an activation function as it speeds up training and fixes dying neuron problem. Leaky ReLU prevents dying neurons since it does not have zero-slope chunks and contains a small epsilon value.

$$y = \begin{cases} 0.01x \ \forall x < 0 \\ x \quad \forall x \geq 0 \end{cases} \tag{2}$$

Max pooling is utilized as it (i) extracts low-level features and summarizes the presence of features, and (ii) reduces the variance and computation. Adam optimizer is used for updating the weights, the binary cross-entropy is employed for computing the loss function as the Layered DarkNet is a binary classifier and the hyperparameters used for training the LDN are learning rate $= 0.0001$, batch size $= 16$ and the number of epochs $= 100$. In order to prevent overfitting, early stopping is introduced with patience $= 10$ and min_delta $= 0$.

3.3 Novel Stacked Dark COVID-Net

To perform multi-class classification, Layered DarkNets are stacked as three-fold (Fig. 3). The first LDN is trained and validated with normal and pneumonia infected (bacterial pneumonia, viral pneumonia & COVID-19) samples. Similarly, the second LDN is trained and validated using bacterial & viral pneumonia (viral pneumonia & COVID-19) samples and the third LDN is trained and validated using viral pneumonia & COVID-19 samples.

The intuition behind the proposed Stacked Dark COVID-Net, in [30] it is stated that the radiographic images of other types of viral pneumonia & COVID-19 has similar features and is quite challenging for the skilled radiologists to discriminate the images. Thus to extract the most significant features and to identify the minuscule difference in the radiographic images, the Layered DarkNets are trained using CLAHE processed X-ray images separately with the respective classes and stacked together using a meta-learner which ends-up as a novel Stacked Dark COVID-Net.

To the best of the authors' knowledge, the proposed model is unique which can perform multi-class multi-label classification of this kind. To combine the prediction results of LDN, multinomial logistic regression is utilized as a meta-learner and is trained on the predictions made using LDNs. Multinomial logistic regression is preferred, as it provides a smooth interpretation of the results predicted by the stacked LDNs. The multi-label

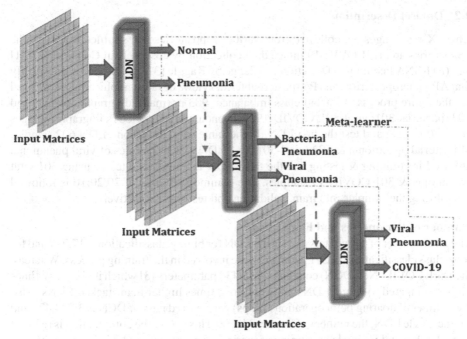

Fig. 3. Stacked Dark COVID Net: multi-class multi-label classifier

notion is as explained with an example where, while performing multinomial logistic regression, single decision class labels are replaced with multi-labels. For instance, COVID-19 sample is labelled as 111, which means the result of LDN1 is pneumonia infected (1) also, the results of LDN2 & LDN3 are viral pneumonia (1) and COVID-19 (1) respectively. Thus a sample with multi-label '111' is classified as COVID-19 sample.

4   Experimental Setup and Discussions

This section describes the overall performance of the proposed Stacked Dark COVID-Net and supporting aids to prove the claim. This section includes (i) Experimental Setup, (ii) Dataset description and (iii) Discussions with proper justifications.

4.1   Experimental Setup

The implementation of the proposed Stacked Dark COVID-Net model is carried out using Python 3.7 by utilizing Keras with a Tensorflow backend from Google Colaboratory. Besides NumPy, pandas, Matplotlib, seaborn, sci-kit learn and OpenCV are used to perform intended tasks. Investigations are carried out in the machine with 13 GB of Primary Memory, Intel(R) Xeon(R) 2vCPU @ 2.20 GHz.

4.2 Dataset Description

Chest X-ray images are collected from various repositories and shuffled together. The repositories are, (i) COVID-19 image data collection by Joseph Paul Cohen et al. [31] and (ii) RSNA Pneumonia Detection Challenge by Kaggle [32]. It is important to specify that AP (anteroposterior) and PA (posteroanterior) views of radiographic images are used for the entire process. To avoid class imbalance, 903 normal radiographic images and 903 (bacterial-301; viral-301; COVID-19-301) pneumonia infected radiographic images are used to train and test the first LDN. In the same way, for second LDN 602 samples of bacterial pneumonia & 602 (viral-301; COVID-19-301) samples of viral pneumonia are used for training & testing and the third LDN is trained and tested using 301 viral pneumonia & 301 COVID-19 samples. The common practice of 70:20:10 is followed for splitting the samples into train, validation and test sets respectively.

Number of Parameters and Flops Used

The total number of parameters used in the LDN for binary classification is 17,747 and for four-class classification 53,241 parameters are involved in the training process. Whereas, the Dark COVID-Net (DCN) contains 1,164,434 parameters [3] which is sixty-five times higher compared to single LDN and twenty-one times higher than stacked LDNs. Also the number of floating point operations (flops) per forward pass of DCN is 3,734,470 and for the single LDN, the number of flops is 34,978. This shows the computation is reduced considerably and in the deep learning scenario, the proposed model is lightweight.

Performance of the Proposed Stacked Dark COVID-Net

The proposed model is compared with the existing classifiers in terms of classification accuracy, sensitivity and specificity (Table 1). For four-class classification, the proposed model achieves 88.70% accuracy and it is observed that the bacterial & viral pneumonia are misclassified to some extent and there is no misclassification takes place in the COVID-19 & normal classes. Also, the proposed Stacked Dark COVID-Net attains 86.59% sensitivity and 94.35% specificity which confirms the proposed model is robust towards false positives. The reasons behind this splendid performance are, (i) the radiographic images are pre-processed using CLAHE which enhances the X-ray image and equipped it suitable for classification, and (ii) the predominant features to identify the minuscule difference that present in the radiographic images are extracted in each stack.

The performance graphs of the three LDNs are depicted to portray the learning process. From Figs. 4 and 5 it is witnessed that the LDNs are learning steadily and it is free from overfitting. However, from the performance graphs of LDN2 it is observed that, while training the LDN with bacterial and viral pneumonia, owing to the similarity pathological impact, the learning model suffers to complete the training process successfully. Thus, it leads to an infinitesimal performance gap between the training and validation curve.

Comparison with the Existing Classifiers

Table 2 shows that the proposed model clearly outperforms other classifiers in terms of accuracy, sensitivity, and specificity. Also, it is vibrant that other than the proposed model, all the existing classifiers fail to attain better generalization. It is worth mentioning that CLAHE processed radiographic images are provided as an input for all the classifiers.

Table 1. Performance metrics

S. No.	Performance metrics	Formula
1	Classification accuracy	$\frac{TP+TN}{TP+TN+FP+FN}$
2	Sensitivity	$\frac{TP}{TP+FN}$
3	Specificity	$\frac{TN}{TN+FP}$

TP: True Positives
TN: True Negatives
FP: False Negatives
FN: False Negatives

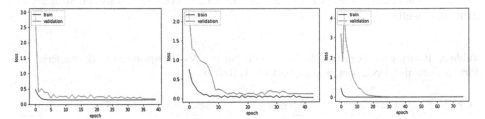

Fig. 4. Loss Vs Epoch graph: LDN1, LDN2 & LDN3 with CLAHE processing

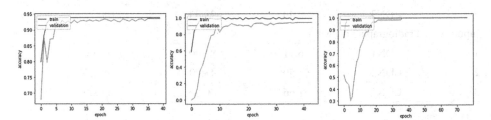

Fig. 5. Accuracy Vs Epoch graph: LDN1, LDN2 & LDN3 with CLAHE processing

Table 2. Four-class classification (Normal Vs Bacterial Vs Viral pneumonia Vs COVID-19) comparison

S. No.	Classifier	Accuracy	Sensitivity	Specificity
1	CNN	77.49	77.50	92.25
2	Dark COVID-Net (DCN)	74.16	74.00	91.00
3	Single LDN	77.50	77.50	92.48
4	**Stacked Dark COVID-Net (Proposed)**	**88.70**	**86.59**	**94.35**

In [3], for three-class classification (COVID-19 Vs Pneumonia Vs No findings) using DCN the accuracy reported is 87.02%. However, the DCN model struggles to perform well owing to poor generalization when extended to four-class classification. The same DCN architecture is trained and validated with four class classification and the accuracy obtained is 74.16% which is comparatively lower than the CNN (77.49%) designed with 17 convolutional layers, 5 MaxPooling layers followed by flatten & dense layer and configured with ReLU as an activation function. Also, Single LDN for four-class classification fails to extract the minuscule difference that exists between the classes.

Table 3 shows the metrics computed for all the LDNs fed with CLAHE processed radiographic images and the results are compared with the LDNs trained and validated with actual radiographic images. It is obvious that the LDNs with CLAHE processed radiographic images perform well and the interesting thing to be renowned is since the network architecture is relatively small the importance of CLAHE is highly pronounced. If the LDN deepens further it may undergo possible overfitting issues and struggle to generalize well.

Table 3. Binary classification of LDNs (LDN1: Normal Vs Pneumonia; LDN2: Bacterial Vs Viral pneumonia LDN3: Viral pneumonia Vs COVID-19)

S. No.	Classifier	Accuracy	Sensitivity	Specificity
Input: CLAHE processed radiographic images				
1	LDN1	93.52	94.73	95.33
2	LDN2	91.86	87.35	98.50
3	LDN3	99.40	99.33	100
Input: Actual radiographic images				
1	LDN1	86.11	86.00	87.00
2	LDN2	67.50	43.00	92.00
3	LDN3	51.66	00.00	100.00

Distribution Plot

In order to show the stability of the Stacked Dark COVID-Net and to provide better transparency, the individual LDNs are assessed by comparing them with the Dark COVID-Net (DCN) using distribution plot (Figs. 6, 7 and 8) and the stability of all the LDNs outperforms. The reasons behind the comparison among the binary classifiers (LDN) are, as the four-class classification of all the other existing classifiers suffer due to overfitting and the performance of the Stacked Dark COVID-Net purely relies on the performance of the individual LDNs.

Ablation Study

Ablation study is carried out to interpret the major contribution of the novel components involved. Thus, in this work two scenarios are taken into account.

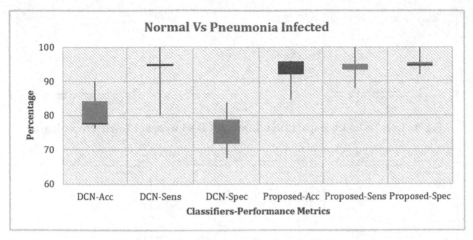

Fig. 6. Comparison between Dark COVID-Net and LDN1 (Normal Vs Pneumonia Infected)

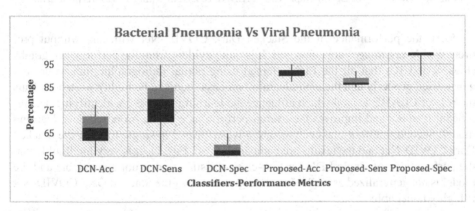

Fig. 7. Comparison between Dark COVID-Net and LDN2 (Bacterial Vs Viral Pneumonia)

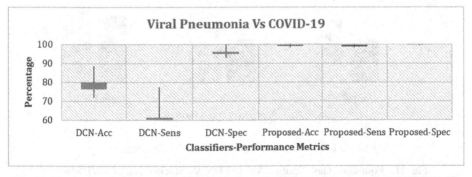

Fig. 8. Comparison between Dark COVID-Net and LDN3 (Viral Pneumonia Vs COVID-19)

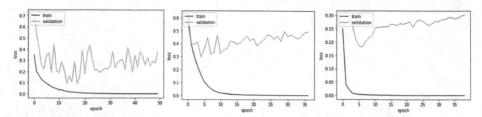

Fig. 9. Loss Vs Epoch graph: LDN1, LDN2 & LDN3 without CLAHE processing

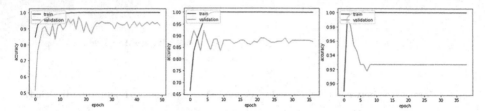

Fig. 10. Accuracy Vs Epoch graph: LDN1, LDN2 & LDN3 without CLAHE processing

First, the performance of the Stacked Dark COVID-Net with and without pre-processed X-ray images are compared. It is quite evident from the performance graphs (Figs. 9 and 10) that all the LDNs trained using actual radiographic images are not generalised properly and the entire learning process seems to be highly wretched. Thus the role of CLAHE is vital which affluence the learning process by identifying the significant features and improves the overall performance of the proposed deep learning model. Second, the four-class classification is performed in single LDN & the Stacked Dark COVID-Net and the results are compared. From Fig. 11, it is very intelligible that the performance of single LDN for four-class classification is not appreciable and the model is not generalized as well. Thus the significance of the Stacked Dark COVID-Net is highly noticeable.

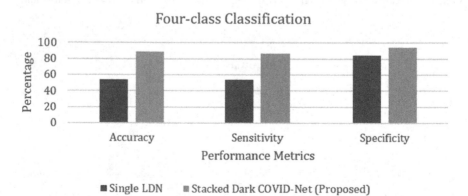

Fig. 11. Four-class classification: Single LDN Vs Stacked Dark COVID-Net

5 Conclusions

The most alarming prerequisite to safeguard people from this highly communicable life-threatening disease is proper and accurate diagnosis of COVID-19. The proposed multi-class multi-label COVID-19 detection model can automatically evaluate the lung structure of victims using X-ray images and diagnose the abnormalities with greater accuracy and minimal false positives. Radiographic images are pre-processed using CLAHE and classified using Stacked Dark COVID-Net which yields promising results. The proposed Stacked Dark COVID-Net and the physicians review together can accelerate the diagnosis process and aid clinicians to improve screening and providing deeper insights into life-threatening factors related to COVID-19. Stacked Dark COVID-Net is validated using shuffled radiographic images obtained from various repositories in terms of sensitivity, specificity, classification accuracy & stability and the results confirm the supremacy of the proposed model. The notable downside of the proposed model is, as the number of class labels increases, that many LDNs to be stacked and the misclassification at a single LDN propagates till the end. Nevertheless, the proposed multi-class multi-label COVID-19 detection model helps to detect COVID-19 using chest X-ray images with 88.7% accuracy (Normal Vs Bacterial pneumonia Vs Viral pneumonia Vs COVID-19). It is worthy to mention that the work can further be extended to identify the stages of lung abnormalities of the COVID-19 victim.

Acknowledgements. This work was supported by The IBM Shared University Research Grant 2017, New York, USA. The authors would like to thank Vigneswaran C. for his valuable inputs in drafting the manuscript.

Conflict of Interest. All the authors declare that they do not have any conflict of interest.

References

1. COVID-19 Coronavirus Pandemic, 09:23 GMT. https://www.worldometers.info/corona virus/. Accessed 24 July 2021
2. Messages and Actions. https://www.who.int/docs/default-source/coronaviruse/key-mes sages-and-actions-for-covid-19-prevention-and-control-in-schools-march-2020.pdf
3. Ozturk, T., Talo, M., Yildirim, E.A., Baloglu, U.B., Yildirim, O., Rajendra Acharya, U.: Automated detection of COVID-19 cases using deep neural networks with X-ray images. Comput. Biol. Med. **121**, 103792 (2020). https://doi.org/10.1016/j.compbiomed.2020.103792
4. Symptoms of Coronavirus. https://www.cdc.gov/coronavirus/2019-ncov/symptoms-testing/ symptoms.html
5. Lau, S.K.P., Che, X., Woo, P.C.Y., Wong, B.H.L., Chan, K., Peiris, J.S.M.: SARS Coronavirus detection methods. Emerg. Infect. Dis. **11**, 7–10 (2005)
6. McCall, B.: COVID-19 and artificial intelligence: protecting health-care workers and curbing the spread. Lancet Digit. Heal. **2**, e166–e167 (2020). https://doi.org/10.1016/s2589-750 0(20)30054-6
7. Lee, E.Y.P., Ng, M.Y., Khong, P.L.: COVID-19 pneumonia: what has CT taught us? Lancet Infect. Dis. **20**, 384–385 (2020). https://doi.org/10.1016/S1473-3099(20)30134-1

8. Chan, J.F.W., et al.: A familial cluster of pneumonia associated with the 2019 novel coronavirus indicating person-to-person transmission: a study of a family cluster. Lancet **395**, 514–523 (2020). https://doi.org/10.1016/S0140-6736(20)30154-9

9. Gauthama Raman, M.R., Somu, N., Kirthivasan, K., Liscano, R., Shankar Sriram, V.S.: An efficient intrusion detection system based on hypergraph - genetic algorithm for parameter optimization and feature selection in support vector machine. Knowl.-Based Syst. **134**, 1–12 (2017). https://doi.org/10.1016/j.knosys.2017.07.005

10. Zu, Z.Y., et al.: Coronavirus disease 2019 (COVID-19): a perspective from China. Radiology **2019**, 200490 (2020). https://doi.org/10.1148/radiol.2020200490

11. Sirazitdinov, I., Kholiavchenko, M., Mustafaev, T., Yixuan, Y., Kuleev, R., Ibragimov, B.: Deep neural network ensemble for pneumonia localization from a large-scale chest X-ray database. Comput. Electr. Eng. **78**, 388–399 (2019). https://doi.org/10.1016/j.compeleceng.2019.08.004

12. Bhandary, A., et al.: Deep-learning framework to detect lung abnormality – a study with chest X-Ray and lung CT scan images. Pattern Recognit. Lett. **129**, 271–278 (2020). https://doi.org/10.1016/j.patrec.2019.11.013

13. Kumar, A., Tiwari, P., Kumar, S., Gupta, D., Khanna, A.: Identifying pneumonia in chest X-rays: a deep learning approach. Measurement **145**, 511–518 (2019). https://doi.org/10.1016/j.measurement.2019.05.076

14. Behzadi-Khormouji, H., et al.: Deep learning, reusable and problem-based architectures for detection of consolidation on chest X-ray images. Comput. Methods Programs Biomed. **185**, 105162 (2020). https://doi.org/10.1016/j.cmpb.2019.105162

15. Kumar, A., Tripathi, A.R., Satapathy, S.C., Zhang, Y.-D.: SARS-Net: COVID-19 detection from chest X-rays by combining graph convolutional network and convolutional neural network. Pattern Recogn. **122**, 108255 (2021). https://doi.org/10.1016/j.patcog.2021.108255

16. Vinod, D.N., Jeyavadhanam, B.R., Zungeru, A.M., Prabaharan, S.R.S.: Fully automated unified prognosis of Covid-19 chest X-ray/CT scan images using Deep Covix-Net model. Comput. Biol. Med. **136**, 104729 (2021). https://doi.org/10.1016/j.compbiomed.2021.104729

17. Song, Y., et al.: Deep learning enables accurate diagnosis of novel coronavirus (COVID-19) with CT images. medRxiv, 2020.02.23.20026930 (2020). https://doi.org/10.1101/2020.02.23.20026930

18. Barstugan, M., Ozkaya, U., Ozturk, S.: Coronavirus (COVID-19) classification using CT images by machine learning methods, pp. 1–10 (2020)

19. Chen, X., Yao, L., Zhang, Y.: Residual attention U-Net for automated multi-class segmentation of COVID-19 chest CT images, vol. 14, pp. 1–7 (2020)

20. Hemdan, E.E.-D., Shouman, M.A., Karar, M.E.: COVIDX-Net: a framework of deep learning classifiers to diagnose COVID-19 in X-Ray images (2020)

21. Wang, L., Wong, A.: COVID-Net: a tailored deep convolutional neural network design for detection of COVID-19 cases from chest X-Ray images, pp. 1–12 (2020)

22. Apostolopoulos, I.D., Mpesiana, T.A.: Covid-19: automatic detection from X-ray images utilizing transfer learning with convolutional neural networks. Phys. Eng. Sci. Med. **43**(2), 635–640 (2020). https://doi.org/10.1007/s13246-020-00865-4

23. Narin, A., Kaya, C., Pamuk, Z.: Automatic Detection of Coronavirus Disease (COVID-19) Using X-ray Images and Deep Convolutional Neural Networks (2020)

24. Kumar, P., Kumari, S.: Detection of coronavirus Disease (COVID-19) based on Deep Features (2020). https://doi.org/10.20944/preprints202003.0300.v1

25. de Moura, J., Novo, J., Ortega, M., Detection, P.D., Imaging, X.: Fully automatic deep convolutional approaches for the analysis of Covid-19 using chest X-ray images. Medrxiv, pp. 1–13 (2020). https://doi.org/10.1101/2020.05.01.20087254

26. Zuiderveld, K.: Contrast limited adaptive histogram eqn. Graph. Gems. 474–485 (1994)

27. Mangeruga, M., Bruno, F., Cozza, M., Agrafiotis, P., Skarlatos, D.: Guidelines for underwater image enhancement based on benchmarking of different methods. Remote Sens. **10**, 1–27 (2018). https://doi.org/10.3390/rs10101652
28. Bendjillali, R.I., Beladgham, M., Merit, K., Taleb-Ahmed, A.: Improved facial expression recognition based on DWT feature for deep CNN. Electron. **8**, 324 (2019). https://doi.org/10.3390/electronics8030324
29. Redmon, J., Farhadi, A.: YOLO9000: better, faster, stronger. In: Computer Vision, pp. 7263–7271
30. Oh, Y., Park, S., Ye, J.C.: Deep learning COVID-19 features on CXR using limited training data sets. IEEE Trans. Med. Imaging **39**, 1 (2020). https://doi.org/10.1109/tmi.2020.2993291
31. Cohen, J.P., Morrison, P., Dao, L.: COVID-19 image data collection. https://github.com/ieee8023/covid-chestxray-dataset
32. RSNA Pneumonia Detection Challenge. https://www.kaggle.com/c/rsna-pneumonia-detection-challenge

Image Augmentation for Improving Automated Eligibility-Classification for Cervical Precancer Ablation Treatment

Peng Guo[1(✉)], Zhiyun Xue[1], Jose Jeronimo[2], Julia C. Gage[2], Kanan T. Desai[2], Brian Befano[3], Francisco García[4], Mark Schiffman[2], and Sameer Antani[1]

[1] National Library of Medicine, Bethesda, MD 20894, USA
peng.guo@nih.gov
[2] National Cancer Institutes, Rockville, MD 20850, USA
[3] Information Management Services, Inc., Rockville, MD 20850, USA
[4] Pima County, Tucson, AZ 85701, USA

Abstract. Cervical tissue ablation is an effective treatment approach for excising high-grade precancerous lesions, which are a direct precursor to invasive cervical cancer. However, not all women are eligible for this ablative treatment due to their cervical characteristics. In our previous study, we presented a deep learning network that used pyramidal features to determine if a cervix is eligible for ablative treatment based on visual characteristics presented in the image. Our method demonstrated promising performance and valid visualization in the task of "treatability classification". In this work, we propose using an image augmenter followed by a customized classification convolutional neural network (CNN) to overcome the challenges due to insufficient training data. We build the image augmenter using a CycleGAN model that is trained using three different datasets to ensure that the augmented images contain clinically significant morphological features. A gynecologic oncologist with more than 20 years of experience validated the augmented images. These are mixed into the set of original images to train our customized CNN. We note a performance improvement of 3.3% (to 89.8%) in treatability classification. We believe that a similar technique can also be applied to other automatic image classification applications for cervical cancer screening.

Keywords: Cervical cancer · CycleGAN · RetinaNet · Pyramidal feature · Data augmentation · Ablative treatment

1 Introduction

Uterine cervix cancer is the fourth most common cancer in women causing more than 311,000 death every year [1]. The mortality rate of this disease can be reduced if eligible women are treated at precancer, i.e., before cancer invades the cervical tissue. Treatment (ablation) eligibility is determined through expert visual assessment of the cervix with/without histological confirmation of high-grade Cervical Intraepithelial Neoplasia (CIN) [2]. Cryotherapy and thermal ablation (thermocoagulation) are typical ablative

KC Santosh et al. (Eds.): RTIP2R 2021, CCIS 1576, pp. 76–84, 2022.
https://doi.org/10.1007/978-3-031-07005-1_8

treatments. While cryotherapy is an effective technique, it is limited by the cost to transport and store the coolant gas used in the treatment. This makes it difficult for use in low and middle resource regions (LMRRs) of the world where the disease is most prevalent. In contrast, thermal ablation is easier to adopt and effective. Eligible women are treated using a reusable metallic probe that is electrically heated to approximately 100 °C for 20–40 s leading to epithelial and stromal destruction [3]. The exposure may be repeated as needed. The simplicity and low cost of the setup make it particularly suitable for use in LMRRs. However, not all women are eligible for a cervical ablative treatment due to the characteristics of their cervix and precancerous lesions. The eligibility for applying thermal ablation is determined by visual examination with/without a colposcopy of the cervix after the application of 3–5% acetic acid. Eligibility guidelines for thermal ablation and cryotherapy published by the WHO are concluded in Table 1 [3].

Table 1. WHO guideline: eligibility for thermal ablation and cryotherapy.

Eligibility	Description
Treatable	**Prerequisite:** i. screen positive ii. without suspicion of invasive or glandular disease (i.e., adenocarcinoma or adenocarcinoma in situ) **Guidelines:** • the transformation zone (TZ) is fully visible, the whole lesion is visible, and it does not extend into the endocervix, or • the lesion is type 1 TZ; or • the lesion is type 2 TZ where the probe tip will achieve complete ablation of the SCJ epithelium, i.e., where it can reach the upper limit of the TZ. Sometimes the SCJ can be seen high in the canal but a probe tip would not reach it
Not treatable	**Prerequisite:** i. screen positive ii. with suspicion of invasive or glandular disease **Guidelines:** • the TZ is not fully visible because it is endocervical (Type 3 TZ); or it is a Type 2 TZ where the SCJ is out of reach of the probe tip

We have previously reported [4] our deep learning method using the pyramidal features of RetinaNet architecture for automatically determining the eligibility of a cervix for thermal ablation. The method achieved a classification accuracy of 86.5%. A subset of 1033 images used in that study was selected from the National Cancer Institute (NCI)'s Guanacaste study data [5]. An expert identified 729 images as clear cases of "treatable" and 304 images as "not treatable". We noted that the lack of sufficient training data might have been a key factor in limiting the classifier's performance. Extraction of additional image data from the study is hindered by the effort needed in expert manual review for selecting and labeling candidate data. In this work, we present a strategy to complement the expert effort using "data augmentation" machine learning methods. Many data augmentation methods have been successfully applied in training deep learning neural networks and improving network performance [6]. The technique enlarges the data pool by creating modified copies of existing data or by creating synthetic data from existing data. In this study, we are not focusing on including as many augmentation methods as we can, rather on investigating a Generative Adversarial Network (GAN) based technique that can retain the clinically relevant morphological features of the cervix visible in the image. CycleGAN [7] is a member of the GAN [8] family which was originally developed for image-to-image translation, was determined to be a suitable candidate. As described in [7], the before-and-after-CycleGAN translation changes in the imaged objects' shape and edges are much subtler than of objects' color tone and environmental lighting. This property of the underscores CycleGAN's potential value toward our goals. In our case, the eligibility of ablative treatment is decided based on several factors that include cervix visibility, Transformation Zone (TZ) morphology, and Squamocolumnar Junction (SCJ) positioning, which are shown in Table 1. These regions are of clinical importance for treatability classification because most cervical abnormalities are found to develop in these regions [9]. Their morphological characteristics are unique in each cervix image and might be irreversible once augmented. The retention of these features is considered important in our study, especially for explaining the network prediction and aligning it with expert opinion. For our experiments, we use three cervix image datasets for the model training. Each dataset contains cervix images captured from different subjects under varying device settings thereby providing greater image variation in CycleGAN training.

To summarize, our goals are to investigate the use of state-of-the-art deep learning technology for augmenting cervical images while retaining clinically significant features; and, to combine the augmentation technique with a customized convolutional neural network derived from a SOTA deep learning architecture toward gaining better performance for treatability classification for cervical precancer.

2 Methods

2.1 Dataset and Annotation

- Dataset A: The images in this dataset were selected from the longitudinal cohort study of HPV and cervical cancer, provided by the NCI-funded Proyecto Epidemiologico Guanacaste [5]. After the photographic images were captured on slides, they were digitized by the National Library of Medicine (NLM). The images were presented via a software tool developed by the NLM and the NCI to two highly experienced medical experts who labeled the cervix in the images as "treatable" or "not treatable" [10]. Disagreements were discussed and resolved by consensus. We randomly split the dataset into 80/20 for training and testing, respectively, at the "woman level", i.e., ensuring that no subject data used for training was also used in testing. This dataset is used to train CycleGAN networks as well as our customized classification network.
- Datasets B and C: As reported in [11], the atypical squamous cells of undetermined significance/low-grade squamous intraepithelial lesion (ASCUS/LSIL) Triage Study (ALTS), also conducted by the NCI, was a randomized clinical trial conducted in the

United States that was designed to determine the optimal management plan for low-grade cervical abnormalities. Datasets B and C used in this study are subsets taken from the ALTS to study observer variability in the visual interpretation of cervical abnormalities. These images were used for landmark annotation using the NLM-developed Boundary Marking Tool (BMT) by several medical experts in cervical oncology. Although both datasets B and C were digitized from the same photographic slides, they have different visual characteristics, such as color tone, resolution, and brightness, due to different scanner settings (See Fig. 1). We randomly selected 2,300 images (1,300 for training, 1,000 for validation) from each of Dataset B and C, to train the CycleGAN models. Data quantity is empirically determined based on our observations.

2.2 CycleGan

CycleGAN is an unpaired image-to-image translation approach that attempts to establish a computational relationship between two image data domains, X and Y [8]. The model contains two mapping functions G: X $\rightarrow$ Y and F: Y $\rightarrow$ X, associated with discriminators DG and DF. DG encourages G to translate X into outputs that can identify with characteristics exhibited in domain Y, while DF encourages F to translate Y into outputs that can, correspondingly, identify with domain X.

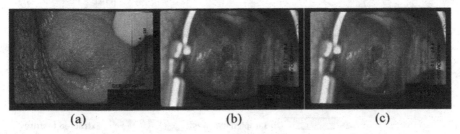

(a)   (b)   (c)

Fig. 1. Examples of Dataset A, B, and C. (a) is an image sample from Dataset A. (b) and (c) are examples from Dataset B and C, respectively. (b) and (c) are digital scans from an identical film, however, they look different (color, lighting, margin, etc.) due to device settings and operations.

There are two cycle consistency losses introduced: a) forward cycle-consistency loss: x $\rightarrow$ G(x) $\rightarrow$ F(G(x)) $\approx$ x, and (b) backward cycle-consistency loss: y $\rightarrow$ F(y) $\rightarrow$ G(F(y)) $\approx$ y [8]. The losses are used to achieve the goal that if one image I_X is translated from domain X to Y and back again it should be indistinguishable to I_X. The losses supervise the network training while ensuring that the two mappings G and F are mutually consistent.

In our study, we trained the CycleGAN models using our original dataset of 1,033 cervix images (dataset A) as domain X and another dataset (dataset B and C, respectively) as domain Y. We use the generator G as our image augmenter upon convergence.

2.3 Customized CNN

We constructed our classification model from a pre-trained RetinaNet [12] (see [4] for details). From the Feature Pyramid Network in RetinaNet, we selected 3 pyramidal layers: (1) P3, the 3×3 convolutional output of L (the weighted sum of up-sampled P4 and 1×1 convolutional output of C3 in ResNet50); (2) P6, the 3×3 convolutional output of C5 in ResNet50; and, (3) P7, the 3×3 convolutional output of P6; The low dimensional feature layers are up-sampled and concatenated with other high dimensional features to make the last convolutional layer of the network, which is then connected to a Global Average Pooling (GAP) and a Fully Connected (FC) layer. As shown in Fig. 2, we employed the trained CyleGAN network models as image augmenters. The output of CycleGAN's generator was incorporated with the original training images to construct a complete input set for training this CNN.

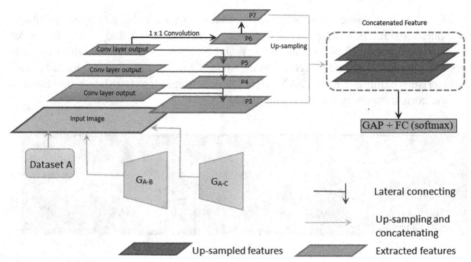

Fig. 2. Method flowchart for the customized CNN classification network using CycleGAN in data augmentation.

3 Experiments

3.1 Augmented Images

The entire dataset A was split into a training set and a testing set, in an 80/20 ratio. We used the 80% split in Dataset A to train two CycleGAN models: (1) a model using Dataset A and B, and (2) a model using dataset A and C. Due to GPU memory limitation, images were resized to have a width of 2,600 pixels, followed by a random cropping step with cropping size of 512 pixels. No other preprocessing technique is used in our CycleGAN training. For both experiments using Dataset B and C, we trained the network for 120 epochs with a batch size of 1. The deep neural network trainings are powered by two GeForce 2080 Ti GPUs.

We extracted the generators of the CycleGAN models after convergence and denoted them as GA-B and GA-C corresponding to steps (1) and (2) above. We clinically validated the generated images from a point of view of making treatability classification and find that: a) almost all the translated images had subtler sharpness degradation compared with original images; b) in over 95% of cases, both the original image and the translated image were given the same diagnostic decision which was made by our medical expert (a gynecologic oncologist with many years' experience in specializing in cervical screening and outpatient treatment); and, c) 1% translated images might exhibit subtle blur effect on lesion area, which could add difficulty to manual classification (Fig. 3).

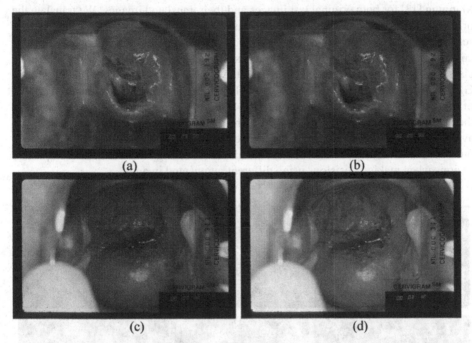

(a)   (b)

(c)   (d)

Fig. 3. CycleGAN translated samples. (a) and (b) are the original image and translated image from GA-B, correspondingly. (c) and (d) are the original image and translated image from GA-C, correspondingly.

3.2   Treatability Classification Performance

In each training, we randomly initialized the model weights and used both the images generated from GA-B, GA-C and original training images in Dataset A as our entire training set. All images were resized to have the longer border to be 1200 pixels while maintaining the original aspect ratio. The models were trained with a learning rate of 1e−6 using an NVIDIA GeForce 2080 Ti GPU.

Using one GA-B and one GA-C trained with different images in B and C each time, we obtained 10 classification models. The highest accuracy of 89.8% (88.9% ± 0.9%) was obtained for classifying the cervix images into "treatable" and "not treatable (Table 2). The model outperformed our best model in [4] (accuracy = 86.5%) which was trained without using any augmented images. Furthermore, we also trained a RetinaNet model using ImageNet weights for initialization and obtain the best accuracy of 84.0% which is 3.9% better than what we obtained in [4].

3.3   Comparing the Visualization

We were also interested in visualizing the network to examine whether the predictions are explainable from the aspect of medical interpretation. We apply Class-Relevance Mapping [13] for both original test images and their translated images. We translate the original test images in Dataset A into two sets using G_{A-B} and G_{A-C} and then test each set separately using our best-performing model. We compare the heatmap coverage of an image sample if the original sample I, its translated I_{A-B} and I_{A-C} are all correctly classified. For the positive category ("not treatable"), heatmap coverage is 2.3% higher in G_{A-B} translated images and 3.1% higher in G_{A-C} translated images, compared with that of original images (examples shown in Fig. 4). For the negative category ("treatable"), the coverage difference is 0.6% and 0.8%, respectively. Changes are calculated as an average over all the tests. Compared with the visualization of our previous models [4], our model in this study remains relatively stable on focusing on anatomically important regions when making decisions using different augmented images.

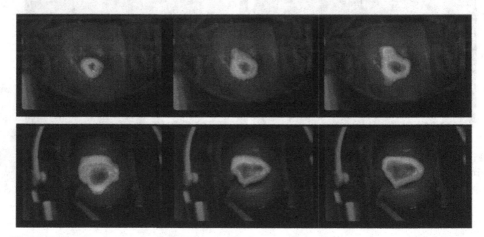

Fig. 4. Heatmap samples for correctly classified images. Top row images are labeled as "treatable", bottom images are labeled as "not treatable". In each row, left, middle, and right images are heatmaps of the original image, translated image from GA-B, and translated image from GA-C respectively.

Table 2. Classification performance using translated images.

Last convolutional layer	Accuracy	F1-score
RetinaNet	0.840 ± 0.007	0.887 ± 0.013
Customized CNN	0.889 ± 0.009	0.927 ± 0.017

4 Conclusion

Data shortage is a limiting factor for the performance of cervix treatability classification and other medical imaging applications. In this study, we investigated state-of-the-art deep learning architectures, including CycleGAN (an image-to-image translation network), and a customized classification CNN that we developed. We take advantage of CycleGAN's power for image domain transformation and its merit of not requiring "paired image" samples to build a data augmenter in our pipeline for training the customized deep learning method. Based on our observation, the trained CycleGAN generator can translate the original cervix images into different domains represented by other datasets while retaining the important morphological features. By adding the translated images to the training input, we have observed performance gain in the architectures proposed in our previous study. Furthermore, we also examine the visualization of correctly classified samples and observe the subtle variance in heatmaps compared with previous results. These findings provide useful information for optimizing the classification model, data acquisition, and data preparation. As the next step, we plan to continue optimizing the algorithm by generating synthetic images with enhanced features.

References

1. World Health Organization: Human papillomavirus (HPV) and cervical cancer. World Health Organization, 24 January 2019. https://www.who.int/en/news-room/fact-sheets/detail/human-papillomavirus-(hpv)-and-cervical-cancer. Accessed 24 Feb 21
2. Jeronimo, J., Schiffman, M.: Colposcopy at a crossroads. Am. J. Obstet. Gynecol **195**(6), 349–353 (2006)
3. World Health Organization: WHO Guidelines for the Use of Thermal Ablation for Cervical Pre-Cancer Lesions. World Health Organization (2019). https://www.who.int/reproductive health/publications/thermal-ablation-for-cervical-pre-cancer-lesions/en/. Accessed 24 Feb 21
4. Guo, P., et al.: Network visualization and pyramidal feature comparison for ablative treatability classification using digitized cervix images. J. Clin. Med. **10**(5), 953 (2021)
5. Bratti, M., Rodriguez, A., Schiffman, M., et al.: Description of a seven-year prospective study of human papillomavirus infection and cervical neoplasia among 10000 women in Guanacaste. Costa Rica. Rev. Panam. Salud Publica **15**(2), 75–89 (2004)
6. Shorten, C., Khoshgoftaar, T.M.: A survey on image data augmentation for deep learning. J. Big Data **6**(1), 1–48 (2019). https://doi.org/10.1186/s40537-019-0197-0
7. Zhu, J., Park, T., Isola, P., Efros, A.A.: Unpaired image-to-image translation using cycle-consistent adversarial networks. In: 2017 IEEE International Conference on Computer Vision (ICCV), pp. 2242–2251 (2017). https://doi.org/10.1109/ICCV.2017.244
8. Goodfellow, I., et al.: Generative adversarial networks. In: Proceedings of the International Conference on Neural Information Processing Systems (NIPS 2014) (2014)

9. Jordan, J., Singer, A., Jones, H., Shafi, M.: The Cervix. Wiley, Hoboken (2009)
10. Gage, J.C., et al.: Treatability by cryotherapy in a screen-and-treat strategy. J. Low. Genit. Tract Dis. **13**, 172–181 (2009)
11. The Atypical Squamous Cells of Undetermined Significance/Low-Grade Squamous Intraepithelial Lesions Triage Study (ALTS) Group: Human papillomavirus testing for triage of women with cytologic evidence of low-grade squamous intraepithelial lesions: baseline data from a randomized trial. J. Nat. Cancer Inst. **92**, 397–402 (2000)
12. Lin, T.Y., Goyal, P., Girshick, R., He, K., Dollar, P.: Focal loss for dense object detection. In: Proceedings of the IEEE International Conference on Computer Vision (ICCV), Venice, Italy, pp. 2999–3007 (2017)
13. Kim, I., Rajaraman, S., Antani, S.: Visual interpretation of convolutional neural network predictions in classifying medical image modalities. Diagnostics **9**(2), 38 (2019)

Osteoarthritis Detection Using Densely Connected Neural Network

Sushma Chaugule$^{(\boxtimes)}$ and V. S. Malemath

Department of Computer Science and Engineering, KLE DR. M. S. Sheshgiri College
of Engineering and Technology, Belagavi, India
vidhu_sun@yahoo.co.in

Abstract. Osteoarthritis (OA) is progressive deterioration kind of bone
joint disease. Knee OA is most common type of OA, which affect loco-
motion. Pain in joint, swelling, stiffness and trouble in walking happens
to be foremost symptoms of knee OA. KOA detection by medical practitioner is most commonly done with the help of radiographs. The radiographic findings in knee OA are joint space narrowing, formation of bone
spurs and increased bone density. In this study, we bring out a method
to detect knee OA using knee x-ray images, implemented in MATLAB.
The detection is based on clinical changes that happen in bone ends.
Nine hundred and fifty knee radiographic images in antero-posterior projection are used, collected from Osteoarthritis Initiative dataset. Those
images are used to train Dense Net Neural Network model. Feature maps
are computed for the given X-ray images to classify into osteoarthritic
knee or normal knee. The trained model gives the validation accuracy of
95.56%. These results indicate the proposed methodology can be used
by medical practitioner for assessment of OA.

Keywords: Osteoarthritis detection · Osteoarthritis classification ·
Knee OA · Biomedical image processing · X-ray images · Radiographs ·
Densely connected neural network · Dense net · OA assessment · OAI

1 Introduction

Osteoarthritis is common inflammatory disease that targets the joints of the
body; specifically knees, fingers, hands and hips. The prime characteristic of
osteoarthritis is loss of cartilage. Cartilage is tissue that covers and protects
ends of the bone; providing easy gliding of bones while walking, because of
its smoothness and elasticity. The major indications of OA are difficulty in joint
motion, hindered joint function, swelling and joint hardness after prolonged rest.
These indications along with clinical examination and radiographic imaging are
used by medical practitioner to examine the progress in knee OA. The typical
findings of OA in x-rays are deterioration of joint cartilage, formation of bone
spurs and increase in bone area [21]. The Fig. 1 shows the normal knee and
osteoarthritic knee.

© Springer Nature Switzerland AG 2022
KC Santosh et al. (Eds.): RTIP2R 2021, CCIS 1576, pp. 85–92, 2022.
https://doi.org/10.1007/978-3-031-07005-1_9

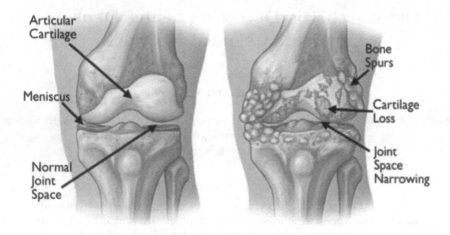

Fig. 1. Normal knee and Osteoarthritic knee [2]

According to WHO, the prevalence of OA is increasing due to population aging and an increase in factors related to obesity. It is estimated that 10–15% of world's population have some degree of OA, who are adults aged over 60 years; with women most commonly affected than men. After prolonged suffering of OA, nearly 75% of patients become disabled. Also life-span of patient may be decreased by 4 to 10 years. So far there is proven remedy for this condition. Therefore, there is need of keeping track of the degree of the disease to build a more significant methods and algorithms to assess the progress in OA.

The present-day advancements in Artificial Intelligence have led to develop a complete automated tool that many a times surpasses human performance. Convolutional Neural Networks can detect objects in the images and classify them into multiple classes more precisely and even quickly when compared to humans. There are other diagnostic methods as well, like Ordinary optical diagnosis, laboratory tests, Vibrational spectroscopy [23].

2   Related Work

Raw data can be processed with a combination of ideas and techniques like digital image processing, pattern recognition and machine learning depending on their applications [8]. To improve in the medical visualizations many authors have contributed to help the medical practitioners, focusing more on X-ray images [12] amongst many of the other modalities like MRI [16]. Generally data is collected clinically or the data is got from the standard dataset [6]. This data is pre-processed i.e. denoising of images [9,13] is done using suitable filters like circular fourier filter [5], contrast enhancement, histogram equalization, thresholding and canny edge detection [4], edge detection techniques [3] like Sobel, Prewitt, Robert, Zero Cross and Canny Edge detection algorithms [11,17,20]. Later these images are further processed to build a fully automated system [1,5,13] or semi-automated systems. During this development process many techniques have been used such as machine learning algorithms [5] with classification rate of 82.98%, feature extraction [14] with accuracy of 66.6%. Other feature extraction techniques like Haralick [20], fisher score [17] with accuracy of 91.5%, wavelets [7], different image segmentation [11,13] like Watershed, Otsu's segmentation [19], ASM [9], pixel segmentation [21], thresholding, region based, clustering, Markov random field, artificial neural network, deformable and atlas guided method [16], some have come up with cartilage maps used for segmentation [18], morphological techniques [1], Densely connected Convolutional Neural Network [12], classification techniques like Naive Bayes, random forest classifiers [5], ANN [14], SVM [20], KNN [18] with cartilage classification rate of 78.2% and tibial cartilage classification rate to be 82.6% were used.

From this literature it is given to learn that many authors have carried out their research with different imaging techniques for OA detection and assessment. Some papers have drawback that they give accurate results for grade 2 and 3 but poor results for grade 1. Some papers used different techniques and then gave the comparison [16]. But the work using machine learning can still be explored and is very challenging and motivating. There is also scope for using recent advancements in machine learning for the implementation of the problem statement i.e. Dense Net can extract information from x-ray images and can give precise and accurate results.

3   Architecture of Dense Net

In this paper, our motive is to use recent advancement in Neural Network called Dense Net to develop a precise method for automatic knee OA severity diagnosis using knee X-ray images that are provided by public dataset Osteoarthritis Initiative (OAI).

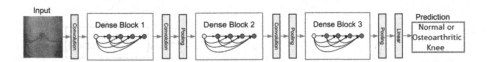

Fig. 2. Dense Net architecture with three dense blocks

Dense Convolutional Network (Dense Net) as shown in Fig. 2 is a trending architecture in convolutional networks that is deeper to a great extent with increased accuracy and more efficient in training. Dense Net connects every layer within in a feed forward way. Consider traditional convolutional network with N layers, having N connections, between every layer and its subsequent layer. Whereas Dense Net has

$$\frac{N(N+2)}{2} \tag{1}$$

direct connections. Equation 1 shows the total number of direct connections. Here, feature maps of preceding layers are the input for each layer and its own feature maps are used as input for subsequent layer. Dense Net requires fewer parameters than traditional convolutional network as there is no need of re-learning redundant feature maps.

The advantages of Dense Net are

1. Build up feature propagation.
2. Helps in feature reuse.
3. Reduces the number of parameters.
4. Improved flow of information and gradient in the network, making them easy to train.

Key observation of paper by Huang G. et al., 2017 is that by creating short paths from early layers (closer to input layer) to the later layers (closer to output layer), Dense Net architecture uses ImageNet classification and shows exceptional classification accuracy with fewer number of parameters (Fig. 3).

4   Design of OA Detection and Classification Model

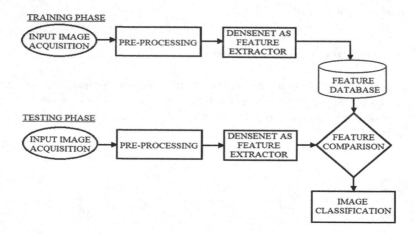

Fig. 3. Proposed method flow diagram

4.1   Input Image Acquisition

Image acquisition is action of getting an input image which is further processed to get a finer image.

Dataset Used: The Osteoarthritis Initiative (OAI) [6] is a ten-year observational study of radiographs of both genders, sponsored by the National Institutes of Health with a goal providing resources to provide a better knowledge in prevention and treatment of KOA. All the images are in antero-posterior projection and used in PNG format. In this work, two categories viz. images with OA and Images with Non-OA are considered from OAI dataset. In each category, for every experimentation 900 randomly selected images from the dataset are considered, which is further divided into 90/10 split, resulting in 810 training images and the rest for validation. The test images are any antero-posterior projected knee x-ray images with PNG format. The training/validation/testing split is made such that images in testing are completely different from training and validation in order to guarantee generalizability of model performance.

4.2 Pre-processing

This step strengthen some important features that are applicable for better understanding of image. In this study, pre-processing is carried out by converting image to grayscale and also cropping & resizing image to 224×224 pixels, however any size can be considered.

4.3 Feature Extraction

In this work, feature extraction technique used is Neural Network model called Dense Net. Dense Net architecture has a series of concatenating previous layer's features together but keeps the same number of features generated by each convolutional functions. Dense Net contains multiple dense blocks. Each block contains convolutional layer and pooling layers. The convolutional layer draws out features from input image by sliding the kernel over the image. Pooling layer is used to reduce dimensionality of feature maps. The dense block are threaded together which helps to learn from features in previous layers, preserving the no. of learning parameters to be low that would avoid over-fitting the model. All Dense Net are trained with training dataset with learning rate of $3e^{-4}$ for 40 epochs on NVIDIA GEFORCE X GPU, implemented on MATLAB 2019b.

4.4 Image Classification

This step in the algorithm deals with the categorizing the input knee x-ray into osteoarthritic or non-osteoarthritic knee.

Classification layer in network is fully connected; every unit in next layer connected to unit in previous layer. The global max pooling is performed on feature maps to reduce the dimensions of the maps. The softmax activation function is used on the feature maps to compute probabilities of classes. The class with highest probability is the class of output value. Equation 2 specifies the softmax function

$$P\left(x_i\right) = \frac{e^{x_i}}{\sum_{i \epsilon K} e^{x_i}} \tag{2}$$

where $P\left(x_i\right)$ is probability score of x_i and x_i are input value in vector of Real number of K numbers.

5   Results and Discussion

In this paper our goal is to provide the automatic and non-invasive method to diagnose OA using knee radiographic images. Depending on the clinical changes that appears in knee x-ray, the Dense Net model classifies knee into Osteoarthritic or Non-osteoarthritic knee. Figure 4 shows the plot of accuracy against No. of iterations.

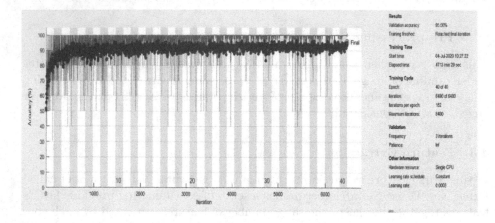

Fig. 4. Training process

As specified, a total of 900 images are divided into 90/10 split, resulting in 810 training images and 90 validation images. For testing any random image are chosen from the remaining images in the dataset and are tested. The model is trained for 40 epochs, with each epoch having 162 iterations. After the completion of training process the model gave validation accuracy of 95.56%.

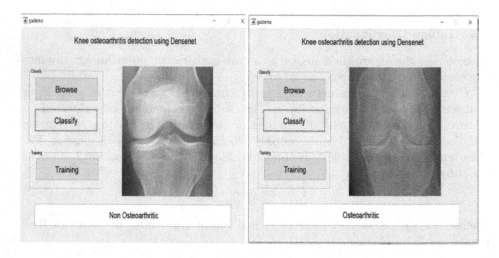

Fig. 5. Results of OA detection and Classification

Table 1. Comparative analysis

Author	Dataset and no. of images	Images resized to	Method	Accuracy in %
Norman et al. [12]	OAI – 4905 Knee radiographs	500 × 500	CNN-Denseblock convolution	91.52
Wahyuningrum et al. [15]	OAI – 4796 Knee radiographs	400 × 100	CNN-LSTM	75.28
Liu et al. [10]	OAI – 2105 Knee radiographs	1024 × 1024	R-CNN	77.88
Proposed work	OAI – 5778 Knee radiographs	224 × 224	CNN-Dense Net	95.56

The Fig. 5 shows that the trained model has correctly classified given test x-ray images.

Comparative analysis is carried out based on methods adopted, image size, dataset, total number of images used for experimentation and their relative accuracy. From Table 1 it's clearly evident that our proposed method outperforms all other methods mentioned in terms of accuracy.

6   Conclusion

In this work, Dense Net neural network is used to develop an accurate automatic knee OA classifier using knee radiographs. The classifier classifies the input knee x-ray into OA or Non-OA class. Thus providing the assistance to medical practitioners in making precise and detailed diagnosis with increasing number of x-rays images.

References

1. Anifah, L., Purnama, I.K.E., Hariadi, M., Purnomo, M.H.: Automatic segmentation of impaired joint space area for osteoarthritis knee on X-ray image using gabor filter based morphology process. IPTEK J. Technol. Sci. **22**(3) (2011)
2. Arthritis of the Knee - Orthoinfo - AAOS. OrthoInfo (n.d.). https://orthoinfo.aaos.org/en/diseases-conditions/arthritis-of-the-knee/. Accessed Feb 2021
3. Bandyopadhyay, S.K.: An edge detection algorithm for human knee osteoarthritis images. J. Glob. Res. Comput. Sci. **2**(2) (2011)
4. Bindushree, R., Kubakaddi, S., Urs, N.: Detection of knee osteoarthritis by measuring the joint space width in knee X-ray images. Int. J. Electron. Commun. **3**, 18–21 (2015)
5. Brahim, A., et al.: A decision support tool for early detection of knee osteoarthritis using X-ray imaging and Machine Learning: data from the osteoarthritis initiative. Comput. Med. Imaging Graph. **73**, 11–18 (2019). https://doi.org/10.1016/j.compmedimag.2019.01.007
6. Chen, P.: Knee Osteoarthritis Severity Grading Dataset. Mendeley Data, V1 (2018). https://doi.org/10.17632/56rmx5bjcr.1

7. Gornale, S.S., Patravali, P.U., Hiremath, P.S.: Osteoarthritis detection in knee radiographic images using multiresolution wavelet filters. In: Santosh, K.C., Gawali, B. (eds.) RTIP2R 2020. CCIS, vol. 1381, pp. 36–49. Springer, Singapore (2021). https://doi.org/10.1007/978-981-16-0493-5_4

8. Gornale, S.S., Patravali, P.U., Manza, R.R.: A survey on exploration and classification of osteoarthritis using image processing techniques. Int. J. Sci. Eng. Res. **7**(6), 334–355 (2016)

9. Lee, H.C., Lee, J.S., Lin, M.C.J., Wu, C.H., Sun, Y.N.: Automatic assessment of knee osteoarthritis parameters from two-dimensional X-ray image. In: First International Conference on Innovative Computing, Information and Control-Volume I (ICICIC 2006), vol. 2, pp. 673–676. IEEE, August 2006

10. Liu, B., Luo, J., Huang, H.: Toward automatic quantification of knee osteoarthritis severity using improved Faster R-CNN. Int. J. Comput. Assist. Radiol. Surg. **15**(3), 457–466 (2020). https://doi.org/10.1007/s11548-019-02096-9

11. Mahmood, N., Shah, A., Waqas, A., Abubakar, A., Kamran, S., Zaidi, S.B.: Image segmentation methods and edge detection: an application to knee joint articular cartilage edge detection. J. Theor. Appl. Inf. Tech. **71**(1), 87–96 (2015)

12. Norman, B., Pedoia, V., Noworolski, A., Link, T.M., Majumdar, S.: Applying densely connected convolutional neural networks for staging osteoarthritis severity from plain radiographs. J. Digit. Imaging **32**(3), 471–477 (2019)

13. Pandey, M.S., Rajitha, B., Agarwal, S.: Computer assisted automated detection of knee osteoarthritis using X-ray images. Sci. Technol. **1**(2), 74–79 (2015)

14. Pratiwi, D., Santika, D.D., Pardamean, B.: An application of backpropagation artificial neural network method for measuring the severity of Osteoarthritis. arXiv preprint arXiv:1309.7522 (2013)

15. Wahyuningrum, R.T., Anifah, L., Eddy Purnama, I.K., Hery Purnomo, M.: A new approach to classify knee osteoarthritis severity from radiographic images based on CNN-LSTM method. In: 2019 IEEE 10th International Conference on Awareness Science and Technology (iCAST), pp. 1–6 (2019). https://doi.org/10.1109/ICAwST.2019.8923284

16. Shaikh, M.H., Panbude, S., Joshi, A.: Image segmentation techniques and its applications for knee joints: a survey. IOSR J. Electron. Commun. Eng. (IOSR-JECE) **9**(5), 23–28 (2014)

17. Shamir, L., et al.: Knee X-ray image analysis method for automated detection of osteoarthritis. IEEE Trans. Biomed. Eng. **56**(2), 407–415 (2008)

18. Shan, L., Zach, C., Charles, C., Niethammer, M.: Automatic atlas-based three-label cartilage segmentation from MR knee images. Med. Image Anal. **18**(7), 1233–1246 (2014)

19. Sharma, P., Singh, J.M.: A novel approach towards X-ray bone image segmentation using discrete step algorithm. Int. J. Emerg. Trends Technol. Comput. Sci. **2**(5), 191–195 (2013)

20. Subramoniam, B.: A non-invasive computer aided diagnosis of osteoarthritis from digital X-ray images 2015

21. Wagaj, B.L., Patil, M.M.: Osteoarthritis disease detection with the help of image processing technique. Int. J. Comput. Appl. **975**, 8887 (2015)

22. Wittenauer, R., Smith, L., Aden, K.: Background Paper 6.12 Osteoarthritis. World Health Organisation (2013)

23. Yu, C., Zhao, B., Li, Y., Zang, H., Li, L.: Vibrational spectroscopy in assessment of early osteoarthritis–a narrative review. Int. J. Mol. Sci. **22**, 5235 (2021). https://doi.org/10.3390/ijms22105235

Generic Foreign Object Detection
in Chest X-rays

KC Santosh$^{(\boxtimes)}$![ORCID], Shotabdi Roy$^{(\boxtimes)}$, and Siva Allu

2AI: Applied Artificial Intelligence Research Lab, Computer Science,
University of South Dakota, Vermillion, SD 57069, USA
santosh.kc@usd.edu,
{shotabdi.roy,SivaSaiVenkata.Allu}@coyotes.usd.edu

Abstract. In an automated Chest X-Ray (CXR) screening process, foreign objects such as coins, buttons, medical tubes, and devices and jewelry can adversely influence the performance of abnormality screening tools. As machine learning algorithms did not separately consider them into account, they result in false-positive cases. In our work, we employ You Only Look Once (YOLOv4) algorithm - a Deep Neural Network - to detect foreign objects in CXR images. Considering its genericity, on a dataset of 400 publicly available CXR images hosted by LHNCBC, U.S National Library of Medicine (NLM), National Institutes of Health (NIH), we achieve the following performance scores: accuracy of 91.00%, precision of 85.00%, recall of 93.00% and f1-score of 89.00%. Unlike state-of-art works, where they are limited to specific type of foreign object (e.g., circle-like objects), this is the first time we report experimental results on all possible types of foreign object.

Keywords: Chest X-ray · Foreign objects · Pulmonary abnormality · AI-guided tools

1 Introduction

Chest radiography is found to be the most common and affordable diagnostic imaging technique for cardiothoracic as well as pulmonary disorders [1]. Lung and heart pathologies include atelectasis, consolidation, pneumothorax, pleural and pericardial effusion, cardiac hypertrophy, Tuberculosis (TB), and hyperinflation. Regarding pulmonary abnormality screening tool, if we consider TB, the presence of foreign objects such as coins, buttons, and medical tubes, and devices hinder the performance of the Computer-Aided Detection/Diagnosis (CAD) tools [2]. Therefore, foreign objects (especially the ones located within the lung region) should not be considered in automated abnormality screening process. For example, from our prior works [3–5], foreign objects (see Fig. 1) such as ring/buttons, cardiac pacemakers, and other medical devices result in CXR screening errors

---

Authors Credit Statement. The first two authors contributed equally to the paper.

as their algorithms considered them pulmonary abnormalities [6–8]. In an auto-mated screening process, machine learning tools typically follow conventional train, validate, and test mechanism. They typically employ handcrafted features from CXRs. As foreign objects are not detected and localized separately from abnormal patterns/regions, the performance can be negatively impacted. As in feature engineering, high-end machine learning algorithms such as deep learning are no exception. In other words, as foreign objects are required to be discarded, detecting them in CXRs can help build a successful abnormality CXR screening tool (with minimum false positives).

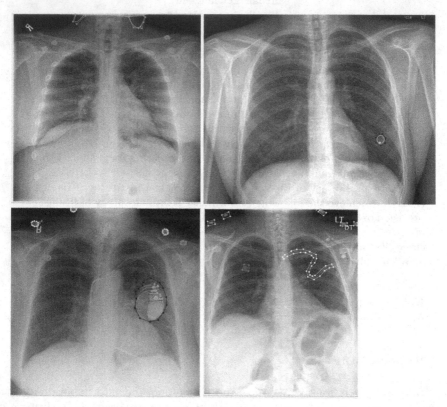

Fig. 1. Foreign objects (annotated/labeled) in chest x-rays: jewelry, buttons and pinn-ode (upper-left), ring (upper-right); pacemaker (lower-left), and medical tube (lower-right)

As opposed to feature engineering in shallow learning mechanism, the use of deep learning idea inherently supports variation/change in dataset(s). It also helps build robust cross-population train/test model [9]. With this concept, in this paper, we employed You Only Look Once (YOLOv4) [10] – a well-known deep learning model – to detect foreign objects in CXR images. We validated the proposed tool on a dataset of 400 publicly available images hosted by LHNCBC, U.S. National Library of Medicine (NLM), National Institutes of Health (NIH).

The remainder of the paper can be summarized as follows. In Sect. 2, we review previous studies/works. In Sect. 3, we provide YOLOv4 architecture and implementation for foreign object detection. Section 4 includes evaluation protocol, performance metrics, and results analysis. The latter of the section includes comparative study. In Sect. 5, we conclude the paper.

2 Related Works

In the literature, numerous clinical methods as well as AI-guided tools were used to identify foreign objects from CXRs. Critical patients in intensive care unit (ICU) often have (bio)medical devices such as endotracheal tubes, prosthetic valves, chest tubes and pacemaker wires to control upcoming serious possible complications [11–14]. On the other hand, people mistakenly swallowed foreign objects (coin, button, scarf pin, and sharp object, for example) [15]. Further, battery and magnets are common cases in children. In [16], authors reported a 15-year single centered review from through 2015 based on clinical reports and images in Cincinnati Children's Hospital Medical Center, where 276 cases of battery ingestion/insertions were confirmed. Such foreign objects, if not detected and removed, can cause serious health issues.

Automatically detecting foreign objects in CXRs is not trivial [17], and it does not have rich state-of-the-art literature. Often, shallow learning algorithms are used, feature engineering covers most of it, where basic image processing and pattern recognition techniques are common. It typically includes Viola-Jones and circular Hough transform (CHT) to detect circle-like foreign objects CXRs. In 2018, Zohora et al. [18] introduced normalized cross-correlation that employed few templates to collect potential circle-like objects, which then followed by unsupervised clustering. Recently in [19], Santosh et al. employed a Faster Region-based Convolutional Neural Network (R-CNN). All of these reported works are limited to circle-like foreign object detection.

Overall, we observe that there exist two groups of foreign object: biomedical foreign object (BFO) and non-biomedical foreign object (NBFO). BFOs are required to control possible serious threats. While, NBFOs, if stays there longer, bring serious threats. Either of them negatively impact when we consider automated CXR screening tools i.e., AI-guided tools. We, therefore, employed YOLOv4 to detect both NBFO and BFO.

3 YOLOv4, Architecture and Implementation

YOLO is a simple one-step detection algorithm. A single convolutional network predicts multiple bounding boxes and their class probabilities at the same time. YOLO trains with complete images and directly optimizes cognitive performance. This integrated model has several advantages over traditional methods of object recognition [20]. YOLO is extremely fast, averaging more than twice the accuracy of other real-time systems. Unlike sliding window and region proposal-based techniques, YOLO implicitly encodes contextual information about a class and its appearance to see the big picture (both in training/testing). In contrast to Fast RCNN [21], YOLO raises less than half of the background errors.

Single-stage detection algorithms mainly include SSD [22], YOLO [20], YOLOv2 [23], YOLOv3 [24], YOLOv4 [10]. Algorithms based on anchor-free target detection primarily include CornerNet [25] and CenterNet [26], and a priori boxes are no longer used. In our work, we adopted the idea of implementing YOLOv4 [27] to detect foreign objects from CXR.

Following Fig. 2, YOLOv4 consists of:

1. Cross stage partial darknet53 (CSPDarknet53) [28];
2. Spatial pyramid pooling (SPP) [29];
3. Path aggregation network (PANet) [30]; and
4. YOLOv3 network.

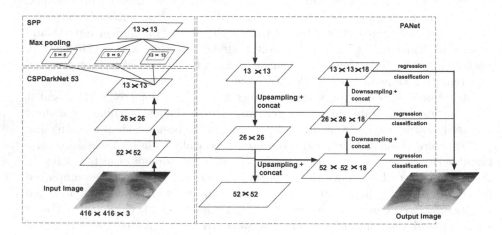

Index:
CSPDarkNet53 = Cross Stage Partial Darknet53
SPP = Spatial Pyramid Pooling
PANet = Path Aggregation

Fig. 2. YOLOV4 architecture

To improve the detection accuracy of YOLOv4 several techniques were introduced. For example, path aggregation network (PANet), spatial pyramid pooling (SPP), mosaic data expansion, mish activation function, and many other techniques for significant improvement in accuracy. The backbone of the network uses CSPDarknet53. It integrates interstage subnetworks (CSPNets), reducing computational overhead while maintaining accuracy, and achieving the perfect combination of speed and accuracy. Figure 2 shows the network structure of YOLOv4. In the Fig. 2, the input image is sent to the backbone network to extract the features and merge the features (feature maps of different scales) via

SPP and PANet. Next, a three-scale characteristic map is created to predict the bounding box, category, and confidence so that the head of YOLOv4 matches YOLOv3. During training, the image is scaled to a size of 416×416 before being sent to the convolutional neural network. After performing $3 \times 3/2$ convolution 5 times (convolution core size is 3×3, the step size is 2), the size is reduced to 13×13, and there are 3 types: 52×52, 26×26, and 13×13.

The functional fusion network YOLOv4 includes PANet and SPP. The function of the SPP module is not to limit the input of the convolutional neural network to a fixed size, but to expand the receptive field and effectively isolate important contextual functions without slowing down the network execution. The SPP model is based on the CSPDarknet53 feature extraction network. The SPP network uses four different maximum pooling scales to process the input feature map. The pooling kernel sizes are 1×1, 5×5, 9×9, 13×13, and these four feature maps are subject to concatenation operations. Maximum pooling uses a padding operation, the move step is 1, and the feature map size does not change after the pooling layer. According to the SPP, YOLOv4 uses PANet instead of the YOLOv3 function pyramid as the parameter aggregation method. YOLOv4 outputs three feature maps on different scales to predict the location of the bounding box, the corresponding category, and the reliability of the target. YOLOv4 continues the basic idea of YOLOv3's bounding box forecasting and adopts a priori box-based forecasting scheme.

4 Experiments

This section includes dataset collection, evaluation metrics, experiment, results and analysis.

4.1 Dataset

As in previous works, we used 400 CXRs from the Indiana CXR dataset maintained by the U.S. National Library of Medication (NLM), National Institutes of Health (NIH). In 400 CXRs, we considered and annotated the following foreign objects: buttons, pinnode, ring, chain, medical tube and devices. In Table 1, we categorize them into three types: a) Circle-like objects, b) medical devices, and c) objects with no shapes.

Table 1. Foreign object: types and total cases.

Types	Total
T1. Circle-like objects (button, pinnode and ring)	1282
T2. Medical devices (tubes and pacemaker)	47
T3. Objects with no specific shape (chain)	25

In our experimental set up, we annotated images using *labelme*[1] annotation tool that provides the poly-line annotating method for better precision (see Fig. 1 for better visual understanding).

4.2 Results and Analysis

To measure how well the proposed tool works, we computed mean Average Precision (mAP), Accuracy (ACC), Precision (PREC), Recall (REC) and F1-score.

AP is used to evaluate the index of target detection performance. AP value also is the area under the PREC-REC curve. To calculate AP, we need Intersection over Union (IoU), and is given by the ratio of the area of intersection to area of union of the predicted bounding box and ground truth bounding box:

$$IoU = \frac{\text{Area of overlap}}{\text{Area of union}}.$$

With this, mean average accuracy (mAP) represents the average accuracy of all categories. For example, mAP_{50} represents a mAP value with an IoU greater than 0.5 in the predictor and ground truth boxes, and mAP_{75} represents an mAP value with an IoU threshold greater than 0.75. map It can be calculated as follows:

$$mAP = \frac{1}{N} \sum_{i=1}^{N} \int_0^1 PREC \, dREC,$$

where N is the number of detected objects. In our experiment, after 2000 iterations, we received mAP_{50} of 83.75% and an average loss of 1.0025 (see Fig. 3). In a similar manner ACC, PREC, REC and F1-score can be computed as follows:

$$ACC = \frac{TP+TN}{TP+FP+TN+FN},$$

$$PREC = \frac{TP}{TP+FP},$$

$$REC = \frac{TP}{TP+FN}, \text{ and}$$

$$F1\text{-score} = 2 \times \left(\frac{PREC \times REC}{PREC+REC}\right),$$

where TP, FP,TN and FN refer to true positive, false positive, true negative and false negative, respectively.

---

[1] https://en.wikipedia.org/wiki/LabelMe.

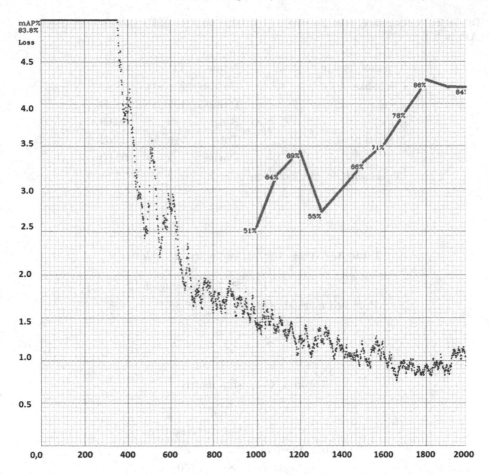

Fig. 3. Total iteration (2000), average loss 1.0025 and mAP$_{50}$ 83.75%

In our experiment, we followed hold-out method. In other words, the dataset was split into standard 80/20% train/test mechanism, where 320 CXRs were used for training and remaining 80 of them were used for testing. We used YOLOv4 architecture for training and Google collaborator notebook platform for training the model. The YOLOv4 configuration was changed to batch size of 64, sub-division of 12 and image size of 416 × 416. The weights generated after 2000 iterations were used for testing the model, and an average mAP$_{50}$ of 83.75% was achieved. In Table 2 we provide individual TP, FP, AP for all types of foreign objects, and in Table 3 we summarize TP, FP and FN values from Table 2 with an average IoU of 69.89%. In Table 4, for better understanding, we create a confusion matrix, actual versus detected (output).

Table 2. Performance: true positive (TP), false positive (FP) and average precision (AP, in %).

Types of foreign object	Name	TP	FP	AP
Circle-like objects	Button	248	33	98.48
	Pinnode	195	27	98.29
	Ring	19	5	90.00
Medical device	Tube	16	16	45.62
	Device	3	0	100.00
Object with no specific shape	Chain	2	2	70.11

Table 3. Average results: summary of Table 2.

	TP	FP	FN	Average IoU
Proposed method	483	83	38	69.89%

Table 4. Confusion matrix

		Actual	
		Positive	Negative
Detected	Positive	483	83
	Negative	38	750

Overall, considering all types of foreign object, we have achieved 91% accuracy, 85% precision, 93% recall, 89% F1-score (see Table 5). Regarding comparative study, we took previous results in Table 6. Previous works are limited to circle-like objects such as buttons and coins [2,17–19]. As they were limited to circle-like foreign objects, shallow learning algorithms (e.g., Viola-Jones, circular Hough transform, normalized correlation and unsupervised clustering) were mostly adopted except Santosh et al. (2020) [18]. Unlike previous studies, the proposed work is generic enough to detect all types of foreign objects. For better understanding, we provide qualitative output samples for various foreign objects such as button, pinnode, devices, chain, ring, medical tubes, and other devices (Fig. 4).

Table 5. Results: accuracy, precision, recall, and f1-score

Method	ACC	PREC	REC	F1-score
Proposed	0.91	0.85	0.93	0.89

Table 6. Comparative results

Authors	PREC	REC	F1-score
Xue et al. (Voila-Jones) [17]	0.37	0.94	0.53
Zohora et al. (CS + CHT) [2]	0.85	0.54	0.66
Zohora et al. (Normalized Correlation + Unsupervised Clustering) [18]	0.76	0.88	0.81
Santosh et al. (R-CNN) [19]	0.90	0.92	0.91
Proposed (YOLOv4)	0.85	0.93	0.89

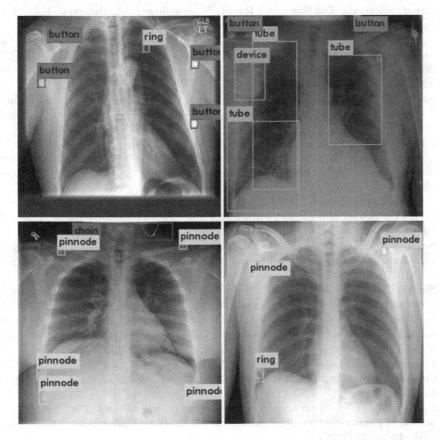

Fig. 4. Qualitative output: ring and button (upper-left), medical tubes, button and devices (upper-right), chain and pinnode (lower-left), and pinnode and ring (lower-right)

5   Conclusions

In this work, we have employed a Deep Neural Network (You Only Look Once (YOLOv4)) to detect NBFO and BFO in chest X-Rays. The network was validated on a set of 400 publicly available CXRs hosted by the U.S. NLM, National Institutes of Health (NIH), and have achieved 91% accuracy, 85% precision, 93% recall, 89% F1-score, and an average mAP_{50} of 83.75% with average IoU 69.89%. Our results are encouraging. To the best of our knowledge, this is the first time we reported a generic foreign object detection in chest x-rays, since previous works are limited to circle-like foreign objects. With this, our immediate plan is to integrate with abnormality screening with and without foreign object detection.

References

1. Raoof, S., Feigin, D., Sung, A., Raoof, S., Irugulpati, L., Rosenow, E.C., III.: Interpretation of plain chest roentgenogram. Chest **141**(2), 545–558 (2012)
2. Zohora, F.T., Santosh, K.C.: Circular foreign object detection in chest X-ray images. In: Santosh, K.C., Hangarge, M., Bevilacqua, V., Negi, A. (eds.) RTIP2R 2016. CCIS, vol. 709, pp. 391–401. Springer, Singapore (2017). https://doi.org/10.1007/978-981-10-4859-3_35
3. Santosh, K.C., Vajda, S., Antani, S., Thoma, G.R.: Edge map analysis in chest X-rays for automatic pulmonary abnormality screening. Int. J. Comput. Assisted Radiol. Surg. **11**(9), 1637–1646 (2016)
4. Ding, M., et al.: Local-global classifier fusion for screening chest radiographs. In: Medical Imaging 2017: Imaging Informatics for Healthcare, Research, and Applications, vol. 10138, p. 101380A. International Society for Optics and Photonics (2017)
5. Mahbub, Md.K., Biswas, M., Gaur, L., Alenezi, F., Santosh, K.C.: Deep features to detect pulmonary abnormalities in chest X-rays due to infectious diseaseX: Covid-19, pneumonia, and tuberculosis. Inf. Sci. **592**, 389–401 (2022)
6. Sakai, S., et al.: Computer-aided nodule detection on digital chest radiography: validation test on consecutive T1 cases of resectable lung cancer. J. Digit. Imaging **19**(4), 376–382 (2006)
7. Simkó, G., Orbán, G., Máday, P., Horváth, G.: Elimination of clavicle shadows to help automatic lung nodule detection on chest radiographs. In: Vander Sloten, J., Verdonck, P., Nyssen, M., Haueisen, J. (eds.) 4th European Conference of the International Federation for Medical and Biological Engineering, pp. 488–491. Springer, Cham (2009). https://doi.org/10.1007/978-3-540-89208-3_116
8. Freedman, M.T., Lo, S.-C.B., Seibel, J.C., Bromley, C.M.: Lung nodules: improved detection with software that suppresses the rib and clavicle on chest radiographs. Radiology **260**(1), 265–273 (2011)
9. Santosh, K.C.: AI-driven tools for coronavirus outbreak: need of active learning and cross-population train/test models on multitudinal/multimodal data. J. Med. Syst. **44**(5), 93 (2020)
10. Bochkovskiy, A., Wang, C.-Y., Liao, H.-Y.M.: YOLOv4: optimal speed and accuracy of object detection. arXiv preprint arXiv:2004.10934 (2020)

11. Thompson, M.J., Kubicka, R.A., Smith, C.: Evaluation of cardiopulmonary devices on chest radiographs: digital vs analog radiographs. Am. J. Roentgenol. **153**(6), 1165–1168 (1989)
12. Godoy, M.C.B., Leitman, B.S., De Groot, P.M., Vlahos, I., Naidich, D.P.: Chest radiography in the ICU: Part 2, evaluation of cardiovascular lines and other devices. Am. J. Roentgenol. **198**(3), 572–581 (2012)
13. Godoy, M.C.B., Leitman, B.S., de Groot, P.M., Vlahos, I., Naidich, D.P.: Chest radiography in the ICU: Part 1, evaluation of airway, enteric, and pleural tubes. Am. J. Roentgenol. **198**(3), 563–571 (2012)
14. Jennings, P., Padley, S.P.G., Hansell, D.M.: Portable chest radiography in intensive care: a comparison of computed and conventional radiography. Br. J. Radiol. **65**(778), 852–856 (1992)
15. Murthy, P.S.N., Ingle, V.S., George, E., Ramakrishna, S., Shah, F.A.: Sharp foreign bodies in the tracheobronchial tree. Am. J. Otolaryngol. **22**(2), 154–156 (2001)
16. Pugmire, B.S., Lin, T.K., Pentiuk, S., de Alarcon, A., Hart, C.K., Trout, A.T.: Imaging button battery ingestions and insertions in children: a 15-year single-center review. Pediatr. Radiol. **47**(2), 178–185 (2016). https://doi.org/10.1007/s00247-016-3751-3
17. Xue, Z., et al.: Foreign object detection in chest X-rays. In: 2015 IEEE International Conference on Bioinformatics and Biomedicine (BIBM), pp. 956–961. IEEE (2015)
18. Zohora, F.T., Antani, S., Santosh, K.C.: Circle-like foreign element detection in chest X-rays using normalized cross-correlation and unsupervised clustering. In: Medical Imaging 2018: Image Processing, vol. 10574, p. 105741V. International Society for Optics and Photonics (2018)
19. Santosh, K.C., Dhar, M.K., Rajbhandari, R., Neupane, A.: Deep neural network for foreign object detection in chest X-rays. In: 2020 IEEE 33rd International Symposium on Computer-Based Medical Systems (CBMS), pp. 538–541. IEEE (2020)
20. Redmon, J., Divvala, S., Girshick, R., Farhadi, A.: You only look once: unified, real-time object detection. In: Proceedings of the IEEE Conference on Computer Vision and Pattern Recognition, pp. 779–788 (2016)
21. Girshick, R.B.: Fast R-CNN. CORR, abs/1504.08083 (2015)
22. Liu, W., et al.: SSD: single shot multibox detector. In: Leibe, B., Matas, J., Sebe, N., Welling, M. (eds.) ECCV 2016. LNCS, vol. 9905, pp. 21–37. Springer, Cham (2016). https://doi.org/10.1007/978-3-319-46448-0_2
23. Redmon, J., Farhadi, A.: YOLO9000: better, faster, stronger. In: Proceedings of the IEEE Conference on Computer Vision and Pattern Recognition, pp. 7263–7271 (2017)
24. Redmon, J., Farhadi, A.: YOLOv3: an incremental improvement. arXiv preprint arXiv:1804.02767 (2018)
25. Law, H., Deng, J.: CornerNet: detecting objects as paired keypoints. In: Proceedings of the European Conference on Computer Vision (ECCV), pp. 734–750 (2018)
26. Duan, K., Bai, S., Xie, L., Qi, H., Huang, Q., Tian, Q.: CenterNet: keypoint triplets for object detection. In: Proceedings of the IEEE/CVF International Conference on Computer Vision, pp. 6569–6578 (2019)
27. Huixuan, F., Song, G., Wang, Y.: Improved YOLOv4 marine target detection combined with CBAM. Symmetry **13**(4), 623 (2021)
28. Wang, C.-Y., et al.: CSPNet: a new backbone that can enhance learning capability of CNN. In: Proceedings of the IEEE/CVF Conference on Computer Vision and Pattern Recognition Workshops, pp. 390–391 (2020)

29. He, K., Zhang, X., Ren, S., Sun, J.: Spatial pyramid pooling in deep convolutional networks for visual recognition. IEEE Trans. Pattern Anal. Mach. Intell. **37**(9), 1904–1916 (2015)
30. Liu, S., Qi, L., Qin, H., Shi, J., Jia, J.: Path aggregation network for instance segmentation. In: Proceedings of the IEEE Conference on Computer Vision and Pattern Recognition, pp. 8759–8768 (2018)

Mammogram Mass Classification: A CNN-Based Technique Applied to Different Age Groups

Sk Md Obaidullah[1], Himadri Mukherjee[2], Ankita Dhar[2], Teresa Goncalves[3], KC Santosh[4], and Kaushik Roy[2(✉)]

[1] Department of Computer Science and Engineering, Aliah University, Kolkata, India
sk.obaidullah@aliah.ac.in
[2] Department of Computer Science, West Bengal State University, Kolkata, India
kaushik.mrg@gmail.com
[3] Department of Informatics, University of Evora, Evora, Portugal
tcg@uevora.pt
[4] 2AI: Applied AI Research Lab, Department of Computer Science, University of South Dakota, Vermillion, SD, USA
santosh.kc@ieee.org

Abstract. The World Health Organization (WHO) reports that breast cancer is one of the most frequent cancers among women, affecting almost 2.1 million women/year. As a consequence, fatality rate is high: 627,000 women died from breast cancer in 2018, which is approximately 15% [1] of all cancer deaths among women. Early detection (using AI-driven tools) can prevent from being worse. In this paper, we propose a Convolutional Neural Network (CNN) based approach for mammogram mass classification. The proposed method outperforms our existing feature-learning based model [2] on the same dataset. We experimentally achieved the best average recognition accuracy of 95.25% in separating malignant from benign masses. In our study on different age groups for mammogram mass classification, better results were observed from the age group: 61–75 years.

Keywords: Mammogram mass classification · Breast cancer · Convolutional Neural Network

The World Health Organization (WHO) reported breast cancer as the most frequent cancer among women, affecting almost 2.1 million women/year. In the last year, the WHO estimated that 627,000 women died from breast cancer [1], which is about 15% of all cancer deaths among women. The rates of breast cancer effect nowadays are not limited to only developed regions, rather it is now effecting globally across every regions of the world. So early detection is inevitable in order to improve the breast cancer results and survival. The detection strategies for breast cancer are mainly two types: (i) early diagnosis and (ii) screening. The main problem of breast cancer diagnosis is limited resource

© Springer Nature Switzerland AG 2022
KC Santosh et al. (Eds.): RTIP2R 2021, CCIS 1576, pp. 105–116, 2022.
https://doi.org/10.1007/978-3-031-07005-1_11

with very weak public health system, which causes diagnosis at a very late stage among the majority of women. Therefore, early diagnosis programs should be prioritize based on awareness of early signs and symptoms and then prompt referral to suitable treatment. A general view of radiologists is, early detection of breast cancer makes this one of the most treatable and curable one. There are several methods for screening like: mammography based screening, clinical breast exam and breast self-exam.

We have a specific type of breast imaging known as screening mammography that uses low-energy x-rays to identify abnormalities in the breast i.e. to detect the cancer at an early stage before women experience symptoms. During this time, the cancer is most treatable. In general, mammography based screening are classified into two types: (i) Screen Film Mammography (SFM) and (i) Full Field Digital Mammography (FFDM), based on the processing modalities. As the name suggests, in case of SFM, thin films are used to capture the images, on the other hand for FFDM, the captured images are stored digitally without printing in any film type materials. As per studies [3–5], both type of mammography, i.e. either SFM or FFDM, having almost similar kind of capability to detect suspicious breast lesions. However, as FFDM are stored is digital computer so they can be further customized easily for enhancement, cross section, zooming kind of study, which is a constraint for SFM type. The present work deals with the SFM images which are available through the BCDR-F03 dataset [6–8], one of the latest and most popular breast imaging film mammography benchmark datasets.

To avoid proportion of the missed cases of breast cancer double reading of the mammograms is commonly suggested. But the problem of such double reading is workload and cost associated which is very are high. Computational approach for early diagnosis of diseases is know as Computer-Aided Diagnostics (CAD). It can help radiologists verify their readings which eventually eliminates the requirement of other radiologists. CAD systems are designed to produce classification accuracies, finding distortions in masses etc. In recent years several CAD methods has been proposed in literature for early diagnosis of breast cancer too. The main utility of CAD systems is: it enable the radiologists for double checking their views. By double checking the number of false-negative cases can be reduced to a significant amount in comparison to single checking by one doctor. This in turn depicts the importance of developing CAD systems. In literature various types of CAD system has been proposed. A CAD system normally has three different parts: (i) extracting the region of interests (ROI) and further preprocessing to enhance the contrast or remove noise(ii) computation of suitable feature set to categorize normal image from defected one and finally (iii) learning those features extracted in step (ii) using the traditional classifiers and classification. Nowadays deep learning based approaches has been widely used by the researchers which replaces the hand crafted feature extraction step and combines step (ii) and (iii) as mentioned earlier. Sometimes image descriptors are merged with clinical information for better classification as reported in literature [9]. The present work focuses on convolutional neural network based classification of

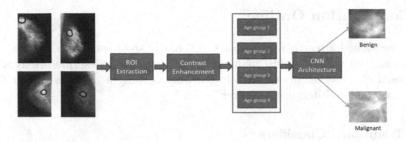

Fig. 1. Overview of the proposed method.

masses from mammogram images. No clinical information is considered during our experimentation.

Calcification and masses are being classified using Haralick texture features[10] as reported in literature [11–15]. This has been used in disparate areas [16] and a comparison between texture based hand crafted features and deep learning is reported in [17]. Wavelet [18,19] and curvelet [20] are two popular feature descriptors which are employed by different authors. Combination of intensity and texture feature to built a hybrid descriptor was explored by Ramos et al. [21]. Moura and Guevara [9] used HOG (Histogram of oriented gradient) and clinical information to classify mammogram masses. Arevalo et al. [8] separated benign and malignant masses with CNN without any clinicla information thereby proving the efficacy of deep learning. In our earlier work [2] we proposed a hand-crafted feature based mammogram mass classification from BCDR dataset. In this work, RMID (Radon Multi-resolution Image Descriptor) was proposed which works on the idea of radon transform and multi-resolution image decomposition. Though we obtained encouraging results but main limitation of this work was its dependency on hand-crafted feature descriptor.

In this paper, we propose a novel Convolutional Neural Network (CNN) based approach to separate benign and malignant masses from mammogram images. Not stopping there, we also studied the performance of CNN while mammogram images are considered based on different age groups. The block diagram of the proposed system is shown in Fig. 1. From BCDR dataset film mammogram images are considered and they are categorized based on CC and MLO views; Region of Interests (ROI) are then extracted and further contrast enhancement algorithm is applied; next images are grouped based on different ages where each age group contains benign and malignant categories. These images are fed to CNN block and classification results for different age groups are obtained.

The rest of the paper is organized as follows. Section 1 reports the contribution, where we discuss the proposed CNN architecture. Experiments are reported in Sect. 2, where we discuss about dataset description, experimental setup, and analysis of results. We conclude the paper in Sect. 3.

1   Contribution Outline

As we mentioned already, we propose CNN based architecture for classification of mammogram masses amidst malignant and benign. We describe briefly about traditional classifiers that use feature learning paradigm along with our CNN based proposed architecture hereafter.

1.1   Traditional Classifiers

Feature-based learning was very common to the machine learning researcher. We compute hand-crafted feature based on some visual or analytical aspects of our domain knowledge and then these features are learned by the classifier to build a model. The idea of deep learning differs from feature learning paradigm is that here we do not have to compute the features from the inputs based on our observation. Rather, the input is provided and deep learning model computes the features, learns based on the features and finally produce classification results. For present work in addition with the proposed CNN model some well known classifiers are studied namely: Bayesian network, Multilayer perceptron, Linear discriminant analysis, Logistic, Random Forest, and Support vector machine. Performance comparison of proposed CNN model with the traditional classifiers are also reported. A brief nutshell about these classifiers are discussed below.

1. Bayesian network
   K2 was used as a bayesian network, a hill-climbing algorithm that determines the distribution in a directed acyclic graph form in an efficient way. It is discussed in detail in [22].
2. Linear discriminant analysis
   LDA [23] treats the data as a group of multivariate normal distributions where the covariance matrix reside with mean vectors for various categories. LDA categories the data based on a hyper plane. The side of the plane is determined from the feature of the categories derived from the test set.
3. Logistic
   Logistic regression assigns the studies to a distinct set of classes based on the features. It maps the output using a sigmoid function and produces a probability rate which is further mapped into categories [24].
4. Support vector machine
   SVM distinguishes data by engendering a hyper-plane (HP)on high dimensional input. It involves the use of multifarious kernels which can be either linear or non-linear. Here, the SVM was tuned with a linear kernel because of it's fast execution.
5. Multilayer Perceptron
   MLP is one of the most popular classifiers. In this experiment, a *56-hl-2* setup was used, where 56 corresponds to the number of features, hl represents the neurons in the hidden layer and 2 depicts the output classes. hl was determined experimentally, as a function of the input and output dimensions. Here, hl was set to 29, i.e. $(56 + 2)/2$.

6. Random Forest

A RF is composed of decision trees. These trained using bootstrapping along with random feature selection. During decision making phase, each tree provides prediction which are combined towards the final decision [25].

1.2 CNN Architecture

Artificial Intelligence (AI) has been witnessing a tremendous growth to bridge the gap between the capabilities of humans and machines. The journey from machine learning to modern deep learning has made possible to solve many complex pattern recognition problem with high degree of accuracy.

Deep learning [26] based classification of data has recently been an interesting and very much effective technique of handling data. Convolutional neural networks (CNNs) are a type of neural networks which adopt a deep learning-based approach. It has three main components namely convolution layer, pooling layer and dense layer. The convolution layer is responsible for analysis of data in different ways. The pooling layer is used to reduce the dimension of the output from a convolution layer. The dense layer is a fully connected layer which forms the final stages of a CNN. In the present experiment, the images were first fed to a 5×5 convolution layer. The output was max pooled and then passed on to a second 3×3 convolution layer. This was again max pooled and passed on to a 256 dimensional dense layer. This layer had ReLU activation (Eq. (1)) whose output was passed on to a second dense layer of 60 dimension.

$$f(x) = max(0, x),$$ (1)

where, x is the input to a neuron. This also had the same activation as the previous layer. Finally, the output was routed to a 2 dimensional dense layer (2 classes) with softmax activation (Eq. (3)).

$$\sigma(z)_j = \frac{e^{z_j}}{\sum_{k=1}^{K} e^{z_k}},$$ (2)

where z is an input vector of length K. The CNN architecture is illustrated in Fig. 2. Initially, we had used a 5 fold cross validation scheme with 50 training iterations. The batch size was set at 100.

2   Experiments

2.1   Dataset and Pre-processing

For any kind of medical imaging work, getting standard data is the crucial issue. For present work we have used one of the benchmark film mammography dataset named BCDR-F03 [8,9]. The data is available from the Breast Cancer Digital

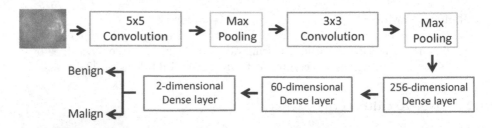

Fig. 2. The proposed CNN architecture.

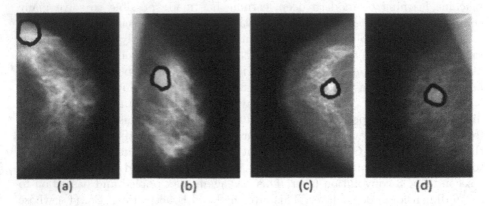

Fig. 3. Different mammogram views, (a) LCC, (b) LO, (c) RCC, (d) RO. The green boundary is the ROI. (Color figure online)

Repository, which is a well known public dataset repository that was built from Cancer patients' cases of Portugal [7]. Here in total 736 film images were used out of which 426 were benign and the rest were malignant. They were collected from 344 patients. The variability of these data samples lies into different mammogram views namely: carniocaudal (CC) and mediolateral oblique (MLO) view. We used both types of data to maintain the variability among the dataset. Figure 3 shows different mammogram views with the lesions marked.

Most of the medical image data are of low contrast. So our primary task is to pre-process those data. Here we did the following pre-processing steps: firstly, ROI extraction where we extract the exact local of our interest that we want to deal with; this ROI must be extracted as per the clinical information provided by the radiologists and we also followed the same procedure. The extracted ROIs were subjected to contrast enhancement of by following standard algorithm which compute by subtracting the mean of the intensities in the image to each pixel. Figure 4 shows one original ROI and its contrast enhanced version.

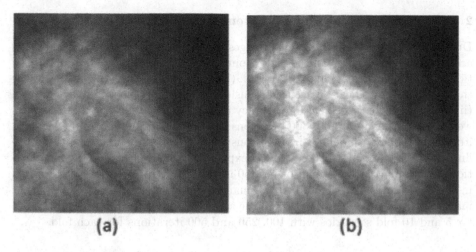

Fig. 4. Contrast enhancement, (a) original low contrast ROI, (b) contrast enhanced image

2.2 Age Grouping

Is there any effect of age for mammography based breast cancer screening? In this paper we also tries to answer the same. To study the age effect for mammogram based breast cancer classification, we divided the BCDR dataset into different age groups along with their respective data distributions:

AG0: Age Group 0 includes cases of age 40 or less (benign cases = 197, malignant cases = 148, and total = 345);

AG0: Age Group 1 includes cases of age between 41 to 60 (benign cases = 33, malignant cases = 19, and total = 52);

AG2: Age Group 2 includes cases of age between 61 to 75; (benign cases = 105, malignant cases = 103, and total = 208); and

AG3: Age Group 3 includes cases of age more than 75 (benign cases = 70, malignant cases = 30, and total = 70).

2.3 Evaluation Metrics

To measure the performance, we computed classification accuracy. Classification Accuracy (CA) is the ratio of number of correct predictions to the total number of input samples, which can simply be computed as,

$$AC = (NCA/TNP) \times 100, \tag{3}$$

where NCA refers to number of correct predictions and TNP, total number of predictions.

2.4   Evaluation Strategy and System Configuration

During experimentation the benign images are labelled as 1 and malignant cases are labelled as 2. The default setup for our CNN model was 5 fold and 50 iterations. Our experimentation was two fold: (i) Our primary objective was to study the number of classification accuracy considering all the images of all age groups. (ii) we studied the classification accuracy age group wise. For the first scenario, we have experimented up to 300 iterations in 5-fold environment to find the best iterations. Then with default 50 iterations we have experimented up to k fold to find the best value of k. Then, we did experimentation with the best combinations from previous two scenarios i.e. 250 iterations with 11 fold cross validation in our case. Secondly, we studied the mammogram image classification performance on different age groups. To do the same, experimentation was carried out for 5 and 10 fold scenarios with 100, 250 and 500 iterations for each fold.

2.5   Results and Analysis

Table 1 shows experimental results for 5 fold cross validations with varying iterations at 50 to 300 with 50 intervals. Here we found the best accuracy of 91.26% with 250 iterations. In another experiment we fixed the number of iterations with the default value i.e. at 50 iterations and experimentations was done for varying number of fold. Best outcome was found at 11 fold with 89.33% classification accuracy. The result is reported in Table 2. Finally, experimentation was carried out with previous two best case scenarios i.e. 250 iterations and 11 fold cross validation. In this experiment we found out of 675 mammogram images 643 images are correctly classified resulting an average classification accuracy of 95.25%. The confusion matrix for the best case scenario is shown in Table 3.

Table 4 shows the experimental results on different age groups. Our objective was to study the effect of different age groups for mammogram mass classification. For experimentation we have chosen 5 and 10 fold cross validation scenarios with 100, 250 and 500 iterations for each cross validation. Using 5 fold cross validation an average classification accuracy of 88.88% is obtained for AG1 (age between 41 to 60 years). While performing 10 fold cross validation, we found the highest average classification accuracy of 93.11% for AG2 (age between 61 to 75 years). This results yields the fact that mammogram images of early age people

Table 1. Overall accuracy (in %): all images are considered for 5-fold cross validations and varying number of iterations.

No. of iterations	50	100	150	200	250	300
% of Accuracy	81.04	84.74	88.89	90.22	**91.26**	90.96

Table 2. Reported accuracy (%) for varying fold with 50 iterations for each fold.

No. of fold	5	6	7	8	9	10	11	12
% of Accuracy	81.04	83.41	84	84.74	88	84.74	**89.33**	81.93

Table 3. Best case scenarios of Table 1 & Table 2 i.e. for 250 iterations and 11 fold.

Mammogram types	Benign	Malignant
Benign	362	13
Malignant	19	281

Table 4. Experimental results (accuracy) for different age groups based classification

Age groups	5 fold				10 fold			
	100	250	500	Avg	100	250	500	Avg
AG0	80.77	88.46	92.31	87.18	90.38	90.38	96.15	92.30
AG1	84.64	90.43	91.59	88.88	88.99	94.20	94.20	92.46
AG2	78.37	87.98	87.98	84.77	91.35	92.31	95.67	**93.11**
AG3	80.00	85.71	87.14	84.28	90.00	92.86	87.14	90.00

is more tough to detect by automated system compared to elderly age cases. So, radiologists need to be more and more careful to avoid false negative cases.

2.6   Comparative Analysis with Previous Relevant Work

Very recently one work on BCDR dataset was proposed [2] where radon multi-resolution based image descriptor was reported where performance of different machine learning classifiers were compared. The machine learning classifiers chosen were namely: Baysian Network, Multilayer Perceptron, Logistic, Linear Discriminant Analysis, Support Vector Machine, and Random Forest. Among all, Logistic and Support Vector Machine shows promising performance of 77.73% and 77.35% classification accuracy. In present work we employed Convolutional Neural Network model on the same dataset and compared the performance with previously reported one. Figure 5 shows the comparative analysis results as mentioned.

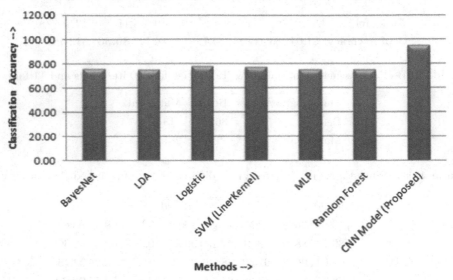

Fig. 5. Performance comparison of traditional machine learning classifiers and proposed CNN model on the same dataset. Here CNN outperform other machine learning classifiers with moderately large margin.

3   Conclusions and Future Work

Undoubtedly breast cancer is one of the most common types of cancer which attach millions of women every year across the world. For an early detected breast cancer, treatment is more successful and the recovery rate is higher. Computer aided diagnostics made it possible for the radiologists for more accurately making the early detection by double checking through automated analysis. Our work reports a deep learning based model using convolutional network on a publicly available dataset and found encouraging outcome. The average classification accuracy of 95.25% is found in our experiment considering all the mammogram images. During age group based analysis we found that: for the age group AG2 (age between 61 to 75 years) average classification accuracy of 93.11% is obtained. This results demonstrates the fact that mammogram images of early age people is more tough to detect by automated system compared to elderly age cases. So, radiologists need to be more and more careful to avoid false negative cases. In future, we will extend our research study by taking fuzzy binarization into account before applying CNN [27]. In addition, ensembling model could potentially work better [28].

References

1. http://www.who.int/cancer/prevention/diagnosis-screening/breast-cancer/en/. Accessed 15 Nov 2019
2. Obaidullah, S.M., Ahmed, S., Gonçalves, T., Rato, L.: RMID: a novel and efficient image descriptor for mammogram mass classification. In: Kulczycki, P., Kacprzyk, J., Kóczy, L.T., Mesiar, R., Wisniewski, R. (eds.) ITSRCP 2018. AISC, vol. 945, pp. 229–240. Springer, Cham (2020). https://doi.org/10.1007/978-3-030-18058-4_18
3. Skaane, P., Hofvind, S., Skjennald, A.: Randomized trial of screen-film versus full-field digital mammography with soft-copy reading in population-based screening program: follow-up and final results of Oslo II study. Radiology **244**(3), 708–17 (2007)
4. Pisano, E.D., Gatsonis, C., Hendrick, E., et al.: Diagnostic performance of digital versus film mammography for breast-cancer screening. N. Engl. J. Med. **353**(17), 1773–83 (2005). For the Digital Mammographic Imaging Screening Trial (DMIST) Investigators Group
5. Pisano, E.D., Hendrick, R.E., Yaffe, M.J., et al.: Diagnostic accuracy of digital versus film mammography: exploratory analysis of selected population subgroups in DMIST. Radiology **246**(2), 376–83 (2008). For the Digital Mammographic Imaging Screening Trial (DMIST) Investigators Group
6. Arevalo, J., González, F.A., Ramos-Pollán, R., Oliveira, J.L., Lopez, M.A.G.: Convolutional neural networks for mammography mass lesion classification. In: IEEE 37th Annual International Conference of the Engineering in Medicine and Biology Society (EMBC) (2015)
7. http://bcdr.inegi.up.pt . Accessed 25 Jan 2018
8. Arevalo, J., González, F.A., Ramos-Pollán, R., Oliveira, J.L., Lopez, M.A.G.: Representation learning for mammography mass lesion classification with convolutional neural networks. Comput. Methods Program. Biomed. **127**, 248–257 (2016)
9. Moura, D.C., López, M.A.G.: An evaluation of image descriptors combined with clinical data for breast cancer diagnosis. Int. J. Comput. Assist. Radiol. Surg. **8**, 561–574 (2013)
10. Haralick, R.M., Shanmuga, K., Dinstein, I.: Textural features for image classification. IEEE Tran. Syst. Man Cybern. **3**(6), 610–621 (1973)
11. Yu, S.Y., Guan, L.: A CAD system for the automatic detection of clustered microcalcifications in digitized mammogram films. IEEE Trans. Med. Imaging **19**(2), 115–126 (2000)
12. Dhawan, A.P., Chitre, Y., Kaiser, B.C., Moskowitz, M.: Analysis of mammographic microcalcifications using gray-level image structure features. IEEE Trans. Med. Imaging **15**(3), 246–259 (1996)
13. Wang, D., Shi, L., Ann, H.P.: Automatic detection of breast cancers in mammograms using structured support vector machines. Neurocomputing **72**(13–15), 3296–3302 (2009)
14. Dua, S., Singh, H., Thompson, H.W.: Associative classification of mammograms using weighted rules. Expert Syst. Appl. **36**(5), 9250–9259 (2009)
15. Sahiner, B., Chan, H.P., Petrick, N., Helvie, M.A., Hadjiiski, L.M.: Improvement of mammographic mass characterization using spiculation measures and morphological features. Med. Phys. **28**(7), 1455–1465 (2001)
16. Mazo, C., Alegre, E., Trujillo, M., González-Castro, V.: Tissues classification of the cardiovascular system using texture descriptors. In: Valdés Hernández, M., González-Castro, V. (eds.) MIUA 2017. CCIS, vol. 723, pp. 123–132. Springer, Cham (2017). https://doi.org/10.1007/978-3-319-60964-5_11

17. O'Neil, A., Shepherd, M., Beveridge, E., Goatman, K.: A comparison of texture features versus deep learning for image classification in interstitial lung disease. In: Valdés Hernández, M., González-Castro, V. (eds.) MIUA 2017. CCIS, vol. 723, pp. 743–753. Springer, Cham (2017). https://doi.org/10.1007/978-3-319-60964-5_65
18. Ferreira, C.B.R., Borges, D.B.L.: Analysis of mammogram classification using a wavelet transform decomposition. Pattern Recogn. Lett. **24**(7), 973–982 (2003)
19. Rashed, E.A., Ismail, I.A., Zaki, S.I.: Multiresolution mammogram analysis in multilevel decomposition. Pattern Recogn. Lett. **28**(2), 286–292 (2007)
20. Meselhy, E.M., Faye, I., Belhaouari, S.B.: A comparison of wavelet and curvelet for breast cancer diagnosis in digital mammogram. Comput BiolMed. **40**(4), 384–391 (2010). https://doi.org/10.1016/j.compbiomed.2010.02.002
21. Ramos-Pollán, R., et al.: Discovering mammography-based machine learning classifiers for breast cancer diagnosis. J. Med. Syst. **36**(4), 2259–69 (2011)
22. Bielza, C., Li, G., Larrañaga, P.: Multi-dimensional classification with Bayesian networks. Int. J. Approx. Reason. **52**, 705–727 (2011)
23. Mika, S., Ratsch, G., Weston, J.: Fisher discriminant analysis with kernels. In: IEEE Conference on Neural Networks for Signal Processing IX, pp. 41–48 (1999)
24. http://mlcheatsheet.readthedocs.io/en/latest/logistic_regression.html. Accessed 15 Nov 2019
25. Santosh, K.C., Antani, S.: Automated chest X-ray screening: can lung region symmetry help detect pulmonary abnormalities. IEEE Trans. Med. Imaging (2017). https://doi.org/10.1109/TMI.2017.2775636
26. Mukherjee, H., et al.: Deep learning for spoken language identification: can we visualize speech signal patterns? Neural Comput. Appl. **31**, 8483–8501 (2019)
27. Santosh, K.C., Wendling, L., Antani, S.K., Thoma, G.R.: Overlaid arrow detection for labeling regions of interest in biomedical images. IEEE Intell. Syst. **31**(3), 66–75 (2016)
28. Ghosh, S., Bandyopadhyay, A., Sahay, S., Ghosh, R., Kundu, I., Santosh, K.C.: Colorectal histology tumor detection using ensemble deep neural network. Eng. Appl. Artif. Intell. **100**, 104202 (2021)

Computer Vision and Pattern Recognition

Complex Object Detection Using Light-Field Plenoptic Camera

Edgar S. Correa$^{(\boxtimes)}$, Carlos A. Parra, Pedro R. Vizcaya,
Francisco Carlos Calderon, and Julian D. Colorado

School of Engineering, Pontificia Universidad Javeriana Bogota,
Cra. 7 No. 40-62, Bogota 110311, Colombia
{e_correa,carlos.parra,pvizcaya,calderonf,coloradoj}@javeriana.edu.co

Abstract. Identifying objects with a lot of complex features in an uncontrolled scene is a challenging task in the image processing research field. This article presents the application of robust and invariant feature descriptors together with an optimal, iterative and probabilistic methodology. These methods let to achieve an application of object detection through a homographic transformation matrix. This work is built on the Raytrix R42 Plenoptic camera, for which the camera calibration process is introduced. The results present a homographic transformation that relates spatial information of the reference object in an uncontrolled scene. This approach put forward an efficient performance that overcomes bad lighting and occlusion problems.

Keywords: Robust descriptor · Homography transform · Optimal
statistic approach · Plenoptic camera

1 Introduction

Images registration has been presented as a research task that addresses processing images captured from different frames, with different sensors, and at different times [1,2]. Image registration consists of estimating the best spatial transformation that allows the images to be related. These images must meet the condition of having common information of the scene, for example, containing the object of interest. This approach makes it possible to find the object's position in the uncontrolled scene, knowing a clear image of the object. The biggest challenges consist of three key points: (i) identifying complex objects, that is, with great content of details in color and shape, (ii) some objects in the scene with great content of similar characteristics, and (iii) uncontrolled environmental conditions, such as uneven lighting and occlusions.

The feature in the space is the representation of data and determines correspondences. The similarity metric determines how matches are scored and is calculated using both images for each test. The first is the image of the object,

Supported by ÓMICAS Program.

KC Santosh et al. (Eds.): RTIP2R 2021, CCIS 1576, pp. 119–133, 2022.
https://doi.org/10.1007/978-3-031-07005-1_12

and the second is an image of an uncontrolled scene, that is, with the three complexity challenges mentioned. Feature space is determined by raw pixel values, commonly is used intensities, edges, contours, and surfaces; however, other approach use (i) outstanding features such as very curved corners, line intersections, and points; (ii) statistical characteristics such as moment in-variants or centroids and (iii) high-level syntactic and structural descriptions [4,5].

Outstanding features refer to specific pixels in the image that contains significant information about the scene. There are two approaches to characterize these relevant features, the first consists of comparing the intensity patterns in the images through correlation metrics that record complete images or subimages using moments that are invariant to changes in perspectives or rotations on an axis [3–5]. The second consists of finding correspondence between image features such as points of interest, establishing point-to-point correspondence between the reference and the target images [6,7], these features are invariant to the scale, translation, and rotation of the image also invariant to changes in lighting and 3D projection [4,8,9].

After characterizing the most salient information of the scene must be select measures of similarity, this step is closely related to the selection of the matching feature. Evaluating all matches is computationally very expensive, for this, the last step is to select a search strategy. The iterative method Random sample consensus (RANSAC) is implemented to estimate the parameters of a mathematical model. This allows generating the spatial transform using the homography matrix. This methodology tackles the problem of object recognition, motion detection, stereopsis, change detection, image mosaicking, super-resolution, and geographic information systems [10,11].

This approach can be used primarily to recognize objects and develop applications that require user interaction [12,13]. However, in the OMICAS research platform, it is planned to use as an algorithm to achieve sensory fusion between the light-field of the plenoptic camera and a multispectral camera in the task of phenotyping crops [14–16].

This research covers the problem of matching two or more photographs to work up an object recognition application, with the characteristic of using a plenoptic camera, this technology is recent and therefore of research interest, however, it works with any type of camera. This paper introduces the plenoptic camera calibration in Sect. 2, presents the methodology in Sect. 3, which is made up of four stages, the first stage is feature detection, the second is feature matching, the third is homography matrix estimation and the last stage is image transformation. Finally, Sect. 3.4 presents the results and Sect. 3.5 presents the conclusions. The experiments cover the three challenges mentioned at the beginning of this section: identifying complex objects, scenes with several similar complex objects, and environments with occlusions and non-uniform lighting conditions.

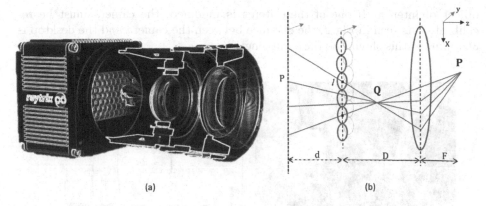

Fig. 1. Plenoptic camera. (a) 3D light field camera [9]. (b) Projective model of Plenoptic camera based on the micro-lenses array.

2   Plenoptic Camera Calibration

The light field technology of the plenoptic cameras has been arousing interest due to the innovation and potential that it presents. It not only captures the intensity of light like a conventional camera, but it also captures the direction in which the rays travel in space. Figure 1 - a shows the structure of the plenoptic sensor developed by Raytrix, this image shows that it is necessary to calibrate the camera due to the micro-lens architecture. Figure 1 - b presents the general projective model of a Plenoptic camera based on literature [20,21], point P is the real spatial information of the scene (P_x, P_y, P_z). The light rays make up the image in the scene and is captured from points P through the main lens, and correspond to points Q that makes up the image captured by the camera. l is the set of micro-lenses on which the plenoptic technology is based, and has a direct relationship with the generation of pixels p. For $P_z > 0$ the relation of Eq. 1 is observed, where d is the distance between the camera sensor and the microlens array, D is the distance between the microlens array and the main lens, and F is the focal length of the main lens and the object in the scene.

$$\frac{1}{F} = \frac{1}{P_z} - \frac{1}{Q_z} \tag{1}$$

The camera calibration process is developed with the RxLive tool and requires two important elements: the calibration filter and a light source. The arrangement of the elements is observed in Fig. 2.

Three key elements intervene in the calibration process, which is the physical-manual configuration: The main lens of the camera, in this case, is 12 mm, the aperture of the diaphragm that affects the amount of light that reaches the sensor, and the focus that defines the distance between the camera and the object of interest. If one of these items is modified, the camera must be re-calibrated. As seen in Fig. 2, the distance between the camera and the desktop is 360 mm, so this should be the focal length.

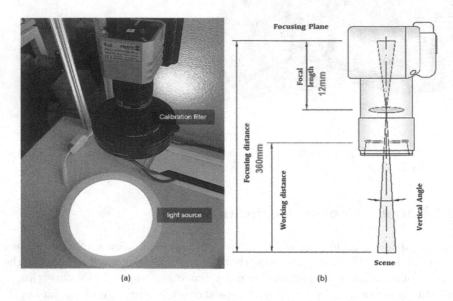

Fig. 2. Camera Ratrix R42 with filter calibration disk and light source.

The illumination of the images is set through the exposure time because the aperture is set fixed. An exposure time of 55 ms is set for these lighting conditions. In Fig. 3 - a is observed overexposure, this is normal due to having the light source direct to the camera. Figure 3 - b a correct exposure is observed, and in Fig. 3 - c the calibration of the micro lens array is presented, and the images captured with the calibrated camera can be seen in Fig. 4.

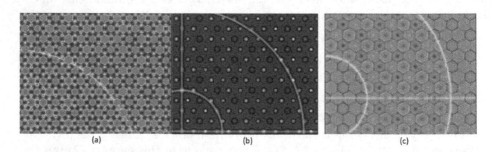

Fig. 3. (a) Conditions of overexposure. (b) Good lighting conditions. (c) Micro lens array calibration

Fig. 4. Light field image captured with a R42 Raytrix plenoptic camera, at a focal length of 360 mm.

3 Methods

Figure 5 shows the experiment design. It consists of having the interest object on the right, in this case, it is a poker card. On the left, the scene in which is desired to detect this object.

The methodology is expanded in four stages, the first is the feature detection through descriptors vectors, the second is the match of these characteristics, the third is the estimation of the spatial transformation model through a probabilistic technique, and finally the implementation of the spatial transformation to validate the methodology.

Fig. 5. Topology of the experiment design, on the right the object of interest, and on the left, a scene containing several objects with many similar characteristics.

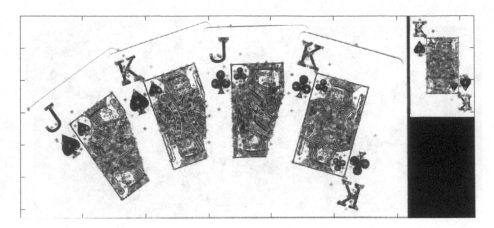

Fig. 6. The composition of images, indicating with an asterisk marks the position of the descriptors generated with SIFT algorithm for each image.

3.1   Feature Detection

To obtain the accurate characterization of the scene must be detected prominent and distinctive areas of the image. The robustness of the object detector application depends on the descriptor. The features should be invariant to illumination, 3D projective transforms, and common object variations. In this research work is used the Scale Invariant Feature Transform approach (SIFT). This approach transforms an image into a large collection of local feature vectors. The SIFT algorithm is conceptualized in the response of neurons of the inferior temporal cortex to the primates vision [19].

The result is a feature vector with a composition of one hundred and twenty-eight dimensions. Each descriptor has its position in the image assigned with the coordinate (X, Y). If the analyzed image is more complex, that is, with a large number of details, it will contain a greater number of descriptors.

Figure 6 shows with an asterisk mark the position (x, y) of each descriptor found in each image.

Algorithm 1: Feature matching by force.
Inputs: A : features of reference image B : features of scene.

---

    for i = 1 : size(A) **do**
      $\mathbf{X}$: cos^{-1} ($A(i)$ * B)
      Match grater values of $'X'$ and Sort
      if $Match(1) < distRatio * Match(2)$ **then**
        MatchTable(i) = $Match(1)$
      else
        MatchTable(i) = 0
      end if
    end for

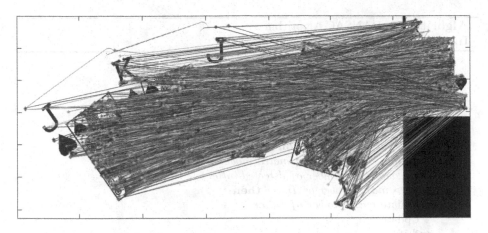

Fig. 7. All possible matches between the two images, 3254 matches.

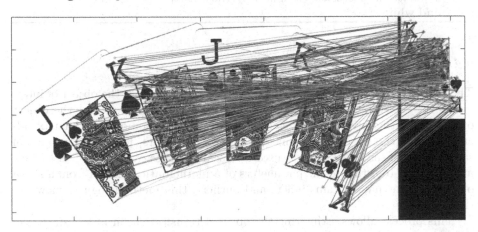

Fig. 8. Matches generated with the Algorithm 1, 257 matches

3.2   Feature Matching

The matching stage relates the information generated between two images. This correspondence link up each of the features through the distance metric between the descriptors. 3254 features are generated in the scene, and 593 features in the interest object image, consequently, Fig. 7 shown 3254 matches generated. To have a better performance of the pattern recognition application, it is sought to process the least amount of information possible. To achieve this, in Algorithm 1 the features correspondence by force is presented, this is done through the security metric *distRatio* to establish the most prominent matches. Figure 8 shows the force matching filter of Fig. 7.

Algorithm 2: RANSAC Algorithm
Inputs: $MatchTable$ from Algorithm 1

$max\ number\ of\ Inlier \leftarrow 0$
Calculate maximum iteration based on termination criterion
while $number\ of\ Iterations < N$ **do**
    I. Hypothesis generation
    $S_i \leftarrow select\ minimal\ subset\ of\ samples\ randomly.$
    $M_i \leftarrow generate\ a\ hypothesis\ (model)\ from\ s_i$
    II. Hypothesis evaluation
    $Calculate\ error\ from\ estimated\ model$
    $I_i \leftarrow count\ the\ number\ of\ detected\ inliers$
    if $I_i > max\ number\ of\ Inlier$ **then**
        Update $max\ number\ of\ Inlier$
        Update N
    end if
    $number\ of\ Iteration \leftarrow number\ of\ Iteration + 1$
end while

3.3 Transform Model Estimation

The transformation model is a mapping function that relates the object of interest in the scene with the reference image, the latter only contains the object of interest in the foreground. This is done through the homography matrix calculated with the position information of the descriptors, for this, the random samples consensus (RANSAC) is used as a search strategy. RANSAC is an iterative method to estimate the parameters of a mathematical model from a set of observed data that contains inliers and outliers, this methodology is shown in the Algorithm 2.

This process allows estimating the optimal transformation in the statistical sense, it is based on a chi-square probability distribution. The probability that the point is an inlier is $\alpha = 0.95$ and to calculate the homography, $\sigma^2 = 5.99$ [1,18].

This approach guarantees that the number of samples chosen is representative, ensuring with a probability "p" that at least one of the random samples of points "s" is free of outliers, that is, the estimate of the transformation is free of outliers with probability p = 0.99. Defining w as the probability of any selected data is inlier, and ϵ as 1-w the probability of outlier be selected. A least N selections features of s points are required to warranty: $(1 - w^s)^N = 1 - p$, as a result Eq. 2 model with ϵ in Eq. 3.

$$N = \frac{log(1 - p)}{log(1 - (1 - \epsilon^s))} \qquad (2)$$

$$\epsilon = \frac{1 - number\ of\ inlier}{Total\ number\ of\ points} \qquad (3)$$

The consensus ends when the probability modeled by this approach is greater than the number of events. The spatial transformation is carried out through the homographic matrix of Eq. 4 to 6. The first relates a rotation transformation, the second integrates linear transformations in the (x, y) axes, and the third is a complete homography transformation in space. The last is used in this work,the transformation is expressed in Eq. 7.

$$\begin{vmatrix} X_T \\ Y_T \\ 1 \end{vmatrix} = \begin{vmatrix} Cos(\theta) & -Sen(\theta) & 0 \\ Sen(\theta) & Cos(\theta) & 0 \\ 0 & 0 & 1 \end{vmatrix} \begin{vmatrix} X_R \\ Y_R \\ 1 \end{vmatrix} \tag{4}$$

$$\begin{vmatrix} X_T \\ Y_T \\ 1 \end{vmatrix} = \begin{vmatrix} a_{11} & a_{12} & t_x \\ a_{21} & a_{22} & t_y \\ 0 & 0 & 1 \end{vmatrix} \begin{vmatrix} X_R \\ Y_R \\ 1 \end{vmatrix} \tag{5}$$

$$\begin{vmatrix} X_T \\ Y_T \\ 1 \end{vmatrix} = \begin{vmatrix} h_{11} & h_{12} & h_{13} \\ h_{21} & h_{22} & h_{23} \\ h_{31} & h_{32} & h_{33} \end{vmatrix} \begin{vmatrix} X_R \\ Y_R \\ 1 \end{vmatrix} \tag{6}$$

$$X_T = H.X_R \tag{7}$$

The goal is to find $h = \begin{vmatrix} h_{11} & h_{12} & h_{13} & h_{21} & h_{22} & h_{23} & h_{31} & h_{32} & h_{33} \end{vmatrix}$. The transformation $X_T = H.X_R$ can be expressed as a linear system $Ah = 0$.

This is solving using Gaussian elimination whit a pseudo-inverse method, as seen in Eq. 8. Matrix resolution is implemented with A and B and are shown in Eq. 9 and 10 respectively.

$$h = (A'^T.A')^{-1} A'^T.b' \tag{8}$$

$$A = \begin{vmatrix} X_{R1} & Y_{R1} & 1 & 0 & 0 & 0 & -X_{R1}.X_{T1} & -Y_{R1}.X_{T1} & -X_{T1} \\ 0 & 0 & 0 & X_{R1} & Y_{R1} & 1 & -X_{R1}.Y_{T1} & -Y_{R1}.y_{T1} & -y_{T1} \\ \cdot & \cdot & \cdot & \cdot & \cdot & \cdot & \cdot & & \cdot \\ \cdot & \cdot & \cdot & \cdot & \cdot & \cdot & \cdot & & \cdot \\ X_{Rn} & x_{Rn} & 1 & 0 & 0 & 0 & -X_{Rn}.X_{Tn} & -Y_{Rn}.X_{Tn} & -X_{Tn} \\ 0 & 0 & 0 & X_{Rn} & Y_{Rn} & 1 & -X_{Rn}.Y_{Tn} & -Y_{Rn}.Y_{Tn} & -Y_{Tn} \end{vmatrix} \tag{9}$$

$$b = \begin{vmatrix} X_{T1} \\ Y_{T1} \\ \cdot \\ \cdot \\ X_{Tn} \\ Y_{Tn} \end{vmatrix} = \begin{vmatrix} X_{R1} & Y_{R1} & 1 & 0 & 0 & 0 & -X_{R1}.X_{T1} & -Y_{R1}.X_{T1} & -X_{T1} \\ 0 & 0 & 0 & X_{R1} & Y_{R1} & 1 & -X_{R1}.Y_{T1} & -Y_{R1}.y_{T1} & -y_{T1} \\ \cdot & \cdot & \cdot & \cdot & \cdot & \cdot & \cdot & & \cdot \\ \cdot & \cdot & \cdot & \cdot & \cdot & \cdot & \cdot & & \cdot \\ X_{Rn} & x_{Rn} & 1 & 0 & 0 & 0 & -X_{Rn}.X_{Tn} & -Y_{Rn}.X_{Tn} & -X_{Tn} \\ 0 & 0 & 0 & X_{Rn} & Y_{Rn} & 1 & -X_{Rn}.Y_{Tn} & -Y_{Rn}.Y_{Tn} & -Y_{Tn} \end{vmatrix} . \begin{vmatrix} h_{11} \\ h_{12} \\ h_{13} \\ h_{21} \\ h_{22} \\ h_{23} \\ h_{31} \\ h_{32} \\ h_{33} \end{vmatrix} \tag{10}$$

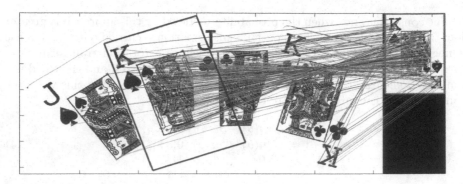

Fig. 9. Object recognition with occlusion of twenty percent under controlled conditions.

Image Transformation. In Fig. 9 the reference image is observed in red, and the same object is observed in blue in the image of the scene. The transformation is carried out using the homographic matrix 'h', the transformation is carried out for each corners of the poker card. Figure 10 shows two characteristics of complexity, an occlusion of approximately fifty percent and a scene with several very similar objects.

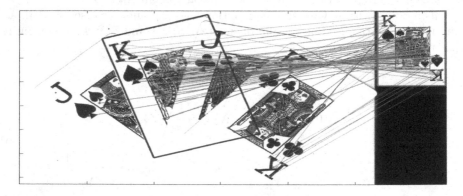

Fig. 10. Object recognition with occlusion of fifty percent under controlled conditions.

3.4   Results

The tests are divided into two groups, the first is seen in Fig. 9 and in Fig. 10, these consist of images under controlled lighting conditions. In these tests a good performance is observed at different levels of occlusion. The second group consists of uncontrolled conditions. Figure 11 shows the identification of a complex object, that is, with many details of shape and color, and in addition, a significant occlusion is shown in Fig. 12. The system presents a good performance in the identification of this object.

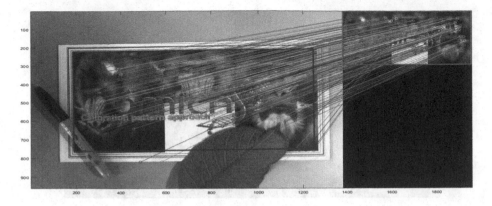

Fig. 11. Object recognition.

Figure 13 shows an identification of the object of interest in the context of an uncontrolled scene. The main characteristic is the presence of two very similar objects, however, the system is able to recognize the object very well.

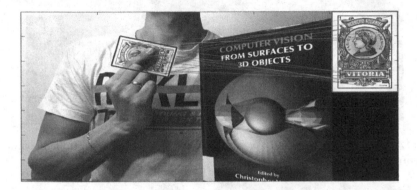

Fig. 12. Object recognition with a significant occlusion under uncontrolled conditions.

Finally, the most challenging test identifies an object of interest with four characteristics: (i) with many characteristics in color and shape, also (ii) in the presence of other objects with a level of very similar characteristics, (iii) in occlusion conditions and (iv) in an uncontrolled lighting scene. In Fig. 13 and 14 the result is observed, the first one presents a greater intensity of illumination compared to the second one. In both cases, good results are presented. Table 1 shows the execution time of the application for each image in column third, the first column links the image, and the second column shows the time of descriptor, match, and transformation stage respectively.

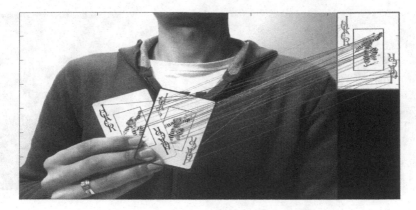

Fig. 13. Object recognition with an occlusion under uncontrolled conditions with two similar objects.

Fig. 14. Complex object recognition with an occlusion under uncontrolled conditions with some similar objects.

Fig. 15. Complex object recognition with an occlusion under uncontrolled conditions with some similar objects, and bad lighting

Table 1. Time it takes the application to recognize the object. Feature, Match and RANSAC for each image.

Image	Time (Seg)	Total time
Figure 9	[3.16, 0.28, 0.55]	3.99
Figure 10	[3.22, 0.20, 0.45]	3.87
Figure 12	[3.55, 0.30, 0.31]	4.16
Figure 13	[3.48, 0.16, 0.27]	3.91
Figure 14	[4.10, 0.31, 0.32]	4.73
Figure 15	[3.56, 1.17, 0.19]	4.92

Face recognition is another option to use this application, as shown in Fig. 16. The face recognition approach is not the motivation of this research paper. However, it could be an interesting future research work.

Fig. 16. Face recognition under uncontrolled conditions. Roger Federer at Australian open 2008, screenshot of [14].

3.5 Conclusions

Feature space is a fundamental aspect in object recognition application. If invariant moments are implemented, the final application is limited to rigid transformations. In this research work is using the robust descriptor SIFT, this has the potential to work with complex scenes and even it can be used to development to three-dimensional space applications. The complexity addressed are: uncontrolled lighting conditions, occlusions, and recurrence of patterns in the scene that are not part of the object of interest. In all cases, the methodology shows good results. From the execution times shown in Table 1, it can be concluded that the highest computational cost is related to the extraction of features. The images with more detail in color, shape and size, present more characteristics to be calculated. The RANSAC algorithm execution time is highly variable due to the random component, especially, when selecting the features to evaluate the model. The average recognition time is 3.93 Seg. for controlled environment and 4.4 Seg for uncontrolled environment.

As future work, it is planned to duplicate the work on a multispectral camera to evaluate the effects of using it in the IR wavelength. The transformations will allow generating a sensory fusion system between the two cameras. As a result, it is expected to achieve the composition of multispectral images with the models generated with the plenoptic camera in the task of phenotyping plants. In this context, the average time of 4 sec is sufficient to achieve the sensory fusion goal, since it only needs to be done once as calibration, and run the model in real-time.

Funding. This work was funded by the OMICAS program: "Optimización Multiescala In-silico de Cultivos Agrícolas Sostenibles (Infraestructura y validación en Arroz y Caña de Azúcar)", anchored at the Pontificia Universidad Javeriana in Cali and funded within the Colombian Scientific Ecosystem by The World Bank, the Colombian Ministry of Science, Technology and Innovation, the Colombian Ministry of Education, the Colombian Ministry of Industry and Tourism, and ICETEX, under grant ID: FP44842-217-2018 and OMICAS Award ID: 792-61187.

References

1. Zitova, B., Flusser, J.: Image registration methods: a survey. Image Vis. Comput. **21**(11), 977–1000 (2003). https://doi.org/10.1016/S0262-8856(03)00137-9
2. dos Santos Júnior, J.G., do Monte Lima, J.P.S., Teichrieb, V.: Occlusion-robust method for RGB-D 6-DOF object tracking with particle swarm optimization. Expert Systems with Applications, **174**, 114736 (2021). https://doi.org/10.1016/j.eswa.2021.114736
3. Mustafa, A., Kim, H., Hilton, A.: MSFD: multi-scale segmentation-based feature detection for wide-baseline scene reconstruction. IEEE Trans. Image Process. **28**(3), 1118–1132 (2018). https://doi.org/10.1109/TIP.2018.2872906
4. Wattanapanich, C., Wei, H., Petchkit, W.: Investigation of robust gait recognition for different appearances and camera view angles. Int. J. Electr. Comput. Eng. (2088–8708), **11**(5) (2021). https://doi.org/10.11591/ijece.v11i5.pp3977-3987
5. Hu, M.K.: Visual pattern recognition by moment invariants. IRE Trans. Inf. Theory **8**(2), 179–187 (1962). https://doi.org/10.1109/TIT.1962.1057692
6. Merkle, N., Auer, S., Müller, R., Reinartz, P.: Exploring the potential of conditional adversarial networks for optical and SAR image matching. IEEE J. Sel. Top. Appl. Earth Observ. Remote Sens. **11**(6), 1811–1820 (2018). https://doi.org/10.1109/JSTARS.2018.2803212
7. Velastin Carroza, S.A., Nazir, S., Yousaf, H.M.: Evaluating a bag-of-visual features approach using spatio-temporal features for action recognition (2018). https://doi.org/10.1016/j.compeleceng.2018.01.037
8. Lowe, D.G.: Object recognition from local scale-invariant features. In: Proceedings of the IEEE International Conference on Computer Vision, vol. 2, pp. 1150–1157 (1999). https://doi.org/10.1109/iccv.1999.790410

9. Zhang, L., Li, K., Qi, Y., Wang, F.: Local feature extracted by the improved bag of features method for person re-identification. Neurocomputing **458**, 690–700 (2021). https://doi.org/10.1016/j.neucom.2019.12.142

10. Zhang, J., Chen, G., Jia, Z.: An image stitching algorithm based on histogram matching and SIFT algorithm. Int. J. Pattern Recognit. Artif. Intell. **31**(04), 1754006 (2017). https://doi.org/10.1142/S0218001417540064

11. Shen, Y., Zhu, J., Liu, H., Sun, L.: Plant image mosaic based on depth and color dual information feature source from kinect. Trans. Chin. Soc. Agric. Eng. **34**(5), 176–182 (2018). https://doi.org/10.11975/j.issn.1002-6819.2018.05.023

12. Mousavi, S., Charmi, M., Hassanpoor, H.: A distinctive landmark-based face recognition system for identical twins by extracting novel weighted features. Comput. Electr. Eng. **94**, 107326 (2021). https://doi.org/10.1016/j.compeleceng.2021.107326

13. Cachique, S.M., Correa, E.S., Rodriguez-Garavito, C.H.: Intelligent digital tutor to assemble puzzles based on artificial intelligence techniques. In: Florez, H., Misra, S. (eds.) ICAI 2020. CCIS, vol. 1277, pp. 56–71. Springer, Cham (2020). https://doi.org/10.1007/978-3-030-61702-8_5

14. Colorado, J.D., et al.: A novel NIR-image segmentation method for the precise estimation of above-ground biomass in rice crops. PLoS ONE **15**(10), e0239591 (2020). https://doi.org/10.1371/journal.pone.0239591

15. Jimenez-Sierra, D.A., Correa, E.S., Benítez-Restrepo, H.D., Calderon, F.C., Mondragon, I.F., Colorado, J.D.: Novel feature-extraction methods for the estimation of above-ground biomass in rice crops. Sensors **21**(13), 4369 (2021). https://doi.org/10.3390/s21134369

16. Correa, E.S., Calderon, F., Colorado, J.D.: GFkuts: a novel multispectral image segmentation method applied to precision agriculture. In: 2020 Virtual Symposium in Plant Omics Sciences (OMICAS), pp. 1–6 (2020). https://doi.org/10.1109/OMICAS52284.2020.9535659

17. 3D Light-Field Cameras with 4D Plenoptic Depth Sensors. https://raytrix.de/products/. Accessed 20 June 2021

18. Fotouhi, M., Hekmatian, H., Kashani-Nezhad, M.A., Kasaei, S.: SC-RANSAC: spatial consistency on RANSAC. Multimed. Tools Appl. **78**(7), 9429–9461 (2018). https://doi.org/10.1007/s11042-018-6475-6

19. Lowe, D.G.: Distinctive image features from scale-invariant keypoints. Int. J. Comput. Vis. **60**, 91–110 (2004). https://doi.org/10.1023/B:VISI.0000029664.99615.94

20. O'brien, S., Trumpf, J., Ila, V., Mahony, R.: Calibrating light-field cameras using plenoptic disc features. In: IEEE International Conference on 3D Vision (3DV), pp. 286–294 (2018). https://doi.org/10.1109/3DV.2018.00041

21. Zhang, C., Ji, Z., Wang, Q.: Decoding and calibration method on focused plenoptic camera. Comput. Vis. Media **2**(1), 57–69 (2016). https://doi.org/10.1007/s41095-016-0040-x

22. Roger Federer's emotional winning speech—Australian Open 2018 Final. https://www.youtube.com/watch?v=A72M2mZ2wHA. Accessed 20 June 2021

Real-Time Face Recognition for Organisational Attendance Systems

Divyagna Bavikadi[1], A. Manjunatha[1], Abhishek Pol[2], Akshat Kadam[3]([✉]),
Prajakta Kulkarni[3], Aparna Singh[3], P. M. Kamble[1], and Ravindra Hegadi[1]

[1] Central University of Karnataka, Kalaburgi 585367, Karnataka, India
[2] Walchand College of Engineering, Sangli 416415, Maharashtra, India
[3] Develearn Technologies Pvt Ltd., Mumbai 400019, Maharashtra, India
akshat.kadam@develearn.in

Abstract. Today we are in an era of feasible biometric solutions to the age-old problem of verifying personal identity. As a form of identity that is verified through inseparable and unique characteristics of a person: their face - facial recognition is now one of the most popular methods in use. We propose an automated real-time facial attendance system where the users can verify their identity without physical contact with any surface. This is achieved through a conjunction of a mobile and platform-independent web application over a shared cloud database. The system is powered by a Face Recognition module to authenticate the users and demonstrated 99.7% of test accuracy, with an improved true positivity rate of 96.14% compared to some existing literature. Our system processes and aligns input face images before utilizing a deep convolutional neural network model to recognize the user's identity. To test the efficacy of our system, we have built a database of over 800 unique individuals of Indian descent. Our tests showed a superior true-positivity rate on our tweaked model demonstrating its efficacy in comparison with the reference literature. We also share some of the methods employed to raise system redundancy and minimize false negativity; a vital metric in any authentication application.

Keywords: Deep convolutional neural network · Face recognition · Attendance system

1 Introduction

Artificial Intelligence is rapidly updating the world and notably boosting the state-of-the-art in many applications including healthcare, security, academics, marketing, etc. In the sense of the attendance system, each organization has its unique process. At present, most of them do it manually by using the paper or file-based approach while few of them are marking automatic attendance using some biometric techniques.

© Springer Nature Switzerland AG 2022
KC Santosh et al. (Eds.): RTIP2R 2021, CCIS 1576, pp. 134–145, 2022.
https://doi.org/10.1007/978-3-031-07005-1_13

Generally, all biometric systems begin with an enrolment process in which a person's unique characteristics are registered, followed by identification procedures. These two phases verify a specific user's biometric feature to a formerly stored template taken upon enrolment. The templates for biometrics can be of many types like Fingerprints, Hand Geometry, Voice, Signature, Face, Gait, and Iris, however, the key authentications remain the same across all modalities. However, facial recognition has its own set of issues, finding it challenging to execute. Influences like variation in pose, facial hair, lighting based on the face location, background in the image, and facial or emotional expressions affect the image, and the result can vary accordingly. The face may not be detected in instances where the face is not visible or obscured from the camera. The majority of the existing systems have mobility, cost, security, accessibility, authenticity restrictions. Users must wait a long time in line while entering the organization via these techniques and involves the user giving actions that require physical contact with the external equipment.

An endeavor to conquer the inadequacies of the existing systems leads to the building of a Real-Time Face Recognition for Organisational Attendance System which will especially be useful in situations or future pandemic situations (Fig. 1).

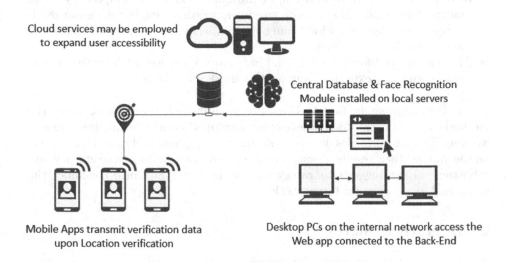

Cloud services may be employed
to expand user accessibility

Central Database & Face Recognition
Module installed on local servers

Mobile Apps transmit verification data
upon Location verification

Desktop PCs on the internal network access the
Web app connected to the Back-End

Fig. 1. Cross-device system design

Real-Time Face Recognition for Organisational Attendance Systems introduces a standalone application that includes a built-in responsive user interface with both web-based and mobile app-based versions, to make the attendance procedure seamless.

A note on the system design, it contains access levels that represent the end user's permissions and privileges across the system or within the corresponding class. The front-end access is given to all the users, though the dashboard and usable features have limited scope for basic/staff level users. The users have limited access to the database server depending on their respective access levels. The Super Admin governs all the users including editing and deleting user details from the system. The Admin-level access has extended permissions and full authority over features and user members within the respective department unit. Admins will govern the staff-level users whose usage of the program is limited to Marking attendance, examining their details and attendance log. The access levels control tool lowers the danger of a privacy breach while also tackling a wide range of security concerns. The architecture mainly consists of three layers, an application layer, a server layer, and a backend database framework.

This work has the following contributions:

- Information Architecture of the system and how a web + mobile app works in tandem to fulfill base requirements.
- Unique checks and balances:
  - Intranet-connection-based verification layer for Web app version.
  - The local network (wi-fi) + geolocation-based verification layer for the mobile app version.
- Algorithm: How Facenet architecture was used to create a database-query protocol and how TP maximization/FP minimization was attempted by using multiple face vectors in a decision tree format rather than tweaking the architecture of the network. Fine tuning the similarity threshold with respect to the custom dataset created.
- There is no need for any additional hardware. User doesn't have to come in contact with any external equipment to mark attendance.

Paper Organization: In Sect. 2, literature is discussed. Section 3 provides the methodology of the end-to-end developed novel method and its architecture and working. Section 4 provides details about the testing phase and experiments done on the system, their results, discussion on experimental findings, the efficacy and robustness of the suggested strategy and architecture. Section 5 concludes the paper and gives scope for future works.

2   Literature Survey

Attendance can be recorded using numerous biometric approaches like retinal scan, fingerprint, iris recognition, face recognition, etc., that are used by many systems. D. Feng et al. [1] worked on marking the student attendance, where the fingerprint is used. The major drawback of this system is the time taken to process and the need for users to physically go to the installed machines. M. Ali et al. [2] used an iris-based attendance system. The issue with this approach is its sensitivity to environmental factors such as illumination changes.

S. Joardar et al. [3] have developed an attendance management system on the basis of the palm dorsal subcutaneous vein pattern of individuals. PDSVP is used as a physiological biometric feature.

Jomon Joseph et al. [4] the author proposed a face recognition attendance system using Eigenface recognition. However, this system is sensitive to faces in the background and head orientation and will fail if the person is wearing eyeglasses or even facial hair etc.

Evta Indra et al. [5] used Haar-like features to recognize faces of the students where they have to line up in front of the camera at a fixed position which is to be installed externally in the institute. But B. Tej Chinimilli et al. [6], proposed a system with the state-of-the-art results using Haar Cascade and Local Binary Pattern Histogram (LBPH) algorithm.

Alghali et al. [7] have presented a model that will identify individuals in every set of conditions especially in pose illumination conditions. A CNN architecture is applied to the complete system. The recognition operation is done by identifying indexes with a 99% accuracy.

In Jinhua Zeng et al. [8], 33 face images were taken for forensic identification. It showed exceptional results on standard datasets such as labeled faces in the wild and YouTube datasets. The accuracy is similar to human prediction at 99%. The wide variability of face appearance and background noise of the image will be the challenge for face recognition [11].

In [12], the authors introduced a new facial recognition technique, that will compute 25 local autocorrelation coefficients. The proposed method in [13] includes detection and recognition for visually impaired people. In [14], the authors proposed an analysis of the Fast Gradient Sign Method. Used for biometric authentication. In [15], the authors proposed an open-source tool Mask-TheFace to create a masked dataset. [16] proposed a modified CNN by adding two normalization operations to the layers. In [17], the authors proposed a face recognition algorithm The main aim of the system is to reduce the feature. In [18], the authors proposed an expression invariant 3D face recognition system. In [19], the authors proposed a model using PCA under the broad heading of factor analysis. In [17], the authors of the article propose a 3-D pose invariant approach based on subject-specific descriptors.

3 Methodology

The proposed method contains a face recognition framework integrated with the web application and the mobile android app, where the web application is built using the MVT (Model View Template) framework and a FaceNet [10] with InceptionResnetv2 framework in python is integrated. The Multi-Task Cascaded Convolutional Neural Network was used for face detection and a deep convolutional neural network for face recognition. Compared to the monotonic grayscale-based transformations, this detector is robust and performs well in terms of detection accuracy.

Figures 2 represents the user journey flow. Whenever the user accessing an application through the web app they will navigate to the home page (Which contains two features: Mark Attendance and Login) and when they are accessing the mobile app, an OTP is sent and verified, and then the user is redirected

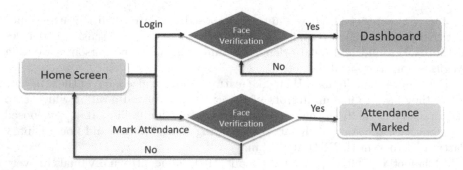

Fig. 2. Flow diagram of the user journey for the joint application

to the home page. The user employees have the privilege where they can also login into the app either with a face id or with login credentials to check their attendance log, request for leave, modify details/check the attendance log of sub-level employees under their respective user access level, upcoming holidays, etc. The logged-in device location is tracked by the system. The user can mark attendance even without logging in and the admin(s) can monitor user activity.

The entire system's basic unit can be considered as the face verification/authentication unit. For the basic unit, a target face feature embedding is given and directly the recognized faces from the database are fetched.

Registering Employees: Each user can only be invited by a user with a higher access level. The invite is sent via email with an auto-generated username, password, registration link which redirects the user to the app where they can update their credentials and register their face in different angles. In order to feed the facial information into the backend database, an approach is employed where input is taken from the capturing module. In this module, a video camera is accessed in the front end interface and the individual frames from the real-time stream are captured and given to the processing module. This module performs: Face detection (identifying the placement of the face in the separated frame from the live stream and resizing the frame to fit the face only) from the frame using MTCNN (Multi-task Cascaded Convolutional Networks), a powerful face detector that has high detection accuracy. The faces stripped from the frame can be positioned in a way that the face verification unit might mistake it to be a different user. As a result, the picture used as input to the basic unit might be in a different state from the image to be analyzed. To resolve that issue, repositioning and alignment of the face detected in the image is done, which increases the accuracy of the face recognition model raising it from 98.9% to 99.7%. Here certain facial feature points that exist on the face are used to distinguish the face, its boundaries, the location of eyes, mouth and lips and then rotation is done on the face such that this transformation is similar to a perfectly centered face as possible. Therefore the face verification unit will not classify the projected faces as different. As a result, the redundant data that is not required for the face authentication unit is removed and the amount of pixels the model needs to work with is reduced, enhancing overall throughput. The processed image is taken and mapped into a compact Euclidean space. We are extracting the high-quality facial feature embeddings using a deep CNN, FaceNet model with an InceptionResNetv2 framework and then represent the face as a 128-dimensional NumPy array that doesn't contain any redundant information of the face. The CNN's convolutional base is frozen which is responsible for the main feature extraction and the last fully connected layer is removed. The model used for face recognition is a deep convolutional network trained using a triplet loss function [10]. No intermediate layer is there to extract the feature set. These embeddings are stored in an array as a cube in the facial database table instead of storing images directly with the corresponding employee's id. Hence the required data of all the registering employees are fed to the system.

Marking Attendance: We employ motion detection when detecting the user's face in order to eliminate the possibility of proxy (holding a picture of another user's face) during authentication. The extracted face encodings of the user trying to mark attendance are taken from the live stream in a similar fashion as explained above and fed to the face authentication unit. The face authentication unit uses Euclidean distance similarity to find the distance between the vectors as a measure of facial similarity. Based on this facial similarity metric, identification of the face can be done. The distance similarity function is as below, using which, similar facial embeddings can be identified:

$$d(p,q) = \sqrt{\sum_{i=1}^{n}(q_i - p_i)^2}. \tag{1}$$

The basic unit takes the input encodings and compares them with the existing system database. The unit decides if they are the same person or different based on the threshold value which is set to 11.370 units. A similarity measure more than the threshold value is considered as a different face. The threshold value of '11.370' is fine-tuned with our custom dataset based on a decision tree algorithm as it splits the database where the gain is maximized for that particular value. The decision tree is built using a part of the database mentioned in the next section by forming a dataset with pairs of similar facial images as well as pairs of different facial images whose distribution is shown in the Fig. 3, where the blue line depicts the similar faces and the orange line depicts the dissimilar faces. As seen in the figure, below approximately 11 units, it can be considered of similar faces. Hence, we tuned the threshold to 11.37 (which is an output from the decision tree) as it gives the most optimised results without compromising the performance of the method as a whole.

To recognize the user, a query is used to directly fetch the employee id of the recognized face by contacting the backend database. This makes the overall process faster than that of the literature and also reduces the computational power required. Then automatically depending on the corresponding employee's id, the attendance is updated with the time stamp in the database's timesheet (Figs. 4, 5 and 6).

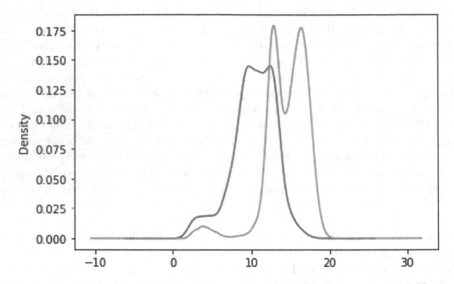

Fig. 3. Distribution plot of corresponding similar and dissimilar faces of the created dataset with Indian ethnicities.

Fig. 4. Output of capturing module

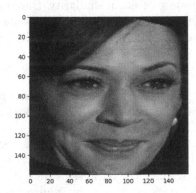

Fig. 5. Output of processing module

Fig. 6. Detected face vs Registered face

4   Experimental Results and Discussion

In a real-time situation, gathering large volumes of data is a tough, monotonous, and time-consuming process. The initial samples collected were using various standard facial datasets and on the LFW (labeled faces in the wild) dataset (has 13,233 images), the developed method gave 99.7% accuracy. But there isn't any standard dataset that is best suited for this project since various angles, expressions, illumination, obstacles, all for a single individual are desired, however, most typical datasets contain millions of single faces, merely various illuminations, expressions of different humans. Illumination and pose of the input facial images affects the efficacy of face detection which affects the overall accuracy. Our pre-processing methods are designed to eliminate pose artifacts(through the face alignment and cropping part) but large variations such as looking sideways/occlusions due to objects/accessories not accounted for can affect the detection of faces.

The optimized and altered in the wild database was created from scratch which consists of 830 individuals with images in the wild ranging from 5 to 20 per individual (out of which one or two images is kept aside for validation of the method) in various expressions, lightings, with and without glasses, angles, projections have been taken for this experiment. In the database, 135 individuals are considered for the purpose of intruder testing, where the method's reliability of whether or not it recognizes the unknown person as its own is tested and hence not stored in the main database of the system. The majority of the database consists of Indian faces, which does not overlap with LFW. Our dataset, unlike other standardised benchmarks, does not solely concentrate on caucasian faces and by extension, helps our proposed method capture facial features of Indian ethnicities in greater detail.

The data is fed to the database and then the validation dataset is fed in the application layer to get the test accuracy and the evaluation metrics of this developed method. Testing of this method is done with the use of live video streaming where employees as well as the people who are foreign to the system use the app. The faces that are foreign to the system are detected and saved which helps to identify intruders and also reduce the incorrect authentication of the users to a Jane Doe (an intruder/faces foreign to the system).

The model and similarity measure used in this method gave more accuracy than those with other combinations (Example: FaceNet with InceptionResnetv2 and cosine similarity metric, OpenFace and euclidean distance, etc.). The similarity measure threshold was finetuned in face recognition with the custom dataset with south asian faces in the wild. After experimenting with different face recognition models in combination with a detector, the best combination that gives an accurate performance is used, which is MTCNN for face detection and the FaceNet with InceptionResnetv2 model for face recognition. MTCNN outperforms haar cascade, dlib based approaches in the proposed architecture. This detector also detects the user from a distance upto 16 feet given the most of the face is covered in the stream, head movements and extracts facial landmarks like eyes, nose, mouth which is important in the processing module for face alignment as that improves the overall accuracy, precision of the facial recognition module. Since it performs well compared to those of the other modules. Even though the method gives a state of art accuracy, the entire system architecture results in an improved true positive, false negative, false-positive rates for both existing registered databases and the foreign individuals who are unknown to the system.

Results: Table 1 gives the experimental results as compared to that of the existing literature. The existing architecture results can be found in [6] for true positive, false positive rates. Table 2 gives the results obtained from the developed method which is tested from the 830 individuals of the dataset.

Table 1. Benchmark comparison

Performance metric	Existing method	Developed method
True positive rate	77%	96.14%
False positive rate	28%	14.61%
False positive rate (user foreign to system)	14%	6.66%
False negative rate	23%	3.86%
True negative rate	72%	85.39%

Table 2. Confusion matrix

	Predicted: No	Predicted: Yes
Actual: No	TN: 222	FP: 38
Actual: Yes	FN: 22	TP: 548

The performance of such attendance marking systems is based on how accurately the users are authenticated and they are measured using the true positive rate, true negative rate, false positive rate, and false negative rates. The true positivity rate of the proposed method is 96.14% (19% greater than that found in existing literature). The tests conducted accounted for varying environmental setups ranging from illumination changes (Outdoors, Indoors, partially outdoors) to presence of occluding accessories, glasses, cap, with dyed hair etc. Even cases where the user may attempt to proxy another user's face with a picture were added in order to raise the robustness of the method. For faces that are foreign to the system, the false positivity rate is 6.66% which is 8% less than that of the state of art, making the system more secure. The false positive rate for the users of the system is 14.61% while it is 28% for some of the existing systems. The false-negativity rate was found to be 3.86%, making the system architecture more reliable as the registered employees will not be rejected wrongfully. The true negative rate is 85.39%, which implies the method will detect the non-users of the system correctly. The overall system time complexity is also improved compared to the literature as well the recognition rate and its instant updation to the main database takes approximately 5 s, unlike an existing attendance system [9] which takes 120 s.

Table 3. Experimental results with finetuning

Framework	Accuracy
Facenet	92.9%
Facenet fine-tuned	99.7%
VGG-face	95.5%
VGG-face fine-tuned	99.2%
OpenFace	93.8%
OpenFace fine-tuned	98.7%

The method was implemented using various state-of-the-art frameworks for face recognition like Facenet, VGG-Face, OpenFace, and their fine-tuned version with respect to threshold value with the custom dataset in the wild. The basic authentication unit was fine-tuned for optimal threshold value with respect to the custom dataset. Their corresponding accuracies as shown in Table 3. The state-of-the-art frameworks were pre-trained with mostly caucassian faces and hence gave less accuracy when tested with Indian faces due to difference in detail of the facial features.

The developed method is working with real-time input and obtaining robust and accurate results with less time and space complexity without requiring a larger database. The existing methods that use face recognition need a large amount of data per face which is 70 images per person which thereby increases the false positives inside the system whereas the developed method requires fewer facial images per person and yet gives a more optimal false positive rate within the system than literature.

The proposed efficient architecture also reduces the risk of a data breach and mitigates a wide range of security issues. It has an improved face recognition runtime than existing methods where even if a separate microprocessor is used which takes time to load, the weights of the model and process the recognition module. Here, the recognized individual id is directly fetched from the database. The proposed architecture, despite using a Deep CNN requires less computational power, is less time consuming for the user and is capable of handling a large data without compromising its performance, making it suitable for use in a large organization, unlike the existing methods in the literature considering the number of students, employees, teaching and non-teaching faculty, and departments.

5   Conclusion

This article describes a smart end-to-end approach for an automated method that successfully marks attendance of the staff, maintains a log of details of the staff, gives various features for the staff to check upcoming holidays, apply for leave, attendance log inquiry etc. The method uses an MTCNN, InceptionRes-netv2 based Facenet framework integrated with an MVT framework architecture on a web-based as well as an android mobile platform. It is a multi-purpose application for the employees in an institute/organization/university/office that makes most of the processes done online without any physical contact and without intermedial delay or any human intervention. It also follows a specifically designed user access management policy. It is easy to deploy and maintain and in order to deploy the system in the institute or workplace environment, no specific hardware gear is required. The end product is a user-convenient system that makes a contribution to the creation of a better, healthier educational institute/work environment. Furthermore, the developed method can be used in a variety of fields where automatic attendance management is required or made more efficient without physical intervention. The users won't need to worry about their privacy since the original face images aren't saved in the system server/backend database. External hardware gear isn't required to be installed or to come in contact with. The attendance records for all dates are likewise stored in the system. As a result, it will be easy to keep track of attendance data.

In the future, for augmenting the core algorithmic performance of the system architecture, the current network used in the method can be retrained over an additional structured dataset of the current version and experiment it with more benchmarks. In the processing module, detection and alignment of faces in the wild such as conditions of strong sunlight and other illumination challenges can also be improved. Also, the scope of this method can be expanded by enabling it to handle multiple users within a single frame for effective use in public locations.

References

1. Feng, D., Wang, P., Zu, L.: Design of attendance checking management system for college classroom students based on fingerprint recognition. In: Chinese Control And Decision Conference (CCDC), pp. 555–559 (2020)
2. Ali, M., Usman Zahoor, H., Ali, A., Ali Qureshi, M.: Smart multiple attendance system through single image. In: IEEE 23rd International Multitopic Conference (INMIC), pp. 1–5. IEEE (2020)
3. Joardar, S., Chatterjee, A., Rakshit, A.: A real-time palm dorsa subcutaneous vein pattern recognition system using collaborative representation-based classification. IEEE Trans. Instrum. Meas. **64**(4), 959–966 (2015)
4. Joseph, J., Zacharia, K.P.: Automatic attendance management system using face recognition. Int. J. Sci. Res. IJSR **2**(11), 327–330 (2013)
5. Indra, E., et al.: Design and implementation of student attendance system based on face recognition by Haar-like features methods. In: 3rd International Conference on Mechanical, Electronics, Computer, and Industrial Technology (MECnIT), pp. 336–342 (2020)

6. Chinimilli, B.T., Anjali, T., Kotturi, A.: Face recognition based attendance system using Haar cascade and local binary pattern histogram algorithm. In: 2020 Fourth International Conference on Trends in Electronics and Informatics (ICOEI) (48184), pp. 701–704 (2020)
7. Alghaili, M., Li, Z., Ali, H.A.R.: FaceFilter: face identification with deep learning and filter algorithm. Hindawi Sci. Program. **2020**, 9 (2020). Article ID 7846264
8. Zeng, J., Qiu, X., Shi, S.: Image processing effects on the deep face recognition system. Math. Biosci. Eng. **18**(2), 1187–1200 (2021)
9. Dev, S., Patnaik, T.: Student attendance system using face recognition. In: International Conference on Smart Electronics and Communication (ICOSEC), pp. 90–96. IEEE (2020)
10. Schroff, F., Kalenichenko, D., Philbin, J.: FaceNet: a unified embedding for face recognition and clustering. In: Proceedings of the IEEE Computer Society Conference on Computer Vision and Pattern Recognition, pp. 815–823. IEEE (2015)
11. Nandini, M., Bhargavi, P., Raja Sekhar, G.: Face recognition using neural networks. Int. J. Sci. Res. Publ. **3**(3) (2013)
12. Goudail, F., Lange, E., Iwamoto, T., Kyuma, K., Otsu, N.: Face recognition system using local autocorrelations and multiscale integration. IEEE Trans. Pattern Anal. Mach. Intell. **18**(10), 1024–1028 (1996)
13. Arun Francis, G., Karthigaikumar, P., Arun Kumar, G.: Face recognition system for visually impaired people. J. Crit. Rev. **7**(17), 2760–2764 (2020)
14. Musa, A., Vishi, K., Rexha, B.: Attack analysis of face recognition authentication systems using fast gradient sign method. Appl. Artif. Intell. (2021)
15. Anwar, A., Raychowdhury, A.: Masked face recognition for secure authentication. arXiv:2008.11104 (2020)
16. Coşkun, M., Uçar, A., Yildirim, Ö., Demir, Y.: Face recognition based on convolutional neural network. In: 2017 International Conference on Modern Electrical and Energy Systems (MEES), pp. 376–379 (2017)
17. Chen, H., Haoyu, C.: Face recognition algorithm based on VGG network model and SVM. In: 2019 3rd International Conference on Machine Vision and Information Technology (CMVIT 2019), Guangzhou, China, vol. 1229, pp. 22–24 (2019)
18. Brostein, A.M., Brostein, M.M., Kimmel, R.: Three-dimensional face recognition. Int. J. Comput. Vis. **64**(1), 5–30 (2005)
19. Khan, M., Chakraborty, S., Astya, R., Khepra, S.: Face detection and recognition using OpenCV. In: 2019 International Conference on Computing, Communication, and Intelligent Systems (ICCCIS), pp. 116–119 (2019)
20. Ratyal, N.I., Taj, I.A., Sajid, M., Ali, N., Mahmood, A., Razzaq, S.: Three-dimensional face recognition using variance-based registration and subject-specific descriptors. Int. J. Adv. Robot. Syst. **6**(3) (2019)

Harnessing Sustainable Development in Image Recognition Through No-Code AI Applications: A Comparative Analysis

Nico Kling[1], Chantal Runte[1], Sajal Kabiraj[2(✉)], and Christian-Andreas Schumann[1]

[1] West Saxon University of Applied Sciences of Zwickau, Kornmarkt 1, 08056 Zwickau, Germany
`nico.kling@fh-zwickau.de`
[2] Häme University of Applied Sciences, Vankanlähde 9, 13100 Hämeenlinna, Finland
`sajal.kabiraj@hamk.fi`

Abstract. Artificial intelligence (AI) solutions and sustainable development have increasingly received public attention and research interest. In this study, the authors discuss the emerging trend of no-code AI solutions, with regards to their contribution to achieving the Sustainable Development Goals, specifically goal 8 (decent work and economic growth) and goal 10 (reduced inequalities). To demonstrate the opportunities that no-code AI may facilitate, the authors compare the performance of conventionally coded models with a no-code model created in Microsoft Lobe, based on secondary data from a dataset offered by Kermany et al. [1] of chest x-rays for pneumonia detection. A total of 5840 JPEG images is used for training and testing, 1575 for normal and 4265 for pneumonia, respectively. Results indicate that the output generated by the studied no-code solution can keep up with coded ones, and partly even outperform them. Possible applications for industries and society include usability cases beyond image recognition, the application in citizen science as well as the exploration of economic development opportunities of no-code AI. Finally, no-code AI could perhaps offer an alternative and emerge as an industry best practice for delivering efficient low-cost solutions in emerging markets, where demographic data is scattered across various homogenous groups.

Keywords: No-code AI · Sustainable development · SDGs · Inequality · Labour market shift

1 Introduction

Both artificial intelligence (AI) and sustainable development have increasingly received public attention over the last decades [2]. Lately, this attention has been expanded to the complex connection between these two essential matters [2]. With the aggravation of complexity of global challenges, coordinated efforts across different spatial and governmental scales are a crucial requirement to facilitate a development in line with the United Nation's (UN) Sustainable Development Goals (SDGs) [3].

© Springer Nature Switzerland AG 2022
KC Santosh et al. (Eds.): RTIP2R 2021, CCIS 1576, pp. 146–155, 2022.
https://doi.org/10.1007/978-3-031-07005-1_14

An ethical perspective on AI became a focal point of the discussion in this matter. The progress in artificial intelligence (AI) and machine learning (ML) plays a pivotal role in addressing the crucial global challenges of the present and the future and thereby also have the potential to positively affect the conation for the SDGs [3]. A study by Vinuesa et al. [4] found that AI has the potential to substantially contribute to 134 out of the 169 targets (79%) of all SDGs, while the efforts for 59 of the targets (35%) might be hampered by AI. In regard to the SDGs 8 (decent work and economic growth) and 10 (reduced inequalities) a negative impact of AI has been discussed in the sense that AI will create labour market dislocations and reduce the employability of certain types of workers [5, 6] and thereby aggravate economic inequality within and between countries [7].

Means to anticipate unintended damage in designing and governing AI have so far been mostly addressed in terms of social policy suggestions as well as the introduction of ethical standards for AI applications. For instance, the European Commission issued an ethics guideline for AI [8] which among other aspects included human agency and oversight. The content of the principles comprise that AI systems "should empower human beings (…)" and be designed to facilitate legitimate supervision "(…) through human-in-the-loop, human-on-the-loop, and human-in-command approaches". Improving the employability and data literacy of employees through training, and education in combination with transparency and openness of AI solutions have been in the focus of this empowerment of employees [7]. However, the potential to spread and develop accessible AI applications that require minimal training have only received superficial attention. For this reason, this paper focuses on the potential of no-code AI applications by comparing models of conventionally programmed AI solutions in medical image recognition of a chest x-ray data set by Kermany et al. [1] to a no-code drag-and-drop software.

2   Literature Review

Globalization and technological progress have significantly shaped the labour market in regards to the requirements for certain skills and competences and the organization of production processes in high- as well as low-and middle-income countries [9]. The impact of transformative technologies such as Big Data, AI or Internet of Things on the labour market are widely discussed in policy debates [9]. The advancements in these technologies have already established themselves in tasks that have previously been impossible to be automated such as customer service through chatbots and virtual assistants or self-checkout cash registers [10]. While the enthusiasm about the potential of transformative technology to boost economic growth is prominent, concerns have emerged about the fate of human workers in a labour market in which many tasks can be performed by AI as several studies covered [9–11]. From creating new jobs to majorly affecting skill and qualification requirements in existing positions and substituting other occupations completely [9], the central question is how to govern this development in a way that does not raise unemployment significantly and generating new or deepening pre-existing inequality.

The UN has published a report [12] in 2019 in which they state that the advances in technology require an improvement in data literacy and a responsible approach to AI research and application to maintain the support of the SDGs. So far, the 'openness' of AI solutions has been addressed in this regard, which describes the practice of publishing all relevant source code and algorithms, research findings and ideas but can also expand to data, safety techniques, or be about the capabilities, expectations, aims, plans and governance structure of AI initiatives to democratize AI [7]. However, in which way this openness reduces entry barriers for workforce that has not been in contact with AI yet, remains unclear.

A study by Tomašev [3] has formulated guidelines on AI solutions that support the SDGs (AI4SG). Among other things these guidelines include that AI4SG projects should aim to be cost-effective and in certain cases may profit from solutions with minimum complexity as they speed up the implementation phase, simplify maintenance and interpretation and still solve practical issues of value [3]. This simplification could be especially important in preparing workforce for the transition in the labour market with its changing requirements of skills and competences. One concern about transformative technologies is that changes will happen in a pace with which the training of staff cannot keep up leading to large segments of the population being temporarily unemployed [10].

For that, low-code and no-code AI solutions might be impactful means. Low-code AI describes solutions that uses visual, model-based development methods and only require minimal coding to create and deploy models [13]. However, these tools are still made for coders and do not synthesize code but support the programmers in writing code faster and more successfully [14]. No-code AI in contrast does not require any coding, and only minimal previous knowledge. It simplifies the application through a drag-and-drop platform and generates applications from predefined elements [14].

In this paper we will apply the example of a no-code AI solution in image recognition to present the current state-of-the-art of these kinds of platforms. Image recognition describes the computer vision task that works to identify the various elements of videos or images in order to classify them in a fast and accurate manner. A deep learning architecture that is commonly used for image classification is the Convolutional Neural Network (CNN) [15].

2.1 Previous Research

A lot of work is done in pneumonia detection with image recognition, specifically with the dataset published by Kermany et al. [1]. Nearly all of the most recent previous research, however, is done through coding, utilizing either Python or Matlab [1, 16–19]. The results can be seen in Table 1.

In their comprehensive study, Kermany et al. [1] establish a diagnostic tool for pneumonia detection based on transfer learning through utilizing a CNN, amongst other things. They stopped training after 100 epochs of the model, and achieved an accuracy of 92.8%, a sensitivity of 93.2%, and a specificity of 90.1%.

Akgundogdu [16] proposed a model based on two steps, feature extraction based on 2D discrete wavelet transform, followed by a classification done through a Random Forest algorithm. To avoid overfitting, the author introduced a 10-fold cross validation method, and achieved an AUC value of 0.99, accuracy of 97.11%, specificity of 99.09%, and a sensitivity of 91.79%.

Liz et al. [17] designed an explainable machine learning model system based on ensembles, through testing different architectures of their CNNs with 3 to 4 convolutional layers and trained them by Adam optimizer. To increase performance, they used ensembles formed by five CNNs. As their goal was to have an explainable output, they used heatmaps to explain their results visually. Using the Kermany et al. [1] dataset, Liz et al. [17] were able to achieve an AUC value of 0.964 for their Arch 1 ensemble, and a sensitivity of 0.791.

In a comparative analysis, Silva et al. [18] implemented five different CNNs, namely ResNet50, VGG-16, InceptionV3, InceptionResNetV2 and ResNeXt50, for pneumonia detection, and introduced Data Augmentation to reduce overfitting. It was shown that ResNeXt50 was the most balanced architecture in their research, with a precision of 97.50% ± 0.0033, recall of 97.80% ± 0.0036, and a F1-score of 97.65% ± 0.0022 for the pneumonia class.

Toğaçar et al. [19] utilized three different CNN models as feature extractors, AlexNet, VGG-16, and VGG-19, reduced those deep features utilizing the minimum redundancy maximum relevance (mRMR) algorithm, in order to feed different classification algorithms, namely decision tree, k-nearest neighbors, linear discriminant analysis, linear regression and support vector machine. Their best performing combination, selecting all features provided by the mRMR method and classifying with linear discriminant analysis, achieved an accuracy of 99.41%, sensitivity of 99.61% and specificity of 99.22%.

Table 1. Results of related work

Reference	Authors	Methods	Accuracy	Recall/Sensitivity	Specificity	Precision
[1]	Kermany et al	Transfer Learning, CNN	92.8%	93.2%	90.1%	–
[16]	Akgundogdu	Random Forest, 2D Discrete Wavelet Transform	97.11%	91.79%	99.09%	–
[17]	Liz et al	Adam optimizer, CNN Ensembles	–	79.1%	–	–
[18]	Silva et al	ResNeXt50	–	97.80% ± 0.0036	–	97.50% ± 0.0033
[19]	Toğaçar et al	Linear Discriminant Analysis, mRMR	99.41%	99.61%	99.22%	–

3 Methodology

3.1 Dataset

For this paper, the authors used secondary data with a public dataset offered by Kermany et al. [1], consisting of validated and labelled chest x-ray as well as optical coherence tomography, using the chest x-rays for the creation of their no-code artificial intelligence model. A total of 5840 JPEG images is used for training and testing, 1575 and 4265 for normal and pneumonia, respectively. The anterior-posterior images were part of the patients' routine clinical care and were selected from retrospective groups of pediatric patients aged 1 to 5 years from Guangzhou Medical Center for Women and Children, Guangzhou. Quality control was ensured through the removal of both unreadable and low-quality scans, as well as grading of the x-ray images through three different medical experts.

3.2 Hardware

For this research, the scientists used a personal laptop with a NVIDIA GeForce GTX 1650 GPU, an AMD Ryzen 5 3350H processor, 8 GB RAM, 512 GB SSD, and Windows 10 Pro.

3.3 Software

The no-code machine learning platform used for the research was Microsoft Lobe [20], an image recognition software currently in open beta. The image recognition model development process of Lobe is displayed in Fig. 1.

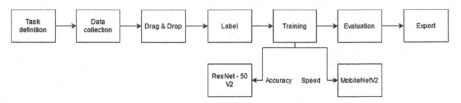

Fig. 1. Lobe development process

After the task definition and the different steps of data collection, users can drag & drop their image data into the program, label it, and Lobe will automatically start with the model creation, either with the ResNet-50 V2 (accuracy option) architecture or the MobileNetV2 (speed option) architecture. Both are CNNs. Training is finished after its initial 25 epochs, where the program uses a cache of five variations per image, as data augmentation is automatically introduced. Afterwards the model can be optimized, and if done so will be trained with early stopping until loss stops decreasing. Subsequently, the model can be evaluated through a graphical display of the training and testing results, which are automatically generated by Lobe. The model files, consisting of the structure and weights, can be used as a local API for app development, in most major cloud platforms to create an API, or locally in other software.

3.4 ResNet – 50 V2

Lobe uses ResNet – 50 V2, a 50-layer residual network, for its accuracy architecture. The original residual network ResNet was introduced at the ILSVRC2015 and uses heavy batch normalization to increase the networks performance, which is done through adjusting the input layer [21]. In order to protect it from the vanishing gradient problem, it features identity connections.

ResNet V2 is a changed version of the ResNet, and uses pre-activation of weight layers instead of post-activation [22] (Fig. 2).

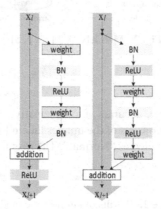

Fig. 2. (left) ResNet Residual Unit, (right) ResNet V2 Residual Unit [22, p. 2]

3.5 MobileNetV2

For its speed architecture, Lobe uses MobileNetV2, a convolutional neural network created by Sanders et al. [23], created for a good performance on mobile devices. The main feature is the inverted residual with linear bottleneck, which is a novel layer module. A low-dimensional compressed representation is the input of their model, which is filtered with a lightweight depth-wise convolution after it is expanded to a high dimension. This leads to features being projected back to a low-dimensional representation with a linear convolution (Fig. 3).

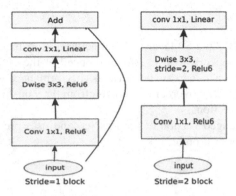

Fig. 3. MobileNetV2 [23, p. 5]

4 Results

Table 2 shows the architecture, accuracy, recall/sensitivity, specificity, precision, and time to train in hours. Class 1 consists of the images labeled as "Pneumonia"; the second class consists of the images labeled as "Normal". The respective confusion matrixes can be seen in Fig. 4, 5, 6 and 7.

Table 2. Results of our no-code model

Architecture	Accuracy	Recall/Sensitivity	Specificity	Precision	Time to train in hours
ResNet – 50 V2	93.66%	95.01%	90.03%	96.27%	1
MobileNet V2	95.03%	98.01%	86.98%	95.32%	0.5
ResNet – 50 V2 optimized	96.56%	95.99%	98.03%	99.25%	10
MobileNet V2 optimized	95.12%	97.00%	90.03%	96.34%	7

ResNet 50 – V2 in its optimized version has the highest accuracy (96.56%), specificity (98.03%), precision (99.25%), and took the longest to train with 10 h, out of the four different architectures. MobileNet V2 has the highest recall/sensitivity (98.01%), the lowest specificity (86.98%), and took the least time to train with 0.5 h. All architectures were able to produce metrics above 90%, apart from MobileNets V2 specificity.

n = 5840	Pneumonia	Normal	
Predicted Pneumonia	4052	157	4209
Predicted Normal	213	1418	1631
	4265	1575	

Fig. 4. Confusion Matrix ResNet – 50 V2

n = 5840	Pneumonia	Normal	
Predicted Pneumonia	4180	205	4385
Predicted Normal	85	1370	1455
	4265	1575	

Fig. 5. Confusion Matrix MobileNetV2

n = 5840	Pneumonia	Normal	
Predicted Pneumonia	4094	31	4125
Predicted Normal	171	1544	1715
	4265	1575	

Fig. 6. Confusion Matrix ResNet – 50 V2 optimized

n = 5840	Pneumonia	Normal	
Predicted Pneumonia	4137	157	4294
Predicted Normal	128	1418	1546
	4265	1575	

Fig. 7. Confusion Matrix MobileNetV2 optimized

5   Discussion

In this paper, the authors compared a no-code AI solution made with Lobe with those that were either coded in Python or Matlab. The research showed that software where no previous experience whatsoever is needed to create a model can indeed compare to ones where programming knowledge is needed. Both underlying architectures of Lobe, ResNet-50 V2 and MobileNetV2, as well as their optimized versions, produced results with high accuracy, recall, specificity and precision, and even outperformed many of the models named earlier, while only requiring minimum monetary, temporal, and technical resources.

A limitation of Lobe is the black-box nature of the software. While it was able to classify our examples very precisely, there was no possibility to understand why and how the algorithms came to their respective results, which contradicts the AI ethic guidelines published by the UN. Furthermore, more in-depth performance metrics, such as recall or precision, had to be calculated outside of the program. A general limitation of no-code AI solutions could be the missing customizability.

Regarding the SDGs 8 (Decent work and economic growth) and 10 (Reduced inequalities), the role of AI in unemployment in certain types of occupations as well as its potential contribution to inequality trends within and between countries has been highlighted.

As a viable, easily accessible, and low-cost solution, the example of using Lobe in image recognition has provided promising results that highlight the potential that these types of AI solutions have for the future. While not necessarily providing transparency, the solutions might lower the entry barrier for people who have not been in contact with AI so far and could benefit and advance the democratization of AI.

Still, different usability cases beyond image recognition need to be explored to indicate the limits and potential of no-code solutions. Other interesting future research topics could be addressing the potential of no-code AI in citizen science in order to even further support the SDGs and democratization. Another possibility could be a study to test economic development opportunities through no-code AI. Moreover, no-code AI could perhaps offer an alternative and emerge as an industry best practice for delivering efficient low-cost solutions in emerging markets, where demographic data is scattered across various homogeneous groups. In the end, AI design does not need to be oriented to be the most intelligent but the most sustainable and socially beneficial. Accessibility represents an integral part of this orientation.

References

1. Kermany, D.S., et al.: Identifying medical diagnoses and treatable diseases by image-based deep learning. Cell **172**(5), 1122-1131.e9 (2018). https://doi.org/10.1016/j.cell.2018.02.010
2. Liengpunsakul, S.: Artificial intelligence and sustainable development in China. Chin. Econ. **54**(4), 235–248 (2021). https://doi.org/10.1080/10971475.2020.1857062
3. Tomašev, N., et al.: AI for social good: unlocking the opportunity for positive impact. Nat. Commun. **11**(1), 2468 (2020). https://doi.org/10.1038/s41467-020-15871-z
4. Vinuesa, R., et al.: The role of artificial intelligence in achieving the sustainable development goals. Nat. Commun. **11**(1), 233 (2020). https://doi.org/10.1038/s41467-019-14108-y
5. Autor, D.H.: Why are there still so many jobs? The history and future of workplace automation. J. Econ. Perspect. **29**(3), 3–30 (2015). https://doi.org/10.1257/jep.29.3.3
6. Brynjolfsson, E., McAfee, A.: The Second Machine Age: Work, Progress, and Prosperity in a Time of Brilliant Technologies. W. W. Norton & Company, New York (2014)
7. Bostrom, N.: Strategic implications of openness in AI development. Glob. Policy **8**(2), 135–148 (2017). https://doi.org/10.1111/1758-5899.12403
8. European Commission: Ethics Guidelines for Trustworthy AI|Shaping Europe's Digital Future. https://digital-strategy.ec.europa.eu/en/library/ethics-guidelines-trustworthy-ai. Accessed 20 July 2021
9. Colombo, E., Mercorio, F., Mezzanzanica, M.: AI meets labor market: exploring the link between automation and skills. Inf. Econ. Policy **47**, 27–37 (2019). https://doi.org/10.1016/j.infoecopol.2019.05.003
10. Furman, J., Seamans, R.: AI and the Economy, p. 31
11. Frey, C.B., Osborne, M.A.: The future of employment: how susceptible are jobs to computerisation? Technol. Forecast. Soc. Change **114**, 254–280 (2017). https://doi.org/10.1016/j.techhfore.2016.08.019
12. United Nations Activities on Artificial Intelligence (AI) 2019, p. 88

13. Dushnitsky, G., Stroube, B.K.: Low-code entrepreneurship: shopify and the alternative path to growth. J. Bus. Ventur. Insights **16**, e00251 (2021). https://doi.org/10.1016/j.jbvi.2021. e00251

14. Woo, M.: The rise of no/low code software development—No experience needed? Engineering **6**(9), 960–961 (2020). https://doi.org/10.1016/j.eng.2020.07.007

15. Rawat, W., Wang, Z.: Deep convolutional neural networks for image classification: a comprehensive review. Neural Comput. **29**(9), 2352–2449 (2017). https://doi.org/10.1162/neco_a_ 00990

16. Akgundogdu, A.: Detection of pneumonia in chest X-ray images by using 2D discrete wavelet feature extraction with random forest. Int. J. Imaging Syst. Technol. **31**(1), 82–93 (2021). https://doi.org/10.1002/ima.22501

17. Liz, H., Sánchez-Montañés, M., Tagarro, A., Domínguez-Rodríguez, S., Dagan, R., Camacho, D.: Ensembles of convolutional neural networks models for pediatric pneumonia diagnosis. Future Gener. Comput. Syst. **122**, 220–233 (2021). https://doi.org/10.1016/j.future.2021. 04.007

18. Silva, L.O., dos Santos Araújo, L., Souza, V.F., Barros Neto, R.M., Santos, A.: Comparative analysis of convolutional neural networks applied in the detection of pneumonia through X-ray images of children. Learn. Nonlin. Mod. **18**(2), 4–15 (2021). https://doi.org/10.21528/ lnlm-vol18-no2-art1

19. Toğaçar, M., Ergen, B., Cömert, Z., Özyurt, F.: A deep feature learning model for pneumonia detection applying a combination of mRMR feature selection and machine learning models. IRBM **41**(4), 212–222 (2020). https://doi.org/10.1016/j.irbm.2019.10.006

20. Microsoft: Lobe (2020). https://www.lobe.ai

21. He, K., Zhang, X., Ren, S., Sun, J.: Deep residual learning for image recognition. In: 2016 IEEE Conference on Computer Vision and Pattern Recognition (CVPR), Las Vegas, NV, USA, June 2016, pp. 770–778 (2016). https://doi.org/10.1109/CVPR.2016.90

22. He, K., Zhang, X., Ren, S., Sun, J.: Identity Mappings in Deep Residual Networks. ArXiv160305027 Cs, July 2016. http://arxiv.org/abs/1603.05027. Accessed 23 July 2021

23. Sandler, M., Howard, A., Zhu, M., Zhmoginov, A., Chen, L.-C.: MobileNetV2: Inverted Residuals and Linear Bottlenecks. ArXiv180104381 Cs, March 2019. http://arxiv.org/abs/ 1801.04381. Accessed 23 July 2021

Evaluating Performance of Adam Optimization by Proposing Energy Index

Mohan Bhandari[1]($\boxtimes$), Pramod Parajuli[2], Pralhad Chapagain[1],
and Loveleen Gaur[3]($\boxtimes$)

[1] Nepal College of Information Technology, Lalitpur, Nepal
mail2mohanbhandari@gmail.com, pralhad.chapagain@gmail.com
[2] CG Institutue of Management, Kathmandu, Nepal
pramodparajuli@gmail.com
[3] Amity International Business School, Amity University, Noida, India
gaurloveleen@yahoo.com

Abstract. The adjustment of learning rate (η), bias and additional parameters throughout back propagation are crucial for the performance of machine learning algorithms. Regarding optimization for algorithms, adam optimization technique tune the learning parameters by utilising the exponential decay of past gradients and their squares. However, the optimizer requires the engagement of frequently occurring features from the datasets that play a significant role for performance improvement in machine learning algorithms.

In this paper, the energy model of a neuron is designed to calculate the energy index from frequently occurring features and introduced in adam optimizer. The classification performance of the proposed energy modeled adam optimizer is experimented on Logistic Regression (single layered) and Support Vector Machine (hyperplane based) machine learning algorithms utlising CIFAR10, MNIST and Fashion MNIST datasets. Optimized with proposed optimizer, Logistic Regression achieved training accuracy of 90.79%, 99.02% and 95.87% whereas Support Vector Machine achieved training accuracy of 39.04%, 80.80% and 82.29% for CIFAR10, MNIST and Fashion MNIST datasets respectively.

Keywords: Machine learning · Stochastic gradient descent · Adam · Energy index · Logistic regression · Support vector machine

1   Introduction

Inspired from the way that biological nervous system process information, artificial neural network (ANN) is neural structure that constitutes highly organized processing nodes to work together called neurons to solve a specific problem. Using mathematical or computational model for processing information, ANNs are taken under consideration for applications like image recognition, object detection, face recognition, speech recognition, data classification and other aspects, neural networks learn by example.

© Springer Nature Switzerland AG 2022
KC Santosh et al. (Eds.): RTIP2R 2021, CCIS 1576, pp. 156–168, 2022.
https://doi.org/10.1007/978-3-031-07005-1_15

Almost all ANNs have some sort of learning rule that adjusts the weights of nodes in neural networks based on input patterns that are calculated after learning from a supervised process that occurs with each epoch over a forward activation flow of outputs and adjusting weights with back-propagation.

With the help of initial inputs provided, a neural network makes an arbitrary 'guess' about what the input might be and finally compares it's guess with the real input and concludes the differences i.e. loss function. Fundamentally, a loss function is a performance metric on how sound the Neural Network succeeds to grasp its goal of generating outputs, likely to the desired values. Hence, on support of loss function, the network attempts to make fitting adjustment to its weights. During this process, different activation functions help the network to polarize the activities for stability.

Optimization, in the neural network, implies finding the low cost function alternative by increasing the essential factors and reducing the less desirable factors under provided constraints to attain stable convergence. The training of network adjusts the parameters and weights of model while minimising the loss function and providing accurate estimates. The loss function leads the optimizer in the right direction. Further, back-propagation with gradient descents necessitates certain manual adjustment in default learning rate [1].

The training of deep neural networks is a challenging optimization task as it involves maximising or minimisation the scalar-parameterised objective function concerning parameters.

For evaluation function, computational complexity on computing first order partial derivatives concerning all parameters is similar; stochastic gradient descent (SGD), is considered effective and efficient model [2].

While, back-propagation using SGD, necessitates certain manual experimentation with the learning rate's initial value. It is observed that an incorrect learning rate may decelerate convergence, trigger to vibrate, or affect the training process to diverge.

The adjustments in the learning rate are additionally associated with model performance and classification accuracy. Consequently, adjusting and automating of appropriate learning rate are critical problems in the SGD training process [1].

The study is concentrated on introducing energy model in adam optimizer. Though Adam solves the problem of exponential decay of past gradients and the square gradients by adjusting the learning rate only in layers, the optimizer do not consider the significance of frequently occurring features in each neuron.

Considering this fact, the performance of this optimizer can be improved on introducing the Energy Index. As result, the study is focused on introducing the Energy Index in Adam Optimization to tune the learning rate in individual neuron of every layer of neural network and analyze the performance in different machine learning models.

2   Related Work

Several researchers have demonstrated the performance of SGD on precise selection of the learning rate.

2.1   AdaGrad

Authors of [3] offered 'AdaGrad' adaptive learning approach that adjusts the learning rate corresponding to the parameters, with more significant updates for intermittent parameters and lower updates for frequent values. Adaptive altering the proximal feature helps determine a learning rate much more effortless. The results are nearly as good as the optimal proximal function that can be preferred in retrospect.

For every parameter θ_i in each iteration t during learning:

$$\theta_{t,i} = \theta_{t-1,i} - \frac{\eta}{\sqrt{g_{t-1} + \epsilon}} g_{t-1,i} \tag{1}$$

where ϵ is smoothing to avoid division by zero and g_{t-1} is objective function's gradient with respect to the parameter θ_{t-1} at iteration t − 1. Being based on past gradients for θ, At each time step t, Adagrad changes the general learning rate for each parameter θ_i. Using Adagrad in ImageNet image database [4], the Reuters RCV1 text classification [4] the optimizer produced very sparse solutions and performed similarly to dense solutions. In adaptive methods, a diagonal approximation to the matrix was obtained by taking the outer products of subgradients computed along the algorithm's run.

Authors of [5] proposed and analysed differentially private variants of an SGD algorithm with adaptive step sizes. Simultaneously, the AdaGrad algorithm, for differentially private convex optimization. By providing the upper bounds on each algorithm's, the authors attempted to demonstrate that the algorithm is optimal. The findings determined that private versions of AdaGrad are better than adaptive SGD.

AdaGrad, once harnessed to convex objective functions with Lipschitz gradient in [6], the iterates produced by either the scalar step size variation or the coordinatewise form of the AdaGrad method are convergent sequences. The crucial discovery of this research, AdaGrad sequences fulfil a variable metric quasi-Fejér monotonicity characteristic, permitting convergence to be demonstrated. Along with the taylor series expansion as lemma's, for smooth convex goals, authors showed AdaGrad's sequential convergence.

Although AdaGrad eradicates the necessity to regulate the learning rate manually, the denominator's accumulation of squared gradients affects the learning rate to decline, ensuing in a sluggish convergence speed.

2.2   AdaDelta

In [7], the authors have adopted an Adagrad alteration that intends to decelerate the forceful and monotonic learning rate. The concept presented in the paper was extracted from [3] to address the method's two significant flaws:

1. Initial Learning rate is selected manually through out the network
2. The continual decay of learning rates during training

Rather than accumulating all previously squared gradients, Adadelta limits the window of cumulative past slopes to a specified size 'w'. Rather than inefficiently retaining 'w' prior squared gradients, the number of gradients is recursively calculated as a decreasing average of all past squared gradients. The update of AdaDelta is:

$$\theta_t = \theta_{t-1} - \frac{RMS[\Delta\theta]_{t-2}}{RMS[g]_{t-1}} g_{t-1} \tag{2}$$

where $RMS[g]_{t-1}$ is the RMS error for gradient descent $_{t-1}$

In supplement to the conventional stochastic gradient descent, Adadelta dynamically adapts over time, applying only first-order information and has a low computing cost. The approach does not require manual learning rate adjustment and appears to be resilient to noisy gradient knowledge, multiple model architecture choices, various data modalities, and hyperparameter selection.

Authors experimented with the optimizer in MNIST handwriting; throughout the training collection, the system was trained on mini-batches of 100 images per batch for six epochs.

As compared to SGD, the approach had low computational overhead and had a per-dimension learning rate. It is observed that the hyperparameters need not be adjusted, despite a broad range of input data formats, hidden unit numbers, nonlinearities, and distributed replica numbers. It indicates that AdaDelta is a robust learning rate system and may be utilized in various situations.

Researchers used [8], the three different variants of algorithms (such as ResNet50, Inception-v3 and VGG-16), to identify environmental microorganisms from Environmental Microorganism Dataset. They implemented Adadelta and observed better performance than SGD's performance. In fully connected layers, to optimise the weights, they embraced the optimizer, among which Inception-v3 gained the highest 84.9% of the accuracy.

Instead of accruing all previous squared gradients, Adadelta impedes the window of accumulated past gradients to some fixed size 'w'; and restricting the convergence.

2.3   RMSProp

Geoffrey et al. [9], indicated that RMSProp is a mini-batch version of RProp, that is equivalent to gradient with division by size. RMSProp algorithm creates mini-batch learning more efficient. The learning rate in RMSProp adapts centred on a moving average of the magnitudes of the latest past gradients. RMSProp, in other words, keeps a moving average of the squares of recent gradients, denoted by (v). Consequently, current gradients are given more weight. The term beta (β) is used to indicate the forgetting factor.

$$v_t = \beta V_{t-1} + (-\beta) \cdot [grad(\theta)_{t-1}]^2 \tag{3}$$

Abiding for Resilient Propagation, RProp uses the signals of gradients to calculate the updates [9]. The rationale is that the enormity of gradients varies by weight and differences over time, thus, making it difficult to choose a specific learning rate. RMSProp addresses the issue by holding a moving average of the squared gradient and changing the weight updates by magnitude. The gradient changes are carried out as follows:

$$E[G^2]_t = 0.9[g^2]_{t-1} + 0.1\ g^2_{t-1} \tag{4}$$

$$\theta_t = \theta_{t-1} - \frac{\eta}{\sqrt{E[g^2_{t-1}] + \epsilon}} g_{t-1} \tag{5}$$

The researchers [10] proposed a technique for connecting different existing information retrieval tools for change impact analysis; and Bag of Words to recognise the potential consequences of a replacement. To identify similar document, a neural network-based LSTM-RNN algorithm is offered in the study. The RMSprop Optimization model was utilised to decrease vibrations in the upward path; Also improving the learning and accuracy rates. The results of the experiments demonstrate that the suggested technique outperforms the existing methods in terms of accuracy.

With three convolution layers and fully connected layers, the CNN structure was modelled by authors in [11] to provide the voice commands for drone control. Using RMSProp as the optimizer for offline datasets, the model achieved 95.72% accuracy, while for real-time, the accuracy was 92.88%.

2.4   Adam

Alternative technique [12] for learning rate optimization is to compute adaptive learning rates for each parameter. As in Adadelta and RMSProp, Adam holds an exponentially decaying average of prior gradients m_t, which is equivalent to momentum, among an exponentially decaying average of past squared gradients v_t

$$g_t = grad(\theta_{t-1}) \tag{6}$$

The first moment is calculated as:

$$m_t = \beta_1 m_{t-1} + (1 - \beta_1)m_t \tag{7}$$

The second moment is calculated as:

$$v_t = \beta_2 v_{t-1} + (1 - \beta_2)^2_t \tag{8}$$

The final parameters are updated as:

$$\theta_t = \theta_{t-1} - \frac{\eta}{\sqrt{\widehat{v}_{t-1}} + \epsilon} \widehat{m}_{t-1} \tag{9}$$

where,

$$\widehat{m} = \frac{m_t}{1 - \beta_1^t} \tag{10}$$

$$\widehat{v} = \frac{v_t}{1 - \beta_2^t} \tag{11}$$

Adjusting m_t and v_t as vectors, authors observed that results were biased towards zero, essentially during the initial steps and throughout the decay rates being small (i.e. $\beta 1$ and $\beta 2$ are close to 1).

In this study, authors [13] analysed the sentiments of Covid-19 problems utilising Twitter data, and the model achieved an accuracy of 70% applying Adam in MLP architecture.

A comparative study among different optimizers like adam, SGD and RMSProp was done in [14] to detect the early and precise diseases using the transfer learning-based CNN model. The authors claimed to achieve the better performance with the use of adam optimizer.

Adam retains an exponentially decaying average of previous gradients m_t, comparable to Adadelta and RMSProp, in addition to an exponentially decaying average of past squared gradients v_t. The Adam algorithm has yet to explore the recurring characteristics in each layer's neurons that plays an essential part in learning.

2.5   Energy Index Based Optimization Method (EIOM)

EIOM was proposed by Huizhen Zhao [1] to adapt the learning rate in backpropagation automatically by introducing the Energy Index (EI). The research concentrated on the idea that frequently occurring features contribute more to the learning rate during backpropagation. The author claimed to accomplish more descriptive learning as a novel approach that dynamically integrates learning about the neuron's feature frequencies. The learning rate η^l of the neuron in l^{th} layer is defined as [1]:

$$\eta^l = \eta^* \times (1 - EI^l) \tag{12}$$

where, η^* is the default learning rate and EI^l is the EI on l^{th} layer.

Numerous machine learning algorithms (e.g., LR and MLP) for the MNIST dataset and CNN for the CIFAR 10 dataset is recommended by EIOM [1]. To validate the model, the authors evaluated the model with other optimizer techniques where learning parameters were set to the same values.

The authors recommended that the EIOM model outclassed the other optimization approaches in terms of classification accuracy. Thus, restricting the manual adjustment to the default value during testing. By retrieving the appropriate SGD learning rate, the EIOM alleviated the bottleneck in deep learning.

For LR and MLP, the authors used the MNIST dataset to compare EI with other optimizers. Figure 1 depicts that both in LR and MLP, the performance of EI is superior.

The study focuses on the idea; frequently occurring characteristics impact more on the learning rate during backpropagation. Though the author considered the characteristics of often recurring features, they left out exponential decay of the past and squared gradients.

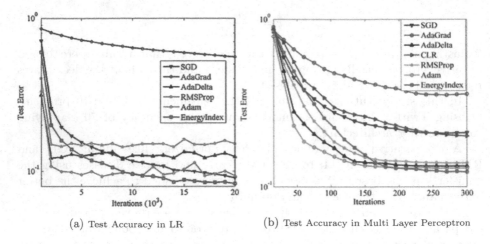

(a) Test Accuracy in LR   (b) Test Accuracy in Multi Layer Perceptron

Fig. 1. Test accuracy comparison of different optimizer with EI

3 Introducing EI to Adam

Features are updated centred on their frequency, while a regularly occurring component is essential than a seldom occurring feature. Alternatively, an often recurring feature should have a lower learning rate to allow for more thorough and thorough learning. In contrast, a rare active feature should have a higher learning rate to allow faster convergence.

The essential components of a neuron in a layer of an artificial network are inputs, outputs, activation function, weights, and biases, which must all be learned and are collectively known as parameters.

Figure 2 defines the energy neuron model in the neural network. An energy neuron model is defined by 6-tuple as [1]:

$$(I, O, P, f, E_{in}, E_{out})$$

where for a individual neuron, I is Input Vector, O is Output Vector, P: Parameters to Learn, f: Activation Function, E_{in} is Input Energy and E_{out} is Output Energy.

The total input energy of all individual neurons in each l layer is defined as:

$$E_{in}^l = \Sigma_{j=1}^m \mid w_j^l \mid \tag{13}$$

where E_{in} is the input energy, w_i^l is the jth column vector of w_l

The output energy of all individual neurons in each layer is defined as:

$$E_{out}^l = \Sigma_{j=1}^m \mid w_j^{l+1} \mid \tag{14}$$

where E_{out} is the output energy, w_i^{l+1} is the ith row vector of w^{l+1}

EI of individual neurons in l^{th} layer EI^l is define as:

$$EI^l = \lambda \frac{E_{in}^l}{\bar{E}_{in}^l} + (1 - \lambda) \frac{(E_{out}^l)^T}{\bar{E}_{out}^l} \tag{15}$$

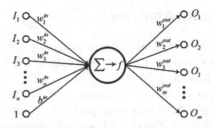

Fig. 2. The structure of energy neuron model [1]

where $\lambda \in [0, 1]$ is EI factor that controls the contribution of input and output energy. $\bar{E}_{in}^l$ and $\bar{E}_{out}^l$ are the expectations of E_{in}^l and E_{out}^l respectively, and $(E_{out}^l)^T$ is the transpose of E_{out}^l Every layer l has a greater EI for a neuron with a higher input and output energy. On the other side, a neuron with lower input and output energy has a lower EI. Finally, EI^l is normalized to a range of $[0, 1]$ as:

$$EI^l = \frac{EI^l}{max(EI^l)} \tag{16}$$

The learning rate η^l of the neuron in l^{th} layer is defined as:

$$\eta^l = \eta^* \times (1 - EI^l) \tag{17}$$

where, η^* is the default value.

First moment (past gradients) is calculated from Eq. 7 and second moment (square gradients) is calculated from Eq. 8. Now, the parameters are updated from Eq. 18

$$\theta_t = \theta_{t-1} - \frac{\eta^l}{\sqrt{\hat{v}_{t-1}} + \epsilon} \hat{m}_{t-1} \tag{18}$$

where, $\hat{m}$ is calculated from Eq. 7 and $\hat{v}$ is calculated from Eq. 8.

Here, η^l (EI based learning rate) is introduced in Adam optimization.

Algorithm 1. Adam optimization with EI

Input: Initial parameters w, b, $\beta1$, $\beta2$ and η^*
1: **for** *For Every Layer in Network* **do**
2:    Calculate input energy using Eq. 13
3:    Calculate output energy using Eq. 14
4:    Calculate EI using Eq. 15
5:    Calculate η^l using Eq. 17
6:    Update parameters using Eq. 18
7: **end for**

---

4   Experiments and Analysis

The experiment is conducted using python language with Intel(R) Core(TM) i5-8250U CPU, windows 10 operating system, with 8 GB RAM and the findings were examined was utilized at 1.60 GHz.

CIFAR10 [15] having 60000 colour images for 10 distinct classifications is obtained from python pickle library and partitioned into training (50000) set and test set (10000). Amongst 32000 black and white images from MNIST handwriting dataset in .csv file 10000 images are taken as test datasets. Similarly, Fashion MNIST dataset in .csv format, 50000 images were used as training data and 10000 images as test data. For both the algorithms and optimizer, applied hyper-parameters are $\beta1 = 0.9$, $\beta2 = 0.999$ and $\epsilon = 1e-8$ [12].

The logistic regression (LR) and SVM machine learning algorithms are utilized to estimate the performance of Adam with the EI (AEI) model; the results are compared to conventional Adam.

4.1   Logistic Regression

Local minima do not affect LR while its goal function is convex; consequently, three distinct datasets are compared. While LR is a single layer, input energy does not exist. Thus, the energy factor λ is set to 0 [1]. After several tests on different learning rates, the best learning rate was 0.001 for 2000 iterations on all three datasets as the initial learning rate.

Figure 3 shows the test results of all the three algorithms where it is demonstrated that AEI and conventional Adam have similar effects. The Table 1, demonstrates that the LR maintained identical results on all the datasets. Having test and train accuracy more than 90%, MNIST dataset performed better, although the cost value for Fashion MNIST is smaller

4.2   Support Vector Machine

The best value for Learning rate as 0.0001 and regularisation parameter as 1.000000e+03 is the final result of cross-validation method for 2000 iteration. Among the different types of kernel, linear kernal is used and for loss function, hinge loss is used. λ is set to 0 [1].

For CIFAR10 dataset, mean of training and test data was calculated and dataset was normalised by subtracting the mean image from the original dataset. Training dimension was 50000×3072 and test dimension was 10000×3072. For AEI, the newly calculated learning rate is of size 3072×10 for multi-class classification.

Cost function, train accuracy and test accuracy between 'SVM with Adam' and 'SVM with AEI' was compared. The result of comparison is shown in Fig. 4(a), Fig. 4(b) and Fig. 4(c) respectively. These figures illustrate that amongst the two models, AEI demonstrates better classification. Although SVM with Adam converged faster, it could not perform better on higher iterations in terms of cost. AEI with higher resistivity started with very low train and

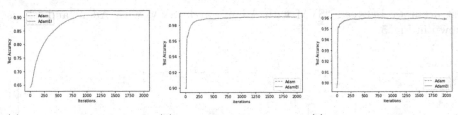

(a) Test accuracy between Adam and AEI for CIFAR10 (b) Test accuracy between Adam and AEI for MNIST (c) Test accuracy between Adam and AEI for Fashion MNIST

Fig. 3. Test accuracy result of LR

Table 1. Comparative analysis of LR for CIFAR10, MNIST and Fashion MNIST

	CIFAR 10		MNIST		Fashion MNIST	
	Adam	Adam with EI	Adam	Adam with EI	Adam	Adam with EI
Cost	0.31	0.31	0.02	0.02	0.09	0.09
Test accuracy	90.79%	90.79%	99.02%	99.02%	95.85%	95.87%
Train accuracy	90.90%	90.79%	99.26%	99.26%	96.23%	96.25%
ROC	0.58	0.58	0.97	0.97	0.87	0.87

test accuracy, but these parameters also performed better on higher iterations. Adam's overall accuracy is 32 %, whereas the accuracy of AEI is 37%.

For the MNIST dataset, The training dimension is 32000 × 784, and the test dimension was 10000 × 3072. The new learning rate of size 784 × 10 is provided for each neuron in the layer. The result of the cost function, train accuracy and

Table 2. Comparative analysis of SVM for CIFAR10, MNIST and Fashion MNIST

	CIFAR 10		MNIST		Fashion MNIST	
	Adam	Adam with EI	Adam	Adam with EI	Adam	Adam with EI
Cost	1.94	1.74	2.32	2.17	0.83	0.73
Test accuracy	34.48%	39.04%	80.25%	80.80%	81.01%	82.29%
Train accuracy	34.95%	40.26%	80.16%	80.92%	80.82%	81.49%
Overall accuracy	32%	37%	80%	81%	81%	82%
ROC	0.65	0.68	0.83	0.83	0.97	0.97

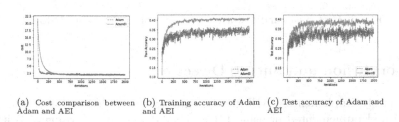

(a) Cost comparison between Adam and AEI (b) Training accuracy of Adam and AEI (c) Test accuracy of Adam and AEI

Fig. 4. Cost, train and test Accuracy of SVM for CIFAR10

test accuracy between "SVM with Adam" and "SVM with Adam and EI" is shown in Fig. 5.

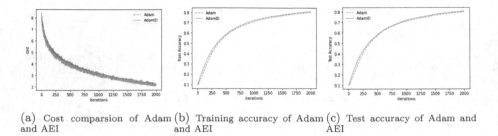

(a) Cost comparsion of Adam and AEI (b) Training accuracy of Adam and AEI (c) Test accuracy of Adam and AEI

Fig. 5. Cost, train and test accuracy of SVM in MNIST

We can see from Table 2 that AEI has demonstrated better performance in comparison to Adam.

For Fashion MNIST, the training dimension is 50000×784 and test dimension is 10000×3072. For AEI, the newly calculated learning rate is of size 784×10. The cost function, train accuracy and test accuracy between 'SVM with Adam' and 'SVM with AEI' is compared. Figure 6 illustrate the results of the comparison. The graphs indicate a higher degree of convergence for both models. Following 200 iterations, both models had a minimal influence of noise and outliers. Table 2 indicates that AEI has an overall superior accuracy than Adam through 1% for MNIST and Fashion MNIST datasets.

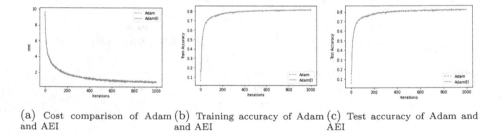

(a) Cost comparison of Adam and AEI (b) Training accuracy of Adam and AEI (c) Test accuracy of Adam and AEI

Fig. 6. Cost, train and test accuracy of SVM for Fashion MNIST

5   Conclusion and Future Direction

In this study, implementing AEI, the learning rate to individual neurons is calculated and implemented utilising LR and SVM machine learning algorithms. The performance of AEI is compared with the conventional Adam optimizer.

The study focused on introducing a faster learning rate to individual neurons, resulting in superior categorisation accuracy.

It is also observed that the calculation for the learning rate for individual neurons may accumulate the time complexity in adam optimization. Though the induction of an AEI to an SVM could not boost performance (37%) on CIFAR10 datasets, however, it outperformed traditional Adam (32%) in terms of accuracy. The SVM has better MNIST and Fashion MNIST Datasets results, but it could not classify better than LR. The LR converged slower for CIFAR10 dataset with a test accuracy of 90.79%, and achieved stability after 1000 iterations. While, the optimizers attained faster convergence speed for both MNIST with accuracy 99.02% and Fashion MNIST with accuracy 95.87%. Outcomes displayed the better performance of LR from all the datasets under consideration.

This study is centred on analysing the performance of adam optimizer with the introduction of EI; the experiments are concentrated only on machine learning algorithms and image classification datasets. The performance of the AEI can be further studied in other deep learning algorithms like multilayer perceptron, convolution neural networks etc. In addition, Comparative analysis of AEI can also be done with other optimisation algorithm with different other datasets. Further, AEI may be realised in typical artificial intelligence applications such as text processing and speech recognition.

References

1. Zhao, H., Liu, F., Zang, H., Liang, Z.: Research on a learning rate with energy index in deep learning. Neural Netw. **110**, 225–231 (2019)
2. Deng, L., et al.: Recent advances in deep learning for speech research at Microsoft. In: IEEE International Conference on Acoustics, Speech and Signal Processing, pp. 8604–8608 (2013)
3. John, D., Elad, H., Yoram, S.: Adaptive Subgradient methods for online learning and stochastic optimization. J. Mach. Learn. Res. **12** (2011). ACMDL
4. Deng, J., Dong, W., Socher, R., Li, L., Kai, L., Li, F.: ImageNet: a large-scale hierarchical image database. In: IEEE Conference on Computer Vision and Pattern Recognition, p. 248 (2009)
5. Asi, H., Duchi, J., Fallah, A.: Private adaptive gradient methods for convex optimization. Proceedings of the 38th International Conference on Machine Learning, vol. 139, pp. 383–392 (2021)
6. Traoré, C., Pauwels, E.: Sequential convergence of AdaGrad algorithm for smooth convex optimization. Oper. Res. Lett. **49**, 452–458 (2021)
7. Matthew, D.Z.: AdaDelta: an adaptive learning rate method. arXiv (2012)
8. Liang, C., Lai, C., Wang, S., Lin, Y.: Environmental microorganism classification using optimized deep learning model. Environ. Sci. Pollut. Res. **28**, 31920–31932 (2021)
9. Hinton, G., Srivastava, N., Swersky, K.: Lecture 6.5-RMSProp, overview of mini-batch, coursera: neural networks for machine learning (2012). http://www.cs.toronto.edu/~hinton/coursera/lecture6/lec6.pdf. Accessed 16 June 2021
10. Nimmani, P., Vodithala, S., Polepally, V. : Neural network based integrated model for information retrieval. In: 5th International Conference on Intelligent Computing and Control Systems, pp. 1286–1289 (2021)

11. Polat, Ö., Polat, A., Ekici, T.: Automatic classification of volcanic rocks from thin section images using transfer learning networks. Neural Comput. Appl. **33**(18), 11531–11540 (2021). https://doi.org/10.1007/s00521-021-05849-3
12. Diederik, P.K., Jimmy, L.B.: Adam: a method for stochastic optimization. arXiv (2015)
13. Hendrawati, T., Purnama, Y.C.: Analysis of Twitter users sentiment against the Covid-19 outbreak using the backpropagation method with Adam optimization. J. Electr. Electron. Inform. **5**, 1 (2021)
14. Thangaraj, R., Anandamurugan, S., Kaliappan, V.K.: Automated tomato leaf disease classification using transfer learning-based deep convolution neural network. J. Plant Dis. Prot. **128**(1), 73–86 (2020). https://doi.org/10.1007/s41348-020-00403-0
15. Krizhevsky, A.: The CIFAR-10 dataset. https://www.cs.toronto.edu/~kriz/cifar.html. Accessed 16 June 2021

An Alignment-Free Fingerprint Template Protection Technique Based on Minutiae Triplets

Afeeza Ali[✉], Vivek Singh Baghel, and Surya Prakash

Department of Computer Science and Engineering,
Indian Institute of Technology Indore, Indore 453552, India
{ms2004101001,phd1801201005,surya}@iiti.ac.in

Abstract. Biometric template protection has been a topic of interest ever since biometrics took over authentication and verification systems. High sensitivity of biometric information of an individual makes it paramount to transform the raw biometric data into an irreversible form that can be enrolled into the database. Fingerprint-based biometric systems make use of minutiae points information. However, it has been shown that the original fingerprint information can be retraced using the measurements of its minutiae points. Consequently, it is essential to ensure that the fingerprint templates in fingerprint-based biometric systems are secure. Fingerprint authentication systems often encounter the problem of variation among fingerprint impressions of the same subject. This arises due to the effect of rotation and translation at the sensor end while capturing the fingerprint data. To eliminate these issues, an alignment-free template protection technique has been proposed in this work, which not only solves the problem of revocability but also provides a secure irreversible transformation without having to compromise the performance of the authentication system. Experimental analysis has been conducted on FVC2002 DB1 and FVC2002 DB2 databases and it depicts highly encouraging performance.

Keywords: Biometric template security · Cancelable biometrics · Biometrics · Fingerprint

1 Introduction

The biometrics has been found to be a highly accurate and reliable user authentication technology [22]. Due to this, it has emerged as an indispensable part of modern identity management and access control systems. Biometric modalities such as fingerprints, face, iris, etc., serve as an efficient means of user authentication. During the enrollment phase of a biometric system, salient features from the biometric sample are extracted and are stored in a database in the form of a biometric template. During authentication, the salient features obtained from the probe biometric sample are compared with the biometric template previously stored in the database for finding out the genuine and imposter users.

© Springer Nature Switzerland AG 2022
KC Santosh et al. (Eds.): RTIP2R 2021, CCIS 1576, pp. 169–182, 2022.
https://doi.org/10.1007/978-3-031-07005-1_16

Although the usage of biometrics for identity verification has countless advantages, there exists numerous security concerns as biometric information is highly sensitive and disclosure of which can pose severe security threats to an user. The biometric features of an individual are unique and permanent, which makes the biometrics an efficient way of authentication. However, their uniqueness poses the risk of them being compromised. Inevitably, once biometrics is compromised, it cannot be reissued as the case in conventional passwords [23] because of its uniqueness and permanence. Hence, the widespread deployment of biometrics-based applications and permanent linkage between users and their biometric features poses a significant threat to the enrolled individuals' biometric information thereby affecting their security and privacy. To mitigate these challenges, it is required that only the templates that are well protected be used for authentication purposes [24].

As discussed above, the privacy and security issues concerning personal information limit the operational use of biometrics. Therefore, it is imperative that biometrics need to be tamper-proof and robust along with being accurate. In the last decade, several methods have been proposed in this regard. Although many of these methods sound theoretically acceptable and produce desired properties of secured biometric authentication, they come at the cost of system performance. In this paper, an alignment-free and non-invertible technique has been proposed to protect the fingerprint template by exploiting the features computed from the minutiae triplets. The proposed technique possesses all essential properties [1] that are required for any fingerprint template protection technique. These properties are briefly discussed below.

- Revocability: In case of a compromised biometric template, the possibility of the biometric template to be revoked and that a new template can be generated based on identical biometric properties must be ensured. Further, it should also be ensured that the multiple unique new user templates can be generated using the original biometric information of an individual.
- Diversity: If multiple applications generate templates that use the same biometric data then biometric templates must ensure that there is no cross-matching between them across applications.
- Security: Reversing the protection techniques applied on the original biometric information must be infeasible. Hence the original features that produced the template must be secure.
- Performance: There must not be any degradation in the performance of the biometric system after applying the template protection technique.

The rest of the paper is organized as follows. Section 2 is dedicated to a literature review wherein we discuss the background on commonly deployed template protection techniques. In Sect. 3, we discuss the proposed methodology for biometric template protection. Section 4 demonstrates the benefits of our methodology through experimentation. Finally, we conclude the paper in Sect. 5.

2 Literature Survey

The biometric template protection techniques that have been developed over the past two decades broadly encompass the following categories: biometric cryptosystems [8] and Cancelable biometrics [12]. While biometric cryptosystems utilize cryptographic techniques to ensure the security of biometric data, cancelable biometrics instead apply some transformation on the biometric features to allow revocability and reissue-ability of biometric templates. Hybrid schemes [4] utilize the benefits of both these techniques to improve performance and security. Apart from these methods, some recent developments use homomorphic encryption [32] on biometrics to allow computation on the encrypted data itself without having to decrypt it. Given the sensitivity of the information of the biometric data of an individual, ensuring the security of biometric templates is imperative. Additionally, in fingerprint based biometric authentication systems, fingerprint information is stored in the form of a template. However, if security of the template is not ensured, then the original fingerprint can be retraced by applying the knowledge of the location and orientation of the minutiae points [3]. In this section, several techniques concerning to biometric template security of fingerprint data have been briefly discussed.

Certain vector-based methods are used to construct feature vectors along with the global texture of fingerprint impressions in [2,3]. Chaotic behavior of logistic map is utilized in [2] to construct a secured fingerprint based biometric template where security of the template is achieved by quantization of a transformed template. A hybrid technique has been proposed by Boult et al. in [4] that integrates encryption and feature transformation to build a protected template. These types of techniques are referred as Biotop, where biotokens provide reasonable security and performance. An alignment-free template transformation technique is devised by Ahn et al. in [5]. A cancelable fingerprint template has been presented by Ahmad et al. in [6] in which pair-polar coordinates of minutiae have been utilized. Another template security technique has been developed by Moujahdi et al. in [7] that makes use of distance between singular point and minutiae points of fingerprint impression and a user-specific key to achieve a secured template in the form of a 2D spiral curve.

In [8], Juels and Wattenberg have put forward a fuzzy commitment scheme. This is a type of cryptographic primitive that combines approaches from cryptography and error correcting codes. Nandkumar in [9] has devised a fixed length binary representation of minutiae and has secured it using the fuzzy commitment scheme. The technique quantizes the spectrum of Fourier phase for a minutia. A popular biometric cryptosystem called fuzzy vault is proposed by Juels and Sudan in [10], which maps the feature on a polynomial to construct a secured vault. In [11], Nagar et al. have used the orientation information of the minutiae points to propose a technique based on fuzzy vault. Ratha et al. in [12] are the first to introduce cancelable biometric by performing template transformation to render the recovery of the original biometric features computationally infeasible. In [13], Tulyakov et al. utilize various polynomial functions thereby generating hashes for minutiae points. A hybrid fingerprint matcher that works along with a local minutiae matching is proposed by Tran et al. in [14]. An alignment-free technique that makes use of a modified Voronoi neighbour structure has been introduced in [15] by Yang et al. Jin at el. in [16] have proposed the usage of kernel methods to generate fixed length representation from minutiae points. An anisotropic Gaussian filter has been developed by Khan et al. in [17]. The technique performs fingerprint image enhancement wherein it decomposes the Gaussian filter to create an oriented Gaussian line and two orthogonal Gaussian filters. Sandhya and Prasad in [18] have proposed a method that uses a k-nearest neighbour approach based cancelable fingerprint template. Si et al. in [19] have put forth a fingerprint technique that uses dense registration to deal with the elastic deformation of finger skin and sparsity of discriminatory components. Wong et al. in [20] introduce a multi-line code (MLC) by describing each minutiae. The method inspects the orientation of each minutiae with respect to a reference minutiae. A user-specific key that computes the permutation order of the MLC ensures the cancelability of the fingerprint template. In their subsequent works, Wong et al. in [21] improvise the MLC performance by using learning-based binarization techniques and different ways of minutia contribution. In the technique, there is a bottleneck of a large storage requirement owing to the bit-string length of 114,688 bits for MLC.

Apparently, the fingerprint template protection is still a challenging problem in the view of template security and alignment issues of fingerprint impression. By considering these challenges, this paper presents an alignment-free and non-invertible fingerprint template protection technique that is further discussed in the following section.

3   Proposed Technique

In the proposed technique, the basic idea is to compute all possible combinations of minutiae points, which form the triplets (triangles) of the fingerprint impression and compute discriminatory features from these triplets in order to generate a secured user template. These discriminatory features are rotation and translation invariant, which make the proposed technique an alignment-free fingerprint template protection technique. Further, the secured template is constructed by computing the discriminatory features of each minutiae triplet separately and then computing a histogram of these features. The secured template is then stored in the repository for the authentication purposes after performing the security enhancement. The overall working of the proposed technique is shown in Fig. 1. Further, the different steps of the technique are discussed in detail below.

3.1   Non-invertible Feature Extraction

Let the set of minutiae points extracted from the fingerprint impression I be represented as $M = \{(x_i, y_i): i = 1, 2, 3 \ldots n\}$, where x_i and y_i, denote the x- and y-coordinates of ith minutia point m_i. From set M, we compute all possible combinations of minutiae points, which form the minutiae triplets. Given

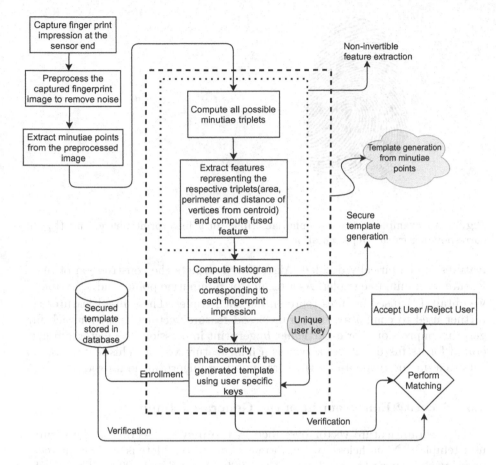

Fig. 1. Block diagram representing the step by step procedure involved in the proposed technique

that there are n minutiae points in M, we get $\binom{n}{3}$ number of triplets where any triplet formed by colinear points is dropped. Figure 2(a) shows one of the minutiae triplets obtained from the fingerprint impression. The obtained triplets (triangles) are further used to compute the rotation and translation invariant features, as shown in Fig. 2(b). The features that we have utilized for the proposed technique are perimeter (P_T), triangular area (A_T) and the sum of distances of vertices from the centroid (DC_T). Therefore, for $\binom{n}{3}$ triplets, we obtain $\binom{n}{3}$ values for each feature. The steps involved in computation of these features from a minutiae triplet are given in Algorithm 1. Further, the generation of secured template from the aforementioned features is discussed in the next section.

3.2   Secured Template Generation

We now take a weighted fusion of the features to produce a discriminatory feature for each triplet that we call the *fused feature* (F_{su}). Weights for corresponding

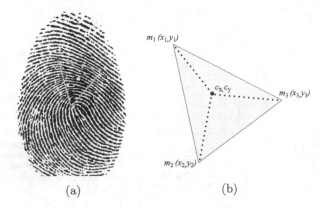

Fig. 2. An example of (a) the minutiae triplet in a fingerprint image, and (b) the corresponding feature representation

features are empirically decided. Algorithm 1 depicts the construction of fused feature for a minutiae triplet. As a result, for n minutiae points and $\binom{n}{3}$ triplets, we obtain $\binom{n}{3}$ fused features representing each triplet. These fused features are further used to compute a histogram based feature vector (H_{Fsu}) for each fingerprint impression. For a particular fingerprint impression, the histogram generated for its fused features serves as a final feature vector. This feature vector acts as a unique template for the corresponding fingerprint impression.

3.3   Security Enhancement of the Generated Template

The histogram feature vector described in the previous section is the secured user template. Nonetheless, the performance of the template is further enhanced by using the key-set (α, β) where $\alpha \in [1, 100000]$ and $\beta \in [1\ 10000]$. The use of a user specific key-set not only provides significant improvement in the recognition performance but also adds a layer of security by further randomizing the values in the feature vector. Equation 1 shows how the key-set is associated with the histogram feature vector.

$$T_H = \alpha H_{Fsu} + \beta J \qquad (1)$$

where, H_{Fsu} is the histogram feature vector, T_H is the security enhanced histogram feature vector, and J is a vector of same size as H_{Fsu}, having all entries one. The T_H is the final secured template that would be stored in the database during the enrollment and is used for matching purpose.

3.4   Matching

To match two secured user templates (which are in the form of vectors), squared error (Euclidean distance) is computed between them. A probe template is considered to be matched with the gallery template if the squared error is less than

---

Algorithm 1. Feature computation from a minutiae triplet

1: **Input:** *Minutiae triplet $\{(x_i, y_i) : i = 1, 2, 3\}$, set of weights $\{w_i : i=1, 2, 3\}$*
2: **Output:** *Fused Feature (F_{su})*
3: */* Compute perimeter P_T, Area A_T, Sum of distances from centroid DC_T */*
4: */* Perimeter P_T */*
5: $a = \sqrt{(x_2 - x_1)^2 + (y_2 - y_1)^2}$
6: $b = \sqrt{(x_2 - x_3)^2 + (y_2 - y_3)^2}$
7: $c = \sqrt{(x_3 - x_1)^2 + (y_3 - y_1)^2}$
8: $P_T = a + b + c$
9:
10: */* Area A_T */*
11: $A_T = \sqrt{(P_T/2) \times ((P_T/2) - a) \times ((P_T/2) - b) \times ((P_T/2) - c)}$
12:
13: */* Sum of Distances from centroid DC_T */*
14: $(C_x, C_y) = ((x_1 + x_2 + x_3)/3, (y_1 + y_2 + y_3)/3)$
15: $DC_a = \sqrt{(x_1 - C_x)^2 + (y_1 - C_y)^2}$
16: $DC_b = \sqrt{(x_2 - C_x)^2 + (y_2 - C_y)^2}$
17: $DC_c = \sqrt{(x_3 - C_x)^2 + (y_3 - C_y)^2}$
18: $DC_T = DC_a + DC_b + DC_c$
19:
20: */* Fused feature using weighted sum */*
21: $F_{su} = w_1 P_T + w_2 A_T + w_3 DC_T$

---

a particular threshold. Equation 2 illustrates the computation of squared error (or distance) (D_{match}) between the two secured templates.

$$D_{match} = \sqrt{\sum_{i=1}^{b}(T_{H\psi}^i - T_{H\omega}^i)^2} \tag{2}$$

where, b is the number of bins in the histogram and $T_{H\psi}$ and $T_{H\omega}$ are the two secured templates generated from different fingerprint impressions.

4   Experimental Analysis

Fingerprint Verification Competition databases, *viz.*, FVC2002 DB1 and FVC2002 DB2, are used for evaluation of the proposed technique where analysis is performed using 1-vs-1 evaluation protocol [25]. Specifics of the databases is given in Table 1. The experimentation is being carried out on a machine with Intel(R) Core(TM) i5-6200CPU@2.30 GHz processor with 8 GB RAM and the minutiae points are extracted using VeriFinger SDK (Demo) version [28]. The experimental analysis of the proposed technique in terms of the four essential criteria is discussed below.

Table 1. Details of the databases used for evaluating the proposed technique

Database	Number of subjects	Samples per subject	Total number of samples
FVC2002 DB1	100	8	800
FVC2002 DB2	100	8	800

4.1 Revocability

A technique is considered revocable given that it is possible to generate another template with the original biometric information as that of the compromised user template. In the proposed technique, if a user template is compromised, it can be easily reconstructed and replaced by altering the key-set of the compromised user template. Although the biometric information used by both the templates is same, each one of them will be considerably distinct from each other due to the use of distinct key-sets. Consequently, non-linkability of both new as well as the old templates remains intact. This implies that the proposed technique is revocable. Revocability is further tested against the revoked template attack [29] wherein an attacker exploits the compromised user template and attempts to gain access of the system. The technique has been analysed for the revoked template attacks of the following types.

- Type I attack: In this case, the attacked user template is revoked, thereby issuing a fresh user template that makes use of a different user key-set on the original fingerprint impression of the particular user. For the purpose of authentication in future, this newly generated user template is replaced in-place of the compromised template in the database. Using the compromised template, an adversary attempts to gain illegitimate access of the system.
- Type II attack: In this case, the attacked user template is revoked, thereby issuing a fresh user template that makes use of a different user key-set on the different fingerprint impression of the particular user. For the purpose of authentication in future, this newly generated user template is replaced in-place of the compromised template in the database. Using the compromised template, an adversary attempts to gain illegitimate access of the system.

We analysed the proposed technique against both of the above mentioned attacks and no user was falsely accepted. Thus, this technique is highly resilient to the revoked template attack. Therefore, it is straightforward that there is no scope of cross-matching between the compromised and the new templates, thereby making the proposed method highly revocable.

4.2 Diversity

The test conducted to assess the diversity in the proposed technique is similar to the ones discussed in [31]. To ensure the same, the proposed technique is analysed

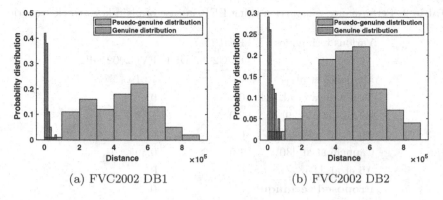

(a) FVC2002 DB1   (b) FVC2002 DB2

Fig. 3. Histogram of genuine and pseudo-genuine score distributions for (a) FVC2002 DB1, (b) FVC2002 DB2 fingerprint databases

by matching the templates constructed using different key-sets. To measure the robustness of the proposed method, we have tested it against cross-matching attack. For instance, we take two separate user key-sets for two cases by selecting two separate ranges for each key. The ranges are chosen in a manner that they do not have any overlap. For the first case, the values for keys α and β are randomly chosen as $\alpha \in [50000, 100000]$ and $\beta \in [1\ 1000]$ whereas for the second case, α and β are selected randomly from the ranges $\alpha \in [1, 50000]$ and $\beta \in [1000, 2000]$. Next, the fingerprint templates for each subject which are generated for above two cases are matched with each other to compute the pseudo-genuine scores. It can be observed from Fig. 3 that the pseudo-genuine and genuine score distributions are clearly distinct from each other. Thus, it shows the unlinkability or diversity of the secured templates, which are computed using the proposed technique.

4.3   Security

A fingerprint template protection scheme is deemed to be secure if in case of an attack it is impossible to retrace any information about the original biometric features that created it. In the discussed technique, even if a user template is compromised, all that is compromised is the histogram feature vector as obtained in Sect. 3.2. As the histogram feature vector has been generated by many-to-one mapping of several values obtained after fusing the discriminatory features of minutiae triplets, it is computationally infeasible to retrace the original information of the minutiae points from the compromised template. In addition to this, the fused features (F_{su}) are produced by combining multiple features, thereby making it impossible to compute the original feature set. Most importantly, in the proposed method, we have not utilized any orientation value of minutiae points and hence it is infeasible to reconstruct the original fingerprint impression. Therefore, it can be concluded that the user templates computed using the proposed technique are highly secure.

178   A. Ali et al.

Table 2. Performance comparison using EER in case of plain-key attack scenario

Various techniques	EER (%)	
	FVC2002 DB1	FVC2002 DB2
Moujahdi et al. [7]	2.03	1.01
M. Sandhya et al. [34]	0	0
Ferrara et al. [29]	2.0	1.1
Ali and Prakash [33]	0	0
Cappelli et al. [30]	1.0	0.49
Ali et al. [31]	0	0
Proposed technique	**0**	**0**

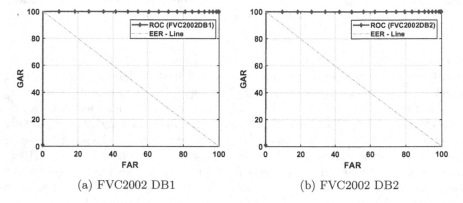

(a) FVC2002 DB1   (b) FVC2002 DB2

Fig. 4. ROC curves for (a) FVC2002 DB1, and (b) FVC2002 DB2 databases for plain-key attack scenario

4.4 Performance

The performance evaluation of the proposed technique has been carried out using four different performance metrics, *viz.*, False Acceptance Rate (FAR), False Rejection Rate (FRR), Genuine Acceptance Rate (GAR), and Equal Error Rate (EER). FAR is defined by the percentage of events wherein unauthorised persons are incorrectly accepted, whereas FRR is given by the percentage of events wherein authorised persons are incorrectly rejected. GAR is given by the percentage of events wherein authorised persons are correctly accepted, which can also be computed as GAR = 100-FRR. We have utilized 1-vs-1 protocol [25] for computing the GAR, FAR, and FRR. In the 1-vs-1 protocol, to compute FAR, the first fingerprint template of a user is compared with every user's first fingerprint template, whereas in FRR, first fingerprint template of every user is compared with the second fingerprint template of the same user.

We have evaluated the technique under two different attack scenarios, one wherein there was no key or same-key associated with the user templates (known as stolen-key attack scenario), and second, where unique keys are assigned to

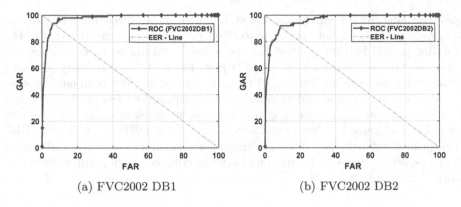

(a) FVC2002 DB1   (b) FVC2002 DB2

Fig. 5. ROC curves for (a) FVC2002 DB1, and (b) FVC2002 DB2 databases for stolen-key attack scenario

different subjects (known as plain-key attack scenario). In the stolen-key attack scenario, we have selected two random samples from each subject to compute the GAR performance metric. Further, Figs. 4(a) and 4(b) depict the plots for the receiver operating characteristics (ROC) in the case of plain-key scenario, whereas Fig. 5(a) and 5(b) show the plots for stolen-key attack scenario for FVC2002 DB1 and FVC2002 DB2 databases respectively. As observed from Table 2, the proposed technique performs better in terms of EER value under plain-key attack scenario as opposed to most of the existing techniques. It can be seen that [31,34] and [33] have produced 0% EER. However, the template generation technique used in [34] and [31] are not alignment free. Moreover, in [33], Ali et al. have utilized singular point information to generate secure finger print shell. One of the major disadvantages of relying on singular point information is that it leads to the overhead of dealing with loss of singular point information in partial, low quality and arch-type images. In the proposed method we have addressed this problem by making the template generation singular point independent. Furthermore, the present technique exhibits quite encouraging results for stolen-key attack scenario as well, as shown in the Figs. 5(a) and 5(b). Hence, the results obtained in terms of the overall performance of a fingerprint verification system show the effectiveness of the proposed technique.

5   Conclusion

The advent of biometrics in authentication systems has resulted in the replacement of traditional methods. Nonetheless, various privacy and security concerns have made it crucial to ensure the security of biometric data. Although numerous techniques have been proposed to achieve the same, it has been somewhat challenging to achieve security without having to trade performance. In this paper, we have proposed an alignment-free and non-invertible secure technique for fingerprint template protection. First, all possible combinations of minutiae points forming the triplets are generated, following which three different features from each minutiae triplet are computed that preserves the local structure of the minutiae points. Further, a fused feature vector is calculated by combining the obtained features from each minutiae triplet. For additional security, we have associated a user-specific key-set with the generated secured template. In case of an attack in the proposed technique, the compromised template is revoked for the particular user, thereby generating a new template using a new set of keys. The technique has been evaluated on FVC2002 DB1 and FVC2002 DB2 fingerprint databases. Outcomes of experimental results exhibit the viability of the proposed technique in terms of all essential criteria of a fingerprint template protection technique.

References

1. Maltoni, D., Maio, D., Jain, A.K., Prabhakar, S.: Handbook of Fingerprint Recognition. Springer, Heidelberg (2009). https://doi.org/10.1007/978-1-84882-254-2
2. Moujahdi, C., Ghouzali, S., Mikram, M., Rziza, M., Bebis, G.: Spiral cube for biometric template protection. In: Elmoataz, A., Mammass, D., Lezoray, O., Nouboud, F., Aboutajdine, D. (eds.) ICISP 2012. LNCS, vol. 7340, pp. 235–244. Springer, Heidelberg (2012). https://doi.org/10.1007/978-3-642-31254-0_27
3. Ross, A.A., Shah, J., Jain, A.K.: Toward reconstructing fingerprints from minutiae points. In: Proceedings of SPIE Conference on Biometric Technology for Human Identification, vol. 5779, pp. 68–80 (2005)
4. Boult, T., Scheirer, W., Woodworth, R.: Revocable fingerprint biotokens: accuracy and security analysis. In: Proceedings of IEEE Conference on Computer Vision and Pattern Recognition, pp. 1–8 (2007)
5. Ahn, D., Kong, S., Chung, Y.-S., Moon, K.Y.: Matching with secure fingerprint templates using non-invertible transform. In: Proceedings of Congress on Image and Signal Processing, vol. 2, pp. 29–33 (2008)
6. Ahmad, T., Hu, J., Wang, S.: Pair-polar coordinate based cancelable fingerprint templates. Pattern Recogn. **44**(10–11), 2555–2564 (2011)
7. Moujahdi, C., Bebis, G., Ghouzali, S., Rziza, M.: Fingerprint shell: secure representation of fingerprint template. Patt. Recogn. Lett. **45**, 189–196 (2014)
8. Juels, A., Wattenberg, M.: A fuzzy commitment scheme. In: 1999 Proceedings of ACM Conference on Computer & Communications Security, pp. 28–36 (1999)
9. Nandakumar, K.: A fingerprint cryptosystem based on minutiae phase spectrum. In: 2010 Proceedings of Workshop on Information Forensics & Security, pp. 1–6 (2010)
10. Juels, A., Sudan, M.: A fuzzy vault scheme. In: Proceedings of IEEE International Symposium on Information Theory, p. 408 (2002)
11. Nagar, A., Nandakumar, K., Jain, A.K.: Securing fingerprint template: fuzzy vault with minutiae descriptors. In: 2008 Proceedings of International Conference on Pattern Recognition, pp. 1–4 (2008)
12. Ratha, N.K., Connell, J.H., Bolle, R.M.: Enhancing security and privacy in biometrics-based authentication systems. IBM Syst. J. **40**(3), 614–634 (2001)
13. Tulyakov, S., Farooq, F., Mansukhani, P., Govindaraju, V.: Symmetric hash functions for secure fingerprint biometric systems. Patt. Recogn. Lett. **28**(16), 2427–2436 (2007)

14. Tran, M.H., Duong, T.N., Nguyen, D.M., Dang, Q.H.: A local feature vector for an adaptive hybrid fingerprint matcher. In: 2017 Proceedings of International Conference on Information and Communications, pp. 249–253 (2017)
15. Yang, W., Hu, J., Wang, S., Stojmenovic, M.: An alignment-free fingerprint bio-cryptosystem based on modified Voronoi neighbor structures. Patt. Recogn. **47**(3), 1309–1320 (2014)
16. Jin, Z., Lim, M.H., Teoh, A.B.J., Goi, B.M., Tay, Y.H.: Generating fixed-length representation from minutiae using kernel methods for fingerprint authentication. IEEE Trans. Syst. Man Cybernet. Syst. **46**(10), 1415–1428 (2016)
17. Khan, T.M., Bailey, D.G., Khan, M.A.U., Kong, Y.: Efficient hardware implementation for fingerprint image enhancement using anisotropic gaussian filter. IEEE Trans. Image Process. **26**(5), 2116–2126 (2017)
18. Sandhya, M., Prasad, M.V.N.K.: k-nearest neighborhood structure (k-NNS) based alignment-free method for fingerprint template protection. In: 2015 Proceedings of International Conference on Biometrics, pp. 386–393 (2015)
19. Si, X., Feng, J., Yuan, B., Zhou, J.: Dense registration of fingerprints. Patt. Recog. **63**, 87–101 (2017)
20. Wong, W.J., Wong, M.L.D., Kho, Y.H.: Multi-line code: a low complexity revocable fingerprint template for cancelable biometrics. J. Cent. South Univ. **20**(5), 1292–1297 (2013)
21. Wong, W.J., Teoh, A.B.J., Wong, M.L.D., Kho, Y.H.: Enhanced multi-line code for minutiae-based fingerprint template protection. Patt. Recogn. Lett. **34**, 1221–1229 (2013)
22. Impedovo, D., Pirlo, G.: Automatic signature verification in the mobile cloud scenario: survey and way ahead. IEEE Trans. Emerg. Top. Comput. **9**(1), 554–568 (2021)
23. Seto, J., Wang, Y., Lin, X.: User-habit-oriented authentication model: toward secure, user-friendly authentication for mobile devices. IEEE Trans. Emerg. Top. Comput. **3**(1), 107–118 (2015)
24. Breebaart, J., Yang, B., Buhan-Dulman, I., Busch, C.: Biometric template protection. Datenschutz Datensicherheit-DuD **33**(5), 299–304 (2009)
25. Ferrara, M., Maltoni, D., Cappelli, R.: Noninvertible minutia cylinder-code representation. IEEE Trans. Inf. Forensics Secur. **7**(6), 1727–1737 (2012)
26. Moujahdi, C., Bebis, G., Ghouzali, S., Rziza, M.: Fingerprint shell: secure representation of fingerprint template. Patt. Recogn. Lett. **45**, 189–196 (2014)
27. Maio, D., Maltoni, D., Cappelli, R., Wayman, J.L., Jain, A.K.: FVC 2000: fingerprint verification competition. IEEE Trans. Pattern Anal. Mach. Intel. **24**(3), 402–412 (2002)
28. Neurotechnology, Verifinger SDK. http://www.neurotechnology.com. Accessed 24 July 2021
29. Ferrara, M., Maltoni, D., Cappelli, R.: A two-factor protection scheme for MCC fingerprint templates. In: Proceedings of Biometrics Special Interest Group (BIOSIG 2014), pp. 1–8 (2014)
30. Cappelli, R., Ferrara, M., Maltoni, D.: Minutia cylinder code: a new representation and matching technique for fingerprint recognition. IEEE Trans. Pattern Anal. Mach. Intell. **32**(12), 2128–2141 (2010)
31. Ali, S.S., Ganapathi, I.I., Prakash, S.: A robust technique for fingerprint template protection. IET Biometr. **7**(6), 536–549 (2018)
32. Luo, Y., Cheung, S.S., Ye, S.: Anonymous biometric access control based on homomorphic encryption. In: Proceedings of IEEE International Conference on Multimedia and Expo, pp. 1046–1049 (2009)

33. Ali, S.S., Prakash, S.: 3-dimensional secured fingerprint Shell. Pattern Recogn. Lett. **126**, 68–77 (2019)
34. Sandhya, M., Prasad, M.V.N.K.: Securing fingerprint templates using fused structures. IET Biom. **6**(3), 173–182 (2017)

Early Prediction of Complex Business Processes Using Association Rule Based Mining

Naveed Khan[1][ID], Zeeshan Tariq[1]([✉])[ID], Aftab Ali[1], Sally McClean[1],
Paul Taylor[2], and Detlef Nauck[2]

[1] School of Computing, Ulster University, Jordanstown BT37 0QB, UK
{n.khan,zeeshan,a.ali,si.mcclean}@ulster.ac.uk
[2] Applied Research, BT, Ipswich, UK
{paul.n.taylor,detlef.nauck}@bt.com

Abstract. Complex business processes are challenging and hard to analyse. The objective here is to enhance delivery of processes in terms of improving quality of service and customer satisfaction. Therefore, an automated process prediction system is desirable to monitor and evaluate complex business processes and forecast process outcome during execution time. The analysis of such processes would help domain experts to make in-time decisions to improve the process. The in-time response greatly effects the quality of service and customer satisfaction. Therefore, in this paper, the early process prediction framework using Classification Based on Association rules (CBA) has been proposed to predict outcomes for such incomplete processes. The essential part of the proposed system is to extract association rules from the process data up to a certain point in time (i.e. the cut-off time) at which the prediction needs to be made; in an live process this would usually be the current time. The CBA algorithm generates rules with user specified support and confidence which are then utilised for early process prediction. The experimental results based on real business process data are presented for on-time and delayed processes. The proposed early process prediction system is evaluated using different metrics such as accuracy, precision, recall and the F-measure. Moreover, the proposed system is also compared with our prior published work in terms of accuracy, recall and F-measure. The analysis shows that the performance of proposed system outperforms schemes in the literature.

Keywords: Complex business processes · Association rules · Process prediction · Event log

1 Introduction

In many businesses, early prediction of business processes can be very useful as a way of making the business process more cost effective. Although such process analysis is usually quite complex and challenging, the ability to predict the

KC Santosh et al. (Eds.): RTIP2R 2021, CCIS 1576, pp. 183–194, 2022.
https://doi.org/10.1007/978-3-031-07005-1_17

likely trajectory of a live process would be a useful aid for business managers to intervene thus avoiding delays or other problems. Here, we focus on prediction of consumer processes for BT, where the data provides details on orders for landline telephone and/or broadband. The focus is on developing a system that will extract features from raw processes for early prediction of an order, where the order can be delayed/cancelled or delivered on-time. The objective of this work is to discover sets of tasks that occur frequently in the processes and could help in identifying the generic structure of the process and also give information about the dependent sets of tasks that are associated. Moreover, it is important to understand sequences of tasks within the process and extract relevant results such as the role of sequences in future process outcomes [11]. Hence, frequent association rules are extracted from successful and unsuccessful processes that can be used for early process prediction. The authors in [11] adapted a similar approach of finding the most suitable rules for the early prediction of business processes. However, rather than utilising the domain expert's knowledge, the proposed system used an automated early business process prediction model to accurately identify delayed and on-time processes without human involvement. A simple sample process with associated sequence of tasks is shown in Fig 1.

Fig. 1. Sample flow of tasks within process.

Here, the processes data is converted into the format such as seq. no, process id, task id and OTD (on-time delivery) for finding frequent sub-sequences. The OTD column is added to identify that either the order has been delivered on time or not i.e. 1 (successful) and 2 (unsuccessful) as presented in Table 1. The objective of adding the OTD column is to facilitate the identification of frequent and discriminant association rules for the successful and unsuccessful orders.

In this paper, a rule mining technique is used to identify and discover informative and interesting rules about the tasks and their sequences towards customer order completion. The objective of using association rule mining is to extract frequent tasks occurring within the process and also give some statistics about each frequent tasks co-occurring in the processes. The aim of using such technique is to identify patterns and uncover deeper insights that are hard to identify through a manual process. Such scrutiny should help experts to manage the process in a timely manner. Furthermore, an early process prediction system using Classification Based on Association rules (CBA) [3] has been developed to predict the process partway through. The CBA algorithm is used to generate rules with user specified support and confidence that are further utilised for early process prediction. The CBA algorithm first generates rules and then builds a model based on selected rules to make predictions. Different metrics such as accuracy, precision, recall and the F-measure are used for early process prediction evaluation. The novelty of this work is to thrive a generic feature selection approach that depends on discovering informative and interesting rules about the tasks

Table 1. Example sequence of a process.

Seq. no	Process-ID	Task-ID	OTD
1	547860605	100332	1
2	547860605	100442	1
3	547860605	100914	1
4	547860605	101002	1
5	547860605	100372	1
6	547860605	100199	1
7	547860605	100500	1
8	547860605	100443	1
9	547860605	100739	1
10	547860605	100602	1
11	547834540	100332	2
12	547834540	100442	2
13	547834540	100914	2
14	547834540	101002	2
15	547834540	100199	2
16	547834540	100500	2
17	547834540	100443	2
18	547834540	100134	2
19	547834540	100202	2
20	547834540	100224	2

and their sequences towards process completion. Such rules are further used as discriminative features for early process prediction.

The rest of the paper is organised as follows: in Sect. 2, the related work is discussed. In Sect. 3, a short description of association rules is given while Sect. 4 presents the CBA-based prediction model. The dataset, experimental results and comparative analysis are discussed in Sect. 5. Finally, a conclusion and future work are presented in Sect. 6.

2   Related Work

Process mining originated at the end of the 20th century with the development of several algorithms, such as the alpha algorithm, designed to learn models from event data, termed as Process Discovery [2]. Over the years, many more advanced algorithms for process mining have been developed, such as the heuristics miner [12], ILP miner [7] and inductive miner [1]. Following process discovery, conformance checking emerged as another important research track within the domain of process mining [4]. The latter is focused on the relationship between event data on the one hand and the process model on the other hand. One of the well-known techniques used by researcher in process mining is rules-based mining. There are two major types of rules-based mining, association-based rules mining and sequence-based rules mining. Association rule mining was initially advocated by Agrawal et al. [1] with the aim of exploring customer's shopping trends in markets. These trends were based upon the set of frequent items purchased together by an individual customer during a shopping trip. Association between items purchased helped businesses defining strategies to increase sales through improved placement of items in shops. On the other hand, sequence mining deals with the temporal relationship of the items purchased by the customers. Several algorithms have been used by researchers, such as AprioriAll, SPADE, GSP and CBA, for mining event sequences in a process log [4]. Sequence mining algorithms identify the frequency and accuracy of a relevant sequences in a log, referred to as a support and confidence [11]. Much industrial research like telecommunications [4], industrial production [8] and the healthcare sector have used these sequence mining algorithms to carry out in-depth analysis of frequent event sequences based upon their support value. Our work is similar to analysis presented by Frank et al. in [4] where authors proposed a methodology for customers' churn prediction considering the individual customer's history of events. In addition, we formulated in this paper a highly accurate framework for future outcomes of a running process based upon frequent sequential rules between events in an individual case.

3   Association Rule Mining

This section demonstrates the initial experiments and results of rule mining techniques to identify and discover informative and interesting rules concerning the tasks and their sequences, towards customer order completion. The objective of using association rule mining is to extract frequent tasks occurring within the process and also give some statistics about frequent tasks co-occurring in the process. The Apriori [2] algorithm has been used for discovering frequent item sets in the data.

The Apriori algorithm is applied to the process dataset to discover and identify useful and interesting rules about the list of tasks in the processes. The Apriori algorithm utilises some interesting measures, for instance support (how frequently an item appear in the dataset), confidence (how often a specific rule has been found to be true) and lift (probability of occurrence of a specific rule in the dataset) for the extracted rules that can help in selecting a specific set of rules which eventually assists in decision mining. The support, confidence and lift are calculated for association rules as is summarised in the following Equations.

$$Rule: X \Rightarrow Y \begin{cases} Support = \dfrac{Frequency(X,Y)}{N} \\[2mm] Confidence = \dfrac{Frequency(X,Y)}{Frequency(X)} \\[2mm] Lift = \dfrac{Support}{Support(X) \times Support(Y)} \end{cases}$$

The BT consumer dataset of business processes has been previously analysed for new orders of land line telephones and/or broadband products in [6]. Initially, a total of 725 on-time delivered processes and 1585 delayed processes were used in experiments to extract useful information and association rules. We now use the Apriori algorithm for extracting association rules using the arules R package to implement the rule mining algorithms. The resulting association rules extracted by Apriori are presented in Table 2.

Table 2. Example of 20 rules from the Apriori algorithm

Seq. no	Rules	Support	Confidence	Lift	Count
1	{100332} ⇒ {100442}	0.813067936	0.993654151	1.212425947	1879
2	{100500} ⇒ {100332}	0.694937257	0.894209354	1.09281746	1606
3	{100500} ⇒ {100442}	0.693206404	0.891982183	1.088368967	1602
4	{100500} ⇒ {100442}	0.693206404	0.891982183	1.088368967	1602
5	{100198} ⇒ {100887}	0.687581134	0.983292079	1.377204845	1589
6	{100887} ⇒ {100198}	0.687581134	0.963030303	1.377204845	1589
7	{100443} ⇒ {100199}	0.683686716	0.985651903	1.413930197	1580
8	{100199} ⇒ {100443}	0.683686716	0.980757294	1.413930197	1580
9	{101046} ⇒ {100958}	0.672868888	0.981691919	1.402157	1555
10	{100958} ⇒ {101046}	0.672868888	0.961063041	1.402157	1555
11	{100197} ⇒ {100500}	0.670272609	0.909037559	1.16970256	1549
12	{100500} ⇒ {100197}	0.670272609	0.86247216	1.16970256	1549
13	{100921} ⇒ {100199}	0.669407183	0.983471074	1.410801771	1547
14	{100199} ⇒ {100921}	0.669407183	0.960273122	1.410801771	1547
15	{100921} ⇒ {100443}	0.667243617	0.980292435	1.413260023	1542
16	{100443} ⇒ {100921}	0.667243617	0.961946351	1.413260023	1542
17	{100197} ⇒ {100332}	0.658156642	0.892605634	1.090857546	1521
18	{100197} ⇒ {100442}	0.657291216	0.891431925	1.08769756	1519
19	{100992} ⇒ {100958}	0.633059282	0.915519399	1.307642356	1463
20	{100958} ⇒ {100992}	0.633059282	0.904202719	1.307642356	1463

4   The CBA-Based Prediction Model

As discussed, the Apriori algorithm is used to generate association rules from the processes which highlight general trends in the data. The Apriori algorithm is used because we are analysing BT customer data which is quite large and require an efficient algorithm for analysis. The support and confidence threshold were set to find the most interesting rules from the data. Since we have more than 10,000 rules, we need to restrict the threshold; initially we choose support ≥0.70 and confidence ≥0.75 to find the most interesting rules. The resulting association rules are presented in Fig. 2.

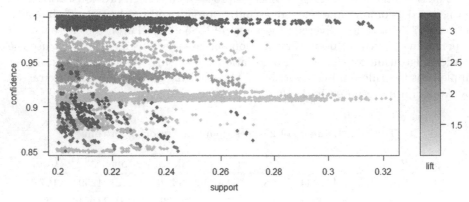

Fig. 2. Rules generation using Apriori algorithm

By restricting confidence to be greater than or equal to 0.75, we intend to choose rules with high frequency of the consequent (right hand side of the rule) occurring given the antecedent (left hand side). As described earlier, the extracted rules from successful on-time processes and delayed processes have been used to predict on-time and delayed/cancelled orders. In our experiments, we have generated rules with support varying from 70% to 80% and with different confidence values varying from 75% to 85% to get more interesting rules for different cut off times of the processes data. The CBA (classification based on association rules) algorithm [3] is implemented in R to use association rules for prediction of process compliance with a target. The CBA technique uses the Apriori algorithm to generate association rules that integrate with a classification rule to produce subsets from effective rules [9]. The CBA algorithm works in two steps: In the association rule generation (CBA_RG) step - it uses the Apriori algorithm to discover the association-based rules, considering user-defined support and confidence thresholds. Then, in the classifier building (CBA-CB) step - a classifier is build based upon non-redundant discovered rules using information about the sets, lists and data dictionaries [5].

CBA has been widely used to build classification system with more predictive and accurate results than traditional methods such as the decision tree [10]. The early process prediction framework using CBA is presented in Fig. 3. The experiments are performed using 60% data for training and 40% data for testing to evaluate the predictive model.

5   Experimental Results

In our experiments, we have analyzed the raw process data from BT, and filtered processes, which are new orders for the land line telephone and/or broadband

[6]. Initially, a total of 15523 on-time delivered processes were extracted, of which only 725 processes were used in our experiments to extract useful information and association rules. Similarly, for delayed/cancelled processes, a total of 5830 processes were extracted, out of which only 1585 processes were used in our experiments to extract useful information and association rules. The extracted association rules from successful on-time processes and unsuccessful processes have been used to predict on-time and delayed/cancelled orders.

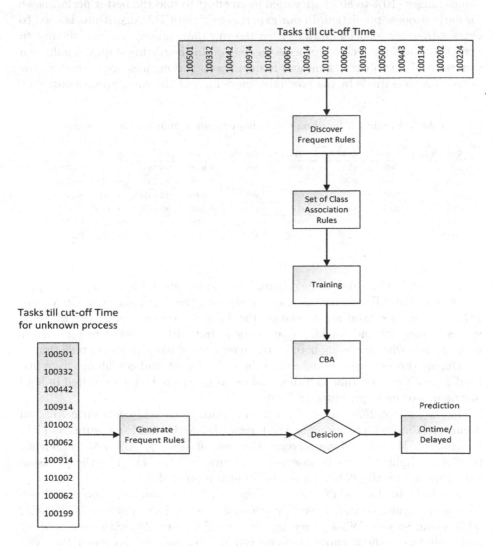

Fig. 3. Early process prediction system using CBA

In the experimental design different cut-off time ratios (25%, 50%, 75%, 85%, 95%, and 100%) are used for early process prediction. The cut-off time, which in a real deployment would often be the current time-point, refers to the percentage of time expired towards target time, so that we can make predictions using data only relating to the history up to this point in time; the prediction is then compared with the actual compliance, or otherwise. Cut-off time here is calculated as a percentage of the target. Moreover, the support and confidence values ranges (10% to 80%) are varied in an effort to find the better performance for early process prediction. In our experiments, the CBA algorithms is used to extract frequent association rules from the raw data taking each cut off time to train the model for accurate process prediction. In the testing step, the unknown process is given to the system and frequent association rules are extracted; the decision is then made by the predictive model about the early process outcome.

Table 3. Prediction based on CBA algorithms for different metric measures

Cut-off time	Support	Confidence	Training	Testing	Accuracy	Precision	Recall	F-measure
25%	80%	75%	60%	40%	75.97%	76.58%	87.56%	85.77%
50%	80%	85%	60%	40%	77.62%	82.14%	89.67%	85.75%
75%	70%	80%	60%	40%	78.09%	82.54%	90.90%	86.48%
85%	70%	80%	60%	40%	80.34%	82.26%	93.63%	88.69%
95%	75%	85%	60%	40%	83.71%	86.73%	95.15%	90.74%
100%	75%	85%	60%	40%	85.81%	87.75%	97.04%	92.16%

As presented in Table 3, the different metric measures such as accuracy, precision, recall and F-measure are used to evaluate the performance of CBA algorithm. In our experiments to choose the best metric measures, the different values of support and confidence are varied (from 10% to 80%) to find better performance with achieving high metric measures of early process prediction.

During the experiments different values of support and confidence were utilized for each cut- off time and those values were selected which resulted in high metric measures as presented in Table 3.

In the case of 25% cut off time, with support 80% and confidence 75%, an accuracy (75.97%), precision (76.58%), recall (87.56%) and F-measure (85.77%) is achieved. However, if we increase the cut off time to 50% and confidence to 85%, a slight increase is observed in accuracy (77.62%) while the precision (82.14%) and recall (89.67%) are significantly improved.

Similarly, in the case of 75% cut off time, with support 70% and confidence 80%, an accuracy, precision, recall and F-measure is achieved of 78.09%, 82.54%, 90.90% and 86.48%. While increasing the cut off time to 85% with same support and confidence, the accuracy is improved to 80.34% but the recall (93.63%) and F-measure (88.69%) are improved significantly. Likewise, in the case of 95% cut off time, with support 75% and confidence 85%, an accuracy (83.71%), precision (86.73%), recall (95.15%) and F-measure (90.74%) is achieved. However, the accuracy (85.81%), precision (87.75%), recall (97.04%) and F-measure

(92.16%) is improved significantly when the cut off time increased to 100%. Overall, we observe a good increase in accuracy, precision, recall and F-measure as we increase the cut off time i.e. 25%, 50%, 75%, 85%, 95%, and 100% as presented in Table 3. This is as expected, since the amount of data available increases as the cut-off time approaches the target. However, the knowledge that a target will be breached is more useful the earlier it is acquired. The experimental results shows that the current approach preform better and achieved high metric measures such as accuracy, recall and F-measure compared to the previous approach presented in [6]. Moreover, the current dataset used in experiments has the class imbalance problem that has great impact on the classification; this can be addressed in our future work.

5.1   Comparative Analysis

In addition, the results of the proposed approach of prediction based on association rules (PBCBA) approach are compared with results using different machine learning approaches and graph-based features, as described in [6] in terms of accuracy, recall and F-measure.

The highest accuracy (75.97%, 77.62%, 78.09%, 80.34%,83.71% and 85.75%) achieved for different cut off time (i.e. 25%, 50%, 75%, 85%, 95% and 100%) when compared with the approach used in [6]. It is observed that as we increase the cut off time the improvement in accuracy is also increased as presented in Fig. 4.

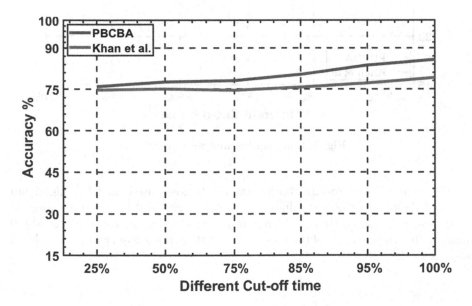

Fig. 4. Comparative analysis of accuracy

Moreover, our approach is also compared in terms of recall where the results show how precisely it predicts the on-time and delayed orders. It is observed that the proposed approach outperforms compared to the results presented in [6] in terms of recall as presented in Fig. 5, which demonstrates that the proposed approach has high prediction potential. Likewise, the proposed approach is also compared with the scheme presented in [6] in terms of the F-measure. The F measure is used to evaluate the performance of the proposed approach. It can be observed that the proposed approach outperforms by achieving high F-measures as compared to the scheme presented in [6]. As we increase the cut-off time, the F-measure is significantly increased as presented in Fig. 6.

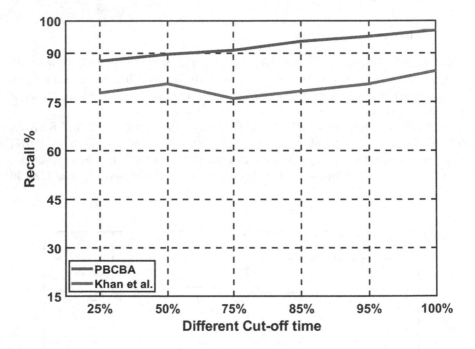

Fig. 5. Comparative analysis of recall

The experimental results shows that prediction based on CBA algorithm achieved significantly higher values of accuracy, recall and F-measure compared to the scheme presented in [6], which indicates that the predictor does a good job in predicting the outcome of the process that either the process will be completed on-time or delayed.

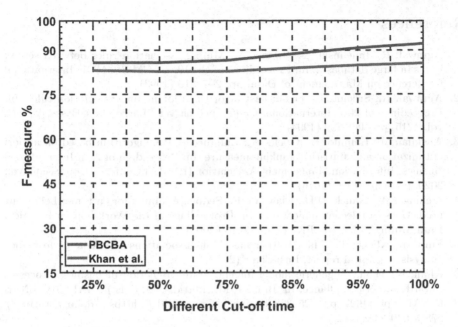

Fig. 6. Comparative analysis of F-measure

6   Conclusion

Process monitoring is crucial in many business organizations to avoid delays in customer orders which can greatly affect customer satisfaction and cause financial loss to the organization. The proposed prediction system uses CBA analyses to identify association rules with high support and confidence from the raw data in real time. Further, these rules are used for early process prediction that might breach the target compliance. The current approach attains a high success rate for early process prediction using different performance metrics such as accuracy, precision, recall and the F-measure when more process data is exposed as the process moves towards the target. Moreover, the results of the proposed system have also been compared with our previous published work, and the results shows that the proposed new scheme performs substantially better in terms of accuracy, recall and the F-measure. In the future work, combinations of rule-mining and sequence mining algorithms will be explored to evaluate business process data for early process prediction.

Acknowledgement. This research is supported by BTIIC (The BT Ireland Innovation Centre) project, funded by BT and Invest Northern Ireland.

References

1. Agrawal, R., Imieliński, T., Swami, A.: Mining association rules between sets of items in large databases. In: Proceedings of the 1993 ACM SIGMOD International Conference on Management of Data, pp. 207–216 (1993)
2. Agrawal, R., Srikant, R., et al.: Fast algorithms for mining association rules. In: Proceedings of 20th International Conference on very Large Data Bases, VLDB, vol. 1215, pp. 487–499 (1994)
3. Alwidian, J., Hammo, B., Obeid, N.: Enhanced CBA algorithm based on apriori optimization and statistical ranking measure. In: Proceeding of 28th International Business Information Management Association (IBIMA) Conference on Vision, vol. 2020, pp. 4291–4306 (2016)
4. Eichinger, F., Nauck, D.D., Klawonn, F.: Sequence mining for customer behaviour predictions in telecommunications. In: Proceedings of the Workshop on Practical Data Mining at ECML/PKDD, pp. 3–10 (2006)
5. Filip, J., Kliegr, T.: Classification based on associations (CBA)-a performance analysis. Technical report, EasyChair (2018)
6. Khan, N., et al.: A generic model for end state prediction of business processes towards target compliance. In: Bramer, M., Petridis, M. (eds.) SGAI 2019. LNCS (LNAI), vol. 11927, pp. 325–335. Springer, Cham (2019). https://doi.org/10.1007/978-3-030-34885-4_25
7. Lim, A.H., Lee, C.S.: Processing online analytics with classification and association rule mining. Knowl.-Based Syst. **23**(3), 248–255 (2010)
8. Lingitz, L., Gallina, V., Ansari, F., Gyulai, D., Pfeiffer, A., Monostori, L.: Lead time prediction using machine learning algorithms: a case study by a semiconductor manufacturer. Proc. CIRP **72**, 1051–1056 (2018)
9. Liu, B., Hsu, W., Ma, Y., et al.: Integrating classification and association rule mining. In: KDD, vol. 98, pp. 80–86 (1998)
10. Nofal, A., Bani-Ahmad, S.: Classification based on association-rule mining techniques: a general survey and empirical comparative evaluation. Ubiquit. Comput. Commun. (UBICC) J. **5**(3) (2010)
11. Taylor, P.N., Kiss, S.: Rule-mining and clustering in business process analysis. In: Bramer, M., Petridis, M. (eds.) SGAI 2018. LNCS (LNAI), vol. 11311, pp. 237–249. Springer, Cham (2018). https://doi.org/10.1007/978-3-030-04191-5_22
12. Weijters, A., van Der Aalst, W.M., De Medeiros, A.A.: Process mining with the heuristics miner-algorithm. Technische Universiteit Eindhoven, Technical report WP, vol. 166, pp. 1–34 (2006)

A Framework for Masked-Image Recognition System in COVID-19 Era

Vijay Prakash[1]([⊠]), Lalit Garg[2], Elena Fomiceva[2], Sergio Vega Pineda[2],
Alex Navia Santos[2], and Seema Bawa[1]

[1] Thapar Institute of Engineering and Technology, Patiala, India
{vijay.prakash,seema}@thapar.edu, vijaysoni200@gmail.com
[2] University of Malta, Msida, Malta
{lalit.garg,elena.fomiceva.19,sergio.vega.20,
alex.navia.20}@um.edu.mt

Abstract. Face Recognition techniques have been widely developed and used for many years. Several approaches and models are adopted and successfully used to perform face recognition in airports, supermarkets, banks, etc. However, with the emergence of the COVID-19 pandemic, the whole world came across the requirement to use face masks. The mask's partial covering of the face makes some well-known face recognition algorithms perform poorly or even fail. This paper has developed a real-time framework to detect, recognize, and identify people to authenticate them before accessing an app, device, or location. The newly created framework offers a unique set of capabilities, including the ability for users to select from various authentication methods based on their preferences or circumstances. The application's face recognition section uses cutting-edge AI and computer vision algorithms to offer the user accurate face detection and recognition, even when the face is partially hidden behind a mask.

Keywords: Face recognition · Computer vision · Masked images · Web application

1 Introduction

Nobody has expected the actual situation in the world one and a half years ago. Nobody was prepared for this, and the new measures that protect us every day also give new problems and difficulties to deal with the situation. One of the technologies with more progress in recent years, facial recognition, has been hampered by the obligation to wear a face mask most of the time [1]. Banks and mobile applications that used this technology to recognize their users have been forced to look for alternatives [2, 3].

This paper aims to create an artificial intelligence-based framework that allows facial recognition given the current circumstances, recognizing the user via computer vision regardless of whether they wear a mask or not [4]. The photos should be stored on the cloud using google cloud or any similar platform as a database and store the hash codes of the images in a blockchain network. Therefore, researchers worldwide are trying new

© Springer Nature Switzerland AG 2022
KC Santosh et al. (Eds.): RTIP2R 2021, CCIS 1576, pp. 195–209, 2022.
https://doi.org/10.1007/978-3-031-07005-1_18

approaches and rapidly developing new techniques to design and implement quality masked face recognition systems.

The scope of this paper is to create a real-time framework to detect, recognize and identify people to authenticate them before accessing an app, device, or place such as a bank. In these times of coronavirus, recognizing people via camera is more challenging than before because everyone must cover half of their faces [5]. The framework must consist of an authentication system via Email and a trained AI that identifies masked faces. The managed data is sensible (photos of people); it must be stored rigorously and safely, like a blockchain network.

1.1 Objectives

The main objectives of this research work are underlines as follows:

1. To detect, recognize and identify people wearing the mask that want to access a device, app, or place somewhere via Computer Vision.
2. To store sensitive data in a secure way that cannot be hacked.
3. To develop a trained AI which can recognize people using photos of their faces.
4. To discuss ethical issues such as asking for consent to record people and store photos of their faces.

The rest of the paper is organized as Sect. 2 discusses the literature review. Section 3 describes the problem formulation. Section 4 discusses the constructs used in the proposed solution. Section 5 describes the specifications and design of proposed solutions. Section 6 discusses the implementations and results analysis followed by conclusions and future scope in Sect. 7.

2   Literature Review

This short literature survey explores the current advances in resolving the relevant problem of masked face recognition. Yande et al. [6] proposed two approaches to masked face recognition: attention-based approach and cropping-based approach. The researchers conducted extensive experiments using SMFRD, CISIA-Web face, AR, and Extend Yela B datasets. In the attention-based approach, the Convolutional Block Attention Module (CBAM) focused on the areas around the eyes. This method demonstrated superior performance results concerning face recognition accuracy. In the cropping-based approach, the authors applied cropping of the occluded (covered by the mask) part of the face image, concentrating only on the area above the face mask. This technique turned out to be effective in two different scenarios: training to recognize masked faces based on standard face images and vice versa.

The authors [7] presents a machine learning algorithm through the image classification method: MobileNetv2. This algorithm is based on the Convolutional Neural Network (CNN) model. This approach was first tested on the Kaggle and the Real-World Masked Face datasets (RMFD). Images from public cameras from 25 cities in Indonesia were used to conduct further experiments. The researchers claim that their implementation of this model allowed them to recognize both mask-less and masked faces with the same 96.85% accuracy. Another article by Walid Hariri [8] also describes pre-trained deep-learning Convolutional Neural Networks (CNN) in combination with the Bag-of-features paradigm and Multilayer Perceptron (MLP). This complex approach was tested on Real-World-Masked-Face-Dataset, and results demonstrated its high performance and efficiency.

Ding et al. [9] analyze the difficulties and issues with face recognition that arose with pervasive mask use in the world. Their work presents a novel latent part detection (LPD) model used to acquire discriminative features from the masked face image. This model was tested in experiments designed based on MFV, MFI, and synthetic masked LFW datasets. Interestingly, these datasets containing masked and mask-less face images were collected explicitly by the researchers to train and test their model. According to the authors, their face recognition algorithm outperforms other methods by a significant margin.

Montero et al. [10] presented their approach based on the ArcFace model used in standard face recognition. The researchers applied enhancements to the existing model. They generated masked versions of three popular face-recognition datasets: Labeled Faces in the Wild (LFW), Celebrities in Frontal-Profile in the Wild (CFP), and Aged. The experiments conducted on these datasets showed that the enhanced ArcFace model was very effective in masked face recognition while preserving the same high level of performance in regular face recognition. In addition, this model showed 99.78% accuracy for checking if a person in the picture is wearing a mask. The framework OpenCV provides real-time object detection using Haar feature-based cascade classifiers. This method was proposed by Paul Viola and Michael Jones in their work [11] in 2001. It is based on a machine learning approach where a cascade function is trained from many positive and negative images. It is then used to detect objects in other images. To make it easier, OpenCV comes with a trainer and a detector that can be used to train our classifier. Furthermore, OpenCV brings us many pre-trained classifiers in XML files for face, eyes, and smile.

This brief literature overview only shows some aspects and directions of research in masked face recognition. It should be mentioned that there is already significant progress and a variety of effective models designed to enable accurate masked face recognition. Moreover, based on the information above, the appearance and availability of extensive masked face datasets for FR system training should also be noted. However, with this area of research being relatively novel and trending, new exciting developments will appear in the coming years. Table 1 depicts the different methods and datasets used in masked face recognition by various authors.

Table 1. Methods and datasets used in masked face recognition

Authors	Method	Dataset	Result
Geng et al. [12]	Novel Identity Aware Mask GAN (IAMGAN) trains the system and Domain Constrained Ranking (DCR) loss function	MFSR: 9,742 masked face images with mask region segmentation and 11,615 images of 1,004 identities with or without masks	Experiments demonstrated the effectiveness of the proposed approach
Lin et al. [13]	Modified LeNet, which changes the number of units in the output layer of LeNet and increases the number of feature maps with smaller filter sizes	Real-world masked face dataset	The accuracy and robustness of the proposed solution have been demonstrated in the experiments
Boutros et al. [14]	Embedding Unmasking Model (EUM) and a novel loss function – the Self-restrained Triplet (SRT)	MS1MV2: 58 m images of 85k different identities	The proposed model demonstrated significantly improvement of performance in the experimental settings
Anwar et al. [15]	Deep network-based face recognition system Facet	VGGFace2-mini: 9131 identities, 42 images per identity without masks VGGFace2-mini SM: same with random application of masks	Authors report an increase of about 38% in the actual positive rate and high face recognition accuracy
Mandal et al. [16]	Deep learning-based model ResNet-50	Real-world masked face recognition dataset (RMFRD): 5,000 masked faces of 525 people and 90,000 unmasked faces	Authors report that their experiments in masked face recognition gave an accuracy of 47.91%. Therefore, they conclude that the model should be further improved

3   Problem Formulation

The initial research revealed some similar applications in the market. Primarily they are developed for mobile devices. However, some of these applications were tested and explored to identify their benefits and limitations. Following is a brief description of some applications in the market that most closely resemble the proposed solution but to overcome the limitations.

BioID Facial Recognition App [17] is an Android and iOS mobile application that provides an authentication service based on face recognition. The testing was conducted with an Android version. In general, the application has a simple, intuitive interface, quick registration process, and relatively efficient facial recognition mechanism. However, the application is too simple, and it does not offer any additional authentication methods. Upon successful authentication, the initial picture of the user or any other information is not shown. The application informs that the verification was successful. The facial recognition is not very accurate: in a test with ten attempts without a mask or any other face cover, the success rate was 7 to 3, while in the same test with a face mask, it gave only a 4 to 6 success rate. Considering these observations, the proposed project can offer substantial advantages in comparison with the BioID app.

Railer Face Recognition Attendance Management Solution [18] is also a mobile application developed for Android and iOS devices. The purpose of this application is slightly different as it is focused on employee or student attendance tracking. But the application presents interest in this context as it tracks employee attendance using face recognition. The testing was conducted with an Android version. Overall, the application is user-friendly and intuitive, offering all the required functionality for attendance tracking. As for the face recognition aspect, the same simple face recognition test was carried out. The application was very accurate in the test without a face mask, recognizing the face 10 times out of 10. However, the face recognition failed when the face mask was on, with no victorious face recognitions and the constant message "No face detected" showing up on the screen. Therefore, it can be concluded that this application is not suitable for face recognition of people wearing face masks.

4 Proposed Solutions

The following constructs have been used to develop the proposed solution to overcome the limitations of the previous section's existing methods.

4.1 Programming Languages and Tools

1. **Python:** This allows us to use open source frameworks related to computer vision, but it can also be used for blockchain.
2. **Typescript:** Open-source programming language built upon JavaScript that allows creating of dynamic web applications
3. **Solidity:** Programming language to develop smart contracts on the Ethereum blockchain.

4.2 Web Application Frameworks

1. **Angular:** Modern framework from Google for development of efficient and dynamic front-end single-page applications.
2. **Django Restful:** The library that works with the standard Django models to create a flexible and powerful back-end API for the project

4.3 Computer Vision Frameworks

1. **OpenCV:** A real-time optimized Computer Vision library and tools.
2. **Face recognition:** The most straightforward face recognition library to manipulate faces in Python. It was built with deep learning and dlib.
3. **Numpy:** The library that allows to create and manage vectors and matrices.
4. **Matplotlib:** The library that allows representing graphics.
5. **Dlib:** The library that includes machine learning algorithms.
6. **Angular:** The framework for web development supported by Google giving features like authentication.

4.4 Algorithms

1. **Haar Cascades:** The ensemble learning is based on the concatenation of several classifiers, using all information collected from the output from a given classifier as additional information for the next classifier in the cascade. Provided Haar cascade by OpenCV for eye recognition: haarcascade_eye.xml.
2. **LPBH:** It is a simple solution to the face recognition problem, recognizing both front and side faces. For this case, it will be used to identify the eyes.

4.5 Approaches

1. **UI front-end:** Develop a login and registration UI with an authentication system via email using Angular.
2. **AI for recognition:** Developed an eyes detector to recognize and identify people wearing masks or not, focusing on the eyes ignoring the rest of the face. We can develop a recognition system using the default Haar Cascades that OpenCV provides with OpenCV and face recognition frameworks. Use the Local Binary Patterns Histogram algorithm that the framework OpenCV provides to identify people with their eyes.
3. **Store data:** Store photos on the cloud using the google cloud platform or any other platform to be discussed as a database. Store the Hash codes of the images on the Ethereum blockchain network.

5 Specification and Design

5.1 System Requirements

The basic requirements for the proposed system were gathered from the initial project outline and further identified and clarified during the first two online meetings with the clients. Based on these discussions and idea exchange, two significant processes representing the main application functionality were established and described. These processes include account registration and user authorization/authentication. Subsequently, three main scenarios for user registration and account creation were defined.

Account Registration Scenarios

1. The user creates the account correctly with a verified email address and can store the photo to verify/authenticate them in the future.
2. The user creates the account with an unverified email address/mobile number. Thus, the registration is denied.
3. The user tries to create an account, but the username is already in use. Thus, the registration is denied as the email used to create the account should be unique. The specifications related to the registration process were defined as follows:

Registration Process

1. The user enters and submits their email address and password; optionally mobile phone number can be provided.
2. The system automatically generates and sends a message containing a random 5-digit confirmation code.
3. The user is required to enter the confirmation code received in the email.
4. The system verifies if the code is correct.
5. Upon code verification, the user is offered to take their picture using their device camera. The image should be without a face mask as this will be the top picture of the user stored in the system to be used for all further authentications.
6. When the picture is taken and uploaded, its hashed value is calculated and stored in the database with other users' details.
7. The user registration is finalized, and the user is redirected to their profile in the system, where they can see the uploaded picture, change security settings or edit their account details. The web application allows registered users to confirm their identities. First, the user gets authorized by providing their email and password. Second, the authentication process can be performed in different ways depending on the settings chosen by the user in their profile. The available authentication settings for the application are as follows:

Security Settings

1. Verification code sent to the registered email (default option).
2. Face recognition verification when the camera's current user picture is compared with the image uploaded at the time of registration.
3. Verification code sent to the registered phone number (available only if the phone number is provided).
4. Access denial setting, when the user will not be authenticated and their picture and details will not be shown in their profile upon login.

Subsequently, six main scenarios for user authorization and authentication were defined.

Login Scenarios

1. The user enters the correct password and username and can proceed to identity verification (based on the option selected).
2. The user tries to access the app but is not registered.
3. The user enters the wrong username and cannot access their account.
4. The user enters the wrong password and cannot access their account.
5. User tries to access their account, but the app cannot verify their face, so they have to try again.
6. The user tries to verify their face but is wearing sunglasses, so the app cannot verify them, and they have to try again.

The specifications related to the authorization and authentication process were defined as follows:

Authorization and Authentication Process

1. The person needing authentication (access to unmasked image/identity information) enters and submits their email address and password when registering the account.
2. This step differs depending on the authentication method selected by the user.

    i) **Email:** The system automatically generates and sends a message containing a random 5-digit confirmation code to the registered email address. The user is required to enter this confirmation code, and the system verifies it. Upon successful verification, the user is authenticated and redirected to the profile that shows the user's picture and details.

    ii) **Face Recognition:** The user is asked to take a picture using their device camera. The image can be with or without a face mask. Then the picture is compared with the one provided at registration. If the pictures match, the user is authenticated and redirected to the profile that shows the user's photo and details. The user's face image hash will be compared with the hash stored in the Blockchain network to have further authentication (at the airport or banks to confirm the identity).

    iii) **iPhone:** The system automatically generates and sends a message containing a random 5-digit confirmation code to the registered phone number (if provided). The user is required to enter this confirmation code, and the system verifies it. Upon successful verification, the user is authenticated and redirected to the profile that shows the user's picture and details.

    iv) **Access denied:** The system does not offer any authentication method and directly loads the user profile, where the user's picture and personal details are hidden. The user is informed that they need to turn on any authentication options to see the personal information.

3. Suppose the user provides incorrect information or fails to provide a matching face picture. In that case, the system will deny access to the user's details stored in their account and redirect the user to the application home page asking for re-attempt the authentication.

Furthermore, the authenticated user can also modify their account information. The user may change the registered email, phone number, or password. The initial picture stored in the system can also be deleted or updated with a new one. This functionality is available in the user profile.

5.2 Principle System Components and Requirements

In the process of initial system discussion and requirements gathering, it has been decided that the client-server web application is the most suitable solution for implementing the mentioned objectives in Sect. 1. The following are the primary considerations that highlight the benefits of such application:

1. The web application does not need direct installation on the client machine and makes its use extremely flexible from different devices and platforms.
2. It is much easier to perform maintenance, introduce updates and fix errors in such an application because the users will not be required to install each new update manually. Therefore, it will exclude the problem of outdated application versions on end-user devices.
3. The web application does not take up any storage space on the user device and is highly efficient and lightweight. Therefore, it can be used even on old devices or devices with limited resources.
4. The development of a web application is more accessible and requires less resources and time. The availability of different web application technologies, frameworks, and libraries enables efficient implementation of all required functionality quickly. It also enables rapid development and presentation of the first working prototype of the application that can be demonstrated to the client and tested in a live environment with the involvement of actual users.
5. The client-server architecture of the application also provides security and protection of vulnerable user data, such as user pictures, emails, phone numbers, etc. The data is stored in the back-end server with limited physical access and a strict access rights management policy. It is also easier to control network traffic in such a system to immediately identify and prevent most security issues and vulnerabilities.

It is considering that the main objective of the proposed solution is to enable quick and efficient authentication services to any user that could require it (e.g., at the airport or bank to confirm the identity). Therefore, the client-server web application will fulfill this requirement and provide services to the vast majority of users in a couple of clicks without the need to install an individual application. The proposed web application is divided into two major parts to benefit from all the mentioned advantages of the client-server architecture. First, the Angular front-end implements a user interface and is responsible for all user interaction functionalities. Second, the Python Django back-end is responsible for internal application logic and data storage.

In terms of the eye's recognition, a real-time video capture needs to be implemented to get an image of the person's face that wants to log in through the camera. As the system works to detect and identify the eyes, the region of interest of that captured frame is the eyes. Hence, a program that detects eyes needs to be done. The next step is to identify the person that wants to access the app. To do that, a local binary pattern histogram algorithm will carry out the person's identification with the eyes. Getting deeper understanding into the recognition part, the following are the primary considerations that highlight the benefits of such application:

1. The script must be installed on the server or user machine to execute the Local Binary Patterns Histogram values stored in a.yml file.
2. The taken photos must be stored in the same folder of the script to run the AI.

6   Implementations and Result Analysis

The individual components that make up the applications front-end are described and discussed below to understand better the user interface, its design, implementations, and functionalities.

6.1   Home Component

Home Component represents the application's main screen, where the user arrives upon loading the page for the first time. It contains the name of the application and a short description of the purpose and primary functionality provided by the service. The user is invited to either register or log in to use the application, as depicted in Fig. 1.

Upon loading the Home screen, there is a check of the user's login status. This check is performed by the NGX Cookie Service [19] library that checks if the client's user agent already has the cookie with the authorization token received from the back-end. If the user has already logged in, the Login and Register buttons below the text will change to the View Profile button, taking them directly to their profile.

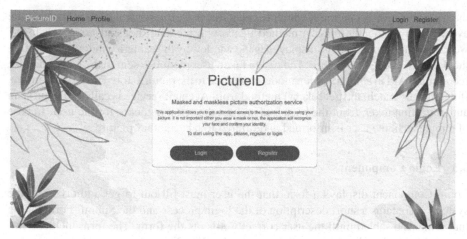

Fig. 1. Home screen with the navigation panel

6.2 Camera Component

The camera Component is intended for taking user face pictures. It is also a reusable component within the application used in registration, authentication (when the face recognition option is turned on), and profile picture update. This component is based on ngx-webcam [20] library that implements easy access to a built-in device web camera, as shown in Fig. 2.

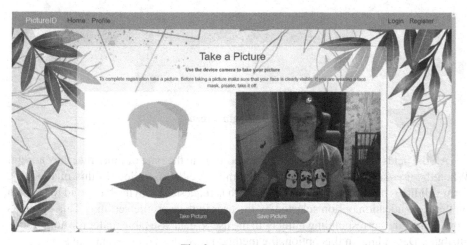

Fig. 2. Camera screen

The component has a brief description of the process, which differs depending on the user's activity. In registration or picture update mode, it asks the user to take off a face mask to make a clear face picture for the profile; in authentication mode, the user can keep the face mask. When the user clicks on the Take Picture button, this calls the triggerSnapshot() method, which triggers the triggerObservable and imageCapture event. Then the handleImage() method deals with the snapshot and assigns it to the webcamImage property to be displayed in the window by the camera window substituting the default placeholder picture. The newly taken user picture is sent to the back-end face recognition API in authentication mode, compared to the picture stored in the user profile. If the images match, the getToken() method from AccountService is called to request an authentication token from the back-end and set the session cookie for the user. In case of a mismatch, the user is informed and offered to take another picture.

6.3 Login Component

Login Component displays a form that the user must fill out to get authorized in the system. It contains a short description of the login process and the Submit Form button that remains disabled until the user correctly fills out the form. The form includes two required fields: Email and password, as shown in Fig. 3.

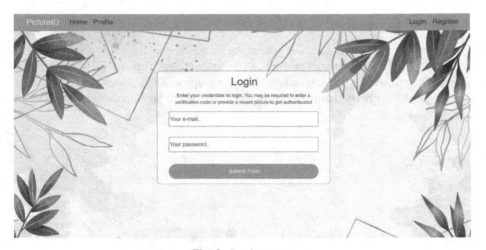

Fig. 3. Login screen

All the fields are client-side validated according to the type of input that they accept. When the user submits the form, the onSubmit() method is called. In this method, the form validity is once again checked. The token is requested from the back-end to get data on the authentication option selected by the user in their profile settings. This option is stored under the corresponding number in the users' database table under the auth_mode attribute. Depending on this option, the method proceeds in 4 different ways.

If authentication mode is set to email, the email model object is created with the values included in the email with confirmation code sent by the getCode() method called from AccountService. If authentication mode is set to face recognition, the user is redirected to Camera Component to take a picture. If authentication mode is set to phone, the user's phone number is obtained from the back-end database, and the method is called to send SMS with verification code to the user's phone. If the user disables authentication, the

Cookie Service [19] library creates a session cookie. However, in this case, the user will not see their picture and detailed information in the profile.

6.4 Profile Component

Profile Component is the most complex in the application as it incorporates various actions that the user can perform on the data stored in their account. The primary function of this component is to display user profile pictures and all other user details retrieved from the database upon login to the application, as shown in Fig. 4. However, if the user has turned off authentication, the picture and phone number will be hidden.

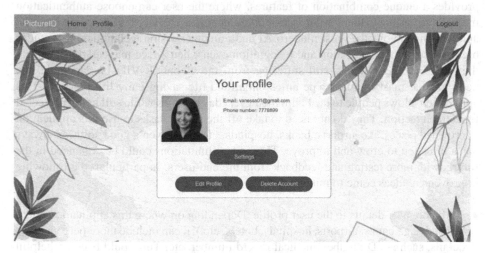

Fig. 4. General profile screen

Upon clicking on the Edit Profile button, the user can make changes to their profile. Here the user can update their profile picture by taking a new snapshot. When the user clicks on the Update Profile Picture button, the onChangePic() method redirects the user to the CameraComponent. By clicking on the Delete Profile Picture button, the user can delete the picture from their profile. This operation will trigger a warning popup that requires the user to confirm picture deletion as it cannot be reverted. Suppose the user confirms their intention to delete the image. In that case, the image is replaced by the default one, and the updateUserInfo() method is called to send the request to delete the user picture reference from the database.

6.5 Results Analysis

Primarily all the requirements gathered and defined during the initial stages of the project planning were implemented. The following testing strategy was to test the application with people who consent to take photos of them, use them as a dataset, and download some free copyright assets. As a result of the tryouts with people, an improvement of the recognition system was detected when the application had more pictures. Hence, a

decision to have 25 photos of the user was taken to improve the AI. The performance of
the eyes recognition system depends on the number of users plus the number of pictures
of each user; thus, we can consider the complexity as O(n^2). Regarding performance,
it is not good to have more than 25 because the AI will delay too much to execute the
Local Binary Pattern Histogram values.

7 Conclusions and Future Work

The resulting product came out to be a nice-looking dynamic web application offering
users a great and intuitive experience along with security and peace of mind. The solution
provides a unique combination of features, where the user can choose authentication
methods according to their preference or circumstances. The face recognition part of the
application employs the most modern AI and computer vision techniques. It provides
highly accurate face detection and recognition even when a face mask partially covers
the face. In today's world, still suffering from the global COVID-19 pandemic, the
need to wear masks has become an essential and life-saving daily life practice. This
application allows people to deal with their everyday routines while still being protected
from the infection. They do not need to take off their face masks to use this application
in crowded places like airports, banks, hospitals, etc. Still, even a good solution always
has a direction to grow and improve. Thus, some limitations could be enhanced in the
future, with more testing and feedback from the end-users. In particular, the following
improvement ideas come to mind:

- Add more user details to the user profile. Depending on where this application could
  be used (e.g., banks, airports, hospitals, hotels, etc.), it can include more personal user
  details, such as ID number, medical record number, etc. This could become helpful
  in places where people need to be quickly and accurately identified.
- Potentially more alternative authentication methods can be added, like fingerprint
  detection, voice recognition, etc. This could give people more choices and, therefore,
  attract more users.

References

1. Talahua, J.S., Buele, J., Calvopiña, P., Varela-Aldás, J.: Facial recognition system for people
   with and without face mask in times of the COVID-19 pandemic. Sustainability 13(12), 6900
   (2021)
2. Hassani, A., Malik, H.: Securing facial recognition: the new spoofs and solutions. Biom.
   Technol. Today 2021(5), 5–9 (2021)
3. Elloumi, W., Cauchois, C., Pasqual, C.: Will face recognition revolutionise the shopping
   experience? Biom. Technol. Today 2021(3), 8–11 (2021)
4. Batagelj, B., Peer, P., Štruc, V., Dobrišek, S.: How to correctly detect face-masks for COVID-
   19 from visual information? Appl. Sci. 11(5), 2070 (2021)
5. Burgoyne, N., Cohn, A.S.: Lessons from the transition to relational teletherapy during COVID-
   19. Fam. Process 59(3), 974–988 (2020)

6. Li, Y., Guo, K., Lu, Y., Liu, L.: Cropping and attention-based approach for masked face recognition. Appl. Intell. **51**(5), 3012–3025 (2021)
7. Sanjaya, S.A., Rakhmawan, S.A.: Face mask detection using MobileNetV2 in the era of COVID-19 pandemic. In: 2020 International Conference on Data Analytics for Business and Industry: Way Towards a Sustainable Economy, ICDABI 2020 (2020)
8. Hariri, W.: Efficient Masked Face Recognition Method During the COVID-19 Pandemic (2021)
9. Ding, F., Peng, P., Huang, Y., Geng, M., Tian, Y.: Masked face recognition with latent part detection. In: MM 2020 - Proceedings of the 28th ACM International Conference on Multimedia, pp. 2281–2289 (2020)
10. Montero, D., Nieto, M., Leskovsky, P., Aginako, N.: Boosting Masked Face Recognition with Multi-Task ArcFace (2021)
11. Viola, P., Jones, M.: Rapid object detection using a boosted cascade of simple features. In: Proceedings of the IEEE Computer Society Conference on Computer Vision and Pattern Recognition, vol. 1 (2001)
12. Geng, M., Peng, P., Huang, Y., Tian, Y.: Masked face recognition with generative data augmentation and domain constrained ranking. In: MM 2020 - Proceedings of the 28th ACM International Conference on Multimedia, pp. 2246–2254 (2020)
13. Lin, S., Cai, L., Lin, X., Ji, R.: Masked face detection via a modified LeNet. Neurocomputing **218**, 197–202 (2016)
14. Boutros, F., Damer, N., Kirchbuchner, F., Kuijper, A.: Unmasking Face Embeddings by Self-restrained Triplet Loss for Accurate Masked Face Recognition (2021)
15. Anwar, A., Raychowdhury, A.: Masked Face Recognition for Secure Authentication, (2020)
16. Mandal, B., Okeukwu, A., Theis, Y.: Masked Face Recognition using ResNet-50 (2021)
17. BioID Facial Recognition App. https://www.bioid.com/facial-recognition-app/. Accessed 25 June 2021
18. Simplified Mobile Face Recognition Attendance Management Solution. https://railer.com/. Accessed 27 June 2021
19. NGX Cookie Service. https://www.npmjs.com/package/ngx-cookie-service. Accessed 05 July 2021
20. ngx-webcam. https://www.npmjs.com/package/ngx-webcam. Accessed 05 July 2021

A Deep-Learning Based Automated COVID-19 Physical Distance Measurement System Using Surveillance Video

Masum Shah Junayed[1,2]([✉])(iD) and Md Baharul Islam[3](iD)

[1] Department of Computer Engineering, Bahcesehir University, Istanbul, Turkey
masumshahjunayed@gmail.com
[2] Department of CSE, Daffodil International University, Dhaka, Bangladesh
[3] College of Data Science and Engineering, American University of Malta, Bormla, Malta

Abstract. The contagious Corona Virus (COVID-19) transmission can be reduced by following and maintaining physical distancing (also known as COVID-19 social distance). The World Health Organisation (WHO) recommends it to prevent COVID-19 from spreading in public areas. On the other hand, people may not be maintaining the required 2-m physical distance as a mandated safety precaution in shopping malls and public places. The spread of the fatal disease may be slowed by an active monitoring system suitable for identifying distances between people and alerting them. This paper introduced a deep learning-based system for automatically detecting physical distance using video from security cameras. The proposed system employed the fine-tuning YOLO v4 for object detection and classification and Deepsort for tracking the detected people using bounding boxes from the video. Pairwise L2 vectorized normalization was utilized to generate a three-dimensional feature space for tracking physical distances and the violation index, determining the number of individuals who follow the distance rules. For training and testing, we use the MS COCO and Oxford Town Centre (OTC) datasets. We compared the proposed system to two well-known object detection models, YOLO v3 and Faster RCNN. Our method obtained a weighted mAP score of 87.8% and an FPS score of 28; both are computationally comparable.

Keywords: COVID-19 Social distancing · Human detection and tracking · Distance measurement · Crowd monitoring · Video surveillance

1 Introduction

Corona Virus (COVID-19) is a highly contagious worldwide virus that has wreaked havoc globally. It has created distance among people. The Corona

© Springer Nature Switzerland AG 2022
KC Santosh et al. (Eds.): RTIP2R 2021, CCIS 1576, pp. 210–222, 2022.
https://doi.org/10.1007/978-3-031-07005-1_19

Pandemic affected about 220 nations and regions worldwide, with roughly 197,201,247 confirmed cases since July 2021 [31]. Numerous COVID-19 virus variants have already been identified worldwide. This virus is continuously evolving due to mutations. Recently, scientists discovered a novel variation in India, dubbed the Delta variant. The Delta strain spreads at a rate that is several times that of other strains [9]. It is dominating the world health sector.

To prevent the massive spread of COVID-19, the WHO establishes specific fundamental guidelines for humans, such as maintaining physical distance from others, wearing a face mask, washing hands for 20 s, wearing PPE, and staying at home. However, it is difficult for the government to control individuals in public areas. As a result, governments in many countries altered their policies to minimize the number of people in public places, such as closing all educational institutions, limiting person attendance in the workplace, and maintaining a distance of at least 2 m for garment workers wearing a face mask. Furthermore, several software firms established their internet offices from home. The physical distance between people contributes to the reduction of COVID - 19 virus transmission. Numerous institutions initiate a program to remove individuals from densely populated regions to reduce the COVID - 19 spread. For instance, the government puts police officers in public areas to ensure public safety, security, and physical distance. The traditional approach (check individuals by security personnel) are tedious, time-consuming, and imprecise. The primary purpose of doing this study is to determine the distance between individuals using a real-time video, which also helps to protect the particular place from the spreading of COVID-19. Our system effectively identifies physical spaces and improves the safety from COVID-19 in specific regions such as constructions and garments areas.

The technology is expected to use the latest machine learning technology, and surveillance cameras in the building to identify whether or not individuals are keeping a safe physical distance from each other based on real-time video feeds [2]. This technology is also said to connect with security cameras at various businesses to prevent employees from working too closely together. Three demonstration steps were provided, each representing a stage in the process of calibration, detection, and measurement.

The development of a wide variety of numerical techniques and models has allowed us to evaluate the evolution of pandemic processes throughout the last two years due to research on the assessment of physical distance in COVID-19 [14,17,23,25]. They spoke about how people's physical distance is affected by their social environment, and they brought up COVID-19's worry. Recently, some commercialized computer vision-based systems [3,7,15] for monitoring physical distance have been established. These methods are intriguing; however, there is no statistical analysis included in the findings. Additionally, there is little discussion of implementation. While the conversations are enlightening, they do not provide concrete results for measuring physical distance, leave the issue open, and may be considered undesirable by others.

Nevertheless, none of these approaches provide in-depth explanations of their methods, performance benchmarks, or logic for their detection algorithm selection. Some work that one must use a theoretical approach for physical distance, but leave out specifics of what steps can be taken in real life. In contrast, we have suggested a real-time automated surveillance system for detecting and monitoring people and measuring inter-distance between humans, assessing risk in real-time by warnings in the form of red text ('Unsafe') and counting them using the bounding boxes. Furthermore, our technology is crucial for observing the physical distance between peoples in density areas and controls entry to a particular location. Listed below are the most important contributions of this paper:

- We introduced a deep learning based automated system for monitoring and detecting people to reduce coronavirus expansion and economic costs.
- A fine-tuning Yolov4 [4] is used to detect and classify objects, while Deepsort [30] is used to track people in this system.
- We utilized pairwise L2 vectorized normalization, which uses the centroid coordinates and dimensions of the bounding box to create 3D feature space. We calculated how many people are not following the physical distance regulation using the violation index.

The following sections comprise the rest of this paper: Sect. 2 summarizes the relevant literature; Sect. 3 elaborates on the proposed approach; Sect. 4 explains the specifics of our experimental results and discussions. Finally, we conclude this article in Sect. 5.

2 Related Works

COVID-19 affects individuals differently, but it mainly spreads via droplet contact, physical touch, and airborne transmission. Physical distance may play an essential role in reducing the spread of COVID-19 [27]. As a result, everyone should be careful and observe the norms of physical distancing, such as keeping a set space (100 cm) between themselves and others. That is why it is also known as "Physical Distancing". Several techniques for detecting objects from movies and pictures have previously been suggested for a variety of applications [1]. This section has been discussed comprehensively in the literature review.

Bouhlel et al. [5] developed a video sequence technique that combines two approaches, the macroscopic and microscopic methods, to calculate the real-time distance between individuals. Based on the techniques, they utilized two kinds of datasets, Mayenberg and Mliki. They used a three-level categorization method to improve performance substantially; however, it is not suited for real-time use.

In the COVID-19 scenario, Razavi et al. [20] devised an automated method to monitor construction workers to guarantee their safety. When the employees are on duty, the system detects the face mask and the physical distance between them. They utilized Faster R-CNN Inception ResNet V2 for image detection to improve the system's accuracy. However, as the quantity of training data decreases, the accuracy decreases. Furthermore, the system is unable to detect the mask when the employees swivel their heads. They used Faster R-CNN Inception V2 to detect the distance between people. They calculated the actual distance traveled by the workers from the image in which the established method did not work effectively because their performance is not good.

Rahim et al. [19] proposed a technique for measuring physical distance in low-light environments. COCO location measurements were used to assess the trained model's performance. After utilizing the YOLO-v4 model for real-time object recognition and physical distance measurement but it's not real time. Two-stage locators achieve better restriction and item recognition accuracy, while one-stage locators achieve faster deduction speed [20]. The technology only works in settings with a fixed physical distance and two target items. Some prototypes that use machine learning and sensing technologies for physical distance tracking have been proposed. Landing AI [2] suggested a physical distance estimator that uses a security camera to identify individuals whose physical distance is less than the acceptable value. In a manufacturing facility, another system [13] was used to control and tracking labor movements and deliver real-time audio warnings. Along with security cameras, systems based on LiDAR and stereo cameras [26] were presented, demonstrating that other kinds of sensors than monitoring cameras can also be beneficial.

Using YOLOv3 and Deepsort, a new approach was presented for locating and tracking individuals [18] that involves monitoring the user's social distance. The procedure also measures the extent to which other non-social-distancing activities occur and then calculates an index of non-social-distancing behaviors. This method seems unique. However, it lacks any statistical analysis.

Rezaei et al. [23] introduced the DeepSOCIAL, which is the DNN based model. It uses cutting-edge deep learning methods to identify, track, and measure social distances. Furthermore, it detected social distance and used dynamic risk assessment. While this paper did not address pure violation detection, it did discover a method to help reduce congestion.

While the methods described above are intriguing, collecting data and issuing invasive warnings may be considered undesirable by some individuals. On the contrary, we present an automated system capable of real-time human identification, tracking, and physical distance measurement and indicating whether a person is safe or unsafe.

3   Proposed Method

This section describes our approach system for physical distancing monitoring consisting of three stages: detection and tracking of persons, inter-distance calculation, and zone-based infection risk evaluations. The system is designed to operate with and is suitable for all types of CCTV security cameras, independent of video quality and real-time depiction of identified people and their distance. Figure 1 shows the flow of the proposed system. The system is divided into three parts: detection, tracking, and distance estimation. The subsections show the full process of our suggested system.

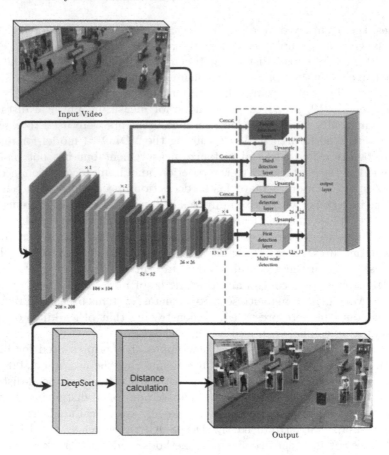

Fig. 1. The architecture of the proposed physical distancing system. Fine tuned Yolo-v4 used for human Detection and classification, deepsort and pairwise L2 norm are used to tracking and physical distancing.

3.1 Human Detection

A real-time human detector is introduced for the complex environment that contains various objects to identify people correctly. This detector has a feature extractor and classification module, which is based on Yolo-v4 [4]. A fundamental strategy of improving the exactness feature extraction of CNN-based detectors [11] is to broaden the receptive field and increase the system's complexity employing additional layers whereas identifying tiny objects more effectively. Instead, for easier training, we utilized a skip-connections method. Consequently, to decrease the size of the parameter, a modified CSPDarknet53 is utilized as a feature extractor for this model. There are few backbones more suited to categorization than detection. For image classification, CSPResNext50 outperforms CSPDarknet53, while CSPDarknet53 outperforms CSPResNext50 in object or human detection [28].

Recently, several recent suggested models have been included layers termed the neck between the feature extraction and classification layers, which are used to gather features from various phases of the backbone network. The neck portion comprises multiple top-down and bottom-up pathways that gather and integrate network characteristics in various layers to produce a more realistic picture and features. We used a pyramid method to increase the receptive field and extract various scales from the feature extraction, followed by multi-scale detection in the head section to identify and categorize tiny objects like people.

We utilize the same setup in the head section as YOLO-v4. YOLO-v4, like many other anchor-based models, detects numerous objects by using preset boxes. The object identification model will next be trained to predict which of the produced anchor boxes belong to which class. Following that, depending on the classification and regression loss, an offset will be utilized to modify the anchor box's size to suit the ground-truth data effectively.

3.2 Human Tracking

Deepsort [30] is used to track people in any video in human tracking. It is created by using discovered from identified humans in pictures pattern, which subsequently is coupled with temporal data to forecast the subjects' trajectories. It maps unique IDs to keep track of each item under investigation for statistical analysis. Deepsort can also be used to deal with occlusion, numerous perspectives, and annotation of training data. In Deepsort, Kalman filter and Hungarian algorithm have been commonly employed for accurate tracking. For improved association, the Kalman filter is employed recursively, and it can forecast future locations based on present positions [29]. We subsequently utilize this time information to assess the severity of physical distance breaches and the presence of high-risk zones on the scene. The status of each individual in a frame is represented by the following this equation:

$$F = [x, y, a, b, x\prime, y\prime, a\prime]^T \tag{1}$$

where (x, y) indicates the target bounding box's horizontal and vertical positions; a signifies the scale (area); and b specifies the bounding box's aspect ratio. $x\prime$, $y\prime$, $a\prime$ are the anticipated values for the horizontal area, vertical area, and bounding box centroid, respectively, as predicted by the Kalman filter.

We performed the following matrix D_t, which contains the position of the n identified persons in the image carrier grid: After completing the detection and tracking procedure (P^t), for each input frame $w * h$ at time t, we define the following matrix:

$$D_t = \{P^t_{x_n, y_n} | x_n \in w, y_n \in h\} \tag{2}$$

3.3 Distance Measurement

Researchers have developed various 2D and 3D depth estimation techniques [8]. We calculated the distance between identified tracked individuals on each image and video.

The deepsort model generates a collection of bounding boxes and an ID for each person detected in the previous phase. When working with bounding boxes (such as rectangular boxes), coordinates (x, y) in the 3D (x, y, d) feature space. However, to the picture that was obtained from the camera, the reduced 2D space of (x, y) correlates to two parameters (x, y) alone, and depth (z) is not accessible. To better visualize the 3D shape of each bounding box, imagine every point in space equates to three values (x, y, z). Using this Eq. 3, the 2D pixel coordinates (x, y) as an input, the world coordinate points are then mapped to the points on the screen (X_w, Y_w, Z_w) [24].

$$[x, y, 1]^T = KRT[X_w, Y_w, Z_w, 1]^T \tag{3}$$

Here, K, R, and T represent the rotation, translation, and intrinsic matrix, respectively. This feature space indicate the coordinates of the centroid, and the value of d describes the depth of each object [16]. We computed the following Eq. 4 to estimate the depth between camera and objects, which can be acquired by studying the form of the image [12].

$$d = \frac{2\pi \times 180}{(w \times h \times 360) \times 1000 + 3} \tag{4}$$

where w denotes the bounding box's width, and h denotes the bounding box's height. The pairwise L2 normalization is calculated for the collection of bounding boxes as provided by the following Eq. 5.

$$|D| = \sqrt{\sum_{i=1}^{n}(q_i - p_i)^2} \tag{5}$$

where we define this equation n = 3. Here, D represent the distance and q_i and p_i represents pixels (range 90 to 170) between two humans. After locating the individual's neighbors using the L2 norm, we allocate them based on their proximity sensitivity. The proximity threshold is constantly updated with a large number of tests using a set of numbers between 90 to 170 pixels wide, depending on the person's position in a particular frame. To use the proximity property, every person in the system must be given at least one neighbor or many additional neighbors to create a group in distinct color-coding. The creation of groups implies the breach of the physical distance practice, which is measured using the following equation:

$$v_i = \frac{n_p}{n_g} \tag{6}$$

where v_i represents the index of violation. To calculate the number of groups or clusters present in the video, the number of separate groups or clusters detected (n_g) and n_p defines the total number of individuals close to those groups or clusters nearby.

4   Experimental Results and Discussions

4.1   Dataset and Training Details

Our proposed system is trained on object detection MS COCO dataset [6] that has 80 classes and 123k images. The bounding box labels on each image were additionally annotated with the matching coordinates. The transfer learning concept was used to train the Yolov4 based model, then fine-tuned and optimized before being used to train the proposed model on the MS COCO dataset. We utilized SGD with warm restarts to alter the learning rate throughout the training phase. It aided in breaking out of local minima in the solution space and saving training time. The technique started with a high learning rate, slowed it down midway, and then decreased the learning rate for each batch with a slight downward slope. It has the effect of jumpstarting the solution space out of local minima, saving the training time. A high learning rate was used in the beginning stage and slowed down midway. Progressively, the learning rate was decreased for each batch, with a minimal drop in speed.

To evaluate the proposed system, we used another dataset, the Oxford town Centre (OTC) dataset [10], an unknown and complex dataset with a high frequency of object recognition overlapping and overcrowded zones. The collection also included a wide range of human clothing and looks in the public location real world. FPS, mAP, and total loss in identifying the individual, as shown in Fig. 2, are constantly measured throughout the validation period.

All training and testing performed on the same PC, which has a Windows 10 operating system, an Intel Core i9-10850K CPU running at 3.6 GHz, 64 GB of RAM, and an NVIDIA GeForce RTX 2080 super GPU. We utilized PyTorch, a CUDA environment, and a vscode editor to implement it.

Table 1. Two well-known object detectors and the proposed YOLO-v4 with two backbones are compared in real-time human detection.

Method	Backbone	mAP	NOI	Total loss	FPS
Faster RCNN [22]	–	0.813	12538	1.98	27
YOLO-v3 [21]	Darknet53	0.839	12135	1.85	26
Modified YOLO-v4	CSPResNext50	0.859	12894	0.96	**29**
	CSPDarknet53	**0.878**	13529	1.71	28

4.2   Results and Discussions

Table 1 shows the performance of human detection with two well-known object detectors and the modified YOLO-v4. The modified YOLO-v4 is evaluated in the proposed system using two alternative backbones: CSPResNext50 and CSPDarknet53. The faster RCNN and the YOLO-v3 models are utilized to compare with the proposed YOLO-v4 for human detection and tracking. The Faster RCNN attained an accuracy of 0.813 mAP and a frame rate (FPS) of 27. The YOLO-v3 achieved an mAP of 0.839 with a frame rate of 26 FPS. It outperforms faster RCNN while falls shorter FPS. This table illustrates the performance of the proposed YOLO-v4 in the two backbones. The mAP, iteration number, training loss (TL), and FPS are compared. The CSPDarknet53 backbone has the highest mAP of 0.878 and TL of 1.71, but CSPResNext50 achieves the highest FPS of 29. The proposed system outperforms the backbone of the CSPDarknet53.

We calculated the evaluation matrics of mean average error (MAE) and average closest physical distance, d_{avg} for the overall frame for measuring physical distance. We calculated the $d_{avg} = \frac{1}{N}\sum_{i=1}^{m} d_i^{min}$, where $d_i^{min} = min(d_{i,j})$, $\forall j \neq i \in \{1,2,..n\}$ is the closest physical distance between number of humans and the MAE of the social distancing violation ratio $r_v = \frac{v}{n}$, where v is the number of humans who break the physical distance and n is total number of people.

Table 2. Performance of physical distance.

Methods	MAE of d_{avg} (meter)	MAE of r_v (count)
Proposed YOLO-v4 (CSPResNext50)	1.516	0.192
Proposed YOLO-v4 (CSPDarknet53)	**0.568**	**0.139**

The performance of physical distance (also known as COVID-19 social distance) is shown in Table 2. It calculates the amount of time it takes to identify breaches of physical distance. The proposed YOLO-v4 with CSPResNext50 and CSPDarknet53 backbones is showed the performance of measuring physical distance and violation of physical distance on the OTC dataset. In the CSPResNext50 backbone, the proposed YOLO-v4 has achieved 1.516 $davg$ and 0.192 rv of MAE. Our proposed method outperforms the CSPDarknet53 backbone, obtaining an MAE of 0.568 $davg$ and 0.139 rv on the OTC dataset. Figure 2 shows the lowest and average closest distances. The blue line shows the average number of individuals who are near each other, while the orange line represents the lowest number of people in this dataset.

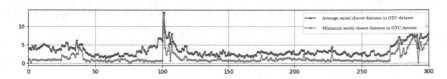

Fig. 2. Minimum vs. average physical closest distance in Oxford Town Center dataset. (Color figure online)

Figure 3 shows how the frequency of social distance violations correlates with the social density $(human/m^2)$ in 2D histograms on the OTC dataset. A violation rises with a rise in social density. It can be seen in the graph where the

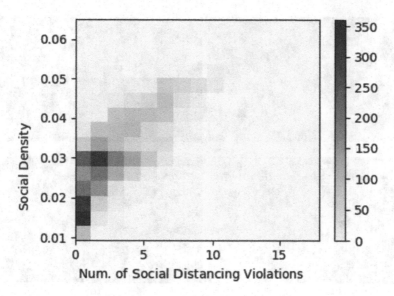

Fig. 3. 2D histograms that visualize the frequency of social distance violations vs. social density. The observation on the histograms correlates with a positive correlation.

two variables (social density and violation) are linearly related to one another. In addition, it is possible to use the suggested linear regression.

Figure 4 depicts the detection and physical distancing outcomes of the proposed approach. The distance between people is shown in this diagram. It shows the safe and count number with a white bounding box if the distance between two people is more than 100 cm. On the other hand, the bounding box was red with the 'unsafe' word and contained a count of dangerous people from the input video.

Table 3. Comparison of the proposed system with the state-of-the-art methods to perform real-time physical distancing measures at frames per second (FPS).

Approaches	Dataset	Input size	FPS
Pouw et al. [17]	OTC	–	10
Punn et al. [18]	OTC	–	23
Rezaei et al. [23]	OTC	512 × 512	24.1
Yang et al. [32]	OTC	1920 × 1080	25
Saponara et al. [25]	OTC	–	27
Ours	OTC	640 × 640	28

To illustrate the efficiency of the suggested approach, we compared our findings to those of previous techniques in Table 3. Rezaei et al. [23], and Yang et al. [25] presented the techniques and obtained fps of 24.1 and 25 with 512 × 512 and

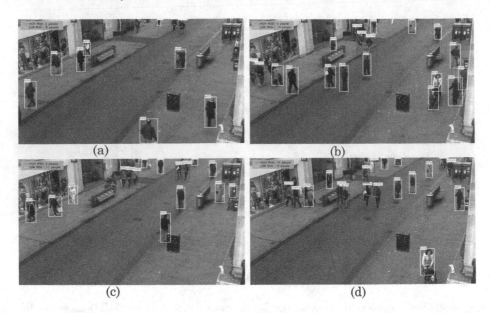

Fig. 4. Output of the proposed physical distancing system. Here, (a), (b), (c), (d) represents the low risk, lower medium risk, medium risk and high risk. (Color figure online)

1920 × 1080 input sizes, indicating that this method works well when the input size is big. In the suggested system, our input size is just 640 × 640. However, our FPS is 28. So, the proposed approach achieves high FPS on the same OTC dataset and received better than the state-of-the-arts.

5 Conclusion

This research introduced a deep learning-based automated system that works on real-time physical distance monitoring, detecting, and tracking people using bounding boxes. We used fine-tune YOLO v4 for object detection and classification in this system, and Deepsort was used for monitoring the human. We calculated the physical distance between two or more peoples using pairwise L2 normalization to create 3D feature space. To monitor the physical distance, we generate a bounding box with text (safe and unsafe) indicating and monitoring who follows/breaks the actual distance. The number of violations is verified by calculating the number of groups created and the violation index term as the ratio of individuals to groups. The suggested approach for detecting people and estimating physical distances is tested using the Oxford Town Centre dataset, including over 7,500 people detection and distance estimates. The system performed well under various conditions, including occlusion, illumination changes, and partial vision. It demonstrated a significant improvement in the mAP score of 0.878 and the speed of 28 FPS, which comparatively outperforms the well-known YOLO v3 and Faster RCNN object detectors. In the future, we apply this technique to mobile cameras, such as those placed on autonomous drones. Drones are thus easier to control and therefore more effective at tracking fast-moving objects in all directions.

References

1. Ahmed, F., Zviedrite, N., Uzicanin, A.: Effectiveness of workplace social distancing measures in reducing influenza transmission: a systematic review. BMC Public Health **18**(1), 1–13 (2018)
2. AI, L.: Landing AI creates an AI tool to help customers monitor social distancing in the workplace (2021). https://landing.ai/. Accessed 07 June 2021
3. Bentafat, E., Rathore, M.M., Bakiras, S.: A practical system for privacy-preserving video surveillance. In: Conti, M., Zhou, J., Casalicchio, E., Spognardi, A. (eds.) Applied Cryptography and Network Security, ACNS 2020. LNCS, vol. 12147, pp. 21–39. Springer, Cham (2020). https://doi.org/10.1007/978-3-030-57878-7_2
4. Bochkovskiy, A., Wang, C.Y., Liao, H.Y.M.: YOLOv4: optimal speed and accuracy of object detection. arXiv preprint arXiv:2004.10934 (2020)
5. Bouhlel, F., Mliki, H., Hammami, M.: Crowd behavior analysis based on convolutional neural network: social distancing control COVID-19. In: VISIGRAPP (5: VISAPP), pp. 273–280 (2021)
6. Chen, X., et al.: Microsoft coco captions: data collection and evaluation server. arXiv preprint arXiv:1504.00325 (2015)
7. Das, S., et al.: Computer vision-based social distancing surveillance solution with optional automated camera calibration for large scale deployment. arXiv preprint arXiv:2104.10891 (2021)
8. Gloudemans, D., Gloudemans, N., Abkowitz, M., Barbour, W., Work, D.B.: Quantifying social distancing compliance and the effects of behavioral interventions using computer vision. In: Proceedings of the Workshop on Data-Driven and Intelligent Cyber-Physical Systems, pp. 1–5 (2021)
9. Guardian, T.: Delta variant of COVID spreading rapidly and detected in 74 countries (2021). https://www.theguardian.com/world/2021/jun/14/. Accessed 25 June 2021
10. Harvey, A., LaPlace, J.: Megapixels: origins, ethics, and privacy implications of publicly available face recognition image datasets. Megapixels **1**, 6 (2019)
11. Junayed, M.S., Islam, M.B., Sadeghzadeh, A., Aydin, T.: Real-time YOLO-based heterogeneous front vehicles detection. In: 2021 International Conference on Innovations in Intelligent Systems and Applications (INISTA), pp. 1–7. IEEE (2021)
12. Khan, M.A., Paul, P., Rashid, M., Hossain, M., Ahad, M.A.R.: An AI-based visual aid with integrated reading assistant for the completely blind. IEEE Trans. Hum.-Mach. Syst. **50**(6), 507–517 (2020)
13. Khandelwal, P., Khandelwal, A., Agarwal, S., Thomas, D., Xavier, N., Raghuraman, A.: Using computer vision to enhance safety of workforce in manufacturing in a post COVID world. arXiv preprint arXiv:2005.05287 (2020)
14. Ksentini, A., Brik, B.: An edge-based social distancing detection service to mitigate COVID-19 propagation. IEEE Internet Things Mag. **3**(3), 35–39 (2020)
15. Nguyen, C.T., et al.: A comprehensive survey of enabling and emerging technologies for social distancing-part II: Emerging technologies and open issues. IEEE Access **8**, 154209–154236 (2020)

16. Pias: object detection and distance measurement (2021). https://github.com/paul-pias/Object-Detection-and-Distance-Measurement/. Accessed 11 Mar 2021

17. Pouw, C.A., Toschi, F., van Schadewijk, F., Corbetta, A.: Monitoring physical distancing for crowd management: real-time trajectory and group analysis. PLoS ONE **15**(10), e0240963 (2020)

18. Punn, N.S., Sonbhadra, S.K., Agarwal, S., Rai, G.: Monitoring COVID-19 social distancing with person detection and tracking via fine-tuned YOLO v3 and deep-sort techniques. arXiv preprint arXiv:2005.01385 (2020)

19. Rahim, A., Maqbool, A., Rana, T.: Monitoring social distancing under various low light conditions with deep learning and a single motionless time of flight camera. PLoS ONE **16**(2), e0247440 (2021)

20. Razavi, M., Alikhani, H., Janfaza, V., Sadeghi, B., Alikhani, E.: An automatic system to monitor the physical distance and face mask wearing of construction workers in COVID-19 pandemic. arXiv preprint arXiv:2101.01373 (2021)

21. Redmon, J., Farhadi, A.: YOLOv3: an incremental improvement. arXiv preprint arXiv:1804.02767 (2018)

22. Ren, S., He, K., Girshick, R., Sun, J.: Faster R-CNN: towards real-time object detection with region proposal networks. IEEE Trans. Pattern Anal. Mach. Intell. **39**(6), 1137–1149 (2016)

23. Rezaei, M., Azarmi, M.: Deepsocial: social distancing monitoring and infection risk assessment in COVID-19 pandemic. Appl. Sci. **10**(21), 7514 (2020)

24. Rezaei, M., Klette, R.: Computer Vision for Driver Assistance. Springer, Cham(2017). https://doi.org/10.1007/978-3-319-50551-0

25. Saponara, S., Elhanashi, A., Gagliardi, A.: Implementing a real-time, AI-based, people detection and social distancing measuring system for COVID-19. J. Real-Time Image Process. **18**, 1–11 (2021). https://doi.org/10.1007/s11554-021-01070-6

26. Supply, L.: Landing AI creates an AI tool to help customers monitor social distancing in the workplace (2021). https://levelfivesupplies.com/social-distance-monitoring/. Accessed 02 June 2021

27. Suresh, K., Bhuvan, S., Palangappa, M.: Social distance identification using optimized faster region-based convolutional neural network. In: 2021 5th International Conference on Computing Methodologies and Communication (ICCMC), pp. 753–760. IEEE (2021)

28. Wang, C.Y., Liao, H.Y.M., Wu, Y.H., Chen, P.Y., Hsieh, J.W., Yeh, I.H.: CSPNet: a new backbone that can enhance learning capability of CNN. In: Proceedings of the IEEE/CVF Conference on Computer Vision and Pattern Recognition Workshops, pp. 390–391 (2020)

29. Wojke, N., Bewley, A.: Deep cosine metric learning for person re-identification. In: 2018 IEEE Winter Conference on Applications of Computer Vision (WACV), pp. 748–756. IEEE (2018)

30. Wojke, N., Bewley, A., Paulus, D.: Simple online and realtime tracking with a deep association metric. In: 2017 IEEE International Conference on Image Processing (ICIP), pp. 3645–3649. IEEE (2017)

31. Worldometer: COVID-19 CORONAVIRUS PANDEMIC (2021). https://www.worldometers.info/coronavirus/?utm_campaign=homeAdvegas1?. Accessed 18 June 2021

32. Yang, D., Yurtsever, E., Renganathan, V., Redmill, K., Özgüner, Ü.: A vision-based social distance and critical density detection system for COVID-19 (2020)

Face Mask Detection Using Deep Hybrid Network Architectures

Aryan Vikas Jain[1](✉), Shubham Chakrabarti[1](✉), and Lalit Garg[2](✉)

[1] SRM Institute of Science and Technology, Ghaziabad, India
aryanvikasjain@gmail.com, shubhamchakrabarti@gmail.com
[2] L-Università ta' Malta, Msida MSD 2080, Malta
lalit.garg@um.edu.mt

Abstract. As the world has been severely affected by Novel Coronavirus, scientists have been working hard to study this rapidly evolving virus, its long-term and short-term implications, and how to stop its spread. As newer variants of the virus are discovered, it has become even more important to enforce the various steps required to curb its spread. We can only fight this virus by wearing masks, using sanitizers, and social distancing. This paper proposes a hybrid masked face detection model for implementing the proper use of face masks. Our study focuses on combining machine learning models and Neural Networks. Even though various models have been proposed in the past for face mask detection, we tried to change the conventional machine learning methods by creating hybrid models like ResNet50 and VGG16 and combining classical machine learning models like SVM and Gradient Booster, and Neural Networks and comparing their performance. The Hybrid model architecture consisting of ResNet50 + SVM significantly outperformed the other models, returning an accuracy and precision of more than 97 and close to 100% each respectively.

Keywords: COVID-19 · Deep learning · ResNet50 · Support vector machine · VGG16 · Transfer learning · Hybrid models

1 Introduction and Problem Understanding

As a pandemic of an unforeseen magnitude disrupted our lives completely, it has become increasingly important to protect ourselves. The virus that causes COVID-19 is mainly transmitted through droplets generated when an infected person coughs, sneezes, or exhales. These droplets are too heavy to hang in the air and quickly fall on floors or surfaces [1]. New research also indicates that airborne transmission of the virus may also occur in the form of aerosol particles that may remain suspended in the air for hours [2]. Cases have been reduced in many countries, but on the other hand, new variants are also found in different parts of the world. Therefore, wearing masks, sanitization, and social distancing is the only way to protect ourselves. We, therefore, decided to use AI to ensure

© Springer Nature Switzerland AG 2022
KC Santosh et al. (Eds.): RTIP2R 2021, CCIS 1576, pp. 223–233, 2022.
https://doi.org/10.1007/978-3-031-07005-1_20

that people wear masks as this is one of the most effective methods to curb the spread of this disease. We trained Deep Learning (ResNet50, DeepNet121) and classical Machine Learning models (Support Vector Machine, Gradient Boosted Decision tree, etc.). We also used transfer learning to create Hybrid Models. Overall we found that Hybrid Models generalised better than classical Machine Learning algorithms (which did not overfit as much as Gradient Boosted Decision Trees, for example) and were quicker overall than Deep Learning Models alone (e.g., ResNet-50 or DenseNet-121). The dataset we used is a state-of-the-art masked-faced dataset consisting of images having various orientations and occlusion degrees, while a mask occludes at least one part of each face.

2   Related Works

Most of the research work priorly is done on Deep learning models, traditional machine algorithms, and pre-trained models. Yande Li et al. [3] propose two approaches to masked face recognition: attention-based approach and cropping-based approach. The researchers conducted extensive experiments using SMFRD, CISIAWebface, AR and Extend Yela B datasets. In the attention-based approach the Convolutional Block Attention Module (CBAM) was used to focus on the areas around the eyes. In [6], authors worked with the MobileNetV2 model and used adam optimizers for classifying images in 2 categories - with mask and without. In [7], the authors developed a face mask-wearing identification method. They classified into three categories for people wearing masks properly, incorrectly no people without a mask. Saber et al. [8] applied the principal component analysis on masked and unmasked face recognition to acknowledge the person. They found that the accuracy of face recognition using the PCA is extremely affected by wearing masks. In [9], authors have worked on various datasets and compared many pre-trained models like AlexNet, ResNet50, VGG16, etc. They have used a high-end GPU system for model training and classified images into three categories: correct, incorrect, and not wearing masks. [10] created the SSDMNV2 model with an architecture consisting of (SSD + ResNet-10 + MobileNetV2) and compared their models with pre-trained models like LeNet - 5 AlexNet, VGG -16, and ResNet - 50. They classified the model into two categories - with a mask or without a mask. In [11], the authors used a hybrid model to detect SARS-CoV-2 using X-ray scans of the chest area. The hybrid model consisted of SVM and ResNet50. They extracted features of ResNet50 and utilized them in SVM Classifier. They achieved excellent model performance across a variety of metrics.

David Montero et al. [12] presented their approach based on the ArcFace model used in normal face recognition. The researchers applied some enhancements to this model and generated masked versions of three popular face-recognition datasets: Labeled Faces in the Wild (LFW), Celebrities in Frontal-Profile in the Wild (CFP) and Aged. The experiments conducted on these datasets showed that the enhanced ArcFace model was very effective in masked face recognition, while still preserving the same high level of performance in normal face recognition. In addition, this model showed 99.78% accuracy for checking if a person in the picture is wearing a mask. S. Lin et al. [13] modified LeNet which changes the number of units in the output layer of LeNet and increases the number of feature maps with smaller filter sizes. B. Mandal et al. [14] Deep learning-based model ResNet-50 real-world masked face recognition dataset (RMFRD): 5,000 masked faces of 525 people and 90,000 unmasked faces. Authors report that their experiments in masked face recognition gave an accuracy of 47.91%. Therefore, they conclude that the model should be further improved. M. Loey et al. [15] in their research also proposed a similar architecture of ResNet50 + SVM and got impressive results on their test data. Their test dataset however consisted of LFW (Labeled Faces in the Wild) which consists of computer-generated images which are of a significantly lower quality as opposed to RMFD and SMFD which led us to conduct our own research on MAFA instead.

3 Dataset and Data Preprocessing

3.1 Data Description

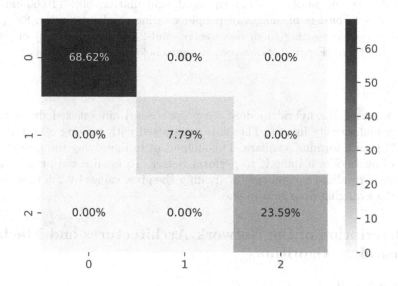

Fig. 1. Confusion matrix of the dataset

The inherent problem with detecting masked faces (i.e., faces with occlusions) is two main reasons: 1) The absence of large datasets of masked faces, and 2) The absence of facial cues from the masked regions. To address these issues, we are using images from the MAFA dataset totalling 23,314 images. From these 15,452 images were used for training and the rest (7862) were used for testing [16].

Fig. 2. Sample photos of the dataset

Different from many previous datasets, each annotated face in MAFA is partially occluded by a mask. Although the dataset is constructed for masked/occluded face reconstruction, its eclectic variety of images belongs to different classes based on race, gender, etc.

In Fig. 1, '0' represents correctly worn masks, '1' represents incorrectly worn and '0' denotes no masks. As per the confusion matrix, 69% (10,603images) of our dataset consists of images of people wearing masks correctly, 8% (1204 images) of people wearing them incorrectly, and 24% (3645 images) of people not wearing them. Figure 2 shows some images belonging to the dataset.

3.2   Resizing

Before applying the hybrid models, we preprocessed our masked dataset. We had very high-quality images. Therefore we started with resizing each image to 244 * 244 pixels, forming a square. This helped us in improving the generalising ability of our model helping it to perform better. To finalize the preprocessing phase, we normalized each image by dividing the pixel values by 255 to scale the pixel values ranging from zero to one.

4   Description of the Network Architectures and Machine Learning Algorithms

4.1   ResNet50

According to [16,17], ResNet-50 has achieved better results when it is used as a feature extractor. Figure 4 illustrates the proposed classical transfer learning model. The ResNet50 was used for the feature extraction phase, while the traditional machine learning model was used in the training, validation, and testing phase.

A residual neural network (ResNet) is a kind of deep transfer learning based on residual learning [18]. All types of ResNet-101, ResNet-50, and ResNet-18 are versions of ResNet to get rid of the problem of vanishing gradients that have their specific residual block. ResNet-50 consists of 50-layers, starting with a convolution layer, and ending with a fully connected layer and in between, followed by 16 residual bottleneck blocks. Each block has three convolution layers.

ResNet50 is a gigantic network architecture consisting of various Conv2D, Activation, and Batch normalization layers, and it consists of 23,587,712 parameters. The last layer of the architecture was the activation function with shape (, 7, 7, 2048). We added a flatten layer as a feature layer with shape (, 100352). These features are then used in machine learning algorithms for model training.

4.2 VGG16

VGG is a very deep convolutional neural network model proposed by K. Simonyan and A. Zisserman, professors and researchers from the Visual Geometry Group at the University of Oxford [19]. By achieving 92.7% test accuracy in ImageNet, a dataset of over 14 million images belonging to 1000 classes.

It follows this sequence of convolution and max pool layers consistently along the entire architecture. Being a very deep network, VGG16 is an incredibly extensive network and has a total of around 138 million parameters. Even today, VGG is one of the most used image-recognition architectures in multiple industries, primarily for face recognition and detection tasks.

VGG16 is not a large deep network architecture like ResNet50, and it has 14,714,688 parameters, but the architecture's combination of Conv2D and Max-Pooling2D makes it different from others and has shown great performance in the past. Its last layer, the MaxPooling2D layer('block5_pool'), has a shape (, 7, 7, 512), we used a flatten layer for creating a feature tensor for feature extraction, and its shape was (, 25088).

4.3 Support Vector Machines

Support Vector Machiner or SVM was developed in the early 1960s s as a way to create nonlinear classifiers by applying the kernel trick to maximum-margin hyperplanes to solve pattern recognition problems. The SVM, originally introduced by Vapnik, is a technique of classification and regression which is now used in a variety of different fields. Various researchers have used the SVM model for face detection and recognition and have achieved satisfactory results.

SVM separates the classes with a decision surface that maximizes the margin between the classes, often referred to as the maximum-margin hyperplane or even the optimal hyperplane, and the data points which lie the closest to the hyperplane are called support vectors. The support vectors are a central element of the training set. An SVM classifier usually employs one of four types of kernels: linear, polynomial, Radial Basis Function (RBF), and sigmoid. The default is the radial basis function kernel, which works well in most cases, however, the parameters of an SVM model have to be properly fine-tuned for each problem to get the best result [20].

4.4   GBDecision Trees

A decision tree is based on a multistage or hierarchical decision scheme or a
tree-like structure consisting of a root node, a set of internal nodes (splits),
and a final set of terminal nodes. Gradient Boosting is, is an ensemble machine
learning model commonly used for classification and regression tasks. It employs
an ensemble of weak learners(usually decision trees) that attempts to reduce bias
and covarianc2e and therefore improve generalization in a variety of practical
tasks. It builds each new tree to approximate the gradients of the current model.
However, all classical boosting algorithms have a tendency to overfit caused by
the problem of biased pointwise gradient estimates. Overall these models are
also faster in comparison to some other ML algorithms.

4.5   Neural Networks

Neural Network (NN) is a classifier that tries to replicate the structure of human
thought, creating an artificial neural network that, via an algorithm, allows the
computer to learn by incorporating new data. The purpose being in the paper is
to use the NN perceptrons in transfer learning and comparing the performance
with other hybrid model architectures. Neural networks have been used for many
decades by researchers and have shown great performances on excess datasets
(Fig. 3).

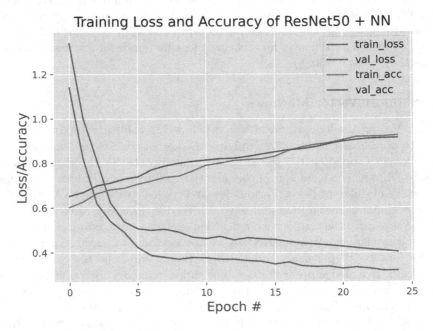

Fig. 3. Loss/accuracy graph of ResNet50+NN

We created a sequential model with some dense layers and 'relu' as an activation function. We also used Dropout to avoid overfitting of our model. The final layer of the model consists of a softmax layer for multi-classification (3 classes). We also used Adam optimizer for model compilation as it is computationally efficient and requires less memory [21]. There were 51,644,931 trainable parameters for ResNet50+NN architecture and 13,109,763 for VGG16 + NN model.

4.6 Hybrid Models

For constructing a hybrid model, various techniques are merged together to form a two-stage system, where first part is a deep learning model, which is used for preprocessing the data. Then, the features are used to train the machine learning classifier for the detection model.

An example of Hybrid Models is Transfer Learning, where we use a previously trained deep neural network architecture's features and use them in machine learning models. They provide higher accuracy and perform better than previously conventional machine learning methods. There are many hybrid models like ARIMA-WNN, which estimate urban traffic flow [22]. Similarly, there are many hybrid models which have provided greater performances than a single learning algorithm alone.

As hybrid models show great performance with better computational complexity, we tried creating better models for multi-classification problems in face mask detection. We chose ResNet50 and VGG16 as our base models for feature extraction, these models have been used by many researchers in the past and have shown great performances in the past for face detection. We also used classical machine learning models like Support Vector Machines (SVM), Gradient Booster (GB), and Neural networks (NN) for model training.

5 Proposed Model: ResNet50 + SVM

After careful deliberations, we concluded that ResNet50 was consistently outperforming VGG16. Therefore, we focused more on the models that used ResNet50 for parameter tuning over those hybrid models using VGG16. Even though the architecture consisting of GB performed better overall than the one using NN, it took longer to train and classify images than SVM. Figure 4 shows the procedure for detection using the proposed model i.e., ResNet50 + SVM.

Our research found that hybrid models showed better results than transfer learning models (ResNet50 +NN and VGG+NN). Also, transfer learning models showed good accuracy after many epochs whereas hybrid architectures performed better with less training time. These models can be implemented in most day-to-day applications. They can even be deployed in real-time scenarios for e.g., enforcing social distancing norms in crowded places where it becomes difficult to implement these guidelines by management bodies, such as Airports, Railway stations, Shopping Malls, Schools, etc.

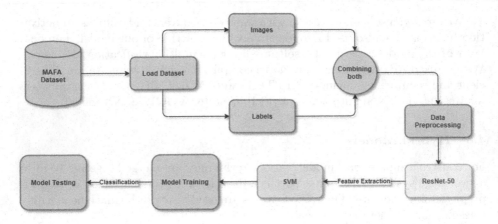

Fig. 4. Flowchart of the proposed model

6   Results and Discussion

As the dataset is slightly skewed in favour of the correctly worn, we decided not to use accuracy alone as a performance metric, since it doesn't give us the complete picture of our model's generalization ability. Instead, we used the combination of F measure, Accuracy, Precision, and Recall to compare our models. The metrics, what are they, along with their formulae, are given below:

Accuracy - the fraction of correctly classified examples divided by the total number of samples.

$$Accuracy = \frac{TP + TN}{TP + TN + FP + FN} \tag{1}$$

Precision - the fraction of correctly classified positive examples from all classified as positive.

$$Precision = \frac{TP}{TP + FP} \tag{2}$$

Recall - actual positive rate of all positive examples, that is, the fraction of correctly classified examples.

$$Recall = \frac{TP}{TP + FN} \tag{3}$$

F-measure - weighted average of Precision and Recall.

$$F - measure = \frac{2}{1/precision + 1/recall} \tag{4}$$

Table 1. Description of metrics achieved by different hybrid models

Hybrid architecture	Accuracy (%)	Precision	Recall	F - measure
ResNet + SVM	**97.24**	**1**	**0.96**	**0.98**
VGG + SVM	94.8	0.98	0.93	0.96
ResNet + GB	93.7	0.98	0.92	0.95
VGG + GB	93.2	0.98	0.91	0.95
ResNet + NN	92.9	0.97	0.91	0.94
VGG + NN	92.7	0.97	0.91	0.94

Table 1 depicts the various models and their respective performance measures, clearly showing the superior performance of the proposed model over the rest of the architectures. The model also has a near-perfect precision while maintaining a respectable recall value, therefore, returning an F-measure of around 0.98 which was the highest among all the models we tested.

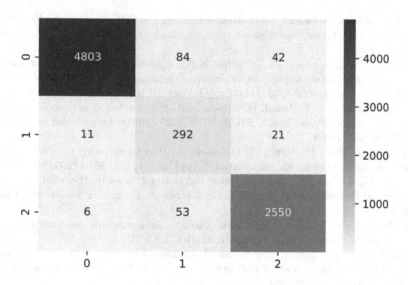

Fig. 5. Confusion matrix for validation dataset

In Fig. 5 we plotted a confusion matrix for predicted vs actual values. Here, the value '0' denotes correctly worn masks, '1' denotes improper masks while '2' denotes no masks. The Model Correctly predicted 97.4% of the images belonging to Class '0', 90.1% of those belonging to class '1' and 97.7% of those belonging to Class '2'. The Model was, therefore, able to model the data well and did not overfit or underfit the data.

7   Conclusion

The world is engulfed in a war against the second and even third covid wave. This acted as a constant reminder of the importance of wearing a mask and adequately wearing it [23]. Although substantial research work has been carried out in masked-face detection, most of it focused on binary classification rather than multi-classification. After extensive research on hybrid models, we chose to implement our model architectures for this particular multi-classification problem. Our choice of the dataset was made keeping in mind the ethnicity, gender, etc., and the dataset's size. Even though our proposed model consisting of ResNet50 and SVM showed promising results, our dataset was somewhat skewed in favour of the correctly worn class. It would also help if we could enforce these guidelines in moving vehicles using the surveillance system used by governments worldwide. Future research can be carried out to find a way to, for instance, locate those individuals who don't wear a mask correctly or at all.

References

1. WHO official website and information regarding COVID protocols and guidelines. https://www.who.int/emergencies/diseases/novel-coronavirus-2019. Accessed 4 Oct 2021
2. Greenhalgh, T., Jimenez, J.L., Prather, K.A., Tufekci, Z., Fisman, D., Schooley, R.: Ten scientific reasons in support of airborne transmission of SARS-CoV-2. Lancet **397**(10285), 1603–1605 (2021). https://doi.org/10.1016/S0140-6736(21)00869-2
3. Li, Y., Guo, K., Lu, Y., Liu, L.: Cropping and attention based approach for masked face recognition. Appl. Intell. **51**(5), 3012–3025 (2021). https://doi.org/10.1007/s10489-020-02100-9
4. Batagelj, B., Peer, P., Štruc, V., Dobrišek, S.: How to correctly detect face-masks for COVID-19 from visual information? Appl. Sci. **11**(5), 2070 (2021)
5. Ge, S., Li, J., Ye, Q., Luo, Z.: Detecting masked faces in the wild with LLE-CNNs. In: Proceedings of the IEEE Conference on Computer Vision and Pattern Recognition, pp. 2682–2690 (2017)
6. Bhadani, A., Sinha, A.: A facemask detector using machine learning and image processing techniques. Eng. Sci. Technol. Int. J. (2020)
7. Qin, B., Li, D.: Identifying facemask-wearing condition using image super-resolution with classification network to prevent COVID-19 (2020). https://doi.org/10.21203/rs.3.rs-28668/v1
8. Ejaz, M.S., Islam, M.R., Sifatullah, M., Sarker, A.: Implementation of principal component analysis on masked and non-masked face recognition. In: 2019 1st International Conference on Advances in Science, Engineering and Robotics Technology (ICASERT), p. 15 (2019). https://doi.org/10.1109/ICASERT.2019.8934543
9. Batagelj, B., Peer, P., Štruc, V., Dobrišek, S.: How to correctly detect face-masks for COVID-19 from visual information? Appl. Sci. **11**(5), 2070 (2021). https://doi.org/10.3390/app11052070
10. Nagrath, P., Jain, R., Madan, A., Arora, R., Kataria, P., Hemanth, J.: SSDMNV2: a real time DNN-based face mask detection system using single shot multibox detector and MobileNetV2. Sustain. Cities Soc. **66**, 102692 (2021). ISSN: 2210-6707, https://doi.org/10.1016/j.scs.2020.102692

11. Enireddy, V., Kumar, M., Donepudi, B., Karthikeyan, C.: Detection of COVID-19 using hybrid ResNet and SVM. IOP Conf. Ser.: Mater. Sci. Eng. **993**, 012046 (2020). https://doi.org/10.1088/1757-899X/993/1/012046
12. Montero, D., Nieto, M., Leskovsky, P., Aginako, N.: Boosting masked face recognition with multi-task arcface. arXiv Preprint arXiv:2104.09874 (2021)
13. Lin, S., et al.: Masked face detection via a modified LeNet. Neurocomputing **218**, 197–202 (2016)
14. Mandal, B., Okeukwu, A., Theis, Y.: Masked face recognition using ResNet-50. arXiv Preprint arXiv:2104.08997 (2021)
15. Loey, M., Manogaran, G., Taha, M.H.N., Khalifa, N.E.M.: A hybrid deep transfer learning model with machine learning methods for face mask detection in the era of the COVID-19 pandemic. Measurement (2021). https://doi.org/10.1016/j.measurement.2020.108288
16. Ge, S., Li, J., Ye, Q., Luo, Z.: Detecting masked faces in the wild with LLE-CNNs. In: IEEE Conference on Computer Vision and Pattern Recognition (CVPR), vol. 2017, pp. 426–434 (2017). https://doi.org/10.1109/CVPR.2017.53
17. Khojasteh, P.: Exudate detection in fundus images using deeply-learnable features. Comput. Biol. Med. **104**, 62–69 (2019). https://doi.org/10.1016/j.compbiomed.2018.10.031
18. Wen, L., Li, X., Gao, L.: A transfer convolutional neural network for fault diagnosis based on ResNet-50. Neural Comput. Appl. **32**(10), 6111–6124 (2019). https://doi.org/10.1007/s00521-019-04097-w
19. He K., Zhang X., Ren S., Sun J.: Deep residual learning for image recognition. In: IEEE Conference on Computer Vision and Pattern Recognition (CVPR), pp. 770–778 (2016)
20. Simonyan, K., Zisserman, A.: Very deep convolutional networks for large-scale image recognition. arXiv arXiv:1409.1556 (2014)
21. Shafri, H.Z.M., Ramle, F.S.H.: A comparison of support vector machine and decision tree classifications using satellite data of Langkawi island. Inf. Technol. J. **8**, 64–70 (2009)
22. Adam: a method for stochastic optimization. arXiv:1412.6980v9 [cs.LG]
23. Ardabili, S., Mosavi, A., Várkonyi-Kóczy, A.R.: Advances in machine learning modeling reviewing hybrid and ensemble methods. In: Várkonyi-Kóczy, A.R. (ed.) Engineering for Sustainable Future, INTER-ACADEMIA 2019. LNNS, vol. 101, pp. 215–227. Springer, Cham (2020). https://doi.org/10.1007/978-3-030-36841-8_21
24. Brooks, J.T., Beezhold, D.H., Noti, J.D., et al.: Maximizing fit for cloth and medical procedure masks to improve performance and reduce SARS-CoV-2 transmission and exposure, 2021. MMWR Morb. Mortal. Wkly Rep. **70**, 254–257 (2021). https://doi.org/10.15585/mmwr.mm7007e1

A Super Feature Transform for Small-Size Image Forgery Detection

M. S. Greeshma$^{(\boxtimes)}$ (ID) and V. R. Bindu$^{(\boxtimes)}$ (ID)

School of Computer Sciences, Mahatma Gandhi University, Kottayam, Kerala, India
{greeshmams,binduvr}@mgu.ac.in

Abstract. In this digital era, we have a wide variety of image editing software that is prone to create malicious alterations on images. Hence, the evaluation for authenticity of image contents and identification of malicious modifications is an open problem. In this work, an efficient small-size image forgery detection algorithm is presented based on Super Feature Transform - combining Super Resolution and Feature Transform. The approach enhances detection of small-size forgery by pre-processing the input image using super resolution algorithm. A robust feature transform is suggested to extract potential feature points from small-size patches with entanglement properties. Subsequently, feature matching and filtering is achieved by fuzzy threshold so that the false matches are filtered out. Also, the feature matching module employs a soft clustering to determine the matching points between identical and semi-identical feature points in different clusters. The experimental evaluations demonstrated that the proposed method outperforms existing techniques particularly when the forgery size is small and detects manifold duplicate forged regions in terms of TPR and FPR recognition rate.

Keywords: Super resolution · Image forgery · Small-image forgery · Copy-move forgery

1 Introduction

The technological advances in image editing software lead to an increased rate of malicious manipulation of digital images in various fields, especially social network, surveillance services etc. This kind of manipulation or alteration of multimedia contents is generally known as image forgery. Fridrich and team proposed the first algorithmic approach to identify copy move forgery. Numerous image forgery detection algorithms have been proposed for Copy Move Forgery Detection (CMFD) that are based on block-based [1–3], key-point based [4–6] and segmentation based approaches [7]. Most forgery detection algorithms focus on forged region localization by inexpensive and accurate ways, and are generally detected by describing the local features of the image such as keypoints. The existing feature points can be distributed into two types: local feature points

Supported by DST-PURSE Phase II, Govt of India.

and global feature points. Local Binary Patterns (LBP), Histogram Oriented Gradients (HOG) and Invariant moments are global feature points that have compact representations of an image, but these features are sensitive to disorder and obstruction, and also feature matching is more expensive due to the high dimension of descriptors. Local feature points such as SIFT [8], SURF [9] and Binary Robust Invariant Scalable Keypoints (BRISK) [10], describe image patches across the multiple interest feature points. Yet, such algorithms may have problems in localizing homogeneous segments; there may not be sufficient keypoints for further analysis. Furthermore, while considering transformations in forgery of small-size, detection becomes more difficult. In order to overcome these weaknesses of above mentioned approaches while improving the performance of feature extraction and filtering, an enhanced feature transform approach Super Feature Transform (SFT) is proposed here. This work proposes a Super Feature Transform algorithm designed for Small-size Image Forgery Detection (SIFD). The key feature of using SFT is that it recognizes the features despite significant disorder and obstruction. The rest of the paper is organized into four sections: Sect. 2 introduces the super resolution algorithms and reviews the forgery detection algorithms, Sect. 3 explains the proposed detection model in detail which includes super resolution process, SFT, filtering, matching and localization and Sect. 4 illustrates the simulation and evaluation of the efficacy of the proposed algorithm. Conclusions and future directions are included in Sect. 5.

2   Related Works and Problem Context

Recognizing the forged regions of small-size and manifold duplicate regions effectively preserves the integrity of image contents. In this work, we introduce a super resolution algorithm to increase the resolution as a preprocessing phase before applying the Super Feature Transform forgery detection algorithm on the host image. The review of super resolution algorithms and forgery detection algorithms are described in the following sections.

2.1   Preliminaries of Super Resolution Algorithms

Super Resolution (SR) is an algorithmic method to increase the resolution of an image from low to high resolution and at the same time preserve feature points and visual quality. Recently, Deep Neural Network has emerged as one of the leading research components in image super resolution [11,12]. Dong and team proposed the first algorithmic approach for image Super Resolution using Convolutional Neural Network [13]. Compared with other learning based SR algorithms, SRCNN algorithm can represent and use hierarchical feature mapping relationship between low resolution and high resolution images, which make the network deeper and reduces the loss of features. The layered approach of feature extraction such as edge and texture information of the image is more accurate and visual quality of HR image is greatly preserved. The mathematical formulation is shortened in Eq. (1) showing the high resolution image F(Y) being recovered from a [Y] image.

$$F(y) = max(0, w * Y + B) \qquad (1)$$

where 'W' and 'B' denote the filters and biases respectively and $*$ represents the convolution operation. Each W matches to n filters of support $c \times f1 \times f1$, where c is the channel and f1 is the size of a filter. Inspired by this fact, we have experimentally chosen fast and deep convolutional neural network for super resolution process of small-size image forgery detection algorithm.

2.2 Review of Forgery Detection Algorithms

In the CMFD algorithms, three broad categories of methods are used to recognize forgery: block-based, keypoint-based and segmentation-based techniques according to significant feature point extraction and representations. In block-based algorithms, the host image is divided into blocks, then feature points are extracted from each block and finally these features are compared and matched to identify tampered blocks. On analysis of block-based algorithms, Fridrich and team proposed a Discrete Cosine Transform (DCT) to the task of forgery detection for the first time [3]. The keypoint based algorithms are an alternative robust category of forgery detection algorithms. In contrary to block-based, these algorithms operate on the host image of size M×N, the points of interest are called keypoints of features in terms of high entropy image regions. David Lowe proposed invariant feature detection for copy move forgery, the most widely used algorithm known as Scale Invariant Feature Transform [8]. Several improved versions of SIFT algorithm have been proposed, which uses SIFT technique to extract keypoints Huang et al. [4]. One more potential local visual feature points approach is Speeded Up Robust Features, which ensures to speed up the feature detection and matching process [9]. Chen et al. proposed Harris Corner points to detect the robust keypoints faster than SIFT and step sector statistics is used to localize the region duplication but do not completely exclude the false matches [14]. To overcome this difficulty, Pun et al. proposed a hybrid approach to combine prominent features of keypoint and block based approaches [15]. Al-Qershi and Khoouses Zernike proposed the detection algorithm, which is considered by moments and locality sensitive hashing (LSH) with K-means clustering [16]. Azrak et al. proposed a combined approach for CMFD; one is DCT-based and other is SURF based transform [17]. The aforementioned algorithms are robust in rotation, scaling and cluttering, but these techniques exhibit ineffective performance when the tampered regions are flatter, smoother and are of small-size, when it is difficult to localize the shape feature of a region. To resolve this problem, we propose a small-size forgery detection algorithm which uses super features and robust matching approach to ensure detection of exact forged regions. The SIFD algorithm follows the general framework of CMFD algorithm such as Christlein et al. [18]; however the dynamic modules of framework are enhanced and innovated in the SIFD algorithm. The simulation result illustrates the suitability of SRCNN for SIFD model since it preserves the structural features and visual quality.

3   Proposed Detection Model

The proposed algorithm for detection of small-size forged region is based on integrating super resolution concepts and adopts the properties of patch computing. For exact detection of the tampered regions, the proposed small-size image forgery detection algorithm extracts the features with entanglement properties, and matches the feature points according to the correlation map. The proposed SIFD detection model is shown in Fig. 1, which comprises of three phases as explained in the sub sections. In the first step, the RGB host image is transformed into YIQ space. The key advantage of YIQ conversion is that highly detailed information such as edge features exist in the luminance element of the images. The first phase in the SIFD detection model is to apply super resolution as a preprocessing step. The supersized image I_H is generated from input image using SRCNN [13], which uses convolutional neural network to perform super resolution by learning the hierarchical relationship between low resolution and high resolution images. The simulation result illustrates the suitability of SRCNN for SIFD model since it preserves the structural features and visual quality.

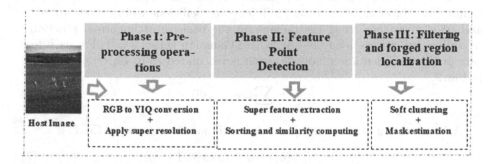

Fig. 1. Small-size image forgery detection model.

3.1   Super Feature Transform (SFT)

Given a high resolution imageI_H, the second step is to extract feature points according to the properties of phenomena, i.e., entanglement, which can be applied to recognize the small-size forgery. Here, SIFD algorithm uses patches as the features to localize the tampered region. In general, global features have dimensionality of feature descriptor 128 to 480; however SFT uses feature descriptor of dimension 80. The feature extraction and filtering process to detect the forged region are executed by the following stages.

3.1.1 Super Feature Extraction Given a super resolved image I_H of size $M \times N$, I_H is transformed into overlapping and averaging patches of $f_{qpatch} \times f_{qpatch} \times c - pixel$, where f_{qpatch} is dimension of patch. In the extraction of features, Fourier-Mellin Transform (FMT) [19] and log polar transform [20] are used to extract feature invariants with respect to geometrical operations (shift, rotation, scale) and the dimensionality is reduced by linear discriminant. While feature extraction is performed using FMT, each patch is denoted by FMT feature coefficients. The FMT feature coefficients of patch are calculated as follows:

$$FC(i,j) = \sum_{(x,y)\epsilon p} I(x,y)K_{i,j}[\rho(x,y), \theta(x,y)] \tag{2}$$

where $FC(i,j)$ is invariant with respect to geometric transformation and (i,j) denotes the coefficient of patch P. $I(x,y)$ Indicates the $(x,y)^{th}$ intensity of the super resolved image patch and $k_{i,j}$ represents the transformation.

$$y = \frac{2 \times y - f_{qpatch-1}}{2}, x = \frac{2 \times x - f_{qpatch-1}}{2} \tag{3}$$

$$\rho(x,y) = \sqrt{x^2 + y^2} \tag{4}$$

$$\theta(x,y) = \tan^{-1}\frac{y}{x} \begin{cases} x = \rho\cos\theta, y = \rho\sin\theta \end{cases} \tag{5}$$

where $\theta(x,y)$ represents the orientation of feature points around patches. Again resampling method is performed to achieve magnitude value in log polar coefficients. The absolute value of the FMT feature coefficient will generate rotation and scale invariance along the radians on the basis of orthonormal functions; $|I(\rho,\theta)| = |\sigma|^{-2}|I(\rho - log\sigma), \theta - \alpha|$, where Gaussian kernel $\sigma = 1$. For each feature point, the orientation θ of the patch is calculated as in Eq. 6 and depicted in Fig. 2.

$$h(\theta) = \sum_{i,j} log(|\rho_j, \theta|) \tag{6}$$

A linear discriminant is estimated for each patch as shown in Eq. 7.

$$f_{[x,y]} = Max(0, 1 - |x|)Max(0, 1 - |y|) \tag{7}$$

The computation of descriptors uses number of keypoints along the radius and circumference. We extract all FMT coefficients with radius at an extreme value and 64×64 vector has been generated using log-polar mapping. The FMT feature descriptor is computed by taking the magnitude of $f(x,y)$ and dividing FMT coefficients of each row in the feature matrix.

$$FMT_F = Bf|I(\rho,\theta), f_{[x,y]}| \tag{8}$$

where Bf is the filter bank. So in brief, given a high resolution image I, a vector of FMT- feature coefficients $FMT_F = FMT_{F1}, FMT_{F2}....FMT_{Fn}$ with dimension 64 is extracted and described by low-pass filters in order to reduce the dimension and at the same time preserving information.

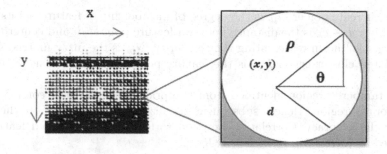

Fig. 2. Patch computation: patches of $M \times N$ image with polar log and orientation.

3.1.2 Feature Point Sorting and Similarity Computing

For later computation, the matrix is sorted in lexicographical order to recover the localization exactness, saving the comparison time. After that, the similarity factor between a row of pair patches is computed, represented as s and s'. We formulate similarity by hamming distance which will compute the distance between smaller regions also.

$$d(H) = \sum_{i=0}^{fpatch} (s_i XOR s_i') \tag{9}$$

where s and s' represent values of rows. The distance values corresponding to each feature patch pair are stored in a matrix.

3.2 Feature Filtering and Forged Region Localization

In the proposed technique of feature point matching, we have adopted a fuzzy threshold [21] for matching technique; the feature points belong to more than one cluster and association of feature points describes the membership values. This proposed technique guarantees the similarity of feature matched pairs via fuzzy threshold, μT. μT is the mean of maximum in the feature class with small centre and the minimum in the class with middle feature centre; $\mu T = mean(max(d_{i1}), min(d_{i2}))$. If the sum of distances between feature points in all clusters is greater than μT, the region is identified as tampered. The SFT feature points are clustered according to their feature descriptors, then some feature points that are closer to the Centre will have high degree of membership, and feature points which are distant from cluster Centre will have lower degree of membership. The 3-class FCM model is as follows:

$$Fm(N_m, C_m, D_m) = \sum_{i=1}^{N} \sum_{k=1}^{c} \mu_{ik}^m \|d_i - c_k\|^2 \tag{10}$$

$$\mu ik = \frac{1}{\sum_{j=1}^{c} \left(\frac{\|d_i - c_k\|}{\|d_i - c_j\|} \right)^{\frac{2}{m-1}}}$$

$$c_k = \frac{\sum_{i=1}^{n} \mu_{ik}^m c_k}{\sum_{i=1}^{n} \mu_{ik}^m}$$

where: m is real number, μ_{ik}^m is the degree of membership of feature points d_i in the cluster k,$d_i - c_k$ is the distance between feature points (d_i and center of the cluster c_k), $\|.\|$ norm representing the similarity, N_m is the fuzzy matrix, C_m is the updated cluster center,D_m is the feature points in the dimensional vector space.

The tampered region identified from the prior steps need not comprise the entire forged region. Hence, subsequent localization is executed on them to improve the accuracy. Correlation between sorted pairs of matched feature is computed as correlation coefficient FC.

$$FC = \frac{\sum_{i=1}^n (f_{xi} - \overline{f_x})(f_{yi} - \overline{f_y})}{\sqrt{\sum_{i=1}^n (f_{xi} - \overline{f_x})^2 (f_{yi} - \overline{f_y})^2}} \tag{11}$$

where f_x and f_y are the patches of FMT coefficient at location I and $\overline{f_x}$ and $\overline{f_y}$) are average of intensities respectively. n is the number of coefficients in the patch and the computed value comes in the range [0, 1]. Once the correlation map is generated, if the correlation $>\mu T$, actual forged region is obtained and the false matches are filtered out. Lastly, morphological operations are used to cover the shape of forged region.

4   Experimentation and Analysis

In this section, a sequence of simulations is executed to assess the excellence of proposed detection model in recognizing the geometric attack of small-sized forgeries. The proposed algorithm was simulated on the database created by Cozzino et al. [7]. This database consists of original images and their corresponding geometric attack- affected images, and images with small size forgeries are selected for evaluation. Super resolution as a preprocessing step is implemented to increase the dimension of 10 images of the database by ×3 zoom ratio. Three performance benchmarks are used for the quantitative analysis of SFT forgery detection - Precision, Recall and F1 Score both at image level and feature level [5]. From the simulation results, it has been proved that the proposed technique SFT is slightly superior to conventional approaches.

4.1   Evaluation of Super Feature Transform

The execution of the proposed SFT algorithm is compared with the existing ap-proaches such as SIFT, SURF algorithms. The enhanced SFT using super resolution is evaluated in comparison with other techniques for SIFD. Table 1 tabulates the detection accuracy of SFT with/without using super resolution, which clearly shows that SFT without super resolution obtains a precision of 97.43% : on the contrary, SFT with super resolution gives *precision* = 98.62% which is slightly better. It is proved that super resolution (preprocessing step) enhances the results of keypoint based detection algorithms, providing the capability to generate enough keypoints and thereby improving the exactness of localization of a forged region. Furthermore, we analyze the performance accuracy of

Table 1. Percentage of detection results before and after applying super resolution process.

Process	Precision (%)	Recall (%)	F_1 (%)
Fig. 4(I1) applied before super resolution	97.43	72.69	83.26
Fig. 4(I1) applied after super resolution	**98.62**	87.92	92.27

conventional CMFD algorithms and SFT with/without super resolution, against certain post-processing alterations (geometric operations -rotation, transformation, scaling, and distortion) as illustrated in Fig. 3. As explained in Sect. 3.1, a different stage of proposed SFT to identify forged regions is depicted in Fig. 4. Figure 4 demonstrates the result of each stage of SFT applied on different images in Cozzolino et al. database, second column shows the tampered image preprocessed using super resolution; thrid column represents the extracted SFT featrure points via FMT tranform with $patches = 0.9 \times 0.9$, fourth coloumn depicts the matching between feature points using fuzzy threshold value; $\mu T = 0.85$ and with minimum distance between regions $= 50 \times 50$; final column shows the detected region using SFT of I1, I2, I3 and I4 images respectively.

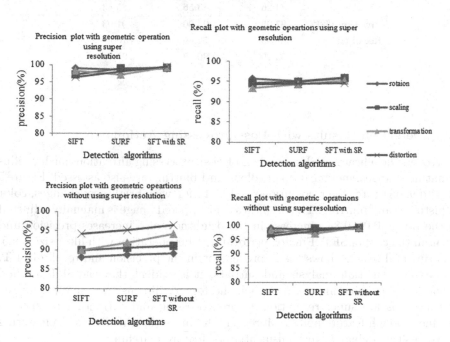

Fig. 3. Testing SFT against geometric operations (rotation, translation, scaling, distortion) and comparison with other CMFD.

Table 2 gives the performance comparison of images at feature point level, comparing SFT with SIFT and SURF features. For image I3, SFT generates better results with *precision* = 94.57%, *recall* = 100% and *F*1 = 85.43% at feature level and for image I4, SFT generates more exact forgery detection results with high *recall* = 100% and at the same time, maintaining good *precision* = 91.93%.

Table 2. Detection results of SIFT/SURF/SFT features with respect to Fig. 4 (I1, I2, I3, and I4 images.)

Host image	Evaluation metric	SIFT features	SURF features	Proposed SFT features
I1	Precision (%)	80.48	88.49	95.84
	Recall (%)	69.75	94.84	99.98
	F1 (%)	75.25	90.94	97.87
I1	Precision (%)	83.18	99.08	98.89
	Recall (%)	66.78	67.86	99.64
	F1 (%)	74.01	81.89	99.26
I3	Precision (%)	97.48	95.69	94.57
	Recall (%)	73.63	74.50	99.99
	F1 (%)	84.26	83.56	85.43
I4	Precision (%)	97.05	93.90	91.93
	Recall (%)	88.93	71.89	100
	F1 (%)	93.29	80.98	95.79

4.2   Detection Results with Post-processing Actions

Moreover, the efficacy of SFT in terms of post processing alterations such as illumination changes, modification of colour and blurring are also assessed. Figure 5 (a–c) demonstrates the recognition results of SFT with brightness changes, color adjustment and blurring. The brightness of tampered image is manually adjusted in the range [0.01–0.88]. Increase in the brightness also increases precision and recall in the case of SFT. Finally, performing blur operation with filter size 5×5, experimental results shows the improvement in the precision and recall of SFT. From the simulation analysis and outputs, it is evident that the SFT method outperforms existing approaches when the forgery dimension is small. The key justifications are super resolution as preprocessing and extracting patches to produce enough feature points. Moreover, the fuzzy threshold via soft clustering decreases the ambiguity and falsification of feature matching.

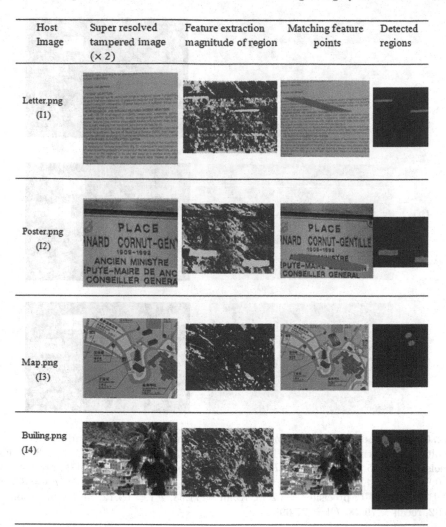

Host Image	Super resolved tampered image (×2)	Feature extraction magnitude of region	Matching feature points	Detected regions

Fig. 4. Example results of the SFT algorithm. Each column represents different stages of SFT.

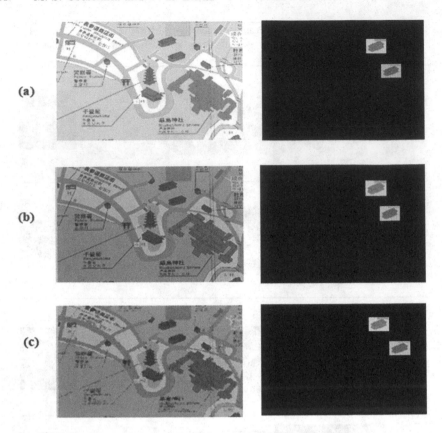

Fig. 5. Post processing operations in tampered image and corresponding detection
results;(a) Brightness change [SIFT: precision = 78.38, recall=75.92 , $F1 = 79.32$; SFT
precision = 85.45, recall = 84.45, $F1 = 83.29$] (b) Color adjustment [SIFT: precision =
70.09, recall = 74.29 , $F1 = 73.25$; SFT : precision = 86.05, recall = 83.26, $F1 = 82.98$]
(c) Blurring [SIFT: precision = 77.48, recall = 71.93, $F1 = 69.12$; SFT : precision =
85.92, recall = 79.48, $F1 = 77.69$].

5   Conclusion

In this work, we have deliberated the problem of small-size image forgery detection. We propose Super Feature Transform algorithm, which uses the supremacy
of super resolution with Fourier-Mellin Transform and soft threshold. The execution of the SFT algorithm was quantitatively assessed with three evaluation
benchmarks: precision, recall and F1score. The proposed approach has been
demonstrated to be robust against the geometric attacks such as brightness
adjustment, color adjustment and blurring. It has been found that the SFT
technique attains improved recognition accuracy and reduces the complexity.
In future, we plan to expand this work to adapt a deep network model to test
small-size forged images.

Acknowledgements. Authors acknowledge the support extended by DST-PURSE Phase II, Govt of India.

References

1. Wang, J., Liu, G., Zhang, Z., Dai, Y., Wang, Z.: Fast and robust forensics for image region-duplication forgery. Acta Autom. Sin. **35**(12), 1488–1495 (2009)
2. Ryu, S.-J., Lee, M.-J., Lee, H.-K.: Detection of copy-rotate-move forgery using Zernike moments. In: Böhme, R., Fong, P.W.L., Safavi-Naini, R. (eds.) Information Hiding, IH 2010. LNCS, vol. 6387, pp. 51–65. Springer, Heidelberg (2010). https://doi.org/10.1007/978-3-642-16435-4_5
3. Fridrich, A.J., Soukal, B.D., Lukas, A.J.: Detection of copy-move forgery in digital images. In: Proceedings of Digital Forensic Research Workshop, Cleveland, Ohio (2003)
4. Huang, H., Guo, W., Zhang, Y.: Detection of copy-move forgery in digital images using SIFT algorithm. In: IEEE Pacific-Asia Workshop on Computational Intelligence and Industrial Application (PACIIA), vol. 2, pp. 272–276 (2008)
5. Amerini, I., Ballan, L., Caldelli, R., Del Bimbo, A., Serra, G.A.: Sift-based forensic method for copy move attack detection and transformation recovery. IEEE Trans. Inf. Forensics Secur. **6**(3), 1099–1110 (2011)
6. Ansari, M.D., Ghrera, S.P., Tyagi, V.: Pixel-based image forgery detection: a review. IETE J. Educ. **55**, 40–46 (2014)
7. Cozzolino, D., Poggi, G., Verdoliva, L.: Efficient dense-field copy move forgery detection. IEEE Trans. Inf. Forensics Secur. **10**(11), 2284–2297 (2015)
8. Lowe, D.G.: Object recognition from local scale-invariant features. In: Proceedings of the Seventh IEEE International Conference on Computer Vision, Kerkyra, Greece, vol. 2, pp. 1150–1157 (1999)
9. Bay, H., Tuytelaars, T., Van Gool, L.: SURF: speeded up robust features. In: Leonardis, A., Bischof, H., Pinz, A. (eds.) Computer Vision – ECCV 2006. LNCS, vol. 3951, pp. 404–417. Springer, Heidelberg (2006). https://doi.org/10.1007/11744023_32
10. Kumar, S., Desai, J.V., Mukherjee, S.A.: Fast keypoint based hybrid method for copy-move forgery detection. Int. J. Comput. Digit. Syst. **4**(2), 91–99 (2015)
11. Kim, J., Lee, J.K., Lee, K.M.: Deeply-recursive convolutional network for image super-resolution. In: Proceedings of the 2016 IEEE Conference on Computer Vision Pattern Recognition, Las Vegas, NV, USA, pp. 1637–1645 (2016)
12. Tai, Y., Yang, J., Liu, X.: Image super-resolution via deep recursive residual network. In: Proceedings of the IEEE Conference on Computer Vision and Pattern Recognition, pp. 3147–3155 (2017)
13. Dong, C., Loy, C.C., He, K.M., Tang, X.O.: Image super-resolution using deep convolutional networks. IEEE Trans. Pattern Anal. Mach. Intell. **38**, 295–303 (2016)
14. Chen, L., Lu, W., Ni, J., Sun, W., Huang, J.: Region duplication detection based on Harris corner points and step sector statistics. J. Vis. Commun. Image Represent. **24**(3), 244–254 (2013)
15. Pun, C.M., Yuan, X.C., Bi, X.L.: Image forgery detection using adaptive oversegmentation and feature point matching. IEEE Trans. Inf. Forensics Secur. **10**(8), 1705–1716 (2015)

16. Al Azrak, F.M., Elsharkawy, Z.F., Elkorany, A.S., El Banby, G.M., Dessowky, M.I., Abd El-Samie, F.E.: Copy-move forgery detection based on discrete and SURF transforms. Wirel. Pers. Commun. **110**(1), 503–530 (2019). https://doi.org/10.1007/s11277-019-06739-7
17. Al-Qershi, O.M., Khoo, B.E.: Enhanced block-based copy-move forgery detection using k-means clustering. Multidimension. Syst. Signal Process. **30**(4), 1671–1695 (2019)
18. Christlein, V., Riess, C., Jordan, J., Riess, C., Angelopoulou, E.: An evaluation of popular copy-move forgery detection approaches. IEEE Trans. Inf. Forensic Secur. **7**(6), 1841–1854 (2012)
19. Derrode, S., Ghorbel, F.: Robust and efficient Fourier-Mellin transform approximations for gray-level image reconstruction and complete invariant description. Comput. Vis. Image Underst. **83**(1), 57–78 (2001)
20. Wolberg, G., Zokai, S.: Robust image registration using log-polar transform. In: Proceedings 2000 International Conference on Image Processing (Cat. No. 00CH37101), pp. 493–496 (2000)
21. Yang, M.S., Nataliani, Y.: Robust-learning fuzzy c-means clustering algorithm with unknown number of clusters. Pattern Recogn. **71**, 45–59 (2017)

Document Analysis and Recognition

UHTelHwCC: A Dataset for Telugu Off-line Handwritten Character Recognition

Rakesh Kummari[✉] and Chakravarthy Bhagvati[✉]

School of Computer and Information Sciences, University of Hyderabad,
Hyderabad 500046, India
rakeshkummarics@gmail.com, chakcs@uohyd.ernet.in

Abstract. This paper describes the creation of UHTelHwCC, a labelled dataset for Telugu off-line handwritten character recognition (HCR), and its characteristics. The form images were scanned at 300dpi and digitised into TIFF images. This paper contains two major aspects: the first, processing the forms and creating a connected component dataset and its statistics; and the second, analysis of the dataset. Preliminary results on this dataset using convolutional neural network (CNN) are presented. UHTelHwCC dataset contains samples written by 84 writers. There are a total of 75K samples of 376 classes, and these samples are divided as 60K, 5K, and 10K into training, validation, and test sets respectively. A large amount of metadata pertaining to the writer's characteristics, class distributions, and variances is also provided. It is hoped that the dataset provides the basis for developing practical Telugu off-line HCR systems and other applications. UHTelHwCC is designed to provide a standard benchmark for comparing different algorithms for Telugu HCR and help in the research and development of Telugu HCR systems. It is expected that UHTelHwCC would be like the extremely well-known handwritten numeral dataset, MNIST but for Telugu script. Our initial experiments using convolutional neural networks show performance accuracies between 84% and 90%.

Keywords: Handwritten character recognition · HCR · Off-line Telugu HCR · UHTelHwCC · Telugu dataset · HCR dataset

1 Introduction

Handwritten character recognition (HCR) is the process of converting handwritten character images into machine editable form. HCR is a well-known problem in the pattern recognition community. The research on Indic HCR has started very late compared to other scripts such Latin, Chinese, and Arabic. The reason for the above is non-availability of standard datasets and the complexity of the scripts. The research progress on Telugu scripts has got less attention than the other Indic scripts due to non-availability of standard datasets. The first and

© Springer Nature Switzerland AG 2022
KC Santosh et al. (Eds.): RTIP2R 2021, CCIS 1576, pp. 249–262, 2022.
https://doi.org/10.1007/978-3-031-07005-1_22

foremost step towards building HCR systems is the creation of the standard dataset. Standard datasets are essential to compare the different algorithms for HCR. In this paper, we are creating a Telugu off-line handwritten character dataset. The dataset serves as a stepping-stone in building HCR systems for Telugu and the comparison of different methods on HCR becomes easier. Telugu is an Indic script. Over 80M people are speaking in Telugu from different parts of the world. The details on the Telugu script can be found in [11,17].

To the best of our knowledge, very few handwritten character datasets for Telugu are available in the literature. The dataset used in [19] contains samples of base character only. The dataset used in [7,21] contains samples from 166 classes. But, the above dataset was originally created in on-line mode, then the obtained character images are made available in off-line mode. The character images obtained using on-line digitising device are very different from the character images which are written on a paper. These 160 classes do not cover all the characters in the Telugu script. To overcome these challenges, we are creating a new dataset with 376 classes which are sufficient to cover the entire script. The details regarding dataset creation and its characteristics are explained in the subsequent sections.

A brief study of related work is mentioned in Sect. 2. Section 3 presents how the dataset is created. Section 4 explains the characteristics of the dataset. The experiments on the dataset are presented in Sect. 5.

2   Related Work

The following handwritten character datasets for non-Indic scripts such as Arabic [2,3,8], Chinese [14,24], Korean [10], Latin [6,13,23], and Parsian [9,16,20] scripts are available in the literature. The Al-ISRA [8] dataset is an Arabic dataset that contains handwritten 10000 digits, 37000 words, 500 sentences, and 2500 signatures. It was developed at the University of British Columbia in Canada. The CENPARMI [3] dataset is an Arabic dataset that contains 13439 digits, 21426 characters, and 11375 words. Three hundred twenty-eight writers wrote these samples. The PE92 [10] dataset is a Korean handwritten character dataset that contains 235000 characters. The ETL-9 dataset is a Japanese handwritten character dataset that contains 607200 characters.

The NIST [23] dataset is an English handwritten text dataset that contains 810000 characters, digits, and 91500 text phrases. Two thousand one hundred writers have written these samples. The MNIST [13] dataset contains 70000 handwritten digits. The CEDAR [6] dataset is a collection of 14000 city and state names, 5000 zip codes, and 49000 characters and digits. The IRONOFF [22] is an on-line and off-line French and English handwritten dataset. It was developed at the University of Nantes, France. It contains 50000 cursive words and 32000 isolated characters.

The CASIA-HWDB [14], is a collection of Chinese handwritten character and text datasets, was built by the National Laboratory of Pattern Recognition (NLPR), Institute of Automation of Chinese Academy of Sciences (CASIA). It is available in both on-line and off-line modes. The character datasets contain 3.9M samples of 7356 classes includes 7185 characters and 171 symbols. The test dataset contains 5090 pages and 1.35M character samples. The HIT-OR3C [24], is a Chinese handwritten character dataset, was built by Harbin Institute of Technology. It contains 832650 characters from 6825 classes. It is available in both on-line and off-line modes.

The following handwritten character datasets for Indic scripts such as Bangla [2,4], Devanagari [21] Oriya [2], Kannada [2,19], Malayalam [15], Telugu [7,19,21], and Tamil [19] are available in the literature. ISI Indic script handwritten databases are a collection of databases for Bangla, Devanagari, and Oriya scripts. Bangla databases contain numerals, base characters, vowel modifiers, and compound characters. Devanagari databases contain numerals and base characters. The Oriya database contains only numerals. The CMATERdb (Center for Microprocessor Applications for Training Education and Research database) [4] consists of unconstrained handwritten document images of pages, lines, words, and characters for Bangla, Devanagari, Arabic, and Telugu scripts. The PHDIndic_11 [18] is a page-level handwritten document image dataset of eleven official Indic scripts for script identification.

The PBOK dataset [2] is a handwritten text (test-line, word, and character) dataset for four different scripts such as Persian, Bangla, Oriya, and Kannada. The PBOK dataset was collected from a total of 707 text pages written by 436 writers in four different scripts. The PBOK dataset contains a total of 12565 text-lines, 104541 words/sub-words, and 553536 characters. The number of text pages for Persian, Bangla, Oriya, and Kannada scripts is 140, 199, 140, and 228 respectively. These text pages are written by 40, 199, 140, and 57 number of writers for Persian, Bangla, Oriya, and Kannada scripts respectively. The PBOK dataset contains 1787, 2820, 3108, and 4850 number of text-lines from Persian, Bangla, Oriya, and Kannada scripts respectively. The PBOK dataset includes 27073, 21255, 27007, and 29206 number of words/sub-words from Persian, Bangla, Oriya, and Kannada scripts respectively. The PBOK dataset contains 106643, 104190, 129556, and 213147 number of characters from Persian, Bangla, Oriya, and Kannada scripts respectively.

The DHCD [1] is a Devanagari handwritten character dataset. It contains 92000 samples from 46 classes and it is a balanced dataset where each class contains 2000 samples. The Amrita-MalCharDb [15], is a Malayalam handwritten character database, was developed at Amrita university. It includes 29302 samples from 85 classes includes vowels, consonants, half-consonants, vowel and consonant modifiers, and conjunct characters. Seventy-seven native Malayalam writers produced these samples.

HPL India has published a collection of handwritten character [7, 21] and word datasets in on-line and off-line mode. There are three isolated character datasets for Telugu, Tamil, and Devanagari scripts. Telugu dataset contains samples from 166 classes where ≈ 270 samples per class. Tamil dataset contains samples from 156 classes where ≈ 500 samples per class. The devanagari dataset contains samples from 111 classes where ≈ 270 samples per class.

Pal et al. [19] used handwritten character datasets for Kannada, Telugu, and Tamil scripts. There are 10779 Kannada handwritten character samples of 48 classes. There are 10872 handwritten Telugu characters of 48 classes. There are 10216 Tamil handwritten character samples of 36 classes.

3   UHTelHwCC Creation

The UHTelHwCC is created from forms designed by Lakshmi et al. [12], and 84 writers fill these forms. There are 11 unique forms, numbered from 0 to 10, were written by a writer. Figure 1 represents a sample form with basic characters. Each form consists of a solid circle, grid, solid rectangles, and writer information such as name, age, and occupation. The solid circle at the top in the forms indicates the form number. The solid rectangles at the bottom of the forms are used to find the skew of the document. Each form grid consists of 180 cells arranged in 18 rows and ten columns. Rows 1,3,.., and 17 corresponds to printed characters, and rows 2,4,.., and 18 corresponds to handwritten characters. Each form contains 90 printed characters and 90 handwritten characters except the final form. Figure 2 shows the final form containing a few empty cells and a few words. The form contents include base characters, *gunitams*, compound characters (*vottus* combined with consonants), Hindu-Arabic numerals, and a few words. Base characters and a few *gunithams* can be seen in Fig. 1, whereas a few *vottus* combined with consonants, Hindu-Arabic numerals, and a few words can be seen in Fig. 2. The form images were scanned at 300dpi and digitised into TIFF images.

The steps in UHTelHwCC creation include 1. Removal of background lines, 2. Textline extraction, 3. Character extraction, and 4. CC extraction and labelling. Figure 3 shows steps involved in creating UHTelHwCC.

First, the input forms are binarized using global thresholding with the threshold value as 220. The binary forms are inverted, where ones represent the foreground. Background lines need to be removed to extract and label Telugu handwritten characters from the forms. The connected component analysis is used to remove background lines. The CCs are extracted from binary and inverted forms. It is observed that the largest CC corresponds to the background and the second-largest CC is corresponds to background lines. All the pixel values of the second-largest CC are replaced with zeros to remove background lines. Figure 4

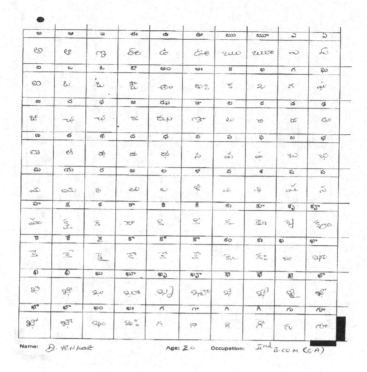

Fig. 1. Sample form with basic characters

is a form without background lines, and it is obtained by removing background lines from the form shown in Fig. 1.

The next step is the extraction of text-lines. Horizontal Projection Profile (HPP) is used for the above task. HPP shows the number of foreground pixels in each row. HPP is applied to the image that is obtained in the previous step. The peaks in HPP correspond to text-lines, and valleys indicate the gap between the text-lines. Figure 5 is HPP of the image shown in Fig. 4. In Fig. 5, X-axis represents the number of pixels, and Y-axis represents row numbers. Figure 6 and 7 show sample printed and handwritten text-lines respectively.

After extraction of text-lines, Vertical Projection Profile (VPP) is applied on each text-line to get individual Telugu characters. VPP shows the number of foreground pixels in each column. Peaks in VPP correspond to the characters, and valleys indicate the gap between characters. Then, extracted characters are labelled based on character position in the text-line. Corresponding handwritten text-lines follow Printed text-lines. Figure 8 shows randomly selected samples from extracted handwritten characters from all the forms.

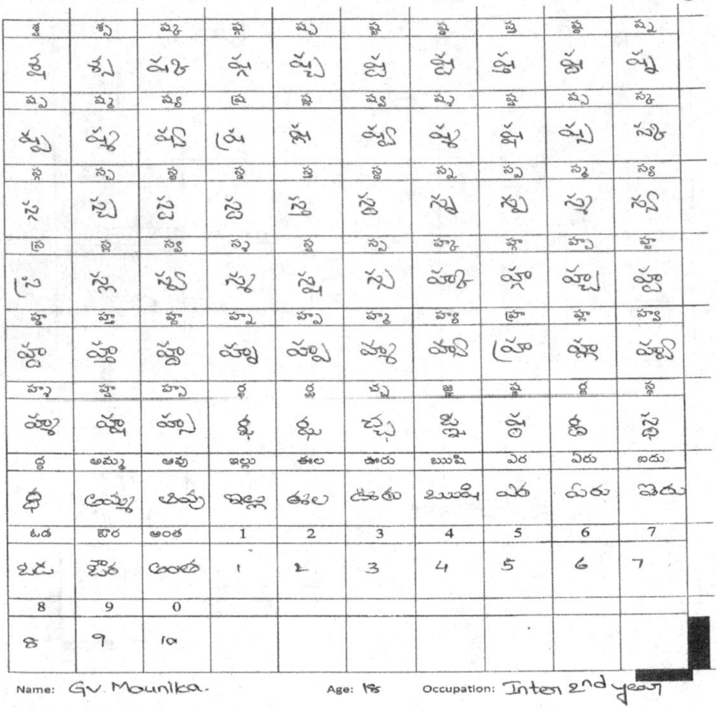

Fig. 2. Sample form with words and numerals

The final step in dataset creation is the extraction and the labelling of connected components from characters obtained in the previous step. A character consists of one or more connected components. All vowels except *ee*, *aM*, and *aH* consist of a single connected component. All consonants except *gha*, *pa*, *pha*, *Sha*, *sa*, *ha*, *tha*, and *Ta* consist of single connected component. Consonants with single CC that are modified by all vowel modifiers except *R*, *RR*, *ai*, *aM*, and *aH* consist of the single connected component. Consonants with two CC that are modified by all vowel modifiers except *aa*, *o*, *oo*, and *au* consist of multiple connected components. Compound characters consist of multiple connected components. Characters with multiple components are segmented and labelled based on the component position. All the CCs are scaled to 32 × 32, and labels are manually verified. For example, *ka vottu* always presents to the right side of the character. Figure 9 shows sample CCs extracted from different forms.

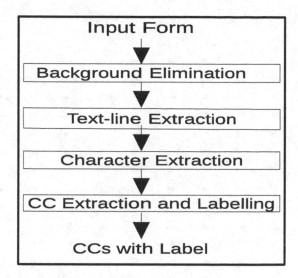

Fig. 3. Steps in UHTelHwCC creation

4 UHTelHwCC Characteristics

This section describes the dataset characteristics such as CC image type and size, writing instrument used, sample distribution, data splits, and writers' details such as the number of writers, histogram of writers' age, educational quali-fication. UHTelHwCC is a Telugu off-line handwritten connected component dataset, and it can be used for character recognition and writer identification. All the connected components are, in binary format, of size 32×32 and labelled. Black color sketch pen is used as a writing instrument for filling forms.

4.1 Sample Distribution

UHTelHwCC contains 75K samples (connected components) of 376 classes (dis-tinct connected components). The number of samples in each class ranges from 1 to 3329. Figure 10 is a horizontal bar graph with the number of classes on the X-axis and number of samples in range on the Y-axis. In UHTelHwCC, 9, 6, 11, 34, 79, 163, 20, 11, 21, 19, and 3 classes are having samples in the range 1–10, 11–20, 21–30, 31–50, 51–75, 76–100, 101–200, 201–500, 501–1000, 1001–2000, and 2001–3500 respectively.

Fig. 4. A form after removing background lines

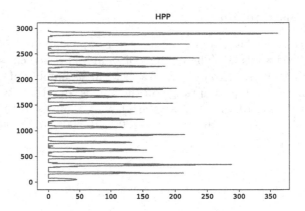

Fig. 5. Horizontal projection profile

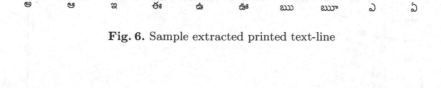

Fig. 6. Sample extracted printed text-line

Fig. 7. Sample extracted handwritten text-line

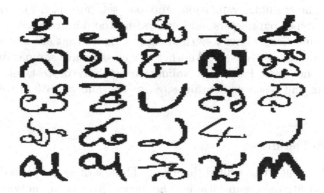

Fig. 8. Sample extracted handwritten characters

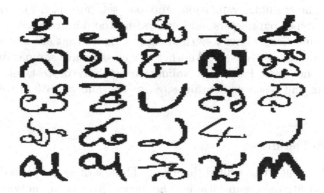

Fig. 9. Sample extracted handwritten connected components

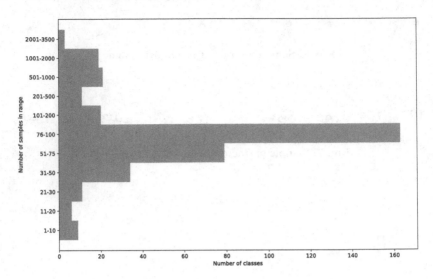

Fig. 10. Sample distribution

4.2   Data Splits

UHTelHwCC consists of 75K samples of size 32×32 in binary format. Each sample can have two values, either zero (background pixel) or one (foreground pixel). There are a total of 75K samples of 376 classes, and these samples are divided as 60K, 5K, and 10K into training, validation, and test sets, respectively. The training, validation, and test sets contain samples of 376, 362, and 367 classes, respectively. The training, validation, and test sets are used for training classifiers, tuning hyper-parameters, and evaluating the performance of the model, respectively. Nine classes have less than eight samples that are neither included in the validation set nor test set. Another five classes have samples in the range 8–15 that are not included in the validation set but the test set. The training, validation, and test sets contain 80%, $\approx$ 7%, and $\approx$ 13% of total samples respectively.

4.3   Writers Details

Eighty-four different writers filled the forms. These writers are from different age groups and educational qualifications. The handwriting of an individual changes with age [5]. Writers are from diverse age groups ranging from 10–80. Figure 11 shows the histogram of the writers' age. In Fig. 11, writes age on the X-axis and number of writers on the Y-axis presented. There are 23, 30, 22, 5, 2, 1, and 1 writers from the age groups 11–20, 21–30, 31–40, 41–50, 51–60, 61–70, and 71–80 respectively. The majority of the writers (≈90%) are from the age 10–40, and the rest of the writers are from age greater than 40.

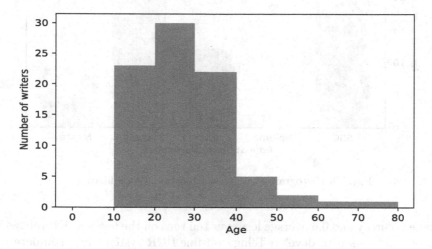

Fig. 11. Histogram of writers' age

The writers are from different educational qualifications ranges from school to master's. Figure 12 shows how many writers are from different educational qualifications. The X-axis represents qualification, and the Y-axis represents the number of writers. 20, 2, 12, 28, and 9 writers are from SSC, intermediate, diploma, bachelors, and master's, respectively.

5   Experiments

We have implemented a Convolutional Neural Network (CNN) to report the baseline accuracies on the UHTelHwCC dataset. The CNN contains 5-layers (two convolution and three fully connected layers) like LeNet-5 [13]. The number of filters in convolutional layers is 32 and 64. There are 1000, 500, and 376 nodes in fully connected layers. *ReLU* activations are used in all the layers except the output layer. *Softmax* activations are used in output layer. The *adam* optimizer and categorical cross-entropy loss function, L_2 regularization (10^{-5}), and dropout (0.5) are used. Figure 13 shows training, validation accuracies, and training, validation loss for 15 epochs. Table 1 shows the CNN accuracy and loss computed on training, validation, and test sets. We have obtained 89.19%

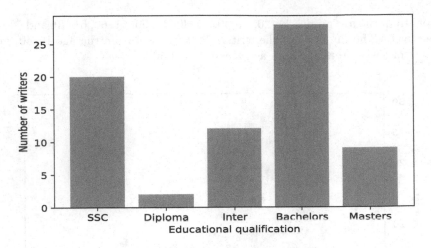

Fig. 12. Histogram of writers' educational qualification

average accuracy and 0.6 average loss over ten runs on the test set. UHTelHwCC dataset can be used to develop Telugu off-line HCR systems and compare the performance of different HCR algorithms.

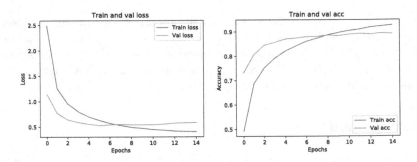

Fig. 13. CNN accuracy and loss

Table 1. CNN accuracy and loss

Data split	Size	Accuracy(%)	Loss
Training set	60K	99.097 ± 0.053	0.216 ± 0.002
Validation set	5K	89.07 ± 0.265	0.599 ± 0.016
Test set	10K	89.195 ± 0.229	0.597 ± 0.011

6   Conclusion

The main contribution of this paper is the creation of UHTelHwCC, a dataset for Telugu off-line handwritten character recognition. This dataset contains 75K samples of 376 classes written by 84 writers. This dataset contains sufficient variations in it and a large number of classes making it suitable for current and future research in HCR. A large number of writers, the variation in their educational qualifications and their ages make the dataset a potential benchmark for handwriting analysis. Connected component analysis, HPP, and VPP are used in form processing to automate labelling of CCs. Manually verified the labels. Finally, we have implemented a CNN and obtained 89.19% average accuracy and 0.597 average loss over ten runs on the test set.

Acknowledgment. We thank Prof. Atul Negi for providing scanned copies of handwritten forms. The first author acknowledges the financial support received from the Council of Scientific and Industrial Research (CSIR), Government of India, in the form of a Senior Research Fellowship.

References

1. Acharya, S., Pant, A.K., Gyawali, P.K.: Deep learning based large scale handwritten Devanagari character recognition. In: 2015 9th International Conference on Software, Knowledge, Information Management and Applications (SKIMA), pp. 1–6. IEEE (2015)
2. Alaei, A., Pal, U., Nagabhushan, P.: Dataset and ground truth for handwritten text in four different scripts. Int. J. Pattern Recogn. Artif. Intell. **26**(04), 1253001 (2012)
3. Alamri, H., Sadri, J., Suen, C.Y., Nobile, N.: A novel comprehensive database for Arabic off-line handwriting recognition. In: Proceedings of 11th International Conference on Frontiers in Handwriting Recognition, ICFHR, vol. 8, pp. 664–669 (2008)
4. Das, N., Acharya, K., Sarkar, R., Basu, S., Kundu, M., Nasipuri, M.: A benchmark image database of isolated Bangla handwritten compound characters. Int. J. Doc. Anal. Recogn. (IJDAR) **17**(4), 413–431 (2014)
5. Huber, R.A., Headrick, A.M.: Handwriting Identification: Facts and Fundamentals. CRC Press, Boca Raton (1999)
6. Hull, J.J.: A database for handwritten text recognition research. IEEE Trans. Pattern Anal. Mach. Intell. **16**(5), 550–554 (1994)
7. Jayaraman, A., Sekhar, C.C., Chakravarthy, V.S.: Modular approach to recognition of strokes in Telugu script. In: Ninth International Conference on Document Analysis and Recognition, ICDAR 2007, vol. 1, pp. 501–505. IEEE (2007)
8. Kharma, N., Ahmed, M., Ward, R.: A new comprehensive database of handwritten arabic words, numbers, and signatures used for ocr testing. In: Engineering Solutions for the Next Millennium. 1999 IEEE Canadian Conference on Electrical and Computer Engineering (Cat. No. 99TH8411). vol. 2, pp. 766–768. IEEE (1999)
9. Khosravi, H., Kabir, E.: Introducing a very large dataset of handwritten Farsi digits and a study on their varieties. Pattern Recogn. Lett. **28**(10), 1133–1141 (2007)

10. Kim, D.H., Hwang, Y.S., Park, S.T., Kim, E.J., Paek, S.H., Bang, S.Y.: Handwritten Korean character image database PE92. IEICE Trans. Inf. Syst. **79**(7), 943–950 (1996)
11. Kummari, R., Bhagvati, C.: UHTelPCC: a dataset for Telugu printed character recognition. In: Santosh, K.C., Hegadi, R.S. (eds.) Recent Trends in Image Processing and Pattern Recognition, RTIP2R 2018. CCIS, vol. 1037, pp. 24–36. Springer, Singapore (2019). https://doi.org/10.1007/978-981-13-9187-3_3
12. Lakshmi, A.V., Krishna, T.S., Negi, A.: Dataset generation for OCR. Int. J. Comput. Trends Technol. (IJCTT) **2**(1), 48–51 (2011)
13. LeCun, Y., Bottou, L., Bengio, Y., Haffner, P.: Gradient-based learning applied to document recognition. Proc. IEEE **86**(11), 2278–2324 (1998)
14. Liu, C.L., Yin, F., Wang, D.H., Wang, Q.F.: CASIA online and offline Chinese handwriting databases. In: 2011 International Conference on Document Analysis and Recognition, pp. 37–41. IEEE (2011)
15. Manjusha, K., Kumar, M.A., Soman, K.: On developing handwritten character image database for Malayalam language script. Eng. Sci. Technol. Int. J. **22**(2), 637–645 (2019)
16. Mozaffari, S., Faez, K., Faradji, F., Ziaratban, M., Golzan, S.M.: A comprehensive isolated Farsi/Arabic character database for handwritten OCR research (2006)
17. Negi, A., Bhagvati, C., Krishna, B.: An OCR system for Telugu. In: Proceedings of Sixth International Conference on Document Analysis and Recognition, pp. 1110–1114. IEEE (2001)
18. Obaidullah, S.M., Halder, C., Santosh, K., Das, N., Roy, K.: PHDIndic_11: page-level handwritten document image dataset of 11 official Indic scripts for script identification. Multimedia Tools Appl. **77**(2), 1643–1678 (2018). https://doi.org/10.1007/s11042-017-4373-y
19. Pal, U., Sharma, N., Wakabayashi, T., Kimura, F.: Handwritten character recognition of popular south Indian scripts. In: Doermann, D., Jaeger, S. (eds.) Arabic and Chinese Handwriting Recognition, SACH 2006. LNCS, vol. 4768, pp. 251–264. Springer, Heidelberg (2008). https://doi.org/10.1007/978-3-540-78199-8_15
20. Solimanpour, F., Sadri, J., Suen, C.Y.: Standard databases for recognition of handwritten digits, numerical strings, legal amounts, letters and dates in Farsi language (2006)
21. Swethalakshmi, H., Jayaraman, A., Chakravarthy, V.S., Sekhar, C.C.: Online handwritten character recognition of Devanagari and Telugu characters using support vector machines. In: Tenth International Workshop on Frontiers in Handwriting Recognition, Suvisoft (2006)
22. Viard-Gaudin, C., Lallican, P.M., Knerr, S., Binter, P.: The IRESTE on/off (IRONOFF) dual handwriting database. In: Proceedings of the Fifth International Conference on Document Analysis and Recognition, ICDAR 1999 (Cat. No. PR00318), pp. 455–458. IEEE (1999)
23. Wilkinson, R., et al.: The first census optical character recognition systems conf.# NISTIR 4912. The US Bureau of Census and the National Institute of Standards and Technology, Gaithersburg, MD (1992)
24. Zhou, S., Chen, Q., Wang, X.: HIT-OR3C: an opening recognition corpus for Chinese characters. In: Proceedings of the 9th IAPR International Workshop on Document Analysis Systems, pp. 223–230. ACM (2010)

Inflectional and Derivational Hybrid Stemmer for Sentiment Analysis: A Case Study with Marathi Tweets

Rupali S. Patil[(✉)] and Satish R. Kolhe

School of Computer Sciences, Kavayitri Bahinabai Chaudhari North Maharashtra University, Jalgaon 425001, Maharashtra, India
rupali.patil173@gmail.com
http://nmu.ac.in/

Abstract. Sentiment Analysis (SA) is more complex in Marathi (Indian Language) than in European languages due to the inflectional words and phrases and comparatively limited resources. SA needs several preprocessing steps, viz., cleaning, stemming, and stopword removal, which reduces the feature set's dimensionality. Stemming, a crucial preprocessing step, converts the inflected words to a root or stem without morphological analysis. The first-ever work presents the inflectional and derivational hybrid stemmer for Marathi Tweets, using a rule-based approach and a dictionary look-up. The 10000 sentences (103789 words) are extracted from the OSCAR (https://oscar-corpus.com/) Marathi corpus to design and develop the stemmer. It achieved an average accuracy of 89.37% for ten random samples of 1000 words each. The performance is investigated using Paice's parameters, i.e., under-stemming and over-stemming errors, Index Compression Factor (ICF), and Mean number of words per signature (MWC). The benchmark dataset of 4,245 Marathi political tweets is constructed to validate the system, and the Marathi lexicons (adjective-adverb) are built from SentiWordNet, and Hindi SentiWordNet are used to classify the tweets as positive or negative. The various experiments are performed to measure the stemmer effect on lexicon-based sentence level SA for Marathi tweets. The outcomes evidence improved accuracy using stemmer from 67.52% to 74.49% with F-measure of 0.75. However, some adverse effects of stemming are observed in the result.

Keywords: Stemmer · Sentiment analysis · Marathi

1   Introduction

In recent years, social media have been reached millions of people around the world, which facilitates interactions on a large scale. Several social media sites like Facebook, Twitter, Instagram, and Google+ carry meaningful insights. Most people use social sites to express their emotions and opinions. English and European languages have dominated the web since its commencement. However, in

© Springer Nature Switzerland AG 2022
KC Santosh et al. (Eds.): RTIP2R 2021, CCIS 1576, pp. 263–279, 2022.
https://doi.org/10.1007/978-3-031-07005-1_23

the last few years, the Indian and Asian language data is significantly increased on the internet. The web data in Indian languages like Hindi, Bengali, Tamil, Telugu, Urdu, and Marathi is now available. Sentiment Analysis (SA) is the evolving field that aims to help people mine web data, find vital information, and detect sentiments. Twitter is a popular micro-blogging site on which people (registered users) can post and interact through messages, termed as Tweet. Initially, tweet characters were restricted to 140, but from November 2017, the character limit has doubled to 280 for all languages, excluding Chinese, Japanese, and Korean. The company reports 126 million daily active users worldwide [1]. It ranks in one of the ten most visited websites in the world [2]. Marathi [3], an Indo-Aryan regional language of central-western India, spoken by 83.1 million people of the Maharashtra state, is one of the 22 scheduled languages of India. It positions 10th in the list of the most spoken languages in the world. After Hindi and Bengali, it has the third-largest native speakers in India. Twitter supports the Marathi language and the other six Indian dialects from August 2015, encouraging more regional people to interact and use the micro-blogging site. Sentiment Analysis is the study of people's emotions, opinions, attitudes, and beliefs. To obtain useful insights about a particular entity, tweets related to this entity can be analyzed. The SA of Marathi tweets is troublesome compared to English and European languages due to the inflectional nature of the language and insufficient resources in Marathi. Before applying sentiment analysis, preprocessing of the data is essential to increase the performance level of the SA system. It is one of the significant steps in the sentiment analysis task, which involves cleaning, stop word removal, and stemming. The cleaning involves the removal of unwanted symbols like # (hashtag), @, RT, and punctuation marks from the tweets filtered by the language Marathi. Stop word removal is the process of eliminating useless words to reduce the size of the data set and improve the overall efficiency of the system [4]. The excess of words appearing in the different morphological forms due to inflection of the terms or the derivation from the root word adversely affects the SA system by endorsing the high dimensionality of the data. For instance, 'विधानसभेच्या' {vidhansabhechyaa} {Of the Legislative Assembly}, 'विधानसभेला' {vidhansabhela} {To the Legislative Assembly}, 'विधानसभेतून' {vidhansabhetun} {From the Legislative Assembly}, 'विधानसभेतील' {vidhansabhetil} {In the Legislative Assembly}, 'विधानसभेसाठी' {vidhansabhesathi} {For the Legislative Assembly}, 'विधानसभेसमोर' {vidhansabhesamor} {In front of the Legislative Assembly} are treated as different words which need to be transformed into only one root 'विधानसभा' {Vidhansabha} {Assembly}. This problem is usually deal by the stemming process. However, the standard stemmer for sentiment analysis of the Marathi language is not readily available. To develop the stemmer, several approaches have been proposed by the researchers, which include rule-based [5–8], dictionary look-up, statistical [9], and hybrid [10–14]. The rule-based approach uses of a set of linguistic rules to strip the suffixes, whereas the dictionary look-up stemmer scans the words in the look-up table and finds the stem to assign for the term. The statistical stemmers are grounded on the corpus statistics like n-gram and HMM. The hybrid stemmers are the combination of any two or more techniques making the best use of them. Each of the stemming methods differs concerning performance and accuracy. The main contributions of research work are in the following:

- Design and development of linguistic rules for stemmer using OCSAR Marathi corpus.
- The manual creation of Marathi stop word list for Marathi text.
- An algorithm for inflectional and derivational hybrid stemmer, a combination of the rule-based and dictionary look-up approach, is proposed for the Marathi text.
- Evaluate the stemmer by performing random sampling of ten test data sets with 1000 unique words each.
- Develop Marathi political tweet dataset, as the standard dataset is not readily available.
- Validate the Marathi stemmer on the benchmark tweet dataset by calculating the standard measures such as accuracy, precision, recall, and F-score.

The rest of the research paper is organized as follows. Section 2 comprises the related work in this area. The morphology of the Marathi language is discussed in Sect. 3. Section 4 presents the proposed methodology for preprocessing steps, including the algorithm for a hybrid stemmer. The experiments and the results are given in Sect. 5. Lastly, the paper concludes in Sect. 6.

2   Related Work

Preprocessing utilizes 85% of the time and efforts [15] of the overall time and efforts of the Knowledge Discovery in Database (KDD), the process of discovering valuable knowledge from a collection of data. SA, as a new trend in KDD, requires many preprocessing steps. The authors [15] presented the design and implementation of a sentiment analysis system for preprocessing and stemming of English tweets. It involved segmentation, cleaning, stop word removing, and stemming on different data sets ranging from 250000 to 1000000 tweets. The system is implemented using MS-SQL and made use of the Porter algorithm [16] for stemming. They accomplished significant data reduction by preserving the attributes of the data sets. The execution time taken by the system was an hour and 32 min for the data set with one million tweets. In the case of stemmer works, many studies have been carried out for English. The authors [17] published the first stemmer based on the context-sensitive longest match in 1968. Later, some of the prominent English stemmers were developed include [18], a very widely used Porter stemmer was designed by Martin Porter [16], which became the standard stemmer algorithm, and [19]. The authors [4] proposed a language-independent unsupervised stemming algorithm. A multipurpose stemmer can be used in Information Retrieval (IR), SA, text classification, and inflection removal. The method employed lexical and corpus-based features to efficiently conflate morphological variations produced by dialectal processes such as suffixation, conversion, and compounding. The algorithm has experimented in IR for English,

Marathi, Hungarian, and Bengali. The performance of the projected approach is compared with baseline algorithms and achieved a significant improvement in all the languages. For the text classification task, the proposed stemmer outperformed the baseline algorithms. The work on stemming for Indian languages began in late 2000. The first stemmer for Hindi lightweight language is proposed by Ramanathan and Rao [20], which used a manually created suffix list with 65 suffixes. It is based on the longest match stripping. The authors [10] have presented two stemmers for the Gujarati language - a lightweight inflectional stemmer using a hybrid method as well as a heavyweight derivational stemmer applying a rule-based method. The average accuracy of 90.7% and 70.7% for inflectional stemmer and derivational stemmer, respectively, is achieved. The authors [21] developed a stemmer named YASS - Yet Another Suffix Stripper. It used a statistical clustering technique based on a string distance measure for the Bengali language. The authors [22] proposed an unsupervised Hindi stemmer. The Hindi documents from the EMILE corpus are used to train the system, and then the stem and suffix probabilities are calculated. The accuracy of this approach is 90%. The authors [5] discussed a rule-based and unsupervised approach to develop a Marathi stemmer. They categorized the Marathi suffixes into three types - plain suffixes, join word suffixes, and complex suffixes. The rule-based stemmer used suffix stripping on morphological features of Marathi, whereas the unsupervised stemmer is based on the n-gram splitting technique. The authors [11] proposed a lightweight Gujarati stemmer using a hybrid method based on Goldsmith's [23] take-all-splits way and a list of manually created Gujarati suffixes. The stemmer removed inflectional suffixes only and achieved an accuracy of 67.86%. The derivational suffixes are not included in the proposed approach. The domain-independent, lightweight Malayalam stemmer LALITHA [24] based on the suffix stripping method has been proposed. The authors [25] proposed a Malayalam stemmer called STHREE using a three-pass algorithm, which reported an accuracy of 97%. The authors [26] discussed the rule-based inflectional and derivational stemmer called Usal for the Urdu language. The system is evaluated on the test data of 3000 Urdu words, which achieved 89.66% accuracy. The authors [27] presented the rule-based Marathi stemmer termed as MarS. The three categories of the Marathi suffixes discussed in [5] are taken into consideration. They experimented on the dataset, which is a Marathi corpus acquired from FIRE (Forum for Information Retrieval for Indian Languages) with 99,275 Marathi documents. The three-step stemming process has been carried out. The first step removed the inflectional suffixes based on the longest common match method. In steps two and three, the plain suffixes and the joint word suffixes are removed, respectively. The system has obtained an average accuracy of 79.97% in nine runs. The under-stemming and over-stemming rates of the system are high. The authors [28] proposed the dictionary-based stemmer for the Marathi language. The dictionary has been manually prepared using the 3000 Marathi documents of the FIRE corpus. The stemmer has got a maximum accuracy of 80.6% when performed the nine different runs. The over-stemming rate is low, but the under-stemming errors are generated. In [29], the comparative study of indexing and the search strategies in the information retrieval area is presented for three Indian languages: Hindi, Marathi, and Bengali. A hybrid stemmer with a rule-based and dictionary look-up method is proposed by the authors [30], in which 3000 FIRE documents are used to create the dictionary, and 500 rules for stemming are proposed. The average accuracy of 84.82% is reported in nine runs. The work stated low over-stemming but high under-stemming errors. The efforts in the state-of-art to develop the Marathi stemmer are towards the information retrieval field. To the best of our knowledge, the proposed work is the first approach to develop the stemmer for the sentiment analysis of the microblogging site - Twitter for the Marathi political tweets.

3   Marathi Morphology

The Marathi phoneme set consists of eleven vowels, forty consonants, and two sound modifiers [31]. It follows the Devanagari script, locally recognized as b¯albodh. In linguistics, morphemes are the smaller meaning-bearing elements [32]. The morpheme is mainly of two types: stem and affix. Stems are the central part providing meaning to the word, and hence stemming has a vital role. An affix is a morpheme attached to a word stem to form a new word or word form. The words are formed by combining the morphemes in two ways: Inflection and derivation. Inflection is the process of word modification with affixation. The Marathi nouns inflect for gender (masculine, feminine, neuter), number (singular, plural), and case; adjectives inflect for gender and number; pronouns inflect for gender, number, case, and person; verbs inflect for gender, number, and person and also for tense, mood, and aspect [33]. For example, the noun 'राणी' {rani} queen is feminine. Its singular form is 'राण्या' {ranyaa} {queens}. Marathi has eight cases [33] viz., a nominative case (kartā- कर्ता), accusative case (karma- कर्म), instrumental case (karaṇa- करण), dative case (sampradāna-सम्प्रदान), ablative case (apadana- अपादान), genitive case (sambandh- संबंध), locative case (adhikaran- अधिकरण), and vocative case (sambhodan- संबोधन). It has three persons- first (pratham purushh- प्रथम पुरुष), second (dwitiya purushh- द्वितिय पुरुष), and third (trutiya purushh- तृतिय पुरुष). The derivation is the formation of a new word from an existing word. The derivational morpheme is attached to the word to add meaning, resulting in a word of a different class. Derivational morphology deals in deriving the new words either by affixation, e.g., 'जबाबदारी' {jababdari} {responsibility} derived from 'जबाबदार' {jababdar} {responsible} or by making variations at the morphemes, e.g., 'प्रादेशिक' {praadeshik} {regional} derived from 'प्रदेश' {pradesh}, {region}. The derivational morphemes [34], affixed to verbs that derive nouns, adjectives, and adverbs termed as Krudanta, as a contrast to Taddhita suffixes affixed to nouns deriving the remaining three linguistic categories by changing the part-of-speech (POS). Due to the complexity of these traditional suffixes, maintaining affix stripping rules for all the forms is not feasible [35], for example, 'देव्हाऱ्याजवळचादेखील' is the complex word variant with 'च्या,' 'जवळ,' 'चा,'

and **'देखील'** as suffixes. Table 1 presents some of the krudanta and taddhita suffixes handled in this work.

Table 1. Krudanta and Taddhita types in Marathi

Derivational Morpheme	Affix Type	Example
Krudanta Affixe (verb + affix -> noun/adj/adv)	त{ta}, ताना {tana}, ला {laa}, ल्या {lyaa}, लेला {lelaa}, णारा {naraa}, वत {vat}, ऊन {oon}, वा {vaa}	बोलणारा {bolnara} {the one who is talking}, करताना {kartana} {while doing}, आणलेला {aanlela} {brought}
Taddhita Affixes (noun + affix -> verb/adj/adv)	कट {kat}, की {ki}, दा {daa}, दार {dar}, पण {pan}, पणा {panaa}, शीर {shir}, सा {sa}	तेलकट {telkat} {oily}, माणुसकी {manuski} {humanity}, एकदा {ekdaa} {once} मूर्खपणा {moorkhpanaa} {foolishness}

4   Marathi Stemming Algorithm

The core objective of the work is to propose efficient preprocessing and stemming algorithms for Marathi text. This step is crucial for any SA system to achieve better analytical results. Figure 1 shows the proposed approach.

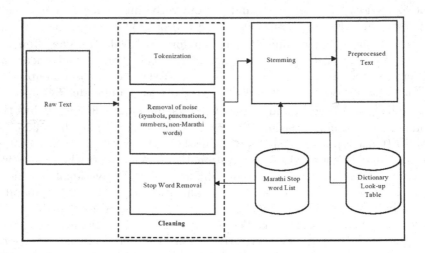

Fig. 1. The proposed architecture

4.1 Data Collection

To design and develop the hybrid Marathi stemmer, the OSCAR (Open Super-large Crawled Aggregated coRpus), a vast multilingual corpus, was primarily developed to train the unsupervised language models in NLP, is used. It includes various languages' sub-corpora. The 1,03,789 words (33,161 unique words) are fetched from the Marathi sub-corpus of the OSCAR corpus. From the Marathi sub-corpus with 1,450,762 KB, only the first 10000 sentences (2018 KB) are considered for the experimentation. The general domain Marathi sentence includes noise such as numbers, punctuation marks, symbols, and non-Marathi (foreign) words that need to be cleaned in further steps. To validate the system, the Marathi tweets corpus composed in this work is used Twitter Achiever Tool [36]. Through the Google Spreadsheet, the Twitter connection was established using Google script. The 4,245 raw political tweets for different political parties, such as BJP (Bhartiya Janta Party), Indian National Congress (Congress), National Congress Party (NCP), and Shivsena, are collected from September 20, 2019, to October 20, 2019, just the one month before Maharashtra's Assembly elections for October 21, 2019.

4.2 Cleaning

SA system requires valuable words that refer to the positive or negative value; hence, it is essential to remove the worthless words and symbols from the data. This process includes the removal of noise from OSCAR Marathi sub-corpus, as well as from the Marathi tweets, such as hashtags, website URLs, Twitter mentions, duplicate tweets, special characters, numbers, and punctuations, and non-Marathi words and letters.

4.3 Stop Word Removal

In SA, the words which do not carry any positive or negative sentiment are treated as stop words [4] and must be removed from the dataset before analysis.

For example, in English, stop words include 'the,' 'to,' 'is,' 'as,' 'of,' 'and.' In Marathi, the stop words contain 'मी,' 'पण,' 'किंवा,' 'म्हणून,' 'आधी,' 'श्री,' 'महासचिव,' 'माजी.' The proposed system uses the 684 stop word list created manually as the standard list is not available.

4.4 Marathi Subjective Lexicon (Adjective-Adverb)

The Marathi subjective lexicon is constructed using Marathi WordNet, Hindi WordNet, and Hindi SentiWordNet (HSWN) [40]. HSWN is the lexical resource designed by working on SentiWordNet and English-Hindi WordNet linking. The Hindi SentiWordNet-Based Marathi Lexicon (HSWNB-ML) covers adjectives and adverbs, along with the three polarities - positive, negative, and neutral, since these words carry most of the sentiments in the sentence. The lexicon contains 220 positive, 397 negative, and 1758 neutral entities. The SentiWordNet-Based Marathi Lexicon (SWNB-ML) created in [40] is constructed using the rich and powerful English SWN3.0. The adjectives and adverbs of SWN3.0 are translated into Marathi using Google Translator, and polarity scores are assigned to corresponding Marathi words. Based on the contexts, the words have various senses in SWN. However, the words with primary sense#1 are targeted by the authors. The lexicon contains the words and their part-of-speeches, the English translation of the word, positive, negative, and neutral score. The lexicon contains 860 positive, 1069 negative, and 8324 neutral entities, and the SWNB-ML was constructed. The two Marathi lexicons HSWNB-ML and SWNB-ML, are used to classify the tweets. The reason for choosing the HSWNB-ML is that the inter-rater agreement is almost perfect with a kappa score of 0.84, but because of its low word coverage, the SWNB-ML with high word coverage is incorporated with the HSWNB-ML by removing the duplicate entries. The resulting Marathi lexicon, with 9,638 adjectives and 1,273 adverbs, is used to classify the benchmark Marathi tweet dataset.

4.5   Stemming

Stemming [15] is the process that transforms the word variants to their root or stem to reduce the adverse effect, considering the crucial preprocessing step before SA. This research proposes the hybrid algorithm based on the affix stripping rule-based and dictionary look-up approach.

Affix Stripping Rule Formation - The work presents three groups of Marathi suffixes created in the form of suffix stripping, orthographic, and substitution rules for the stemmer:

Group 1 - Substitutional suffixes: The words with the morphological variants are replaced to form the stem of a word, e.g., 'नारा' nara replaced with 'णे' ne, 'बोलणारा' bolnara resulting in a root word 'बोलणे' bolne to talk

Group 2 - Vibhakti Pratyaya suffixes: In Marathi, eight vibhakti pratyaya are present which are attached as suffixes to the root word to produce its variant, e.g., 'स' sa, 'ला' laa, 'ते' te, 'ना' naa, 'शी' shi.

Group 3 - Complex and dependent suffixes: The words 'साठी,' 'वर,' 'कडून,' 'मध्ये' combined with the root word to form the morphological variant, e.g., 'माझ्याकडून,' 'फुलासारखा,' 'भारतामध्ये' are the words containing complex suffixes. The vowel signs are also called dependent suffixes, which combine with the root word to form its variant. 'ां,' 'ाों,' 'ा,' 'ि,' 'ों,' 'ु,' 'ू',.. are some of the vowel suffixes combined with vibhakti pratyaya suffixes in Group 1 and with complex suffixes in Group 2.

Creation of Dictionary - The dictionary look-up table has the inflected forms of the words and their stems. The development of the look-up table involves manual efforts by adding the stem of the word variants. The clean and stop word removed tweets are treated as the corpus. The dictionary contains 367 unique stem words obtained from the tweet corpus. It contains all the possible derivational word variants corresponding to the root words. The stemming is performed by searching the index element in the dictionary.

The proposed stemmer algorithm is shown in Fig. 2, which performs root word replacement and stop word removal iteratively to minimize the over-stemming errors.

Algorithm 1: *Marathi Hybrid Stemmer*

Input: input_file, stopset, rootword_dict
Output: stemmed_words
Begin
Read the input_file to be stemmed
Tokenize the input_file and generate the token list T
stopwords_removed_list = remove_stopwords(T, stopset)
rootword_replaced_list =
replace_rootwords(stopwords_removed_list, rootword_dict)
word_list = remove_stopwords(rootword_replaced_list)
for word in word_list do
   if word contains suffix from suffix_group1 then
     wordlist_grp1 = apply rule from Group1
     wordlist_grp1 = remove_stopwords(wordlist_grp1, stopset)
     wordlist_grp1 = replace_rootword(wordlist_grp1,
rootword_dict)
   if word contains suffix from suffix_group2 then
     wordlist_grp2 = apply rule from Group2
     wordlist_grp2 = remove_stopwords(wordlist_grp2, stopset)
     wordlist_grp2 = replace_rootword(wordlist_grp2,
rootword_dict)
   if word contains suffix from suffix_group3 then
     wordlist_grp3 = apply rule from Group3
     wordlist_grp3 = remove_stopwords(wordlist_grp3, stopset)
     wordlist_grp3 = replace_rootword(wordlist_grp3,
rootword_dict)
stemmed_words = remove_stopwords(wordlist_grp3)

Fig. 2. Algorithm for Marathi hybrid stemmer

5   Experiments and Results

5.1   Performance of the Stemmer

The performance of the hybrid stemmer is evaluated using four factors [37]: i) The stemming accuracy, ii) Under-stemming and over- stemming error rate, iii) Index Compression Factor (ICF), and iv) Mean number of words per signature (MWC). The accuracy of the stemmer is calculated using Eq. 1.

$$Accuracy\ (\%) = \frac{Total\ no.\ of\ words\ correctly\ stemmed}{total\ no.\ of\ words\ stemmed} * 10 \tag{1}$$

The correctly stemmed word does not imply linguistic correctness, i.e., the stem need not be the morphological root. For example, the morphological root of the word 'reducing' is 'reduce'; however, a stemmer could produce the stem 'reduce' by removing the suffixing. It will not be considered incorrect for all the morphological variants of 'reduce' such as 'reduced', 'reducing', 'reduces' mapped to 'reduce'.

Stemming errors are of two types: under-stemming, the words that refer to the same root are not reduced to the same stem, and over-stemming, the words are transformed to the same stem even if they refer to different roots [38]. The third factor, Index Compression Factor (ICF), and the fourth factor, the mean number of words per signature (MWC), measure the stemmer strength and are calculated in Eqs. 2 and 3.

$$ICF = \frac{Total\ no.\ of\ unique\ words - Total\ no.\ of\ unique\ stemmed\ words}{Total\ no.\ of\ unique\ words} \tag{2}$$

$$MCW = \frac{Total\ no.\ of\ unique\ stemmed\ words}{Total\ no.\ of\ unique\ words} \tag{3}$$

The test data is distributed in ten runs. Table 2 shows the test data statistics and the stemmer strength in the form of ICF and MWC.

Table 2. Statistics of the test data

Test no.	Total words	StopWord removed words	Unique words before stemming	Total stemmed unique words	Correctly stemmed unique words	ICF	MCW
1	1000	967	699	501	467	0.28	1.40
2	1000	956	670	441	401	0.34	1.52
3	1000	952	668	490	446	0.27	1.36
4	1000	965	752	612	548	0.19	1.23
5	1000	941	671	530	465	0.21	1.27
6	1000	949	706	648	576	0.08	1.09
7	1000	962	657	502	456	0.24	1.31
8	1000	980	414	361	322	0.13	1.15
9	1000	966	736	657	597	0.11	1.12
10	1000	962	724	543	487	0.25	1.33

Table 3. Accuracy and errors of the stemmer

Run no.	Total stemmed words	Incorrect stemmed words	Correct stemmed words	Accuracy (%)	Under-stemming errors (%)	Over-stemming errors (%)
1	501	75	426	85.03	2.99	11.98
2	441	40	401	90.93	2.04	7.03
3	490	44	446	91.02	1.63	7.35
4	612	64	548	89.54	1.96	8.5
5	530	65	465	87.74	2.08	10.19
6	648	72	576	88.89	2.01	9.1
7	502	46	456	90.84	1.39	7.77
8	361	39	322	89.2	0.83	9.97
9	657	60	597	90.87	2.44	6.7
10	543	56	487	89.69	0.92	9.39

Table 3 presents the % accuracy and the stemming errors of the proposed stemmer.

It is observed that the maximum accuracy of 91.02% and minimum accuracy of 85.03% are achieved. The proposed stemmer makes an average of 1.8% under-stemming and 8.79% over-stemming errors. Figure 3 shows the under-stemming and over-stemming errors.

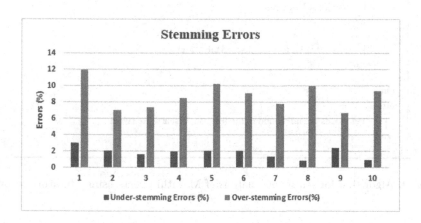

Fig. 3. Under-stemming and over-stemming errors

5.2 Tweet Classification and Stemmer Validation

In order to validate the proposed stemmer, the Marathi tweet corpus with 4,245 tweets is developed for the political domain. With the expert's help, the 2,100

Algorithm 2: *Sentiment Analysis using Marathi Lexicon*

Input: Marathi Lexicon (Lex_file), csv file for containing tweet dataset (D)
Output: Tweets classification (POS, NEG)
Notation: W: word, T: tweet, *pos_score*: positive score, *neg_score*: negative score, O_Pos: overall positive score for a tweet, O_Neg: overall negative score for a tweet
Initialization: $pos\_score = neg\_score = O\_Pos = O\_Neg = 0.0$
while T *in D* **do**
    for W *in T* **do**
        if (W *is present in Lex_file*) **then**
            $pos\_score = get\_pos\_score$ (W)
            $neg\_score = get\_neg\_score$ (W)
            if ($pos\_score >= neg\_score$) **then**
                $O\_Pos = O\_Pos + pos\_score$
            end
            else if ($pos\_score < neg\_score$) **then**
                $O\_Neg = O\_Neg + neg\_score$
            end
        end
        else
            W is not present in *Lex_file*
        end
    end
    if (*Sentiment words are present in T*) **then**
        if ($O\_Pos > O\_Neg$) **then**
            Tweet is Positive
        end
        else if ($O\_Neg > O\_Pos$) **then**
            Tweet is Negative
        end
        else
            Tweet is Objective, discard the tweet
        end
    end
    else
        Tweet words are not found in the lexicon, discard the tweet
    end
end

Fig. 4. Algorithm for sentiment analysis of Marathi tweets using Marathi lexicon

Neutral tweets Out of 4,245 are discarded from further processing as they do not carry any sentiments. The lexicon-based SA module uses the Marathi lexicons generated in [40], which classifies 2,145 tweets as positive, negative, or neutral with and without the stemming process. Figure 4 shows the algorithm for SA using the Marathi lexicon to classify the tweets as positive or negative. The experiment evaluates the system in terms of accuracy, precision, recall, and F-score measures. Table 4 shows the result of the SA module with and without

Table 4. Validation of stemmer on tweet dataset with and without stemmer

Method	Total tweets	Classified tweets	Correctly classified tweets	Accuracy (%)	P	R	F-score
Without stemmer	2145	1755	1185	67.52	0.6257	0.8213	0.7104
With stemmer	2145	1835	1367	74.49	0.6819	0.8325	0.7497

the stemming process. The system, without stemming, could find the adjectives and adverbs of 1755 tweets, where 1,185 tweets are correctly classified. The system could not classify the 390 tweets since the tweets contain sentimental words (adjective-adverb) in either inflected or derived form. Hence the system could not locate them in the Marathi lexicon. For instance, the word 'सुगंध' {fragrance} is present in the Marathi lexicon as 'सुगंध,0.625,0,a' being a positive word. The word inflects by the attachment of the suffixes 'oमुळे' in the tweet text resulting in 'सुगंधामुळे' {because of the fragrance} which the system could not find in the lexicon. With the help of the proposed Marathi stemmer, the inflected and derived words are converted into their root forms. The system, with stemming, could classify 80 more tweets resulting in 1,835 tweets classification, where 1,367 tweets are correctly classified. The more adjectives and adverbs found in the Marathi lexicon by stemming process classified the tweets more accurately. The experiments evidence the rise in the accuracy of sentiment analysis of Marathi tweets from 67.52% to 74.49%. However, the adverse effects of stemming are observed, like under-stemming and over-stemming errors (Tables 5 and 6).

Table 5. Tweet classification (with and without stemmer)

Tweet	Translation	Polarity without stemming	Polarity with stemming
भाजप सरकार भक्कम	The BJP government is strong	Positive	Positive
भाजप आणि देवेंद्र फडणवीस चांगल्या प्रकारे कार्य करत आहेत	BJP and Devendra Fadnavis are doing well	Not classified	Positive
भाजप देशभरात वाढण्यात त्यांच्या कर्तृत्वापेक्षा काँग्रेसचा मूर्खपणा जास्त कारणीभूत	The stupidity of the Congress is more responsible for the growth of the BJP in the country than their deeds	Negative	Negative
राज्यकर्त्यांच्या नाकर्तेपणामुळे मुंबईकरांचे जीव घेणे	Mumbaikars are being killed due to the reluctance of the rulers	Not classified	Negative

Table 6. Comparison with the existing Marathi stemmer

Reference	Approach	Area	Total unique words	Result
[29]	Light and aggressive	IR	NA	Improvements over no stemming: 13.9% with light stemmer, 41.6% with the aggressive stemmer
[5]	Rule-based and unsupervised	IR	1500	Rule-based-80.7%
[27]	Rule-based	IR	4500	79.97
[28]	Dictionary-based	IR	4500	80.6
[30]	Hybrid	IR	4500	84.82
Proposed	Hybrid	SA	6697	89.37

5.3 Comparison with Existing Marathi Stemmers

The work [30] is proposed for the Information Retrieval area. According to [39], stop word removal is advantageous in the text retrieval system, but it is not handled in [30]. The stop words are removed in the proposed work. The morphological resource stemmer is required to reduce the data sparsity in sentiment analysis of the Marathi language.

6 Conclusion

Preparing the data for sentiment analysis needs numerous steps that play a critical role in reducing worthless information without losing meaningful data. Stemming, followed by cleaning and stop word removal, is crucial for making the data valuable for sentiment analysis. This paper first attempts to create the hybrid stemmer for sentiment analysis of Marathi political tweets. The tweet dataset comprising 4,245 Marathi political tweets from different political parties is generated. The algorithms for stop word removal, root word replacement from the dictionary look-up table and hybrid Marathi stemmer are designed and developed using 10,000 sentences from the OSCAR Marathi corpus (103789 words). The proposed stemmer is based on linguistic rules and a dictionary look-up table. The average accuracy of 89.37% is obtained when tested on ten random samples of 1000 words each. The greatly improved result of the proposed approach is due to the well-formed affix stripping rules and maximum coverage of the rules for the dataset used in work. The over-stemming and under-stemming error rates are low due to the adequate word-stem dictionary entries. The system is validated on the benchmark dataset of 4,245 Marathi political tweets and Marathi lexicon's help (adjective-adverb). The accuracy, precision, and recall are measured for the tweet classification with and without the use of the proposed stemmer.

The experiments evidence the improved accuracy using stemmer from 67.52% to 74.49% with F-measure of 0.75. However, the adverse effects are under-stemming and over-stemming, which need to be handled using more linguistic knowledge like Part-Of-Speeches of the words.

References

1. Twitter reveals its daily active user numbers for the first time (2021). https://www.washingtonpost.com/technology/2019/02/07/twitter-reveals-its-daily-active-user-numbers-first-time. Accessed 25 Feb 2021
2. Top websites ranking (2020). https://www.similarweb.com/top-websites. Accessed 7 July 2020
3. Marathi language. https://en.wikipedia.org/w/index.php?title=Marathi_language&oldid=1013782960. Accessed 7 July 2020
4. Singh, J., Gupta, V.: A novel unsupervised corpus-based stemming technique using lexicon and corpus statistics. Knowl. Based Syst. **180**, 147–162 (2019)
5. Majgaonker, M.M., Siddiqui, T.: Discovering suffixes: a case study for Marathi language. Int. J. Comput. Sci. Eng. **2**(8), 2716–2720 (2010)
6. Gupta, V.: Hindi rule-based stemmer for nouns. Int. J. Adv. Res. Comput. Sci. Softw. Eng. **4**(1), 62–65 (2014)
7. Sarkar, S., Bandyopadhyay, S.: Design of a rule-based stemmer for natural language text in Bengali. In: Proceedings of the IJCNLP - 08 Workshop on NLP for Less Privileged Languages, pp. 65–72 (2008)
8. Das, S., Mitra, P.: A rule based approach of stemming for inflectional and derivational words in Bengali. In: IEEE Technology Symposium, pp. 134–136 (2011)
9. Bhat, S.: Statistical stemming for Kannada. In: The 4th Workshop on South and Southeast Asian NLP, International Joint Conference on Natural Language Processing, pp. 25–33 (2013)
10. Suba, K., Jiandani, D., Bhattacharyya, P.: Hybrid inflectional stemmer and rule-based derivational stemmer for Gujarati. In: Proceedings of the 2nd Workshop on South and Southeast Asian Natural Language Processing (WSSANLP), IJCNLP, pp. 1–8 (2011)
11. Patel, P., Popat, K., Bhattacharyya, P.: Hybrid stemmer for Gujarati. In: Proceedings of the 1st Workshop on South and Southeast Asian Natural Processing (WSSANLP), the 23rd International Conference on Computational Linguistics (COLING), pp. 51–55 (2010)
12. Mishra, U., Prakash, C.: MAULIK: an effective stemmer for Hindi language. Int. J. Comput. Sci. Eng. **4**(5), 711–717 (2012)
13. Saharia, N., Konwar, K.M., Sharma, U., Kalita, J.K.: An improved stemming approach using HMM for a highly inflectional language. In: Gelbukh, A. (ed.) Computational Linguistics and Intelligent Text Processing, CICLing 2013. LNCS, vol. 7816, pp. 164–173. Springer, Heidelberg (2013). https://doi.org/10.1007/978-3-642-37247-6_14
14. Meitei, S., Purkayastha, B.S., Devi, H.M.: Development of a Manipuri stemmer: a hybrid approach. In: 2015 International Symposium on Advanced Computing and Communication (ISACC), pp. 128–131 (2015)
15. Al-Khafaji, H.K., Habeeb, A.T.: Efficient algorithms for preprocessing and stemming of tweets in a sentiment analysis system. IOSR J. Comput. Eng. **19**(3), 44–50 (2017)

16. Porter, J.M., John, L.: Economist and Social ScientistKaren Iversen Vaughn Chicago Economist and Social Scientist Karen Iversen Vaughn Chicago, 2nd edn., pp. xiv, 178. University of Chicago Press (1981)
17. Lovins, J.B.: Development of a stemming algorithm. Mech. Transl. Computat. Linguist. **11**, 21–31 (1968)
18. Dawson, J.L.: Suffix removal for word conflation. Bull. Assoc. Lit. Linguist. Comput. **14**(3), 33–46 (1974)
19. Paice, C.D.: Another stemmer. ACM SIGIR Forum **24**(3), 56–61 (1990)
20. Ramanathan, A., Rao, D.D.: A lightweight stemmer for Hindi. In: Workshop on Computational Linguistics for South-Asian Languages, EACL, pp. 1–8 (2003)
21. Majumder, P., Mitra, M., Parui, S.K., Kole, G., Mitra, P., Datta, K.: YASS: yet another suffix stripper. ACM Trans. Inf. Syst. **25**, 18–38 (2007)
22. Pandey, A.K., Siddiqui, T.J.: An unsupervised Hindi stemmer with heuristic improvements. In: Proceedings of the Second Workshop on Analytics for Noisy Unstructured Text Data, AND 2008, pp. 99–105 (2008)
23. Goldsmith, J.A.: Unsupervised learning of the morphology of a natural language. Comput. Linguist. **27**, 353–371 (2001)
24. Prajitha, U., Sreejith, C., Reghuraj, P.C.: LALITHA: a light weight Malayalam stemmer using suffix stripping method. In: 2013 International Conference on Control Communication and Computing (ICCC), pp. 244–248 (2013)
25. Pragisha, K., Reghuraj, P.C.: STHREE: stemmer for Malayalam using three pass algorithm. In: International Conference on Control Communication and Computing (ICCC) (2013)
26. Gupta, V., Joshi, N., Mathur, I.: Design and development of rule based inflectional and derivational Urdu stemmer 'Usal'. In: 2015 International Conference on Futuristic Trends on Computational Analysis and Knowledge Management (ABLAZE) (2015)
27. Patil, H.B., Patil, A.S.: MarS: a rule-based stemmer for morphologically rich language Marathi. In: 2017 International Conference on Computer, Communications and Electronics (Comptelix) (2017). https://doi.org/10.1109/comptelix.2017.8004036
28. Patil, H.B., Mhaske, N.T., Patil, A.S.: Design and development of a dictionary based stemmer for Marathi language. In: Bhattacharyya, P., Sastry, H., Marriboyina, V., Sharma, R. (eds.) Smart and Innovative Trends in Next Generation Computing Technologies, vol. 827, pp. 769–777. Springer, Cham (2018). https://doi.org/10.1007/978-981-10-8657-1_60
29. Dolamic, L., Savoy, J.: Comparative study of indexing and search strategies for the Hindi, Marathi, and Bengali languages. ACM Trans. Asian Lang. Inf. Process. **9**(3), 1–24 (2010)
30. Patil, H.B., Patil, A.S.: A hybrid stemmer for the affix stacking language: Marathi. In: Iyer, B., Deshpande, P.S., Sharma, S.C., Shiurkar, U. (eds.) Computing in Engineering and Technology. AISC, vol. 1025, pp. 441–449. Springer, Singapore (2020). https://doi.org/10.1007/978-981-32-9515-5_42
31. Marathi alphabet (2019). https://en.wikibooks.org/w/index.php?title=Marathi/Alphabet&oldid=3587734. Accessed 27 Nov 2019
32. Jurafsky, D., Martin, J.H.: Speech and Language Processing: An Introduction to Natural Language Processing, Computational Linguistics, and Speech Recognition. Prentice Hall, Englewood Cliffs (2006)
33. Dabre, R., Ambekar, A., Bhattacharyya, P.: Morphological analyzer for affix stacking languages: a case study of Marathi. In: Proceedings of COLING 2012: Posters, COLING 2012, pp. 225–234 (2012)

34. Damale, M.K.: Marathi Shastriy Vyaakarana. Deshmukh and Company, Pune (1970)
35. Bhosale, G., Kembhavi, S., Amberkar, A., Mhatre, S., Popale, L., Bhattacharyya, P.: Processing of Kridanta (participle) in Marathi. In: Proceedings of ICON- 2011: 9th International Conference on Natural Language Processing. Macmillan Publishers (2011)
36. Sharma, Y., Mangat, V., Kaur, M.: A practical approach to sentiment analysis of Hindi tweets. In: 1st International Conference on Next Generation Computing Technologies (NGCT) (2015)
37. Frakes, W.B., Fox, C.J.: Strength and similarity of affix removal stemming algorithms. ACM SIGIR Forum **37**(1), 26–30 (2003). https://doi.org/10.1145/945546.945548
38. Paice, C.D.: An evaluation method for stemming algorithms. In: Croft, B.W., van Rijsbergen, C.J. (eds.) SIGIR '94, pp. 42–50. Springer, Cham (1994). https://doi.org/10.1007/978-1-4471-2099-5_5
39. Pandey, A.K., Siddiqui, T.J.: Evaluating effect of stemming and stop-word removal on Hindi text retrieval. In: Tiwary, U.S., Siddiqui, T.J., Radhakrishna, M., Tiwari, M.D. (eds.) Proceedings of the First International Conference on Intelligent Human Computer Interaction, pp. 316–326. Springer, Cham (2009). https://doi.org/10.1007/978-81-8489-203-1_31
40. Patil, R.S., Kolhe, S.R.: Resource creation for sentiment analysis of under-resourced language: Marathi. In: Santosh, K.C., Gawali, B. (eds.) Recent Trends in Image Processing and Pattern Recognition, RTIP2R 2020. CCIS, vol. 1380, pp. 445–457. Springer, Singapore (2021). https://doi.org/10.1007/978-981-16-0507-9_37

Adaptive Threshold-Based Database Preparation Method for Handwritten Image Classification

Parshuram M. Kamble[1], Darshan D. Ruikar[2(✉)], Kavita V. Houde[1],
and Ravindra S. Hegadi[1]

[1] Department of Computer Science, Central University of Karnataka,
Kalaburagi 585367, India
[2] School of Computer Science, MIT World Peace University, Pune 411038, India
darshanruikar1986@gmail.com

Abstract. Problem-specific, well classified database is primary and most important requirement of all machine learning-based systems. Hand-written character classification and recognition system is also no exception to this. In terms of features the good database must have less intra-class variance and high inter-class variance. However, extracting unique features from digital handwritten character image (HCI) is one of the most challenging task. High variation in the writing style of the writers and similarity in the feature value between multiple classes of characters are the primary hurdles. Unfortunately this scenario leads to high false acceptance rate which interns results drastic decrease in accuracy of the classification and recognition system.

As far as handwritten character classification and recognition system is concerned to overcome this hurdle we have developed a simple but effective adaptive threshold-based database preparation method. In the proposed method, Adaptive Threshold Value (AT_v) is calculated based on the similarity score (SS) of an existing HCI images in the respective class. If the threshold value of a new sample is in acceptable range then it is added into the feature map of respective class. To verify the efficiency and accuracy of the proposed method, the series of experiments are conducted on two standard datasets (MNIST and VDM). For the experimentation high-level features extracted using Deep neural network (DNN) based architecture and the proposed adaptive threshold-based method is applied to place HCI to correct class. Experimental results state that, the proposed adaptive thresholding-based method produces promising results and reduced the false acceptance rate.

Keywords: Handwritten character image (HCI) · Adaptive threshold · Feature extraction · Classification · Recognition

1 Introduction

Handwritten character recognition (HCR) is one of the most interesting and challenging branch of the optical character recognition (OCR). Designing a robust

© Springer Nature Switzerland AG 2022
KC Santosh et al. (Eds.): RTIP2R 2021, CCIS 1576, pp. 280–288, 2022.
https://doi.org/10.1007/978-3-031-07005-1_24

classification and recognition system for handwritten symbols (characters and numerals) is difficult task. Usage of inferior quality handwriting materials, variation in pen ink and thickness and presence of noise in scanned documents are the some basic challenges in the HCR. In addition to these conventional challenges, high variation in writing style of same person over time, mimicking other's handwriting style, and variation in the shape and curvature of the same character are the additional human dependent challenges are there. Due to this the probability of the misclassification is more in the HCR.

As far as HCR is concerned, there is always demand for new methods to emerge as computational technology to solve these challenges. Most of the researchers made several successful attempts to develop the state of the art methods to overcome conventional challenges. Inspite of this a lot of research, must be carried out to develop machine learning-based methods to overcome human dependent challenges and to improve overall system accuracy.

HCR system has two crucial sub-components: feature extraction and classification. In the feature extraction model, unique numerical or strings are extracted from the isolated handwritten sample and inserted into the feature map. Then, the feature map is classified based on the classification parameters. Some sample database is required to train HCR system and to evaluate the performance of system. That is, problem-specific database having sufficiently large amount well categorized samples is mandatory to build a machine learning-based HCR model.

The model tries learn inherent knowledge from that database in terms of features. If the database itself is not well catheterized then model may leads to confusing state and may not produce accurate output. In [5] a trained database is used to verify the class of the query sample. The region of curve (RoC) features were extracted for the classification. By confirming to the result, authors state that, loosely categorized database results increase in the false acceptance rate and also decrease in the overall accuracy of the system.

To overcome above discussed challenges in HCR model. We proposed adaptive threshold based database preparation method to develop automatically categories input handwritten character images (HCI) into correct class. In the experimentation of HCR consist whole feature database. Database contains the feature vectors values extracted from appropriate handwritten character image class.

Each class contains the finite number of the feature of handwritten characters image. Out of the dataset in real recognition model only one feature value is sufficient to recognize the image in the class. If failed in the same class then counted as a failed acceptance sample (FAS). This will help to prevents dales acceptance during character classification at training time. The adaptive threshold value is considered based on the similarity index of all samples with in class.

2 Related Works

Digital document data play a vital role in the field of information processing due to the presence of a vast collection of information [20]. Moreover, digital data processing is more economical than handling traditional paper information [3]. These systems can understand meaningful data stored on historical pages and manuscripts written in handwritten documents and enable to find of unrecognizable through the naked eye [1,5]. Apart from historical revelations, handwritten recognition systems are significant for the digital transformation of any organization [1].

Automatic handwriting recognition systems can have a range of uses: recognition of handwritten medical transcripts would help patients, staff, and chemists [17]. They may assist psychologists who believe that the personality can be judged through handwriting [18]. Handwritten recognition in forensic analyses can interpret handwriting to trace a criminal and help to drastically reduce the crime rates [9]. Automatic recognition of vehicle number plates and postal codes written on envelopes or reading bank cheques [19] are the other uses of automatic handwriting recognition.

All these applications have massive databases, and we need to develop recognition systems with minimum tolerance, computational time, and reliable accuracy. The task of the handwritten character recognition system is to group symbols (character, unique character, and digits) that are involved in writing a similar or multi-script [13]. However, variations in writing styles and patterns, the resemblance between the shapes of characters, and overlapped characters have increased the complexity of recognition systems [6].

Last few decades, researchers were focused on improving of handwritten character recognition. Many experiments are found using low and high-level features with supervised and unsupervised classification techniques. Low-level features are statistical [11], structural and topological based on pixel intensity and density [8]. Histogram Oriented Gradients (HOG) [10,14], Convolutional Neural Network (CNN) [16], Principal Components Analysis, and Local Binary Pattern are utilized to improvement of handwritten character recognition accuracy.

Feature map has been classified using Support Vector Machine, k- Nearest Neighbors (k- NN), and Neural Network [7] classification techniques. After studying existing work, we found that the false acceptance rate is a significant issue in the character recognition system. The database has been prepared based on the extracted features of the training dataset. In the dataset, we have added a threshold parameter that will avoid false entry into the database.

3   Methodology

In the proposed system adaptive threshold-based method is used to prepare the handwritten character database. A deep neural network (DNN) architecture is used to extract feature vector from input HCI [2,12]. During feature extraction process itself, threshold value is calculated and associated with each class. Then same database is used to train and evaluate classification and recognition system. The proposed system structure is illustrated in Fig. 1.

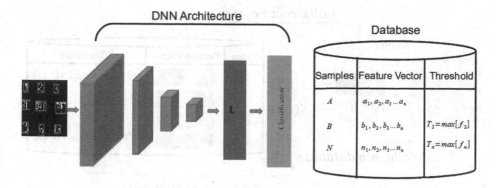

Fig. 1. System architecture

3.1 Deep Neural Network

At first, DNN-based character recognition model with the L normalization layers is trained. The HCI contains exactly one handwritten character which is given as a input to the model. The output of the L layers is extracted and used as the unified handwritten character feature vector. The extracted feature vector may either belongs to a class of the character whose feature has already been extracted or they may belongs to new class, i.e., a class for whom feature vector need to extract.

In L normalization, the inner product between two handwritten character classes is used to compute similarity index between two classes. At the time of feature extraction, a threshold value is associated to the feature extracted character and the threshold of the other feature extracted characters will be modified accordingly.

3.2 Feature Extraction with Adaptive Threshold

The handwritten character database made of images $I = I_1, I_2, I_3, \ldots I_n$. The unique identity label $P = P_1, P_2, P_3, \ldots P_n$ is associated with each image. DNN is used to extract feature vector $F = F_1, F_2, F_3, \ldots F_n$ for each image. Then to prepare a well formed database, the extracted feature vector are classified into respective classes. At the same time threshold value is also calculated and stored into the database. The proposed adaptive threshold-based database preparation system is described in Fig. 2.

Per iteration of each character class, classified feature vector F_n, respective unique feature threshold value t_n and identity label P_n is inserted into the database. Then the similarity score is calculated between two feature vectors F_v and F_d ($d = 1, 2, 3 \ldots n$) using below equation.

$$S(t, v) = F_v \cdot F_d \tag{1}$$

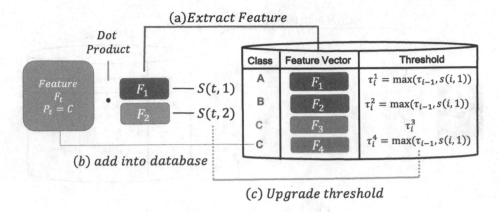

Fig. 2. Incubating threshold value for new class

Then t_i is calculated as the maximum value among all handwritten characters not belonging to the same class. The below formula is used to calculate t_i.

$$t_i = max(S(t, v)), \quad v = 1, 2, 3, \ldots n; \quad where \quad p_n \neq p_d \tag{2}$$

The handwritten images are classified one at a time. Recursive threshold modification approach is adapted to optimize the system performance.

3.3   Classification and Recognition

In a real-time application an input sample image I_λ without respective identity label is given to the proposed model. At first DNN architecture is used to extract feature vector F_λ of the input image I_λ. Then the similarity scores were computed with all the classes those are already stored in the database. Highest score value from the same class is extracted and denoted by index u:

$$u = max(S(\lambda, v)) for \quad v = 1, 2, 3, \ldots n \tag{3}$$

When the most matching class F_u is found, the proposed system compares the associated threshold t_i^u with the similarity score $S(\lambda, u)$. If $S(\lambda, u)$ more significant than t_i^u, then sample image I_λ will be classified as identity p_u. Else that image placed in new class B_new which indicates unknown entry.

The proposed classification and recognition system is illustrated in Fig. 3.

4   Experimental Setup and Evaluation Protocol

The main objective of the proposed work is to minimize the false acceptance rate of the character recognition system moreover to enhance overall classification accuracy. The proposed system is implemented using a Python platform with the additional libraries. All the experiments are tested on an intel core i5 processor 8 GB RAM and an NVIDIA Ge force GT 710 co-processor system.

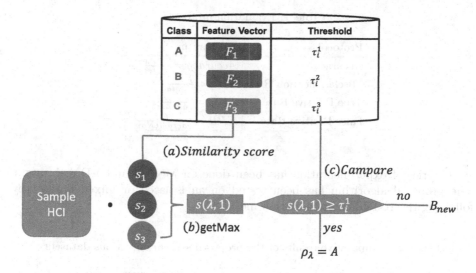

Fig. 3. Classification flowchart for sample HCI

4.1 Dataset and Pre-processing

The MNIST [15] and VDM [4] datasets are used for the experimentation and results were obtained. MNIST (Modified National Institute of Standards and Technology) is a digit dataset for handwritten character research and made it available for use. It has a large collection of handwritten digits. All digits have been written by high school students and employees of the United States Census Bureau. The digit dataset is already pre-processed and size normalized into the 20×20 pixel. MNIST dataset is split into two categories: training dataset with 60000 sample training and 10000 samples in testing.

VDM (Vikas J. Dongare and Vijay H. Mankar) dataset containing 5137 numerals and 20305 characters of Devanagari scripts obtained from 750 writers of different ages, gender, education, and professions. It contains isolated handwritten Devanagari characters in 28×28 pixel binary format. For experimentation, dataset images are converted in uniform dimension 20×20 and classified into training and testing categories.

4.2 Evolution Protocol

MNIST and VMD datasets are mixed and divided into two categories: 70% training and 30% for testing the model. Next, training dataset is sub divided further into subcategories based on character type and assigned the numeral label for the folder. In the testing folder, all characters are mixed with each other. The evaluation of the proposed work has been done by using the standard evaluation protocol summarized in Table 1.

Table 1. Evaluation protocols

Protocol	Mechanism
Accuracy	$Accuracy = \frac{TP+TN}{total}$
Misclassification Rate	$MR = \frac{FP+FN}{total}$
True Positive Rate	$TPR = \frac{TP}{actual(Yes)}$
False Positive Rate	$FPR = \frac{FP}{actual(No)}$

A series of experimentation has been done on MNIST and VDM datasets. The proposed algorithm has been tested on an isolated or mixed dataset by following the 10-fold cross-validation method.

Table 2. Comparative results of the proposed system on various datasets

Datasets	Methods	TPR	FPR	MR
MNIST	DNN	95.61	5.75	3.54
VDM	DNN	97.64	6.45	3.21
MNIST	DNN + fixed threshold	95.63	4.13	2.95
VDM	DNN + fixed threshold	98.01	5.23	3.25
MNIST	DNN + adaptive threshold	96.21	3.25	1.75
VDM	DNN + adaptive threshold	98.53	2.35	1.29

In Table 2 recorded the comparative results of the proposed system on MNIST and VDM datasets. For verification we used very robust recognition DNN model to test performance of proposed model. The model has verified without threshold, with fixed threshold value and fusion of adaptive threshold value. Adaptive threshold value performs better as comparatively without threshold value.

5   Conclusion and Future Scope

A Well categorized database having sufficiently large samples is the mandatory requirement to develop robust machine learning-based models. Randomly classified database will increase false acceptance rate and reduces overall system accuracy. In this paper, a adaptive threshold-based method developed to prepare well formed database for handwritten character recognition. Class specific threshold value is computed automatically. While classifying images to the respective class at first feature vector is extracted with the help of DNN architecture and threshold value is also computed. Then the computed threshold value is used as basis to decide the class of the input image.

After problem-specific database preparation, the database is used to train classification and recognition model. By confirming to the experimental results, the overall classification accuracy significantly improve when the database is classified with the help of proposed adaptive threshold-based method.

References

1. Albahli, S., Nawaz, M., Javed, A., Irtaza, A.: An improved faster-RCNN model for handwritten character recognition. Arab. J. Sci. Eng. **46**, 8509–8523 (2021)
2. Balaha, H.M., Ali, H.A., Saraya, M., Badawy, M.: A new Arabic handwritten character recognition deep learning system (AHCR-DLS). Neural Comput. Appl. **33**(11), 6325–6367 (2021). https://doi.org/10.1007/s00521-020-05397-2
3. Chen, Y.: Analysis of electronic equipment recycling based on environmental economic background. In: IOP Conference Series: Earth and Environmental Science, vol. 631, p. 012040. IOP Publishing (2021)
4. Dongre, V.J., Mankar, V.H.: Development of comprehensive Devanagari numeral and character database for offline handwritten character recognition. Appl. Comput. Intell. Soft Comput. **1** (2012)
5. Guha, R., Das, N., Kundu, M., Nasipuri, M., Santosh, K.: DevNet: an efficient CNN architecture for handwritten Devanagari character recognition. Int. J. Pattern Recogn. Artif. Intell. **34**(12), 2052009 (2020)
6. Gupta, D., Bag, S.: CNN-based multilingual handwritten numeral recognition: a fusion-free approach. Expert Syst. Appl. **165**, 113784 (2021)
7. Hegadi, R.S., Kamble, P.M.: Recognition of Marathi handwritten numerals using multi-layer feed-forward neural network. In: 2014 World Congress on Computing and Communication Technologies, pp. 21–24. IEEE (2014)
8. Hegadi, R.S., Kamble, P.M., Sherikar, A.S., Dhandra, B.: Multiwavelet and connected pixel based feature for handwritten Marathi characters. In: AIP Conference Proceedings, vol. 1989, p. 030010. AIP Publishing LLC (2018)
9. Jenkins, B.D., Le Grand, A.M., Neuschatz, J.S., Golding, J.M., Wetmore, S.A., Price, J.L.: Testing the forensic confirmation bias: how jailhouse informants violate evidentiary independence. J. Police Crim. Psychol. 1–12 (2021)
10. Kamble, P.M., Hegadi, R.S.: Handwritten Marathi character recognition using R-HOG feature. Proc. Comput. Sci. **45**, 266–274 (2015)
11. Kamble, P.M., Hegadi, R.S.: Handwritten Marathi basic character recognition using statistical method. Emerg. Res. Comput. Inf. Commun. Appl. **3**, 28–33 (2014)
12. Kamble, P.M., Hegadi, R.S., Hegadi, R.S.: Distance based edge linking (DEL) for character recognition. In: Santosh, K.C., Hegadi, R.S. (eds.) RTIP2R 2018. CCIS, vol. 1037, pp. 261–268. Springer, Singapore (2019). https://doi.org/10.1007/978-981-13-9187-3_23
13. Kaur, G., Garg, T.: Machine learning for character recognition system. Mach. Vis. Inspect. Syst. Mach. Learn.-Based Approaches **2**, 91–107 (2021)
14. Khuman, Y.L.K., Devi, H.M., Singh, N.A.: Entropy-based skew detection and correction for printed Meitei/Meetei script OCR system. Mater. Today: Proc. **37**, 2666–2669 (2021)
15. LeCun, Y.: The MNIST database of handwritten digits (1998). http://yann.lecun.com/exdb/mnist/
16. Lincy, R.B., Gayathri, R.: Optimally configured convolutional neural network for Tamil handwritten character recognition by improved lion optimization model. Multimed. Tools Appl. **80**(4), 5917–5943 (2021)

17. Padilla, D.A., Vitug, N.K.U., Marquez, J.B.S.: Deep learning approach in Gregg shorthand word to English-word conversion. In: 2020 IEEE 5th International Conference on Image, Vision and Computing (ICIVC), pp. 204–210. IEEE (2020)
18. Peng, Z., Guo, Q., Tsang, K.W., Ma, X.: Exploring the effects of technological writing assistance for support providers in online mental health community. In: Proceedings of the 2020 CHI Conference on Human Factors in Computing Systems, pp. 1–15 (2020)
19. Shaukat, Z., Ali, S., Xiao, C., Sahiba, S., Ditta, A., et al.: Cloud-based efficient scheme for handwritten digit recognition. Multimed. Tools Appl. **79**(39), 29537–29549 (2020)
20. Tekleyohannes, M.K., Rybalkin, V., Ghaffar, M.M., Varela, J.A., Wehn, N., Dengel, A.: I DocChip: a configurable hardware architecture for historical document image processing. Int. J. Parallel Program. **49**(2), 253–284 (2021)

A Graph-Based Holistic Recognition of Handwritten Devanagari Words: An Approach Based on Spectral Graph Embedding

Mohammad Idrees Bhat[1]([✉]), B. Sharada[2], and Manish Kumar Sinha[3]

[1] University Institute of Computing, Chandigarh University, Mohali 140413, India
idrees11@yahoo.com
[2] Department of Studies in Computer Science, University of Mysore, Mysore, India
[3] Department of Computer Science and Engineering (AI & ML), SVIT,
Secunderabad, India

Abstract. In this paper, we make an attempt to give graph representation to handwritten Devanagari words. Each edge in resulted word graph is weighted with its corresponding stretching (or length). For transforming/embedding word graphs into feature vectors their Eigen decomposition *aka* spectral decomposition is carried out from their weighted associated matrices. Since, these associated matrices contain complementary information we fused their sorted Eigen values at decision level by exploiting multi-class support vector machines (SVM). In order to corroborate the experimental results, we employed Legal amount dataset. From the experimentation, we observe some interesting insights that might be useful for future investigations.

Keywords: Graph representation · Eigen/spectral decomposition ·
Graph associated matrices · Multi-class support vector machines

1 Introduction

Handwritten Devanagari word recognition (DWR) approaches are either based on *analytical-based* or *holistic-based* approaches. In case of analytical-based DWR, a single instance of word image is segmented into its constituents, such as characters (or pseudo-characters), graphemes, different zones, etc., identifying each unit and constructing a word level recognizer, by employing a lexicon. In the latter case, a word image is treated as a whole (or an indivisible object), rather than decomposing it into constitutes/sub-units [1].

In analytical-based DWR, versatile approaches have been proposed, such as, water-reservoir [2], headline guided pseudo character segmentation [3], and lexicon-driven [4], etc. However, these approaches are negatively affected by the presence of variability in segmentation, noisy words, and touching characters, etc. [1]. In many cases, these approaches may result over or under-segmentation

KC Santosh et al. (Eds.): RTIP2R 2021, CCIS 1576, pp. 289–301, 2022.
https://doi.org/10.1007/978-3-031-07005-1_25

of characters like, for instance, in cursive handwriting (Fig. 1). In holistic-based DWR, words are either described by different feature representations or matched as a whole viz. graphs. For feature representations, initial and extensively used models are based on hidden markov models (HMM). For example, a two stage HMM-based recognition approach is exploited in [3]. A number of studies can also be traced that investigated efficacy of different feature representational formalisms, and their combinations at various levels of fusion [5–7].

In feature representation, the structure/topology of handwriting is captured only in one direction, despite its rich two-dimensional ($2D$) nature. In addition, the word structure is represented with a fixed number of features. On the contrary, a more robust and natural representation is achieved with graphs. Which preserve inherent two-dimensional structural characteristics of the handwriting through vertices and edges [8]. More importantly, by associating labels to vertices and edges further properties from the application domain ($2D$ handwriting) can be incorporated. Furthermore, Graphs are invariant to image/geometrical transformations [9].

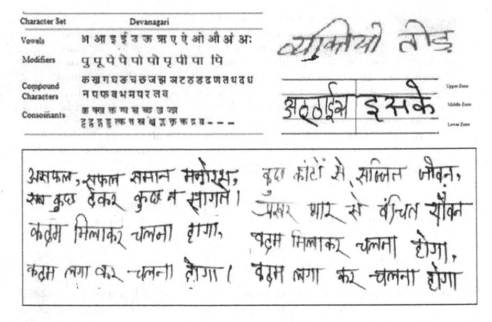

Fig. 1. Illustration of a Devanagari character set, different writing zones, and hand-written text document.

Overall, considering the structure of Devanagari handwriting (Fig. 1), graphs qualify as natural representational formalism. However, their representational flexibility is overshadowed by their computational expensive nature. To overcome this bottleneck various attempts have been carried out [10], spectral graph embedding (SGE) is one such approach. That tries to maximally preserve structure/topological properties of the underlying graph in low dimensional vector/feature space. After, transforming *aka* embedding graphs in terms of associated matrices their Eigen decomposition is carried out, that forms a corresponding feature vector. With this motivation, in this paper, we propose a novel graph representation to handwritten Devanagari words and exploited the concept of SGE for transforming Devanagari word graphs into vectorial/feature description. The rest of the paper is divided into three sections: Sect. 2 provides the complete description of the proposed methodology. Experimentation is given in Sect. 3. Finally, Future work and conclusion is drawn in Sect. 4.

2   Proposed Model

The overview of the proposed model is shown in Fig. 2.

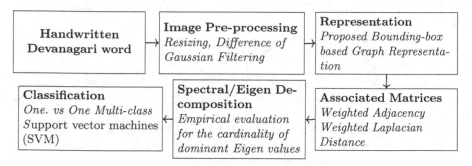

Fig. 2. Illustration of the proposed model

2.1   Pre-processing

At, first, word images are resized to a common size (256 × 256) and filtered with difference of Gaussian (DoG) technique. The motivation of DoG is two-fold: first, to remove the noise, and second, it enhances edge visibility, as the subsequent graph extraction solely depends on preserved edges. Note, we have used σ (variance) set of values in first Gaussian filter as: $\sigma_1 = (0.1, 0.5, 1.0)$ and for the second Gaussian filter as: $\sigma_2 = (10, 40)$. The best combination of σ_1, σ_2 is selected based on manual inspection of the resulting images (Fig. 3). Skew is corrected with the radon transform. Finally, resized, filtered and skew corrected word images are skeletonised with 3 × 3 thinning operator (Fig. 4).

2.2   Proposed Graph Extraction/Representation

Bounding-boxes (BBs) are extensively used in image segmentation [11], object detection [12], and extraction of region of interest in images [13], etc. However, to the best knowledge of ours, BBs have not been exploited for the extraction of underlying graphs from word images. After necessary pre-processing (i.e., resized, filtered, and skeletonized word images, from now on S) branch points of word images are inverted/removed *(see Algorithm 1)*. As a result, word image S is

Fig. 3. Illustrates the difference of Gaussian filtering technique, from left-to-right, first image filtered with σ = 1 second image filtered with σ = 40. Finally, resulting third image obtained after subtracting second image from first image.

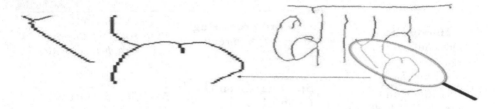

Fig. 4. Skeletonisation of Devanagari word image

decomposed into various connected components (C). If a connected component contains larger foreground pixels than a specified threshold D , it is further decomposed into sub–components C_s *(see lines 3–7 of Algorithm 1)*. Next, for each connected component C_{total} a BB is formed *(see lines 8–10 of Algorithm 1)*. Figure 5 illustrates the main steps.

2.3   Edge Connecting, Labelling and Selection of Graph Associated Matrices

Since the graph extraction is based on, nodes only. In order to extend/connect edges, we used standard edge connecting technique that is based on Delaunay triangulation [14]. A technique which inserts an edge between any two nodes by using the concept of triangulation, such that, for any P set of nodes of an underlying graph a triangle is formed. And, each triangulation formed does not contain any other node of G (Fig. 6).

Afterwards, each node is labelled/weighted[1] with respective (x,y)-coordinates that indicates the location of each node in a two-dimensional plane (Fig. 7). We used Z- score technique for normalising the coordinates of nodes in a word graph and obtained a new (x,y)-coordinates for each node, as expressed in (1). Thereafter, for weighted/labelled graphs each edge $e \in E$ in a word graph is assigned a numerical weight with a Euclidean weighting function:

---

[1] There is a subtle difference between labelled graph and weighted graph, however, in this paper, we have used them interchangeable.

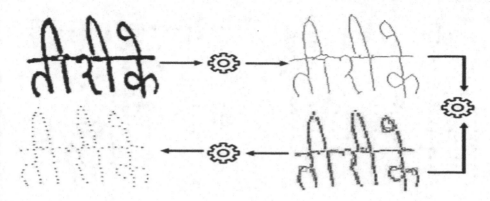

Fig. 5. From left-to-right (Ist row): pre-processed original word image, skeletonized word image. From right-to-left (2nd row): formation of bounding boxes with threshold D = 4, and graph representation by taking centre of each bounding-box.

Algorithm 1: Bounding box based graph representation (BBGR)

Input: Handwritten Devanagari word image S, threshold D
Output: Handwritten Graph $DWG=(V,E)$, where $E \rightarrow \{\}$
1 Function BBGR(S,D)
2 Invert/remove all branch points in S
3 For each connected component C in S do
4   If the number of foreground pixels in C is greater than ($\geq$) D do
5   Split C into connected sub-components C_s such that each C_s, contains at most ($\leq$) D *foreground pixels*
6   End If
7 End For
8 For each connected component $C_{total} = (C \cup C_s)$ in S do
   Form a bounding-box B and each vertex/node V in DWG is represented by the Centre of B.
9 End For
10 Return DWG

$w : E(G) \rightarrow \mathbb{R}^+(2)$. That is computed from respective new (x,y)- coordinates of nodes adjacent with each edge e *in* E in (Fig. 7). The motivation comes from the fact that it is easy to compute and the distance remains the same between any two nodes when the additional nodes are included in analysis [14,15].

$$\bar{x} = \frac{x - \bar{x}}{\sigma_x}, \qquad \bar{y} = \frac{y - \bar{y}}{\sigma_y} \tag{1}$$

$$w(v_i \rightarrow v_j) : \sqrt{(v_{xi} - v_{xj}) + (v_{yi} - v_{yj})} \tag{2}$$

For SGE, it is indispensable to select (or extract) appropriate/relevant matrices from underlying graphs. Such that, structure of the underlying graph is maximally preserved. In view of this, we selected weighted adjacency matrix

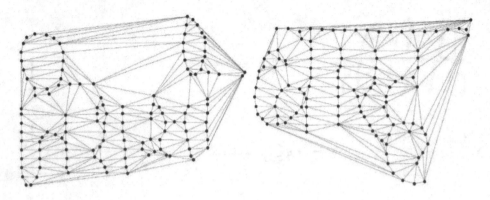

Fig. 6. Illustration for a Delaunay edge connecting technique.

(WA(G)), weighted laplacian matrix *(WL(G))*, and distance matrix *(Dist(G))*. The adequacies of the selected graph associated matrices are described briefly, however, we strongly refer readers to [16,17].

2.3.1 Weighted Adjacency Matrix

In weighted adjacency matrix*(WA(G))* of graph G, each edge of adjacency matrix $A(G)$ is represented by a weight assigned to that edge. Since, we have used undirected graphs for representation, therefore, *WA(G)* is also symmetric. There are various discriminating properties of A(G). Such as, stretching/length of edges, moreover, it has a uniqueness property. These properties are essential for isomorphism and invariance of graphs. Also, each a_{ij} in $WA(G)^k$ gives sum total of walks of length k between adjacent vertices. Finally, information about connectedness of a graph is also conveyed.

2.3.2 Weighted Laplacian Matrix

A Laplacian matrix *L(G)* is defined as:

$$L(G) = D(G) - A(G) \tag{3}$$

Here, D(G) and A(G) are degree and adjacency matrices of a graph G. As a result, each a_{ij} in L(G) is computed as:

$$f(x) = \begin{bmatrix} d_i & \textit{if } (i{=}j) \\ -w_{i,j} & \textit{if}(i \neq j) \\ 0 & \textit{Otherwise} \end{bmatrix} \tag{4}$$

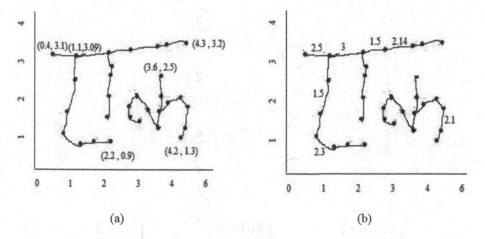

(a)   (b)

Fig. 7. Depiction of node and edge labelling for a word graph (a) nodes are labelled with respective coordinates. (b) Edges are labelled with Euclidean weighting function. Note, for better visualisation we have only showed few nodes and edges

Total number of connected components and spanning trees in a graph G are given by the $L(G)$ These are considered well established invariants in literature [16–18] and leading to other discriminating properties about the underlying graph. Finally, disjoint and isolated graphs are also inspected with the decomposition of $L(G)$.

2.3.3 Distance Matrix

Distance matrix $Dist(G)$ gives distance (computed through the weighting function (2)) between each pair of vertices present in a graph G. Distances are also computed between non-adjacent vertices. With this information, graphs with equal order are also get discriminated (Fig. 8).

2.4 Spectral Decomposition of Word Graph Associated Matrices

Consider M be any associated graph matrix then the Eigen/spectral decomposition[2] of it is carried as follows:

$$M\Phi = \lambda\Phi \tag{5}$$

where Φ is an associated Eigen vector for an Eigen value λ. For each Φ there will be an Eigen value, hence, the spectral decomposition of M is then the set of all Eigen values associated with each Φ. In literature, sorted Eigen values (ascending or descending) have shown substantial recognition performance [19]. Eigen decomposition of the $WA(G)$ is computed as:

---

[2] Eigen decomposition and spectral decomposition refer the same thing.

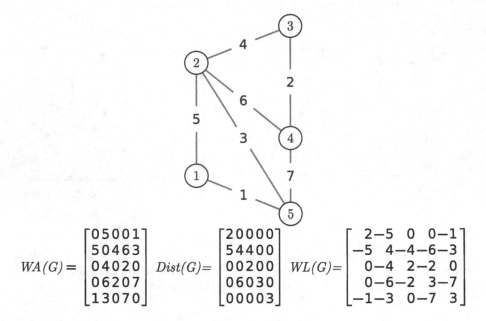

$$WA(G) = \begin{bmatrix} 0&5&0&0&1 \\ 5&0&4&6&3 \\ 0&4&0&2&0 \\ 0&6&2&0&7 \\ 1&3&0&7&0 \end{bmatrix} \quad Dist(G) = \begin{bmatrix} 2&0&0&0&0 \\ 5&4&4&0&0 \\ 0&0&2&0&0 \\ 0&6&0&3&0 \\ 0&0&0&0&3 \end{bmatrix} \quad WL(G) = \begin{bmatrix} 2&-5&0&0&-1 \\ -5&4&-4&-6&-3 \\ 0&-4&2&-2&0 \\ 0&-6&-2&3&-7 \\ -1&-3&0&-7&3 \end{bmatrix}$$

Fig. 8. Weighted Graph G(5,7) with corresponding associated matrices. Note, graph is labelled/weighted arbitrarily

$$WA(G) = \begin{bmatrix} 0&5&0&0&1 \\ 5&0&4&6&3 \\ 0&4&0&2&0 \\ 0&6&2&0&7 \\ 1&3&0&7&0 \end{bmatrix} \Rightarrow \begin{bmatrix} -\lambda & 5 & 0 & 0 & 1 \\ 5 & -\lambda & 4 & 6 & 3 \\ 0 & 4 & -\lambda & 2 & 0 \\ 0 & 6 & 2 & -\lambda & 7 \\ 1 & 3 & 0 & 7 & \lambda \end{bmatrix}$$

Upon simplifying the $-\lambda^5 + 140\lambda^3 + 378\lambda^2 - 1445\lambda + 344$ and sorting (descending) we get following Eigenvalues, 12.6880, 1.9669, 0.2570, −6.0595, −8.8523. Following the same procedure other associated matrices are also decomposed. Finally, we have our feature matrices representing (in terms of Dominant Eigen values) the underlying graph.

3   Adequacy of the Features

Spectral decomposition includes various discriminating properties from the graph associated matrices. The few are stated, however, we refer reader to [16–19].

- If the graph matrix is real and symmetric that means Eigen decomposition is also real and symmetric. More importantly, it projects the graph in a coordinate system afterwards any machine learning approach can be used on them, for example, spectral clustering.

- Sorted Eigen values results in isomorphic graphs as the Eigen decomposition is invariant with respect to graph labelling. Therefore, variation in the order of the graphs has no effect.
- As each Eigen value can describe all the nodes of a graph, therefore, we can use only their subset.
- For disconnected graph G spectrum is the union of the spectra of different components in G.
- With the increase in number of nodes in G or when $|V|$ in approaches to infinity (or significantly large number of nodes) almost all graphs are characterized by their spectrum (from particular associated matrix) is a *well-known* conjecture. That is, non-isomorphic graphs have different spectra. Therefore, the effect of co-spectral graphs (non-isomorphic graphs having same spectra) is minimized with the increase in number of nodes.
- If two underlying graphs only differ in rotation/ (or one is just a flipped version of other) spectrum is unable to differentiate these graphs. However, Eigen decomposition (spectrum) of matrix and inverse of it are same.
- In contrast to graph matching techniques, a graph can be Eigen decomposed in polynomial time $\mathcal{O}(n^3)$ where specifies the order of the graph.
- The important discriminating properties which otherwise are with exponential time complexity can be easy computed with the spectral parameters of the graph. Such as, *chromaticity, sub-graph isomorphism, perturbation*, and *maximal clique*, etc.
- The significance of largest eigenvalue is assertive in spectral clustering approach.

4   Experimentation

4.1   Dataset

We have used Handwritten Devanagari Legal amount dataset [20], for our experimentation. It is the one of the largest publically available word dataset. It nearly contains 26720 handwritten legal amount words extracted from Indian Bank cheques. The dataset is divided into three subsets, first and second sets are written in Marathi language and third set written Hindi language. These sets differ only in number of writers, classes and samples present in each class. We performed experiments on all three subsets and final results are later averaged.

4.2   Experimental Setup

- First we inspected each spectrum individually and finally fused at decision level fusion. For brevity, from now on $WA(G), WL(G), Dist(G)$ are referred as FT1, FT2, FT3, respectively.
- For decision level fusion we employ one.-vs.-one multi-class support vector machines with radial basis (RBF) function.
- We empirically validated the meta-parameters (C, γ) of RBF kernel with a grid search on logarithmic scale of base-2
- Total number of dominant Eigen values are also empirically chosen.

4.3   Experimental Results

Individual recognition performance of different feature types i.e. FT1, FT2, and FT3 are presented in Table 1. Note, experiments were carried out for 20 random trials of training, validation and testing in the ratios of 50:25:25 and 60:20:20, respectively. Recognition performance in each trial was recorded in terms of $F-$ measure. And, the average F-measure is computed from all trails. It was also revealed that the optimised meta-parameters for RBFSVM for FT1, FT2, and FT3 are $C = 0.124$ $\gamma = 0.001$, $C = 0.032$ $\gamma = 0.003$, and $C = 0.001$ $\gamma = 0.003$, respectively.

Table 1. Individual recognition performance of FT1, FT2, and FT3

Dataset	Feature type	Ratio for training, validation and testing	
		50:25:25	60:20:20
Legal amounts [20]	FT1	0.7211 ± 0.111	0.7621 ± 0.110
	FT2	0.6401 ± 0.011	0.6801 ± 0.011
	FT3	0.6010 ± 0.011	0.6211 ± 0.111

We observe individually these features types generate 60 to 76% recognition accuracy. Since, FT1 and FT2 preserve the structure of the word graphs exactly, hence they generate significant recognition accuracies. Since, the used spectra[3] contains non-overlapping information about word graphs, therefore, we achieved one of the pre-requisite for multi-classifier systems i.e., *diversity*. The second perquisite i.e., *accuracy* is achieved by utilising support vector machines. Thereafter, we fused the classifiers at decision level (Table 2). We observe from Table 2 that we were able to augment ≈7% recognition performance. The main observation from Table 2 is that as we increase the number of training samples we observe increase in recognition performance. From Table 3, for first three dominant Eigen values significant recognition performance has been reported. Therefore, for all our experiments we have used first three dominant Eigenvalues for each associated matrix. Although, SGE is not time consuming, however, the approach is sensitive towards word graphs with same graph representations. Moreover, as stated, miss-classification occurs mainly due to the invariance of the spectrum.

5   Comparative Analysis

In literature, we found only one work towards the graph representation [21]. As they have used in-house dataset, which is not publically available. Therefore, we decided to implement their technique on our employed dataset. The technique proposed in [21], is based on stringent exact graph matching (i.e., Subgraph-homeomorphism), which is rarely used in handwritten-domain, rather it

---

[3] Spectrum (Eigen values) is singular but spectra is plural.

Table 2. Recognition performance after fusing the spectra

Dataset	Training, validation and testing	Representation	Recognition rate (average F-measure)	Average recognition accuracy (%)
Legal amounts [20]	50:25:25	BBGR	0.8481 ± 0.011	84.81
	60:20:20		0.8621 ± 0.012	86.21

Table 3. Empirical evaluation for largest n Eigen values

Representation	Training, validation and testing	Largest Eigenvalues 'n'	Average recognition accuracy in terms of F -measure
			Legal Amounts [20]
BBGR	50:25:25	3	0.8481 ± 0.011
		4	0.8271 ± 0.010
	60:20:20	3	0.8621 ± 0.012
		4	0.8312 ± 0.102

is considered too rigid for real-world applications [10]. Moreover, as compared to [21], we have used substantially large number of training and testing word graph samples. In addition, spectral decomposition of word graphs is efficient (in terms of storage and computational complexity). Thus, the efficacy of the proposed method can easily be justified (Table 4).

Table 4. Comparison

Dataset	Approach	Recognition accuracy (%)
Legal amounts [20]	Exact graph matching [21]	82
	Proposed	82 to 86

6   Conclusion and Future Work

In this paper, after proposing bounding box based graph representation, we have extracted spectral graph based features from three associated word graph matrices. The first associated matrix is based on weighted adjacency matrix that encodes stretching information of the graph. The second matrix is based on weighted laplacian matrix that carries the information about connected components and total number of spanning trees present in a graph, etc. In order to differentiate between graphs having equal number of nodes but differ only in stretching, we extracted distance matrix from underlying graphs. Afterwards, each associated matrix underwent Eigen decomposition/spectral decomposition. First we investigated each individual spectra for recognition potential and later fused them at decision level. From the fusion based experiments, we observe that accuracy has been increased significantly. However, we feel proposed approach needs further validation by employing various graph associated matrices with different, graph representations, labelling/weighting functions, and classifiers used. Finally, we strongly feel that the proposed approach (structural approach) can be complemented/used with any statistical feature representation rather than standalone representation.

References

1. Madhvanath, S., Govindaraju, V.: The role of holistic paradigms in handwritten word recognition. IEEE Trans. Pattern Anal. Mach. Intell. **23**(2), 149–64 (2001)
2. Pal, U., Roy, P.P., Tripathy, N., Lladós, J.: Multi-oriented Bangla and Devnagari text recognition. Pattern Recogn. **43**(12), 4124–4136 (2010)
3. Shaw, B., Parui, S.K., Shridhar, M.: Offline handwritten Devanagari word recognition: a segmentation based approach. In: 19th International Conference on Pattern Recognition (ICPR), pp. 1–4 (2008)
4. Pal, U., Roy, R.K., Kimura, F.: Multi-lingual city name recognition for Indian postal automation. In: Proceedings - International Workshop on Frontiers in Handwriting Recognition (IWFHR) (1), pp. 169–173 (2012)
5. Malakar, S., Sharma, P., Singh, P.K., Das, M., Sarkar, R., Nasipuri, M.: A holistic approach for handwritten Hindi word recognition. Int. J. Comput. Vis. Image Process. (IJCVIP) **7**(1), 59–78 (2017)
6. Shaw, B., Bhattacharya, U., Parui, S.K.: Offline handwritten Devanagari word recognition: information fusion at feature and classifier levels. In: 3rd IAPR Asian Conference on Pattern Recognition (ACPR), 09 June 2015 (2015)
7. Bhat, M.I., Sharada, B.: Automatic recognition of legal amounts on Indian bank cheques: a fusion-based approach at feature and decision levels. Int. J. Comput. Vis. Image Process. (IJCVIP) **10**(4), 54–73 (2020)
8. Conte, D., Foggia, P., Sansone, C., Vento, M.: Thirty years of graph matching in pattern recognition. Int. J. Pattern Recogn. Artif. Intell. (IJPRAI) **18**(03), 265–298 (2004)
9. Kandel, A., Bunke, H., Last, M.: Applied Graph Theory in Computer Vision and Pattern Recognition. Studies in Computational Intelligence, vol. 52. Springer, Heidelberg (2007). https://doi.org/10.1007/978-3-540-68020-8
10. Riesen, K., Bunke, H.: Graph classification based on vector space embedding. Int. J. Pattern Recogn. Artif. Intell. (IJPRAI) **23**(06), 1053–1081 (2009)
11. Lempitsky, V., Kohli, P., Rother, C., Sharp, T.: Image segmentation with a bounding box prior. In: Proceedings of the IEEE International Conference on Computer Vision (ICCV), pp. 277–284 (2009)
12. Lee, J.D.: Object Detection. Brigham Young Robotic Vision Class 163050048, 11–26 (2011)
13. Chen, H.M., Varshney, P.K., Slamani, M.A.: On registration of Regions of Interest (ROI) in video sequences. In: Proceedings - IEEE Conference on Advanced Video and Signal Based Surveillance (AVSS), pp. 313–318 (2003)

14. Stauffer, M., Fischer, A., Riesen, K.: A novel graph database for handwritten word images. In: Robles-Kelly, A., Loog, M., Biggio, B., Escolano, F., Wilson, R. (eds.) S+SSPR 2016. LNCS, vol. 10029, pp. 553–563. Springer, Cham (2016). https://doi.org/10.1007/978-3-319-49055-7_49
15. Deza, M.M., Deza, E.: Encyclopedia of Distances. Springer (2012)
16. Schmidt, M., Palm, G., Schwenker, F.: Spectral graph features for the classification of graphs and graph sequences. Comput. Stat. **29**(1–2), 65–80 (2014). https://doi.org/10.1007/s00180-012-0381-6
17. Chung, F.R.K.: Spectral graph theory. ACM SIGACT News **30**, 14 (1999)
18. Brouwer, A.E., Haermers, W.H.: Spectra of Graphs. Universitext. Springer, New York (2012). https://doi.org/10.1007/978-1-4614-1939-6
19. Cvetkovic, D.M., et al.: Recent Results in the Theory of Graph Spectra, vol. 36. Elsevier (1991)
20. Jayadevan, R., Kolhe, S.R., Patil, P.M., Pal, U.: Database development and recognition of handwritten Devanagari legal amount words. In: International Conference on Document Analysis and Recognition (ICDAR), Beijing, pp. 304–308 (2011)
21. Malik, L.: A graph based approach for handwritten Devanagari word recognition. In: International Conference on Emerging Trends in Engineering & Technology, vol. 1 (2012). 2012-42

Signal Processing and Machine Learning

Imagined Object Recognition Using EEG-Based Neurological Brain Signals

Rajkumar Saini[1]([⊠]), Sameer Prabhu[2], Richa Upadhyay[1], Sumit Rakesh[1],
Prakash Chandra Chippa[1], Hamam Mokayed[1], Marcus Liwicki[1],
and Foteini Liwicki[1]

[1] Luleå Tekniska Universitet, Luleå, Sweden
{rajkumar.saini,richa.upadhyay,sumit.rakesh,prakash.chandra.chippa,
hamam.mokayed,marcus.liwicki,foteini.liwicki}@ltu.se
[2] Data Ductus AB, Luleå, Sweden
sameer.prabhu@dataductus.se

Abstract. Researchers have been using Electroencephalography (EEG) to build Brain-Computer Interfaces (BCIs) systems. They have had a lot of success modeling brain signals for applications, including emotion detection, user identification, authentication, and control. The goal of this study is to employ EEG-based neurological brain signals to recognize imagined objects. The user imagines the object after looking at the same on the monitor screen. The EEG signal is recorded when the user thinks up about the object. These EEG signals were processed using signal processing methods, and machine learning algorithms were trained to classify the EEG signals. The study involves coarse and fine level EEG signal classification. The coarse-level classification categorizes the signals into three classes (Char, Digit, Object), whereas the fine-level classification categorizes the EEG signals into 30 classes. The recognition rates of 97.30%, and 93.64% were recorded at coarse and fine level classification, respectively. Experiments indicate the proposed work outperforms the previous methods.

Keywords: Electroencephalography (EEG) · Brain signals · Wavelet · Statistical features · Classification · Random forest (RF) · Emotiv Epoc+

1 Introduction

The study of the electrical activity of the brain is known as electroencephalography (EEG). Invasive methods capture EEG signals by surgically implanting an EEG electrode on the brain's surface or even at a certain depth within the brain. Medical therapy employs such invasive techniques. On the other hand, noninvasive methods capture EEG signals by putting EEG electrodes on the scalp above the skull. Noninvasive EEG sensors such as EEG Emotiv [10] and ActiCHamp [22] are used in non-medical developments. Figure 1 shows typical (a) Emotiv

All authors contributes equal.

Epoc+ and (b) ActiCHamp Plus EEG headsets hardware. For the positioning of EEG electrodes over the head, these EEG headsets employ the conventional 10–20 system. Figure 2(a) depicts the usual placement of a 14-electrode EEG headset and Fig. 2(b) shows an example of the contact quality of the electrodes. The colors green, orange, and red represent good, average, and poor contact quality, respectively, while the black color represents no contact detected.

(a)   (b)

Fig. 1. EEG headsets: (a) Emotive Epoc+ (14 electrode) [10] (b) ActiCHamp Plus (32–160 electrode).

EEG is used for a variety of Brain Computer Interface (BCI) applications which involve the use of Deep Learning (DL) algorithms. Some of them are discussed here. This includes many medical diagnosis applications like, tumor detection [9,24], Alzheimer's disease identification [23,28,29], sleep stage classification [8,20,27] and many more. There are non-medical application as well like, emotion recognition[12,18], biometrics [6,31], control tasks [3,16,30], etc.

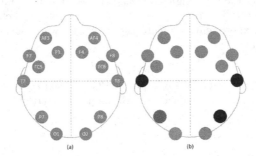

(a)   (b)

Fig. 2. The positioning of an EEG headset with 14 electrodes as per 10–20 system standards: (a) Positioning with electrode names (b) toy example of the contact quality depicted in color; green (good), orange (average), red (poor), and black (no contact detected). (Color figure online)

All these studies focus on classification problems and make use of non-invasive EEG signals for the cause.

Similarly, this article focuses on identification of imagined visual using multi-channel EEG signals. There is an increasing amount of literature in the area of imagery tasks like speech imagery and visual imagery. In [25] hierarchically trained parallel connected Convolutional Neural network (CNN) and Recurrent Neural network (RNN) along with a cascaded deep auto-encoder are used to decode imagined speech from EEG by spatio-temporal features extracted from the variability of the channels. Kernel-based Extreme Learning Machine (kernel ELM) are employed in [29] to identify covert speech, basically mental representations of four words i.e., left, right, up, and down. Article [19], aims to distinguish between imagined vowels using statistical features of EEG signals and Support Vector Machine (SVM) for classification. A very comprehensive survey of many of the studies related classification of EEG signals based on the imagined speech is illustrated in [21]. The study in [14] discusses both imagined speech and visual identification of imagined words by using Regularized Linear Discriminant Analysis (RLDA) on spatial features. This work is extended in [15], which uses three different classifiers RLDA, random forest (RF), and SVM) on the common spatial pattern (CSP) features of the EEG signals. Some other works related to only visual imaginary task are, [7] which uses a CNN for the reconstruction of an image of the imagined object and genetic algorithm for obtaining parameters of the network, and [4] focus on visual perception-based EEG classification using time-frequency analysis and CNN.

The proposed work discusses the EEG signal classification based on the imagined visual using a random forest algorithm on statistical and wavelet features without any coarse-to-fine dependency. There are three coarse classes (*Char*, *Digit*, *Object*), and for each of them, ten different labels making thirty classes at the fine level as presented by Pradeep et al. [13]. Pradeep et al. [13] proposed a two-step classification framework. In the first step, they classify the three primary categories (coarse-level), followed by deeper classification in the second step (fine-level). The classification in the second step depends upon the outcome of the first step. If a sample is classified into primary class, e.g., *Digit*, the corresponding fine-level samples are only investigated for digits (0–9). A similar fashion is done for *Char* and *Object* categories. Therefore, four RF models are trained; one in the first and three in the second step. The recognition rates of 85.20%, and 67.03% were recorded in coarse-level, and fine-level classification, respectively.

The remainder of the paper is structured in the following manner. Section 2 discusses the methodology of the proposed work, including feature extraction and classifiers. Section 3 discusses the experimental results. Finally, the conclusion and future scope are discussed in Sect. 4.

2   Proposed Methodology

In this section, we discuss the proposed methodology, including feature extraction and classifier. The flow diagram of the proposed work is depicted in Fig. 3. A subject sees an object image on the screen and imagines it in a closed eye state. Next, EEG signals are pre-processed, and features are extracted, followed by classification. The classification is done in two levels, namely, coarse and fine, to maintain consistency as done by Pradeep et al. [13]. The coarse-level classification recognizes three primary classes, namely, *Char*, *Digit*, and *Object* representing characters, digits, and object images. The fine-level focuses on 30 classes (ten categories in each primary class). RF classifier is trained to discriminate among all classes.

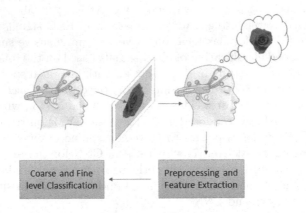

Fig. 3. Workflow of the imagined object recognition.

2.1 Signal Preprocessing

EEG dataset [13] consists of EEG signals collected using 14-electrode EEG Emotiv Epoc+ headset shown in Fig. 1(a). The names and positioning of all electrodes are mentioned in Fig 2(a). Out of these 14 electrodes, the contact quality of $P7$, $P8$, $T7$, and $T8$ was not consistent; either the contact quality was black or red for them. Therefore, the signals from these electrodes were ignored. The EEG signals are split into small non-overlapping partitions as done by Pradeep et al. [13]. The signals were split into samples of 250 ms and 50 ms at coarse and fine levels, respectively. Next, statistical and wavelet-based features were extracted as discussed below.

2.2 Feature Extraction

The goal of a machine learning model is to find a relation or a pattern between the input variables and the target variable. Sometimes raw input data does not give sufficient or optimal information to train a model. Feature extraction is the foremost and an important step in any machine learning pipeline. In this work, various statistical features and wavelet based features are extracted, which are further fed into RF classification model.

Sum of Values (sum): Sum of every element in the signal is calculated using Eq. (1), where N denotes the length of signal of each electrode and x_n denotes the nth element value of the signal.

$$sum = \sum_{n=0}^{N} x_n \tag{1}$$

Energy (E): In discrete domain, energy of a signal is defined by Eq. (2), where N denotes the length of signal of each electrode and x_n denotes the nth element value of the signal.

$$E = \sum_{n=0}^{N} |x_n|^2 \tag{2}$$

Standard Deviation (std): Standard deviation is a measure that describes how the signal values are spread about the mean value. It is an important parameter for EEG signals [13]. Standard deviation is defined in Eq. (3), where N denotes the length of signal of each electrode, x_n denotes the nth element value of the signal and μ_x denotes mean value.

$$std = \sqrt{\frac{1}{(N-1)} \sum_{n=0}^{N} (x_n - \mu_x)^2} \tag{3}$$

Root Mean Square (rms): Root Mean Square is defined as the square root of the arithmetic mean of the square of signal value. It is calculated using Eq. (4), where N denotes the length of signal of each electrode and x_n denotes the nth element value of the signal.

$$rms = \sqrt{\frac{1}{N} \sum_{n=1}^{N} |x_n|^2} \tag{4}$$

Skewness: Skewness [11] describes the distribution of the data, more specifically it defines the symmetry or lack of symmetry in the distribution. If the data is symmetric then skewness is 0. Skewness is defined in Eq. (5), where N denotes the length of signal of each electrode, x_n denotes the nth element value of the signal, μ_x denotes mean value and s denotes the standard deviation.

$$skewness = \frac{\sqrt{N(N-1)}}{N-2} \frac{\sum_{n=1}^{N}(x_n - \mu_x)^3}{Ns^3} \tag{5}$$

Kurtosis: Kurtosis [11] gives information about the tail of the distribution, whether the distribution is heavy tailed or light tailed when compared to normal distribution. Kurtosis is defined in Eq. (6), where N denotes the length of signal of each electrode, x_n denotes the nth element value of the signal, μ_x denotes mean value and s denotes the standard deviation.

$$kurtosis = \frac{\sum_{n=1}^{N}(x_n - \mu_x)^4}{Ns^4} \tag{6}$$

Entropy: Entropy [17] is a measure of amount of information. More amount of information is required to represent rare or surprising events as compared to usual or common events. Entropy is defined in Eq. (7), where N denotes the length of signal of each electrode, x_n denotes the nth element value of the signal and prob represents probability.

$$entropy = -\sum_{n=0}^{N} x_n ln(prob(x_n)) \tag{7}$$

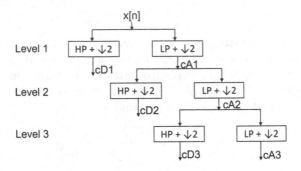

Fig. 4. Wavelet decomposition

Wavelet Features: Wavelet transform is used to identify time localized events making it easier to extract discriminatory features. Also, they are more effective compared to Short Time Fourier Transform for a nonstationary EEG signal [2]. Discrete Wavelet Transform (DWT) decomposes the signal into two components by applying successive high pass filtering using wavelet function and low pass filtering using mirror function. Figure 4 represents the decomposition of the input signal (x[n]), where LP denotes the Low Pass filter, HP is High Pass filter, and ↓ 2 defines decimation by 2. The coefficients at level 1 from the low pass filter correspond to the scaling function, and coefficients from the high pass filter correspond to the wavelet function. They are called Approximate coefficient (cA) and Detailed coefficient (cD), respectively. The output from the low pass filter is further split into approximate and detailed coefficients at level 2, and this continues until a specific number of decomposition is reached which depends on the dominant frequency in the signal [2]. The artifacts in the EEG which contaminates the signal is to be processed and therefore the selection of mother wavelet and the level of decomposition is a critical task. The decomposed EEG signal is conserved and optimal reconstructed signal can be obtained when an orthogonal wavelet function such as Daubechies (DB) wavelet is used [1]. In this paper DB wavelet of order 4 and level 3 decomposition is used [26].

The above discussed features were computed for each electrode. The normalized (using zscore normalization) features were used to train the RF classifier.

2.3   Random Forest (RF)

Proposed initially by Breiman et al. [5], an ensemble of classification trees is made to realize the RF classifier. Each tree contributes to the final decision by designating the test input a class label. Here trees are grown randomly, and posterior distribution is used to estimate the leaf nodes over several classes. The root node is the starting point for the construction of a random tree; in this, splitting of the training data is done based on features and it continues for each feature value. On the other hand, test root node splitting and selection is based on the information gain. Please follow Breiman et al. [5] for more details.

3   Experiments and Results

This section discusses the dataset, experiment protocol, implementation details, and classification results.

3.1   Dataset Description and Experiment Protocol

The EEG dataset [13] consists of EEG recordings collected from 23 subjects aging between 15 and 40. The subjects were shown pictures of 10 characters (A, C, F, H, J, M, P, S, T, Y), 10 digits (0–9), and 10 objects (apple, car, dog, gold, mobile phone, rose, scooter, tiger, wallet, wrist watch) one by one on a monitor screen[1]. Each picture was shown for 10 s, and then the subject imagined it for 10 s. The gap of 20 s was maintained between two EEG recordings. Hence, a total of 690 (23×30) EEG recordings were collected. The EEG signals were split into small non-overlapping partitions as done by Pradeep et al. [13]. Each EEG recording was split into samples of 250 ms and 50 ms at coarse and fine levels, respectively. Therefore, the dataset consisted of 27600, and 138000 instances for coarse, and fine levels, respectively. All the channels except $P7$, $P8$, $T7$, and $T8$ were considered for experiments. The dataset was developed by Pradeep et al. [13] and can be downloaded from their website[2]. A 10-fold cross-validation scheme has been adopted for the experiments, and an average of 10 folds is presented in the results. The experiments have been conducted using statistical and wavelet-based features. The experiments have been conducted on a ThinkPad laptop with a Windows 10 operating system, i7 processor, and 16 GB of RAM.

---

[1] Figure 6 in https://link.springer.com/content/pdf/10.1007/s00779-017-1083-4.pdf.
[2] http://parimal.iitr.ac.in/dataset.

3.2   Experimental Results

The results have been conducted individually with statistical features and wavelet-based features for both coarse and fine levels.

Coarse-Level Results. We extracted seven statistical features (*sum, energy, std, rms, skewness, kurtosis, and entropy*) for each of the ten electrodes. Therefore, statistical features cost 70 dimensions in total. We also extracted 19 wavelet-based features, namely, approximation ($19 \times 10 = 190$ dimensions) and detail coefficients ($19 \times 10 = 190$ dimensions). The total number of instances at coarse-level is 27600. The number of trees in RF was iterated from 1 to 51. For each iteration, 10-fold cross-validation was performed, and average results were reported. Figure 5, Fig. 6, and Fig. 7 show the coarse-level precision, recall, and F1-score graphs, respectively.

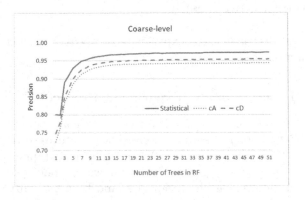

Fig. 5. Coarse-level precision (statistical, and wavelet decomposition cA & cD) vs. number of trees in RF.

The precision Fig. 5 of 97.31%, 94.38%, and 95.45% were recorded with statistical (number of trees = 50), cA (number of trees = 45), and cD (number of trees = 51), respectively.

The recall Fig. 6 of 97.30%, 94.39%, and 95.45% were recorded with statistical (number of trees = 50), cA (number of trees = 45), and cD (number of trees = 51), respectively.

The F1-score Fig. 7 of 97.31%, 94.38%, and 95.43% were recorded with statistical (number of trees = 50), cA (number of trees = 45), and cD (number of trees = 47), respectively. It can be noticed that statistical features perform best as compared to wavelet-based features.

The margin between the best F1-scores and the F1-scores at the number of trees = 50 is negligible. Therefore, we show the confusion matrices for statistical and wavelet-based features with RF (number of trees = 50) in Table 1. The recognition rates of 97.30%, 94.34%, and 95.37% have been recorded with statistical, wavelet (cA), and wavelet (cD), respectively.

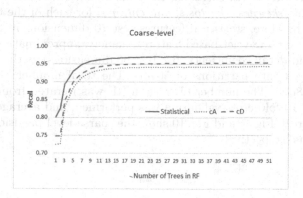

Fig. 6. Coarse-level recall (statistical, and wavelet decomposition cA & cD) vs. number of trees in RF.

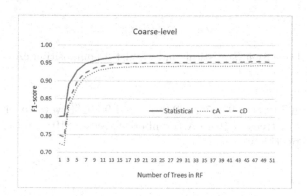

Fig. 7. Coarse-level F1-score (statistical, and wavelet decomposition cA & cD) vs. number of trees in RF.

Table 1. Coarse-level confusion matrices from RF with 50 trees

Statistical				cA				cD		
	Char	Digit	Object		Char	Digit	Object		Char	Digit	Object
Char	97.42	1.52	1.06	Char	94.71	2.67	2.63	Char	95.67	2.56	1.78
Digit	1.64	97.09	1.27	Digit	3.15	94.29	2.56	Digit	2.32	95.02	2.67
Object	1.21	1.39	97.40	Object	3.32	2.65	94.03	Object	1.54	3.03	95.43

Fine-Level Results. We extracted the same seven statistical features (*sum, energy, std, rms, skewness, kurtosis, and entropy*) for each of the ten electrodes at fine-level. Therefore, statistical features cost 70 dimensions in total. At fine-level, we extracted 6 wavelet-based features, namely, approximation ($6 \times 10 = 60$ dimensions) and detail coefficients ($6 \times 10 = 60$ dimensions) as the original EEG signals were split into partitions of 50 ms. The total number of instances at fine-level is 138000. The number of trees in RF was iterated from 1 to 20. For each iteration, 10-fold cross-validation was performed, and average results were reported. Figure 8, Fig. 9, and Fig. 10 show the coarse-level precision, recall, and F1-score graphs, respectively.

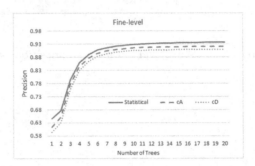

Fig. 8. Fine-level precision (statistical, and wavelet decomposition cA & cD) vs. number of trees in RF.

The precision Fig. 8 of 93.67%, 92.09%, and 90.92% were recorded with statistical (number of trees = 19), cA (number of trees = 19), and cD (number of trees = 20), respectively.

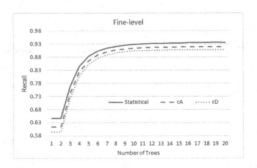

Fig. 9. Fine-level recall (statistical, and wavelet decomposition cA & cD) vs. number of trees in RF.

The recall Fig. 9 of 93.63%, 91.99%, and 90.80% were recorded with statistical (number of trees = 19), cA (number of trees = 19), and cD (number of trees = 20), respectively.

The F1-score Fig. 10 of 93.64%, 92.01%, and 90.83% were recorded with statistical (number of trees = 19), cA (number of trees = 19), and cD (number of trees = 20), respectively. It can be noticed that statistical features perform best as compared to wavelet-based features.

At fine-level, the margin between the best F1-scores and the F1-scores at the number of trees = 19 is negligible. Therefore, we show the confusion matrices for statistical and wavelet-based features (cA and cD) with RF (number of trees = 19) in Tables 2, 3 and 4, respectively. The recognition rates of 93.64%, 91.10%, and 90.79% have been recorded with statistical, wavelet (cA), and wavelet (cD), respectively.

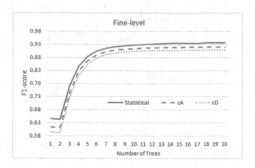

Fig. 10. Fine-level F1-score (statistical, and wavelet decomposition cA & cD) vs. number of trees in RF.

Comparative Analysis. Pradeep et al. [13] proposed a two-step classification framework. In the first step, they classify the three primary categories, followed by deeper classification in the second step. The classification in the second step depends upon the outcome of the first step. If a sample is classified into primary class, e.g., *Digit*, the corresponding fine-level samples are only investigated for digits (0–9). A similar fashion is done for *Char* and *Object* categories. Therefore, four RF models are trained; one in the first and three in the second step. However, we eliminated the dependency and used only two RF models; one for primary classes (3 classes) and one for deeper classification (30 classes). Table 5 shows the comparison of statistical, wavelet features, and with Pradeep et al. [13]. It can be noticed that statistical features perform better than others.

Table 2. Confusion matrix (statistical features at fine level)

PREDICTION

GROUND TRUTH	0	1	2	3	4	5	6	7	8	9	A	C	F	H	J	M	P	S	T	Y	Apple	Dog	Car	Mobile	Tiger	Watch	Wallet	Scooter	Rose	Gold
0	95.51	0.41	0.32	0.27	0.24	0.25	0.25	0.20	0.24	0.18	0.11	0.14	0.15	0.09	0.17	0.15	0.12	0.08	0.08	0.12	0.12	0.10	0.12	0.09	0.08	0.08	0.07	0.10	0.10	0.10
1	0.57	94.15	0.60	0.44	0.38	0.35	0.23	0.22	0.24	0.21	0.14	0.15	0.20	0.12	0.15	0.19	0.11	0.12	0.11	0.12	0.16	0.16	0.12	0.13	0.10	0.16	0.13	0.08	0.09	0.09
2	0.46	0.76	93.99	0.47	0.48	0.37	0.31	0.26	0.25	0.22	0.13	0.14	0.11	0.15	0.15	0.23	0.13	0.11	0.13	0.10	0.12	0.12	0.11	0.09	0.12	0.09	0.10	0.10	0.14	0.09
3	0.40	0.55	0.54	93.97	0.39	0.40	0.36	0.25	0.28	0.17	0.13	0.13	0.15	0.15	0.16	0.21	0.12	0.12	0.15	0.12	0.15	0.10	0.10	0.13	0.18	0.12	0.12	0.14	0.10	0.12
4	0.35	0.56	0.57	0.46	93.37	0.43	0.37	0.31	0.27	0.32	0.16	0.22	0.13	0.17	0.26	0.26	0.12	0.16	0.15	0.09	0.12	0.17	0.11	0.13	0.13	0.14	0.15	0.11	0.11	0.10
5	0.43	0.60	0.50	0.51	0.65	93.42	0.42	0.24	0.27	0.28	0.15	0.20	0.15	0.11	0.18	0.25	0.10	0.10	0.13	0.09	0.11	0.13	0.14	0.11	0.16	0.12	0.13	0.08	0.12	0.10
6	0.43	0.40	0.51	0.44	0.50	0.38	93.52	0.38	0.41	0.35	0.20	0.22	0.14	0.14	0.15	0.23	0.13	0.13	0.11	0.15	0.07	0.10	0.13	0.11	0.11	0.12	0.08	0.13	0.11	0.14
7	0.36	0.44	0.45	0.39	0.41	0.33	0.47	93.95	0.36	0.30	0.15	0.23	0.12	0.13	0.18	0.17	0.14	0.13	0.10	0.11	0.10	0.11	0.11	0.09	0.07	0.09	0.07	0.17	0.11	0.14
8	0.39	0.49	0.39	0.49	0.40	0.31	0.47	0.43	93.16	0.51	0.20	0.22	0.19	0.12	0.19	0.22	0.14	0.14	0.15	0.14	0.10	0.12	0.18	0.08	0.09	0.13	0.11	0.17	0.13	0.15
9	0.38	0.34	0.30	0.26	0.53	0.40	0.40	0.37	0.62	93.42	0.17	0.22	0.21	0.14	0.23	0.16	0.08	0.13	0.20	0.18	0.11	0.13	0.10	0.15	0.09	0.14	0.15	0.13	0.15	0.09
A	0.25	0.24	0.23	0.18	0.30	0.23	0.27	0.22	0.26	0.23	93.75	0.50	0.29	0.43	0.24	0.31	0.19	0.35	0.23	0.37	0.10	0.10	0.08	0.11	0.11	0.10	0.08	0.13	0.08	0.05
C	0.27	0.32	0.27	0.23	0.35	0.23	0.33	0.26	0.30	0.32	0.45	93.32	0.29	0.30	0.29	0.26	0.19	0.26	0.39	0.36	0.10	0.12	0.11	0.11	0.13	0.10	0.08	0.09	0.10	0.07
F	0.32	0.31	0.27	0.25	0.30	0.29	0.26	0.20	0.30	0.36	0.37	0.43	93.74	0.26	0.27	0.37	0.14	0.19	0.28	0.22	0.09	0.08	0.12	0.08	0.07	0.10	0.07	0.09	0.09	0.10
H	0.32	0.25	0.20	0.23	0.28	0.22	0.21	0.22	0.22	0.25	0.53	0.38	0.27	93.95	0.20	0.24	0.22	0.40	0.21	0.31	0.10	0.08	0.11	0.08	0.07	0.11	0.09	0.09	0.08	0.08
J	0.33	0.33	0.33	0.25	0.34	0.31	0.26	0.25	0.29	0.29	0.36	0.37	0.42	0.29	93.30	0.43	0.13	0.20	0.29	0.24	0.16	0.10	0.08	0.10	0.10	0.09	0.08	0.11	0.08	0.08
M	0.35	0.42	0.38	0.35	0.42	0.37	0.27	0.20	0.28	0.23	0.36	0.41	0.40	0.23	0.46	92.97	0.13	0.20	0.25	0.21	0.13	0.10	0.17	0.10	0.10	0.13	0.09	0.11	0.08	0.13
P	0.22	0.31	0.29	0.18	0.26	0.17	0.22	0.18	0.19	0.18	0.31	0.29	0.18	0.20	0.20	0.19	94.95	0.37	0.12	0.16	0.06	0.09	0.07	0.08	0.08	0.10	0.08	0.09	0.09	0.08
S	0.23	0.30	0.24	0.24	0.24	0.27	0.27	0.17	0.29	0.29	0.54	0.26	0.28	0.47	0.22	0.25	0.45	93.57	0.24	0.25	0.11	0.08	0.10	0.08	0.08	0.12	0.12	0.10	0.09	0.05
T	0.30	0.35	0.30	0.31	0.33	0.24	0.22	0.20	0.27	0.30	0.40	0.53	0.51	0.26	0.36	0.34	0.14	0.28	93.12	0.32	0.10	0.12	0.11	0.10	0.12	0.10	0.05	0.09	0.07	0.07
Y	0.37	0.32	0.30	0.24	0.28	0.22	0.23	0.15	0.28	0.28	0.60	0.51	0.39	0.48	0.28	0.32	0.20	0.36	0.32	92.89	0.10	0.08	0.12	0.08	0.14	0.12	0.06	0.13	0.08	0.05
Apple	0.30	0.25	0.31	0.25	0.24	0.23	0.21	0.18	0.23	0.15	0.16	0.17	0.15	0.18	0.20	0.17	0.11	0.12	0.09	0.14	93.73	0.31	0.36	0.27	0.31	0.27	0.28	0.12	0.26	0.26
Dog	0.25	0.35	0.31	0.23	0.35	0.23	0.25	0.18	0.23	0.22	0.13	0.18	0.16	0.12	0.14	0.15	0.12	0.11	0.11	0.11	0.33	93.42	0.26	0.21	0.20	0.45	0.39	0.12	0.40	0.25
Car	0.27	0.32	0.31	0.28	0.32	0.29	0.24	0.21	0.20	0.24	0.15	0.16	0.15	0.15	0.14	0.21	0.11	0.13	0.12	0.16	0.47	0.32	93.12	0.40	0.33	0.27	0.27	0.14	0.27	0.28
Mobile	0.27	0.37	0.31	0.21	0.27	0.24	0.19	0.16	0.17	0.23	0.10	0.15	0.17	0.10	0.19	0.22	0.11	0.13	0.14	0.13	0.33	0.32	0.42	93.58	0.39	0.23	0.17	0.19	0.23	0.20
Tiger	0.19	0.24	0.24	0.29	0.26	0.27	0.23	0.23	0.26	0.22	0.22	0.17	0.13	0.13	0.14	0.18	0.10	0.11	0.12	0.16	0.36	0.30	0.40	0.48	93.67	0.15	0.19	0.25	0.14	0.14
Watch	0.30	0.36	0.28	0.30	0.33	0.24	0.21	0.21	0.26	0.24	0.12	0.17	0.15	0.14	0.19	0.20	0.12	0.13	0.09	0.12	0.35	0.73	0.29	0.19	0.19	92.85	0.55	0.10	0.32	0.30
Wallet	0.27	0.31	0.24	0.23	0.27	0.24	0.18	0.17	0.19	0.18	0.12	0.14	0.13	0.15	0.11	0.20	0.11	0.15	0.11	0.12	0.35	0.45	0.29	0.18	0.16	0.58	93.83	0.09	0.23	0.20
Scooter	0.28	0.28	0.25	0.26	0.23	0.23	0.24	0.22	0.17	0.23	0.17	0.15	0.18	0.17	0.14	0.19	0.14	0.13	0.13	0.12	0.17	0.20	0.21	0.28	0.30	0.15	0.14	94.35	0.12	0.17
Rose	0.29	0.33	0.27	0.30	0.38	0.23	0.21	0.18	0.22	0.21	0.17	0.16	0.12	0.13	0.11	0.20	0.10	0.13	0.14	0.13	0.47	0.52	0.35	0.24	0.18	0.44	0.30	0.15	93.00	0.33
Gold	0.27	0.29	0.30	0.27	0.26	0.22	0.27	0.19	0.21	0.22	0.17	0.15	0.15	0.15	0.16	0.19	0.12	0.12	0.12	0.14	0.45	0.33	0.34	0.24	0.14	0.28	0.25	0.18	0.42	93.41

Table 3. Confusion matrix (approximation coefficients (cA) at fine level)

PREDICTION

GROUND TRUTH	0	1	2	3	4	5	6	7	8	9	A	C	F	H	J	M	P	S	T	Y	Apple	Dog	Car	Mobile	Tiger	Watch	Wallet	Scooter	Rose	Gold
0	94.17	0.46	0.35	0.30	0.29	0.33	0.33	0.25	0.22	0.25	0.22	0.16	0.17	0.18	0.20	0.15	0.15	0.13	0.15	0.15	0.17	0.13	0.15	0.15	0.11	0.10	0.13	0.17	0.15	0.12
1	0.67	92.63	0.49	0.49	0.41	0.33	0.34	0.33	0.33	0.26	0.26	0.25	0.20	0.26	0.22	0.20	0.22	0.20	0.15	0.15	0.16	0.20	0.16	0.14	0.15	0.16	0.21	0.15	0.13	0.16
2	0.55	0.59	92.56	0.45	0.41	0.40	0.39	0.35	0.30	0.27	0.27	0.26	0.22	0.24	0.25	0.22	0.20	0.21	0.15	0.15	0.19	0.20	0.14	0.15	0.17	0.15	0.15	0.15	0.16	0.12
3	0.48	0.54	0.58	92.87	0.43	0.32	0.34	0.31	0.32	0.29	0.27	0.25	0.20	0.22	0.20	0.24	0.21	0.15	0.17	0.14	0.18	0.17	0.13	0.14	0.19	0.13	0.13	0.16	0.13	0.10
4	0.48	0.49	0.52	0.44	92.28	0.41	0.40	0.36	0.40	0.33	0.23	0.24	0.26	0.25	0.22	0.22	0.19	0.21	0.17	0.19	0.18	0.19	0.16	0.18	0.15	0.19	0.17	0.17	0.18	0.16
5	0.54	0.53	0.50	0.48	0.48	91.97	0.38	0.30	0.38	0.33	0.29	0.28	0.28	0.22	0.24	0.28	0.20	0.22	0.19	0.16	0.18	0.18	0.21	0.22	0.16	0.16	0.15	0.21	0.13	0.17
6	0.47	0.50	0.55	0.51	0.47	0.49	92.27	0.40	0.39	0.32	0.28	0.27	0.21	0.24	0.17	0.23	0.17	0.22	0.17	0.17	0.13	0.13	0.18	0.14	0.15	0.17	0.15	0.12	0.15	0.18
7	0.50	0.52	0.54	0.52	0.47	0.45	0.45	92.43	0.33	0.29	0.25	0.23	0.22	0.22	0.19	0.23	0.18	0.19	0.17	0.15	0.19	0.17	0.12	0.13	0.16	0.11	0.14	0.17	0.13	0.14
8	0.54	0.57	0.49	0.45	0.52	0.42	0.48	0.42	91.77	0.35	0.28	0.23	0.30	0.26	0.28	0.25	0.16	0.19	0.16	0.23	0.18	0.18	0.18	0.19	0.14	0.18	0.15	0.18	0.13	0.14
9	0.47	0.53	0.48	0.41	0.53	0.52	0.43	0.38	0.43	91.99	0.31	0.26	0.28	0.26	0.22	0.20	0.21	0.20	0.17	0.20	0.13	0.21	0.10	0.18	0.15	0.13	0.15	0.17	0.15	0.14
A	0.44	0.50	0.44	0.41	0.46	0.42	0.38	0.33	0.33	0.36	91.82	0.34	0.30	0.35	0.26	0.28	0.24	0.27	0.27	0.24	0.15	0.16	0.17	0.17	0.15	0.14	0.16	0.15	0.17	0.15
C	0.46	0.42	0.49	0.45	0.41	0.41	0.38	0.30	0.33	0.34	0.35	91.82	0.27	0.32	0.27	0.30	0.20	0.23	0.30	0.24	0.18	0.21	0.20	0.18	0.20	0.18	0.12	0.13	0.17	0.13
F	0.41	0.44	0.48	0.38	0.44	0.46	0.37	0.28	0.35	0.32	0.35	0.35	92.10	0.31	0.31	0.26	0.16	0.20	0.24	0.22	0.17	0.18	0.15	0.16	0.15	0.17	0.15	0.16	0.15	0.13
H	0.46	0.45	0.43	0.43	0.48	0.45	0.42	0.37	0.30	0.34	0.41	0.35	0.34	91.89	0.25	0.20	0.24	0.28	0.17	0.26	0.15	0.20	0.11	0.14	0.14	0.17	0.14	0.15	0.14	0.15
J	0.42	0.48	0.41	0.45	0.41	0.40	0.35	0.35	0.33	0.30	0.32	0.34	0.37	0.28	91.92	0.31	0.22	0.23	0.22	0.22	0.18	0.18	0.20	0.19	0.18	0.15	0.16	0.14	0.13	0.15
M	0.44	0.49	0.50	0.47	0.49	0.45	0.36	0.34	0.32	0.28	0.37	0.34	0.33	0.26	0.45	91.35	0.20	0.25	0.28	0.24	0.22	0.19	0.21	0.18	0.15	0.20	0.14	0.17	0.14	0.17
P	0.40	0.46	0.36	0.41	0.40	0.34	0.34	0.28	0.32	0.33	0.39	0.29	0.23	0.30	0.21	0.20	92.60	0.26	0.18	0.20	0.16	0.16	0.14	0.15	0.14	0.19	0.14	0.13	0.15	0.13
S	0.43	0.53	0.56	0.42	0.55	0.48	0.32	0.35	0.36	0.34	0.43	0.32	0.29	0.36	0.25	0.25	0.29	91.45	0.22	0.24	0.17	0.20	0.15	0.16	0.13	0.18	0.18	0.12	0.17	0.13
T	0.49	0.45	0.51	0.36	0.45	0.38	0.35	0.34	0.31	0.31	0.34	0.50	0.30	0.28	0.33	0.29	0.22	0.26	91.70	0.21	0.19	0.17	0.19	0.16	0.18	0.17	0.12	0.14	0.14	0.17
Y	0.52	0.51	0.45	0.38	0.46	0.44	0.38	0.32	0.36	0.28	0.43	0.40	0.36	0.32	0.26	0.25	0.26	0.25	0.26	91.41	0.21	0.21	0.21	0.14	0.17	0.15	0.15	0.17	0.18	0.13
Apple	0.50	0.45	0.43	0.34	0.41	0.37	0.29	0.32	0.30	0.25	0.33	0.28	0.28	0.23	0.26	0.22	0.25	0.23	0.21	0.21	91.98	0.25	0.23	0.24	0.26	0.17	0.16	0.15	0.19	0.19
Dog	0.50	0.43	0.42	0.41	0.46	0.40	0.37	0.33	0.33	0.32	0.32	0.29	0.30	0.25	0.29	0.29	0.20	0.27	0.18	0.21	0.26	91.62	0.22	0.21	0.19	0.25	0.19	0.16	0.17	0.18
Car	0.51	0.44	0.50	0.41	0.39	0.45	0.34	0.30	0.35	0.29	0.34	0.33	0.29	0.24	0.26	0.27	0.24	0.23	0.26	0.21	0.26	0.27	91.41	0.22	0.21	0.17	0.16	0.17	0.23	0.23
Mobile	0.50	0.42	0.41	0.36	0.48	0.37	0.34	0.29	0.36	0.34	0.30	0.27	0.30	0.24	0.26	0.28	0.18	0.23	0.21	0.17	0.25	0.28	0.30	91.64	0.28	0.20	0.19	0.19	0.18	0.18
Tiger	0.51	0.43	0.47	0.39	0.44	0.30	0.37	0.31	0.30	0.28	0.31	0.36	0.25	0.24	0.29	0.24	0.19	0.23	0.21	0.21	0.29	0.23	0.25	0.29	91.77	0.15	0.15	0.20	0.15	0.17
Watch	0.48	0.54	0.43	0.42	0.50	0.41	0.35	0.30	0.30	0.31	0.39	0.30	0.25	0.27	0.29	0.27	0.27	0.25	0.21	0.18	0.26	0.28	0.25	0.18	0.19	91.32	0.24	0.14	0.22	0.20
Wallet	0.49	0.57	0.51	0.39	0.37	0.40	0.31	0.31	0.37	0.33	0.32	0.30	0.28	0.27	0.23	0.23	0.20	0.21	0.22	0.20	0.23	0.26	0.24	0.19	0.20	0.21	91.70	0.12	0.16	0.18
Scooter	0.44	0.39	0.47	0.43	0.39	0.36	0.25	0.37	0.27	0.25	0.31	0.21	0.26	0.28	0.25	0.24	0.23	0.17	0.19	0.19	0.22	0.15	0.16	0.17	0.25	0.15	0.13	92.57	0.12	0.17
Rose	0.47	0.44	0.44	0.36	0.47	0.39	0.36	0.33	0.33	0.32	0.33	0.32	0.30	0.31	0.23	0.27	0.19	0.25	0.20	0.21	0.22	0.24	0.25	0.23	0.21	0.22	0.22	0.17	91.55	0.17
Gold	0.48	0.50	0.41	0.42	0.47	0.41	0.39	0.34	0.38	0.26	0.23	0.28	0.30	0.30	0.30	0.30	0.28	0.21	0.20	0.22	0.22	0.26	0.29	0.23	0.22	0.18	0.20	0.15	0.20	91.36

Table 4. Confusion matrix (Detailed coefficients (cD) at fine level)

PREDICTION

GROUND TRUTH	0	1	2	3	4	5	6	7	8	9	A	C	F	H	J	M	P	S	T	Y	Apple	Dog	Car	Mobile	Tiger	Watch	Wallet	Scooter	Rose	Gold
0	91.14	0.92	0.77	0.69	0.55	0.50	0.56	0.35	0.37	0.33	0.23	0.22	0.27	0.21	0.28	0.28	0.17	0.16	0.20	0.15	0.17	0.20	0.17	0.19	0.13	0.17	0.21	0.15	0.14	0.12
1	1.07	91.16	0.84	0.75	0.61	0.52	0.48	0.36	0.40	0.34	0.18	0.21	0.26	0.15	0.23	0.23	0.14	0.14	0.12	0.15	0.17	0.20	0.16	0.18	0.14	0.22	0.18	0.15	0.15	0.12
2	0.93	0.99	90.97	0.75	0.69	0.68	0.55	0.45	0.40	0.34	0.21	0.20	0.22	0.15	0.21	0.26	0.11	0.13	0.16	0.11	0.15	0.19	0.15	0.12	0.17	0.11	0.17	0.15	0.14	0.15
3	0.97	0.95	0.81	90.85	0.73	0.59	0.53	0.50	0.39	0.34	0.24	0.22	0.22	0.19	0.19	0.22	0.14	0.19	0.16	0.13	0.14	0.18	0.13	0.18	0.17	0.14	0.12	0.13	0.13	0.13
4	0.91	0.82	0.86	0.87	90.73	0.66	0.51	0.43	0.39	0.41	0.18	0.20	0.20	0.20	0.21	0.21	0.15	0.16	0.18	0.12	0.19	0.20	0.16	0.12	0.19	0.15	0.17	0.15	0.17	0.12
5	0.87	0.83	0.78	0.75	0.73	90.71	0.59	0.44	0.46	0.43	0.17	0.17	0.20	0.16	0.20	0.18	0.22	0.18	0.18	0.11	0.19	0.15	0.17	0.18	0.17	0.15	0.17	0.16	0.16	0.15
6	0.83	0.78	0.73	0.69	0.68	0.69	90.64	0.55	0.45	0.47	0.19	0.20	0.23	0.17	0.19	0.17	0.16	0.17	0.14	0.17	0.18	0.23	0.20	0.17	0.18	0.17	0.14	0.15	0.13	0.15
7	0.72	0.73	0.67	0.66	0.61	0.56	0.60	90.55	0.59	0.53	0.22	0.20	0.18	0.17	0.23	0.19	0.21	0.14	0.16	0.13	0.23	0.29	0.18	0.17	0.18	0.22	0.17	0.17	0.14	0.17
8	0.71	0.69	0.61	0.68	0.57	0.60	0.57	0.67	90.60	0.60	0.22	0.21	0.16	0.17	0.23	0.21	0.19	0.17	0.13	0.15	0.18	0.24	0.23	0.18	0.16	0.15	0.15	0.21	0.16	0.16
9	0.71	0.63	0.62	0.59	0.63	0.65	0.58	0.60	0.58	90.65	0.23	0.24	0.17	0.20	0.20	0.22	0.19	0.15	0.14	0.18	0.23	0.23	0.18	0.20	0.20	0.17	0.17	0.15	0.16	
A	0.52	0.45	0.42	0.38	0.38	0.27	0.30	0.24	0.27	0.28	91.05	0.70	0.53	0.76	0.40	0.29	0.40	0.50	0.34	0.58	0.11	0.11	0.08	0.09	0.08	0.09	0.11	0.10	0.08	0.10
C	0.48	0.42	0.42	0.39	0.33	0.33	0.28	0.31	0.28	0.29	0.81	91.02	0.63	0.54	0.36	0.32	0.28	0.34	0.54	0.50	0.11	0.13	0.11	0.11	0.14	0.10	0.08	0.12	0.12	0.09
F	0.66	0.53	0.49	0.36	0.33	0.38	0.30	0.32	0.23	0.24	0.67	0.67	90.79	0.39	0.64	0.47	0.26	0.26	0.53	0.40	0.15	0.13	0.13	0.10	0.09	0.10	0.11	0.07	0.10	
H	0.58	0.45	0.43	0.35	0.32	0.28	0.27	0.28	0.30	0.30	0.91	0.58	0.89	90.95	0.33	0.31	0.57	0.69	0.34	0.46	0.10	0.10	0.08	0.09	0.11	0.09	0.08	0.11	0.07	0.09
J	0.67	0.52	0.51	0.42	0.38	0.35	0.28	0.28	0.36	0.28	0.52	0.51	0.72	0.33	90.86	0.58	0.18	0.24	0.50	0.31	0.13	0.11	0.14	0.13	0.13	0.09	0.08	0.16	0.09	0.13
M	0.65	0.56	0.54	0.46	0.38	0.35	0.29	0.31	0.31	0.27	0.47	0.57	0.60	0.36	0.67	90.87	0.14	0.19	0.38	0.31	0.16	0.13	0.15	0.14	0.15	0.08	0.09	0.13	0.10	0.16
P	0.56	0.54	0.44	0.36	0.34	0.34	0.34	0.37	0.31	0.29	0.50	0.38	0.30	0.68	0.22	0.18	91.22	0.79	0.25	0.35	0.13	0.13	0.15	0.14	0.09	0.14	0.13	0.11	0.11	0.11
S	0.57	0.45	0.36	0.43	0.38	0.33	0.31	0.33	0.28	0.26	0.74	0.45	0.30	0.85	0.27	0.21	0.82	90.78	0.28	0.39	0.10	0.17	0.11	0.11	0.11	0.15	0.14	0.12	0.12	0.10
T	0.58	0.45	0.44	0.41	0.35	0.37	0.27	0.28	0.22	0.26	0.63	0.89	0.74	0.43	0.56	0.44	0.27	0.29	90.60	0.44	0.12	0.12	0.14	0.13	0.11	0.11	0.07	0.12	0.09	0.07
Y	0.50	0.44	0.36	0.35	0.39	0.33	0.32	0.27	0.28	0.22	0.97	0.81	0.57	0.67	0.38	0.32	0.38	0.44	0.45	90.59	0.12	0.10	0.09	0.10	0.09	0.08	0.07	0.13	0.09	0.09
Apple	0.56	0.55	0.48	0.38	0.42	0.39	0.38	0.38	0.32	0.18	0.16	0.16	0.14	0.17	0.19	0.15	0.16	0.11	0.13	0.43	90.63	0.38	0.33	0.28	0.50	0.50	0.20	0.48	0.35	
Dog	0.57	0.56	0.51	0.46	0.42	0.38	0.34	0.35	0.38	0.32	0.18	0.15	0.21	0.19	0.16	0.19	0.15	0.16	0.11	0.13	0.43	90.63	0.38	0.33	0.28	0.50	0.50	0.20	0.48	0.35
Car	0.58	0.46	0.38	0.38	0.34	0.41	0.34	0.37	0.33	0.16	0.17	0.17	0.22	0.18	0.18	0.11	0.12	0.67	0.43	90.76	0.52	0.37	0.31	0.31	0.27	0.35	0.38			
Mobile	0.57	0.55	0.50	0.40	0.47	0.41	0.36	0.35	0.33	0.30	0.18	0.18	0.15	0.12	0.22	0.21	0.14	0.12	0.12	0.10	0.57	0.36	0.52	90.88	0.55	0.27	0.27	0.21	0.32	0.28
Tiger	0.52	0.50	0.50	0.50	0.40	0.36	0.40	0.33	0.30	0.19	0.18	0.16	0.16	0.22	0.22	0.15	0.14	0.15	0.13	0.48	0.32	0.44	0.64	90.93	0.32	0.26	0.33	0.24	0.25	
Watch	0.55	0.53	0.45	0.43	0.45	0.37	0.42	0.42	0.39	0.33	0.16	0.16	0.17	0.12	0.14	0.17	0.14	0.13	0.09	0.10	0.48	0.65	0.43	0.33	0.32	90.58	0.52	0.22	0.38	0.32
Wallet	0.57	0.54	0.50	0.48	0.43	0.39	0.36	0.37	0.35	0.32	0.14	0.17	0.17	0.14	0.14	0.15	0.14	0.12	0.10	0.10	0.48	0.61	0.39	0.31	0.30	0.60	90.69	0.21	0.38	0.32
Scooter	0.50	0.50	0.52	0.45	0.40	0.41	0.37	0.43	0.37	0.32	0.23	0.20	0.19	0.22	0.22	0.25	0.19	0.14	0.20	0.37	0.23	0.37	0.36	0.49	0.19	0.24	90.97	0.21	0.21	
Rose	0.54	0.53	0.50	0.48	0.42	0.43	0.36	0.33	0.33	0.36	0.18	0.19	0.21	0.14	0.17	0.14	0.18	0.10	0.10	0.61	0.62	0.43	0.33	0.27	0.40	0.44	0.22	90.42	0.40	
Gold	0.55	0.53	0.38	0.40	0.38	0.36	0.33	0.33	0.36	0.31	0.15	0.17	0.19	0.18	0.20	0.22	0.15	0.17	0.14	0.14	0.81	0.50	0.41	0.35	0.30	0.36	0.37	0.23	0.43	90.58

Table 5. Performance comparison

Coarse-level (%)	
Pradeep et al.	85.20
Our (Statistical)	**97.30**
Our (cA)	94.34
Our (cD)	95.37
Fine-level (%)	
Pradeep et al.	67.03
Our (Statistical)	**93.64**
Our (cA)	91.10
Our (cD)	90.79

4   Conclusion and Future Scope

In this paper, we have focused on imagined object recognition from the EEG-based brain signals. The paper initially (coarse-level) distinguishes between three primary signal classes: *Char*, *Digit* and *Object*. The categorization of EEG signals related to individual characters, digits, and objects in the dataset was further investigated (fine-level) for each primary class. The statistical and wavelet-based features were extracted from the raw EEG signals and used to train the RF classifier. The recognition rates of 97.30%, 94.34%, and 95.37% have been recorded with statistical, wavelet (cA), and wavelet (cD) at coarse-level, respectively. Whereas, the recognition rates of 93.64%, 91.10%, and 90.79% have been recorded with statistical, wavelet (cA), and wavelet (cD), at fine-level, respectively. The results support the hypothesis that the EEG signals contained the information of the imagined objects at both the coarse and fine levels. This study consisted of 10 characters, 10 digits, and 10 object images. In the future, we shall extend the work with more classes. Emotions' influence on classification will also be investigated. It would also be good to examine if these imagined objects can work as biometric.

References

1. Al-Qazzaz, N.K., Hamid Bin Mohd Ali, S., Ahmad, S.A., Islam, M.S., Escudero, J.: Selection of mother wavelet functions for multi-channel EEG signal analysis during a working memory task. Sensors 15(11), 29015–29035 (2015). https://doi.org/10.3390/s151129015
2. Amin, H.U., Mumtaz, W., Subhani, A., Mohamad Saad, M.N., Malik, A.: Classification of EEG signals based on pattern recognition approach. Front. Comput. Neurosci. 11, 103 (2017). https://doi.org/10.3389/fncom.2017.00103
3. Ang, K.K., Guan, C.: EEG-based strategies to detect motor imagery for control and rehabilitation. IEEE Trans. Neural Syst. Rehabil. Eng. 25(4), 392–401 (2016)
4. Bang, J., Jeong, J.H., Won, D.O.: Classification of visual perception and imagery based EEG signals using convolutional neural networks. In: 2021 9th International Winter Conference on Brain-Computer Interface (BCI), pp. 1–6 (2021)
5. Breiman, L.: Random forests. Mach. Learn. 45(1), 5–32 (2001)
6. Carrión-Ojeda, D., Fonseca-Delgado, R., Pineda, I.: Analysis of factors that influence the performance of biometric systems based on EEG signals. Expert Syst. Appl. 165, 113967 (2021). https://doi.org/10.1016/j.eswa.2020.113967
7. Costa, F.R.L., Iáñez, E., Azorín, J., Patow, G.: Classify four imagined objects with EEG signals. Evol. Intel. 1–10 (2021). https://doi.org/10.1007/s12065-021-00577-y
8. Crasto, N., Upadhyay, R.: Wavelet decomposition based automatic sleep stage classification using EEG. In: Rojas, I., Ortuño, F. (eds.) IWBBIO 2017. LNCS, vol. 10208, pp. 508–516. Springer, Cham (2017). https://doi.org/10.1007/978-3-319-56148-6_45
9. Dong, H., Yang, G., Liu, F., Mo, Y., Guo, Y.: Automatic brain tumor detection and segmentation using U-Net based fully convolutional networks. In: Valdés Hernández, M., González-Castro, V. (eds.) MIUA 2017. CCIS, vol. 723, pp. 506–517. Springer, Cham (2017). https://doi.org/10.1007/978-3-319-60964-5_44
10. Emotiv: EEG emotiv epoc+, https://www.emotiv.com/epoc/. Accessed 9 Feb 2020
11. Heckert, N., et al.: Handbook 151: Nist/sematech e-handbook of statistical methods (2002)
12. Kong, W., Song, X., Sun, J.: Emotion recognition based on sparse representation of phase synchronization features. Multimed. Tools. Appl. 80(14), 21203–21217 (2021)
13. Kumar, P., Saini, R., Roy, P.P., Sahu, P.K., Dogra, D.P.: Envisioned speech recognition using EEG sensors. Pers. Ubiquit. Comput. 22(1), 185–199 (2018)
14. Lee, S.H., Lee, M., Jeong, J.H., Lee, S.W.: Towards an EEG-based intuitive BCI communication system using imagined speech and visual imagery. In: 2019 IEEE International Conference on Systems, Man and Cybernetics (SMC), pp. 4409–4414 (2019)
15. Lee, S.H., Lee, M., Lee, S.W.: Neural decoding of imagined speech and visual imagery as intuitive paradigms for BCI communication. IEEE Trans. Neural Syst. Rehabil. Eng. 28, 2647–2659 (2020)

16. Lu, Y., Bi, L.: Eeg signals-based longitudinal control system for a brain-controlled vehicle. IEEE Trans. Neural Syst. Rehabil. Eng. **27**(2), 323–332 (2018)
17. MacKay, D.J.C.: Information Theory, Inference, and Learning Algorithms. Cambridge University Press, Cambridge (2003)
18. Maheshwari, D., Ghosh, S., Tripathy, R., Sharma, M., Acharya, U.R.: Automated accurate emotion recognition system using rhythm-specific deep convolutional neural network technique with multi-channel EEG signals. Comput. Biol. Med. **134**, 104428 (2021). https://doi.org/10.1016/j.compbiomed.2021.104428
19. Min, B., Kim, J., Park, H., Lee, B.: Vowel imagery decoding toward silent speech BCI using extreme learning machine with electroencephalogram. BioMed Research International (2016)
20. Mishra, S., Birok, R.: Literature review: sleep stage classification based on EEG signals using artificial intelligence technique. Recent Trends in Communication and Electronics, pp. 241–244 (2021)
21. Panachakel, J.T., Ramakrishnan, A.G.: Decoding covert speech from EEG-a comprehensive review. Front. Neurosci. **15**, 392 (2021)
22. Products, B.: actiCHamp Plus. https://www.brainproducts.com/productdetails.php?id=74. Accessed 9 Feb 2020
23. Rajagopal, D., Hemanth, S., Yashaswini, N., Sachin, M., Suryakanth, M.: Detection of Alzheimer's disease using BCI. Int. J. Progressive Res. Sci. Eng. **1**(4), 184–190 (2020)
24. Rajinikanth, V., Joseph Raj, A.N., Thanaraj, K.P., Naik, G.R.: A customized VGG19 network with concatenation of deep and handcrafted features for brain tumor detection. Appl. Sci. **10**(10), 3429 (2020)
25. Saha, P., Fels, S.: Hierarchical deep feature learning for decoding imagined speech from EEG. In: Proceedings of the AAAI Conference on Artificial Intelligence. vol. 33, pp. 10019–10020 (2019)
26. Saini, R., et al.: Don't just sign use brain too: a novel multimodal approach for user identification and verification. Inf. Sci. **430**, 163–178 (2018)
27. Santaji, S., Santaji, S., Desai, V.: Automatic sleep stage classification with reduced epoch of EEG. Evolutionary Intelligence, pp. 1–8 (2021)
28. Simpraga, S., et al.: EEG machine learning for accurate detection of cholinergic intervention and Alzheimer's disease. Sci. Rep. **7**(1), 1–11 (2017)
29. Vecchio, F., et al.: Classification of Alzheimer's disease with respect to physiological aging with innovative EEG biomarkers in a machine learning implementation. J. Alzheimers Dis. **75**(4), 1253–1261 (2020)
30. Vidaurre, C., Klauer, C., Schauer, T., Ramos-Murguialday, A., Müller, K.R.: EEG-based BCI for the linear control of an upper-limb neuroprosthesis. Med. Eng. Phys. **38**(11), 1195–1204 (2016)
31. Yang, S., Deravi, F.: On the usability of electroencephalographic signals for biometric recognition: a survey. IEEE Trans. Hum.-Mach. Syst. **47**(6), 958–969 (2017)

A Fast and Efficient K-Nearest Neighbor Classifier Using a Convex Envelope

Hermann Yepdjio[1] and Szilárd Vajda[2(✉)]

[1] Department of Computer Science, Portland State University,
Portland, OR 97201, USA
hermann@pdx.edu
[2] Department of Computer Science, Central Washington University,
Ellensburg, WA 98926, USA
szilard.vajda@cwu.edu

Abstract. In this paper, we propose a fast and efficient method to classify all kinds of patterns using the classical k-nearest neighbor (kNN) classifier. The kNN is one of the most popular supervised classification strategies. However, –for large data collections, the process can be very time consuming due to the tedious distance calculations. Our aim is to provide a generic strategy for all kinds of data collections by calculating fewer distances as in the classical approach. For that reason we propose a data selection technique that reduces the original data to a limited one which contains only some class prototypes. The prototypes are representatives of each class and are selected based on the notion of convex envelope. The experiments on multiple benchmark data collections such as MNIST, Fashion-MNIST and Lampung characters show a considerable speed up (up to *12*x) in the classification, while reporting similar or slightly less classification figures than the classification results obtained using the complete data.

Keywords: K-nearest neighbor · Convex envelope · Digit recognition · Character recognition · Classification

1 Introduction

Classification is an important goal in machine learning. Given a pattern (an image, an object, a (raw) measurement, etc.) a classification algorithm should be able to determine in which group (class) that pattern belongs. For that reason, current algorithms (except [6, 18]) look for similarities to identify relationships between the patterns.

Mainstream machine learning (ML) uses different feature representations and calculates different distance metrics to distinguish the class label for the analyzed pattern. Methods such as kNN (k-nearest neighbor), SOM (Self Organizing Map), GNG (Growing Neural Gas), NN (Neural networks), DTW (Dynamic Time Warping), K-means clustering, etc. rely their decision on distance calculations considering the distance as being the proper metric to decide for a class

© Springer Nature Switzerland AG 2022
KC Santosh et al. (Eds.): RTIP2R 2021, CCIS 1576, pp. 320–329, 2022.
https://doi.org/10.1007/978-3-031-07005-1_27

or another or to back-propagate error in the system in case of neural networks. Using this strategy one pattern is compared to another using only local comparisons based on feature comparisons involving distance metrics such as Euclidean, Hamming, City block, Minkowski, Mahalanobis, Chebychev, Manhattan, Cosine similarity, Jaccard similarity or Spearman coefficient [12].

All these strategies, –even though are very efficient, have a common problem. They are very costly in terms of time. The more data points we have and the higher the dimension of these points is the more time will be consumed to calculate these often very mathematically complex distance measures. If there is no time constraint involved one could calculate all the distances necessary and get the best possible result. However, in modern real-time applications such as postal automation [19,24], face matching [4], road sign recognition [26], etc. the time factor is primordial.

In this paper, we are proposing a data-driven solution to select only a limited number of patterns that can serve as prototypes for the classical kNN classification scheme. Instead of using the whole training set only a limited amount of data points will be selected to serve in the classification. For this purpose, we use the concept of convex set which will guide the selection process of the class prototypes. However, the detection of the convex hull in large data sets considering high dimensional spaces is bounded by the time limits and memory limits [2]. To avoid such limitations the data points are reduced to lower dimensions using Principal Component Analysis (PCA) and Feature Agglomeration (FA), respectively.

The novelty of this paper can be summarized as follows: *i)* reduction of the original training set using only elements from the convex envelope to serve as class prototypes and *ii)* solving the convex envelop problem in high dimensional space by reducing the the dimensionality of the original.

The remainder of this paper is organized as follows. Section 2 discusses the kNN paradigm and the different attempts to reduce the time complexity in this classification scheme. In Sect. 3 we introduce the prototype selection based on the convex hull. Section 4 describes the data collections we used for the experiments and the obtained results. Finally, Sect. 5 reflects on the method, the results and possible future works.

2   Related Work

Unequivocally, the k-nearest neighbor (kNN) is to be considered the most used and the most studied supervised classification method in the field. Originally proposed by Fix and Hodges [7], the kNN is a solution to classify unknown patterns based on distance calculations to existing, –already identified patterns, by inheriting the label of the pattern which resides the closest considering different distance measures. Besides classification, the method can be also used for regression.

Formally, the problem can be stated as follows. Let $P = \{p_1, p_2, \ldots, p_n\}$ be a template or reference set containing n number of points taking values in R^d, where d denotes the dimension of the data space. Let $Q = \{q_1, q_2, \ldots, q_m\}$ be a query set containing m different data points with the same dimension. The k-nearest neighbor problem consists of searching for each point $q_i \in Q$ in the template set P given a specific distance metric.

Despite the rather limited and simple non-parametric strategy, kNN was used with success in many applications [1,20]. Torralba et al. [21] argue that if the size of the data is adequate and the object classes to be recognized are rich there is no need for complex classification models. A kNN type classifier can perform in the same range as many nowadays so popular parametric methods.

However, it is common knowledge that the kNN is limited by the size of the data, the dimensionality of the data and last but not least the complexity of the distance measure. The large amount of data and complexity of the distance measure can lead to tedious and time consuming calculations. In order to reduce the computational complexity of the kNN several attempts were proposed in the literature.

Some methods use graph-based solutions to approximate the nearest neighbor [10]. Some others use a data subsampling strategy to reduce the number of distance calculations by reducing the number of data points [3,8,11] considering different selection mechanisms meant to quantify the quality of the selected so-called reference points. In [13] the authors propose a dimensionality reduction on the original data to reduce the number of calculations. In another attempt [25] the authors consider some preliminary clustering followed by a selection process. Garcia et al. [9] focus more on the implementation of the method by utilizing parallel calculation in the GPU. The recently published extremely fast FAISS [14] implementation is based on building an index in the memory on which the similarity search operates.

In order to avoid hardware-dependent solutions, which are subject to change and solutions which reduce the quality of the information considered in the process, our method is similar to those methods that do not alter the distance metric, do not reduce the feature space but select particular prototypes to represent a larger population of data. Such a solution allows to keep the information intact and speed up the overall process in the kNN classification by considerably reducing the number of calculations.

3   Method

Due to the fact that we want to utilize the kNN as our classifier, the size of the data and the dimension is critical (see Sect. 2). For that reason, instead of using all samples $\forall p_i \in P, i = \overline{1, n}$ as prototypes, the aim is to select only a limited number $p_k \in P, k = \overline{1, k}$ where k is the number ($k \ll n$) of those capable to represent our patterns.

To select the prototypes we combined two methods. For selection, we would like to use the concept of convex set, more specifically the notion of convex hull. The convex hull or convex envelope is the smallest convex set that contains it. Finding the convex hull of a finite set of 2D points or other low dimensional

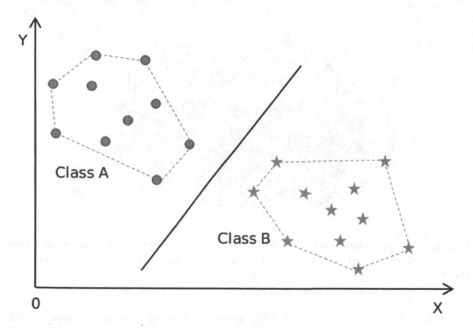

Fig. 1. An intuitive explanation for the convex hull based classification.

Euclidean space is a fundamental algorithm in computational geometry. Usually, for low dimensional spaces the complexity of the algorithm is $\mathcal{O}(nlogn)$ and can be done using an algorithm such as Graham's scan, Chan's algorithm or the Kirkpatrick-Seidel algorithm [2].

An intuitive explanation of our method can be seen in Fig. 1. The elements (data points) constituting the convex hull somehow represent all the points inside the convex envelop, thus we can substitute each class only by those points which build this particular set. A similar concept is applied for the Support Vector Machines (SVM) [5] when the support vectors are identified. While in 2D the solution for the convex hull is straightforward, in higher dimensions the n-dimensional convex envelope inherits the same properties. Therefore, the process is limited to calculate the convex set for each class separately.

However, as mentioned earlier, in high dimensional spaces the convex hull algorithm implementations are bounded by time constraints and memory space. In order to avoid such constraints, we decided to reduce the dimension of the data points using PCA (Principal Component Analysis) and FA (Feature Agglomeration), respectively. PCA is a dimensionality reduction technique that reduces the dimensionality by discarding those features that contain the same information. The reduced dimensions are linear combinations of the original variables and they are independent of each other. The FA used here is also an unsupervised technique using hierarchical clustering to reduce the dimension of the data. **Remark**: We also experimented with an encoder network to reduce the dimensionality of the data. Despite the fact that such reduction was used with success

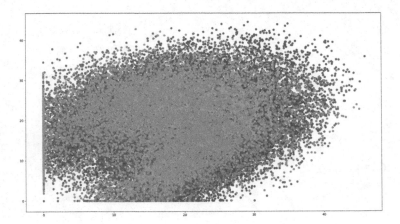

Fig. 2. A 2D representation of the MNIST test collection considering an encoder network to reduce the 784 features to 2. The different colors represent the different digit classes.

in comparable scenarios [23], though admittedly using way more dimensions, the data was not separable in such low dimensions. Therefore, we were not able to identify the convex hulls for the different classes. The representation of the MNIST digits in a 2D space, using an encoder network can be observed in Fig. 2.

Once the convex envelope for each class is identified, those samples which are part of the envelope are considered as being the class prototypes. However, the classification is not happening in this reduced space but in the original space of the data. This mapping to the original space is useful as in this space the data representation is complete. If we would use the reduced space (in our experiments this is set to 6 established based on trial runs) that would suffer from information loss which admittedly is happening using dimensionality reduction techniques such as PCA or FA.

4   Experiments

First, we present briefly the datasets used in these experiments followed by the achieved results. To be able to judge on the quality of the method, we report our accuracy and speed performance compared to the classical k-nearest neighbor utilizing brute force, –which compares each query example with all the reference samples [9].

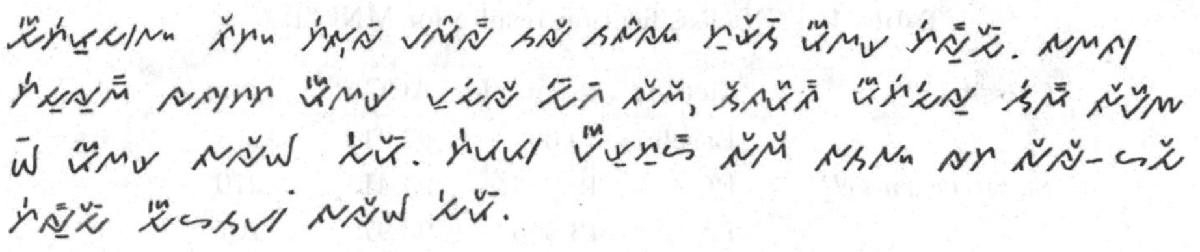

[Text in Lampung script]

Fig. 3. A text written in Lampung script.

4.1 Data Collections

MNIST [16] is a well-known benchmark dataset[1] containing separated digits assigned to 10 different classes. The images coming mainly from US census forms are size normalized and centered to 28 × 28 gray-level images. The data set contains 60,000 and 10,000 images for training and test, respectively.

Fashion-MNIST [27] is a newly introduced benchmark dataset[2] comprising 10 different types of fashion products. The original images are converted to 28 × 28 gray-scale images. The size of the training and the test set is similar to MNIST. 60,000 images are considered for training and 10,000 images can be used for testing.

The Lampung characters used in these experiments were extracted from a multi-writer handwritten collection produced by 82 high school students from Bandar Lampung, Indonesia. The Lampung texts are created as transcriptions of some fairy tales. One exemplary document snippet can be seen in Fig. 3. Some 23,447 characters were collected for training, while 7,853 characters were considered for test. Altogether 18 different character classes were identified. Each character is represented by a centered and normalized 32 × 32 gray-scale image. More details about this publicly available data are to be found in [15,22].

4.2 Experimental System

All our experiments were performed on an Intel 2.8GHz machine equipped with 24GB of RAM running Ubuntu 18.04. For the kNN classification experiments the implementations of FAISS [14] and Scikit-learn [17] were used.

4.3 Results

In this section, we will present several results. Our aim is to show how this method performs with different data collections. For all our experiments we considered accuracy as a measurement of success. We also recorded the elapsed time for each of our experiments to measure the impact on the speed component.

To be able to compare the performances of our strategy, we defined a golden standard, namely the accuracy and the elapsed time when the kNN is applied

---

[1] http://yann.lecun.com/exdb/mnist/.
[2] https://github.com/zalandoresearch/fashion-mnist.

Table 1. kNN classification results for MNIST.

Classifier	Method	# samples	ACC (%)	Time (s)
Scikit-Learn kNN[17]	Baseline	60,000	96.91	1873
	PCA	19,943	94.41	270
	FA	13,555	93.97	167
FAISS kNN[14]	Baseline	60,000	96.91	12
	PCA	19,943	94.41	1
	FA	13,555	93.97	1

to the complete data collection. This will be considered as a baseline system for all our experiments. For all our trials, we considered as distance metric for the kNN the L_2 norm and k (size of the neighborhood) was set to 1.

In Table 1 we can observe that the baseline method, –using all 60.000 MNIST samples from the training, leads us to a score of 96.91%. To achieve this the kNN implementation from [17] spends some 1873 s seconds to calculate all 60.000 Euclidean distances for each test sample. Once we apply the reduction strategy to reduce the number of reference points the time is reduced to 270 s (for PCA) and 167 s (for FA), respectively. This is a speed gain of *6.9*x and *11.2*x. Admittedly, the accuracy has dropped by 2.5% and 2.94%, respectively. A similar trend is to be observed when the FAISS kNN[14] implementation was considered. Here the speed gain is *12*x with the same accuracy losses as for the previous method.

The results for the Fashion-MNIST are shown in Table 2. The baseline system reports 84.97% accuracy when all 60.000 items were considered as training material. With the reduction (see PCA) the accuracy loss is 10.21% but the speed gain is *5.5*x. For the FAISS implementation similar loss can be observed but the speed is increasing with the order of a magnitude.

Similar trend can be observed in Table 3 when the data reduction strategy is applied to Lampung characters. The data is reduced by 65%, the loss is 7.45% and the speed gain almost tripled. Is to be noted that for the FAISS implementation despite the considerable data reduction the speed factor only doubled. This can be explained with the specific building mechanism implemented in this method to create the index tree necessary to operate the fast distance calculations.

While the results are very promising for the MNIST collection (see Table 1), the results for the Fashion-MNIST (see Table 2) and Lampung (see Table 3) are more modest. However, in all the cases the speed gain is very impressive. After analyzing the classes from the Fashion-MNIST and Lampung we can draw the conclusion that the overlap between the classes is bigger than for the digits. This overlap can cause confusion when calculating the distances.

Table 2. kNN classification results for Fashion-MNIST.

Classifier	Method	# samples	ACC (%)	Time (s)
Scikit-Learn kNN[17]	Baseline	60,000	84.97	684
	PCA	10,421	74.76	124
	FA	9,077	73.01	115
FAISS kNN[14]	Baseline	60,000	84.97	10
	PCA	10,421	74.76	≪ 1
	FA	9,077	73.01	≪ 1

Table 3. kNN classification results for Lampung.

Classifier	Method	# samples	ACC (%)	Time (s)
Scikit-Learn kNN[17]	Baseline	23,447	83.94	306
	PCA	8,848	73.97	132
	FA	8,022	76.49	115
FAISS kNN[14]	Baseline	23,447	83.94	2
	PCA	8,848	73.97	1
	FA	8,022	76.49	≪ 1

Another aspect worth to be analyzed is the convex hull. As mentioned in Sect. 3, in high dimensional space the calculation of the convex envelope is quasi impossible mainly due to the memory constraints. For this reason, we reduced the high dimensional spaces (see 784, 784, and 1024) to 6. This can be considered a very drastic data loss in terms of features. This tremendous loss could also be the source of erroneous convex sets for each class.

5 Conclusion

In this paper, we proposed a simple and efficient way to reduce the complexity of the k-nearest neighbor classifier. kKN is known as being a costly classifier scheme due to the tremendous number of distance calculations to be performed among the reference points and each query point. To reduce the linear search we proposed a solution to decrease the number of reference points by using the concept of the convex envelope.

To reduce the number of reference points we used only the data points which build the convex hull of each class separately. However, due to the time and memory complexity of the technical implementation of the algorithm identifying the convex envelope a data reduction strategy was necessary. We experimented with PCA and FA, respectively. The high dimension (see 784 for MNIST, 784 for MNIST-Fashion and 1024 for Lampung) of each data collection was reduced to 6, a condition which ensured to run the convex hull algorithm with success.

For the kNN implementation, we considered two benchmark implementations among which the FAISS, –proposed by Facebook, is a very efficient one in terms of speed. However, with our algorithm, we managed to speed up the calculations in the order of magnitude for the different benchmark collections. The 12x speed factor is impressive considering the need for real-time applications applied to all kinds of embedded devices, where calculation and energy resources are limited. Is also to be noted the fact that some precision was lost in term of accuracy. However, considering the enormous time gain obtained with the sample selection some real-/time applications can afford such precision loss in order to maintain the real-time processing constraints of the applications.

To further improve the method, we are considering in the future a more sophisticated solution to establish the convex envelope. Instead of calculating the convex envelop for each class using all the data from that class, an intermediary clustering will be involved which will considerably reduce the complexity in terms of data points. With more but smaller clusters, one could calculate more convex envelops in higher dimensional spaces. These convex envelops will be later considered to calculate the overall convex envelop for the classes and this could lead to more precision for the final results.

References

1. Agarwal, Y., Poornalatha, G.: Analysis of the nearest neighbor classifiers: a review. In: Chiplunkar, N.N., Fukao, T. (eds.) Advances in Artificial Intelligence and Data Engineering. AISC, vol. 1133, pp. 559–570. Springer, Singapore (2021). https://doi.org/10.1007/978-981-15-3514-7_43
2. Avis, D., Bremner, D.: How good are convex hull algorithms? In: Snoeyink, J. (ed.) Proceedings of the Eleventh Annual Symposium on Computational Geometry, Vancouver, B.C., Canada, June 5–12, 1995, pp. 20–28. ACM (1995)
3. Bentley, J.L.: Multidimensional divide-and-conquer. Commun. ACM **23**(4), 214–229 (1980)
4. Borovikov, E., Vajda, S.: FaceMatch: real-world face image retrieval. In: Santosh, K.C., Hangarge, M., Bevilacqua, V., Negi, A. (eds.) RTIP2R 2016. CCIS, vol. 709, pp. 405–419. Springer, Singapore (2017). https://doi.org/10.1007/978-981-10-4859-3_36
5. Cortes, C., Vapnik, V.: Support-vector networks. Mach. Learn. **20**(3), 273–297 (1995)
6. Duin, R.P.W., Verzakov, S.: Fast kNN mode seeking clustering applied to active learning. CoRR abs/1712.07454 (2017). http://arxiv.org/abs/1712.07454
7. Fix, E., Hodges, J.L.: Discriminatory Analysis: Nonparametric Discrimination. Consistency Properties, USAF School of Aviation Medicine (1951)
8. Friedman, J.H., Bentley, J.L., Finkel, R.A.: An algorithm for finding best matches in logarithmic expected time. ACM Trans. Math. Softw. **3**(3), 209–226 (1977)
9. Garcia, V., Debreuve, E., Barlaud, M.: Fast k nearest neighbor search using GPU. In: 2008 IEEE Computer Society Conference on Computer Vision and Pattern Recognition Workshops, pp. 1–6 (2008)
10. Hajebi, K., Abbasi-Yadkori, Y., Shahbazi, H., Zhang, H.: Fast approximate nearest-neighbor search with k-nearest neighbor graph. In: Proceedings of the Twenty-Second International Joint Conference on Artificial Intelligence - Volume Two, pp. 1312–1317. IJCAI 2011, AAAI Press (2011)

11. Indyk, P., Motwani, R.: Approximate nearest neighbors: towards removing the curse of dimensionality. In: Proceedings of the Thirtieth Annual ACM Symposium on Theory of Computing, pp. 604–613. STOC 1998, ACM, NY (1998)
12. Irani, J., Pise, N., Phatak, M.: Clustering techniques and the similarity measures used in clustering: a survey. Int. J. Comput. Appl. **134**, 9–14 (2016)
13. Jalan, A., Kar, P.: Accelerating extreme classification via adaptive feature agglomeration. CoRR abs/1905.11769 (2019). http://arxiv.org/abs/1905.11769
14. Johnson, J., Douze, M., Jégou, H.: Billion-scale similarity search with GPUs. CoRR abs/1702.08734 (2017). http://arxiv.org/abs/1702.08734
15. Junaidi, A., Vajda, S., Fink, G.A.: Lampung - a new handwritten character benchmark: database, labeling and recognition. In: International Workshop on Multilingual OCR (MOCR), pp. 105–112. ACM, Beijing (2011)
16. LeCun, Y., Bottou, L., Bengio, Y., Haffner, P.: Gradient-based learning applied to document recognition. In: Intelligent Signal Processing, pp. 306–351. IEEE Press (2001)
17. Pedregosa, F., et al.: Scikit-learn: machine learning in Python. J. Mach. Learn. Res. **12**, 2825–2830 (2011)
18. Pekalska, E., Duin, R.P.W., Paclík, P.: Prototype selection for dissimilarity-based classifiers. Pattern Recognit. **39**(2), 189–208 (2006)
19. Sharma, N., Sengupta, A., Sharma, R., Pal, U., Blumenstein, M.: Pincode detection using deep CNN for postal automation. In: 2017 International Conference on Image and Vision Computing New Zealand, IVCNZ 2017, Christchurch, December 4–6, 2017, pp. 1–6. IEEE (2017)
20. Taunk, K., De, S., Verma, S., Swetapadma, A.: A brief review of nearest neighbor algorithm for learning and classification. In: 2019 International Conference on Intelligent Computing and Control Systems (ICCS), pp. 1255–1260 (2019)
21. Torralba, A., Fergus, R., Freeman, W.T.: 80 million tiny images: a large data set for nonparametric object and scene recognition. PAMI **30**(11), 1958–1970 (2008)
22. Vajda, S., Junaidi, A., Fink, G.A.: A semi-supervised ensemble learning approach for character labeling with minimal human effort. In: ICDAR, pp. 259–263 (2011)
23. Vajda, S., Rangoni, Y., Cecotti, H.: Semi-automatic ground truth generation using unsupervised clustering and limited manual labeling: application to handwritten character recognition. Pattern Recognit. Lett. **58**, 23–28 (2015)
24. Vajda, S., Roy, K., Pal, U., Chaudhuri, B.B., Belaïd, A.: Automation of Indian postal documents written in Bangla and English. Int. J. Pattern Recognit Artif Intell. **23**(8), 1599–1632 (2009)
25. Vajda, S., Santosh, K.C.: A fast k-nearest neighbor classifier using unsupervised clustering. In: Santosh, K.C., Hangarge, M., Bevilacqua, V., Negi, A. (eds.) RTIP2R 2016. CCIS, vol. 709, pp. 185–193. Springer, Singapore (2017). https://doi.org/10.1007/978-981-10-4859-3_17
26. Wang, C.: Research and application of traffic sign detection and recognition based on deep learning. In: 2018 International Conference on Robots Intelligent System (ICRIS), pp. 150–152 (2018)
27. Xiao, H., Rasul, K., Vollgraf, R.: Fashion-MNIST: a novel image dataset for benchmarking machine learning algorithms. CoRR abs/1708.07747 (2017). http://arxiv.org/abs/1708.07747

Single Channel Speech Enhancement Using Masking Based on Sinusoidal Modeling

Rantu Buragohain, R. Aditya Reddy, Yenduri Venkatesh,
Gudmalwar Ashishkumar Prabhakar, and Ch. V. Rama Rao[✉]

National Institute of Technology Meghalaya, Shillong 793003, India
{g.ashishkumar,chvramarao}@nitm.ac.in

Abstract. This paper focused on development of single channel speech enhancement method. Conventional noise reduction methods based on filtering like Wiener filtering and masking uses spectral magnitudes. These magnitudes are obtained from time-frequency representation of noisy speech signals. Here, speech signal is analyzed using sinusoidal modelling. Filter gain is developed for masking of the background noise based on sinusoidal components. The developed system's performance is evaluated using Perceptual Evaluation of Speech Quality (PESQ). It is evident from experiments that proposed approach displaying better performance compared to existing approaches.

Keywords: Speech enhancement · Sinusoidal modeling · Masking

1 Introduction

Single channel speech enhancement is crucial and a difficult task in various applications like hands free mobile communications, automatic recognition of speech [1] and hearing aids. We are enhancing the quality and intelligibility of noisy speech signal using speech enhancement. Since the voice communication system's performance is degraded due to background noise. Conventional single channel speech enhancement methods such as power spectral subtraction [2], Minimum Mean Squared Error (MMSE) estimation [3,4], Wiener filtering [5], and optimally modified log-spectral amplitude (OM-LSA) speech estimator [6,7] have been used in the past for several decades and can found in the literature. However, performance of conventional speech enhancement methods is limited in real time noise environments due to unexpected noise components.

This work deals with the development of Wiener filter based single channel speech enhancement system using sinusoidal modeling of speech signals. Sinusoidal modeling is successfully used for speech coding and speech signal representation [8]. In sinusoidal modeling the parameters such as amplitude, frequency and phases are estimated from the peaks of the noisy power spectrum in every frame. In order to match these peaks obtained, a peak matching algorithm is

© Springer Nature Switzerland AG 2022
KC Santosh et al. (Eds.): RTIP2R 2021, CCIS 1576, pp. 330–337, 2022.
https://doi.org/10.1007/978-3-031-07005-1_28

applied and the obtained matched peaks and other parameters are sent to the synthesizer. In conventional Wiener filtering, single weighing factor is used for every frame to multiply the noisy speech magnitudes. In [9] conventional Wiener filter is modified by varying the gain for each frequency sub band.

2 Signal Model and Notation

In real time scenario, the background noise signals are added with clean speech. These additive broadband noise signals are uncorrelated with the clean speech. The noise corrupted speech signal is represented as,

$$x(n) = s(n) + p(n) \tag{1}$$

here the $x(n)$, $p(n)$ and $s(n)$ represents the noisy, noise and clean speech signals in time domain respectively. Furthermore, the noise signal is varying slowly compared to clean speech. Which is treated as a stationary signal. The spectral properties of speech signal vary with time. In order to make the noisy speech signal stationary, divide the noisy speech signal into frames using the windowing. As the short-time spectrum has vast significance in the perception of speech [10], it is one of the primary reasons for working in the frequency domain. The complex spectrum of the noisy speech signal is given by

$$X(m,l) = S(m,l) + P(m,l) \tag{2}$$

here $X(m,l)$, $P(m,l)$ and $S(m,l)$ denotes spectral coefficients of noisy, noise and clean speech signals respectively. Where m and l represents frame and frequency bin indexes. The enhanced signal component is estimated by multiplying the noisy spectral component with filter gain as shown in (3)

$$\tilde{S}(m,l) = G(m,l).X(m,l) \tag{3}$$

where $G(m,l)$ is the Wiener filer gain function. $G(m,l)$ is derived using the MMSE criteria. MMSE estimator is applied between clean speech and estimated speech signal components by defining the cost function as

$$\zeta = E\{(\tilde{S}(m,l) - S(m,l))^2\} \tag{4}$$

$$= E\{(G(m,l)(S(m,l) + P(m,l)) - S(m,l))^2\} \tag{5}$$

By assuming the noise and speech signal are uncorrelated, the (5) will be reduced to

$$\zeta = (1 - G(m,l))^2 E\{S^2(m,l)\} + G^2(m,l)E\{P^2(m,l)\} \tag{6}$$

The optimum filter gain $G(m,l)$ is computed by setting $\frac{\partial \zeta}{\partial G(m,l)} = 0$

$$G(m,l) = \frac{\zeta(m,l)}{\zeta(m,l) + 1} \tag{7}$$

where $\zeta(m,l) = \frac{E\{S^2(m,l)\}}{E\{P^2(m,l)\}}$, is known as apriori signal to noise ratio. $\zeta(m,l)$ is calculated as per the approach in [3]. In this work, Wiener filter gain function is derived based on sinusoidal component magnitudes which are obtained in each frame.

3   Sinusoidal Model Based Speech Enhancement

In Conventional Weiner Filter, filter gain function is obtained based on noisy spectral components in each frame. The clean spectral components will be calculated by multiplying the noisy spectral components with the estimated gain function. In this process, all noisy spectral component magnitudes have to be retained to estimate the gain function. In voice communication, the clean speech is corrupted by environmental noise and it is transmitted to the destination through any transmission medium. At the destination to recover the clean speech signal, it is needed to retain all noisy spectral components. And which leads to the requirement of more storage. This problem will be overcome if we recover the clean signal from only some of the noisy spectral components. This can be achieved by representing the speech signals in terms of its production model. The produced speech is the resultant of time varying linear filtering of glottal excitation signal. In this paper, glottal excitation signal is modeled as set of sinusoidal terms of arbitrary magnitude, frequency and phases. In this work, sinusoidal components are obtained in each noisy frame and only these components will be retained not all noisy speech components. The filter gain is derived using these sinusoidal components. The proposed speech enhancement approach is as follows: (i) obtaining of sinusoidal components in each frame (ii) deriving the Wiener filter gain function based on sinusoidal components (iii) synthesis system. The Fig. 1 illustrates the block diagram of proposed system for noise reduction. Details on sinusoidal modeling for speech analysis and synthesis can be found in [8]. The peaks of the power spectrum represents the sinusoidal components. The frequency, magnitude and phase of the sinusoidal components can be calculated using the peaks of the power spectrum.

3.1   Finding of Peaks of the Power Spectrum

The process of peak estimation gives the significant peaks in a given frame sorted by frequency. The location of these peaks gives us the frequency of the sinusoidal components. Gradient descent algorithm is used to find the peaks in the power spectrum of each frame. Let us assume that peaks up to frame are estimated. In the frame m, the peaks can be identified as we move across the frequency samples while slope changes from positive to negative. The occurrence of number of peaks changes from frame to frame. Figure 2 represents the identified peaks in the power spectrum of a given frame of speech utterance.

3.2   Peak Matching Algorithm

As the number of estimated peaks in every frame are not constant and varying. So a straightforward matching process would not be feasible. In a real case scenario spurious peaks will occur due to the effects of the side lobe interaction. If the pitch varies then the location of the peaks also varies. At voiced/unvoiced transitions which are the rapidly varying regions of the speech will result in very fast changes in the location as well as the number of peaks. These rapid

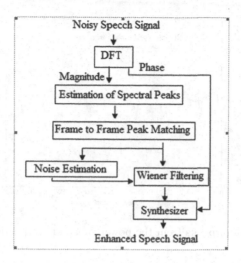

Fig. 1. The proposed system's block diagram for noise reduction

movements in spectral peaks have to be accounted. The "birth" and "death" approach from [11] is considered to interpret these rapid movements. The following procedure is adopted for matching the peaks from one frame to another, for example, matching of the peaks from frame m with the adjacent frame $m+1$.

- In frame m and $m+1$, anchor frame is chosen depending on which frame is having greater energy.
- In this step, we are attempting to match the frequency f_n from the $m+1$ frame for all the frequencies, $k_1, k_1, ...k_p$ of frame m. Notably, k_i of frame m matches to f_n of frame $m+1$, if and only if

$$|k_i - f_n| < |k_i - f_i| < \nabla \qquad (8)$$

i.e. the frequency f_n must lie in the matching interval of k_n and must be the closest such frequency. Here represents matching interval in terms of frequency. Then we assume that a candidate match is obtained. This candidate match is further executed in step 3 to find out the definitive match since there might be frequencies in frame m which may be a better match to f_n. If no match is found, in such a situation, the frequency track k_n is considered "dead" on entering frame $m+1$. Its magnitude is made zero in $m+1$ frame. For the next frequency k_{i+1}, Step 2 is repeated.
- In this step, peak match from earlier step is confirmed. The candidate match from previous step can be declared a definitive match, if f_n has no better match to the remaining unmatched frequencies of frame m. This condition can be given by

$$|f_n - k_i| < |f_n - k_{i+1}| \qquad (9)$$

If this condition is satisfied, frequencies f_n and k_i are eliminated from further discussion. If the above condition is not satisfied then it is concluded that

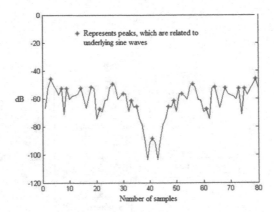

Fig. 2. Representation of peaks from the power spectrum of particular frame of given speech utterance

frequency k_i is matched to itself with zero magnitude and step 2 is repeated for the next frequencies.

- After completion of the matching process for all the frequencies of the frame with adjacent frame, respective frequency track is assigned. There might be frequencies in frame that are not matched. Let us assume presence of one such frequency. Then it is considered as "born" in frame and it will be assigned to a new frequency in the frame with zero magnitude. The procedure will be followed for all the unmatched frequencies.

After the frame to frame peak matching each track has extended itself forward in time or turned off. Thus from these amplitudes obtained at the end of peak matching represents the noisy speech spectral amplitudes. So in order to enhance the speech signal, the amplitudes obtained at the peak matching are sent through the Wiener Filter.

3.3   Wiener Filter Gain Function

Wiener filter gain function is derived using the amplitudes of sinusoidal components instead of noisy spectral amplitudes. Similar procedure has been followed as discussed in the Sect. 2, to obtain gain function in each frame.

3.4   Synthesis System

The sinusoidal components related to clean speech will be estimated by applying the Wiener filter gain to magnitudes of sinusoidal components in each frame. The obtained clean speech sine wave parameters are sent through the synthesizer. The synthesizer combines these estimated clean speech sine wave amplitudes with their respective frequencies and phases using the following equation

$$\hat{s}(n) = \sum_{m=0}^{N-1} \hat{A}_m^l . cos(n\omega_m^l + \phi_m^l) \tag{10}$$

where $\overset{\wedge^l}{A_m}$, ω_m^l and ϕ_m^l represents m^{th} sine wave amplitude, frequency and phase in the lth.

4   Results and Discussion

The proposed approach performance is estimated and measured by carrying out simulations with the NOIZEUS database [12], a noisy speech corpus for evaluation of speech enhancement algorithms. This database contains 30 IEEE sentences (uttered by three female and three male speakers) corrupted by eight various real environment noises at different SNRs. The speech utterances were degraded with seven different noise samples at various SNR levels such as 0 dB, 5 dB, 10 dB and 15 dB. The noises were street, car, restaurant, babble, exhibition hall and airport.

Table 1. Comparison of obtained PESQ values with proposed and existing approaches

Noise type and SNR (dB)		MMSE-STA	PSS	Proposed
Airport	0	1.36	1.03	1.69
	5	1.40	0.95	1.72
	10	2.12	1.61	2.14
	15	2.24	1.13	2.17
Babble	0	1.41	0.91	1.66
	5	1.83	1.11	1.95
	10	1.73	0.96	2.02
	15	2.15	1.56	2.33
Car	0	1.18	0.94	1.81
	5	1.57	0.91	2.01
	10	1.75	1.10	2.07
	15	2.14	1.12	2.29
Exhibition hall	0	1.02	0.90	1.30
	5	1.02	0.90	1.71
	10	1.89	1.14	1.93
	15	2.17	078	2.20
Restaurant	0	0.86	1.25	0.41
	5	1.80	1.15	1.92
	10	1.87	1.12	2.05
	15	2.06	1.30	2.26
Street	0	1.17	0.77	1.37
	5	1.45	1.26	1.63
	10	2.06	2.30	2.09
	15	2.06	1.21	2.17

For the evaluation of proposed approach for speech enhancement, the objective quality measure used is Perceptual Evaluation of Speech Quality (PESQ) measure [13]. In general, the higher PESQ value indicates the more intelligibility of the enhanced speech utterance. The performance of proposed method is compared with MMSE short-time spectral amplitude (MMSE-STA) estimator [3] and power spectral subtraction (PSS) [14].

Table 1 depicts the comparison of PESQ Scores. From Table 1, it is observed that higher PESQ values are obtained with the proposed method. It explains that the proposed method maintains an acceptable level of residual noise, benefits low speech distortion, and improves the intelligible capacity of speech signal.

5   Conclusion

This paper proposed Wiener filter based speech enhancement system using sinusoidal representation of speech signal. Wiener filter gain function is derived by considering sinusoidal components in each frame. Peaks of the power spectrum indicate the sinusoidal components. In conventional Wiener filtering, all noisy speech spectral components have been processed. In the proposed method only magnitude, frequency and phase of sine waves in each frame are processed through the Wiener filter. The proposed method's performance is computed using PESQ values. From the results it is observed that better performance is achieved using the proposed approach.

Acknowledgement. This work is supported by the Science and Engineering Research Board (SERB), Department of Science and Technology (DST), Government of India and, file no. is EEQ/2018/001338, dated 27th February 2019.

References

1. Benesty, J., Makino, S., Chen, J.: Speech Enhancement. Springer, Cham (2005)
2. Boll, S.F.: Supression of acoustic noise in speech using spectral subtraction. IEEE Trans. Acoust. Speech Signal Process. **ASSP 27**, 113–120 (1979)
3. Ephraim, Y., Malah, D.: Speech enhancement using a minimum mean square error log-spectral amplitude estimator. IEEE Trans. Acoust. Speech Signal Process. **32**(6), 1109–1121 (1984)
4. Ephraim, Y., Malah, D.: Speech enhancement using a minimum mean square error log-spectral amplitude estimator. IEEE Trans. Acoust. Speech Signal Process. **33**(1), 443–445 (1985)
5. Lim, J., Oppenheim, A.: All-pole modeling of degraded speech. IEEE Trans. Acoust. Speech Signal Process. **ASSP 26**(3), 197–210 (1978)
6. Cohen, I.: Noise spectrum estimation in adverse environments: improved minima controlled recursive averaging. IEEE Trans. Speech Audio Prcoess. **9**(1), 12–15 (2002)
7. Cohen, I.: Noise spectrum estimation in adverse environments: improved minima controlled recursive averaging. IEEE Trans. Speech Audio Prcoess. **11**(5), 466–475 (2003)

8. McAulay, R.J., Quatieri, T.F.: Speech analysis-synthesis based on a sinusoidal representation. IEEE Trans. Acoust. Speech Signal Process. **ASSP 34**, pp. 744–754, Lincoln Lab., M.I.T (1986)
9. Rao, C.V.R., Murthy, M.R., Rao, K.S.: Speech enhancement using sub-band cross-correlation compensated Wiener filter combined with harmonic regeneration. Int. J. Electron. Commun. **66**(6), 459–464 (2012)
10. Lim, J.S., Oppenheim, A.V.: Enhancement and bandwidth compression of noisy speech. Proc. IEEE **67**(12), 1586–604 (1979)
11. McAulay, R.J., Quatieri, T.F.: Magnitude only reconstruction using a sinusoidal speech model. In: Proceedings International Conference on Acoustics, Speech, and Signal Processing, pp. 27.6.1-27.6.4 (1985)
12. http://www.utdallas.edu/loizou/speech/oizeus/
13. Rix, A., Beerends, J., Hollier, M., Hekstra, A.: Perceptual evaluation of speech quality (PESQ) - a new method for speech quality assessment of telephone networks and codecs. In: Proceedings IEEE International Conference on Acoustics, Speech, and Signal Processing, vol 2, pp. 749–52 (2001)
14. Berouti, M., Schwartz, R., Makhoul, J.: Enhancement of speech corrupted by acoustic noise. In: Proceedings International Conference on Acoustics, Speech, and Signal Processing, pp. 208–211 (1979)

Extraction of Temporal Features on Fibonacci Space for Audio Based Vehicle Classification

Amandeep Sinha, S. Hemanth Kumar, Gudmalwar Ashishkumar Prabhakar, and Ch V. Rama Rao[✉]

National Institute of Technology Meghalaya, Shillong 793003, India
g.ashishkumar@nit.ac.in, chvramarao@nitm.ac.in

Abstract. In this study we address automatic vehicle and engine identification based on audio information. This information be based on many factors, such as vehicle type, tires, speed, wear and tear of vehicles, as well as type of road. We have decided a feature set for discriminating pairs of classes. Feature set include Fibonacci feature space, entropy, skewness and kurtosis. The audio information collected are real time on-road recordings. There are four classes of vehicle sounds. The paper also shows problems related to vehicles classification. Classification on audio-based engine and vehicle type identification are proposed and conclusions are shown.

Keywords: Vehicle sound · Pattern recognition · Temporal features · CNN

1 Introduction

In the current scenario we encounter many noises in our day-to-day life such as speech, vehicle sounds, animal sounds etc. In most of the cases we were not able to distinguish the noises. Especially in the case of traffic we come across with many different sounds like horn, engine, indicators etc. In that case we were unable to identify the type of vehicle approaching or passing by. In this paper we are going to classify the type of vehicle bypassing. We are going to classify them by using audio data of the vehicles. We choose audio because it is easy to collect and there will not be a problem of traffic while collecting data. And we can also collect the data any time irrespective of the light availability. We can extract a greater number of features from the audio data, which can be used to classify the type of vehicle bypassing. Extracting features from the audio data is the big task here that can classify vehicles accurately. The audio data of vehicles depend on many factors. Different vehicles produce different sounds depending on the type of vehicle, type of engine, speed, type of road, type of fuel used etc. Sometimes the same type of vehicles produces different sounds based on their speed. Sometimes vehicles produce different sounds at the same speed depending

KC Santosh et al. (Eds.): RTIP2R 2021, CCIS 1576, pp. 338–345, 2022.
https://doi.org/10.1007/978-3-031-07005-1_29

on the steep slope. Nowadays people are excited using vehicles that produce less sounds. Electric vehicles and cars produce less sound (almost inaudible), in that case we can classify the vehicles by using the sound produced by friction between road and tyres. Sometimes the type of fuel used (petrol, diesel, CNG) varies the sound produced. The above are the key factors that define our audio data.

Travelling and traffic have become a part of our life nowadays. The noise generated on roads can be used to develop an Intelligent Transportation System, which will help smooth and safe travel for commuters and be used for traffic monitoring to ease traffic. In this paper, we address the automatic classification of vehicle type based on audio recording through a microphone. We assume that the vehicles types considered here have similar working condition which generate similar sounds. With the help of sound produced by these sounds is used to classify vehicles. This paper uses the Fibonacci feature space as one of the features for classification. Deep Neural Network has been used for classification purposes. This paper focuses on the classification of four types of vehicles. One of the major advantages of using audio data for classification is that it requires less storage space and is cheaper to obtain. Some other advantages are that it can be recorded bad whether conditions, low visibility or night condition, etc.

Various attempts on vehicle classification based on the audio signal have been made in [1], and authors used an auto regressive modeling for extracting the features from the recorded vehicle sounds. Probabilistic neural network (PNN) models are estimated for distinguishing type of vehicle and its distance. In [2], authors used LPC (Linear Predictive Coding) for vehicle identification based on a moving vehicle's acoustic sound source. An eigenface method to recognize a moving vehicle sound using the frequency vector Principal Component Analysis (PCA) is discussed in [3] for vehicle classification. In [4], the authors implemented neural networks to classify vehicles based on engine sound. The fundamental frequency short-time energy, average zero-crossing rate, and pitch frequency of periodic segments of signals were used for classifying four vehicle sounds such as bus, car, motor and truck [5]. In that work, SVM is used as classifier to classify these vehicle sounds. In [6], authors employed wavelet-based feature extraction for target identification using neural network classifiers.

In this work, we extracted the Fibonacci Feature Space (FSP) based features for classifying four-vehicle sounds. The proposed feature is computed by finding the Fibonacci signal from each frame of the audio signal. The Fibonacci signal is obtained by sampling considered audio signals in Fibonacci sequence indexes. This sampled signal is plotted against the Fibonacci sequence and the area formed in FSP is calculated. The obtained area is used as one of the features along with entropy, skewness and kurtosis. These obtained features are passed through the convolution neural network (CNN) to classify four considered vehicle sounds.

2   Feature Extraction

This section explains about feature extraction using Fibonacci feature space. An audio signal may change its characteristics over time, such as the frequency variation of a signal, rate change of amplitude. The short time analysis on signal seems a better approach to extract useful information. The basic assumption behind this approach is that the signal changes occur slowly. In this work, we have segmented audio signals into smaller duration for feature extraction.

2.1 Fibonacci Series

Fibonacci sequence is series of numbers 0, 1, 1, 2, 3, 5, 8, 13, 21, 34, 55, 89, 144, 233, 377... ... The series starts with a 0 and 1. The next element is obtained by adding the previous two elements in the series. In this study, the Fibonacci sequence is used as an index for extracting features from audio signals. The expression to create the Fibonacci series is defined as follows:

$$if\, n < 0\, fn = 0$$
$$if\, n = 1\, fn = 1$$
$$if\, n > 1\, fn = fn - 1 + fn - 2$$

where fn represents the element of series at index n. In this study, we use the Fibonacci indexed signal's discriminating feature to differentiate between the classes of vehicles. A 2D feature space is plotted from Fibonacci indexed signal to draw a boundary around it to calculate its area.

3   Preprocessing: Segmentation and Windowing

In this study, to perform the feature extraction from the audio signals, we performed segmentation, dividing signals into segments of 25 ms and with an overlap of 50%. Hamming window was used for this purpose. We slide through each segment for extraction of features. With this process, signal gets spectrally smoothed, and frequency resolution increases. It's known that in short duration signal does not show any remarkable changes. Small changes in a short interval of time can provide an advantage while feature extraction, extracting worthwhile information from segments separated by certain intervals. We use each of these segmented signals for processing. We further sample the segmented signal in accordance with Fibonacci indexes for our calculation.

3.1 Algorithm

The Fibonacci series indices are estimated from signal index. Here, A new Fibonacci signal will be generated by using the index value of the specified signal. This process is illustrated in Fig. 1 using an example and Fibonacci sequence is labelled from signal index. It will generate a new signal as shown in Fig. 1B. Here, the purpose for conversion to a new signal is to transfer the information contained in original signal to new signal. The estimated new signal with FSp features information can be used in different scenario. For example, It can be helpful in separating healthy signal from pathological signal or acoustic signal

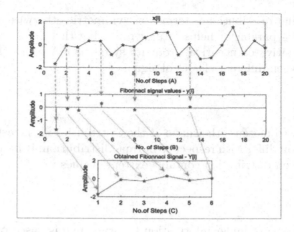

Fig. 1. Procedure to obtain Fibonacci signal

having different characteristics may be distinguished from each other within certain criteria. The Fibonacci signal estimated from signal using its index values is shown in Fig 1C. Here, generate a new Fibonacci signal is Y[i]. We then create a difference signal X[i] from the Fibonacci signal by subtracting the initial value of Y[i] from the rest of the signal. And plot the 2-D feature space and calculate the area. Figure 2 shows the difference operation and its procedure. Then this area is sent to the classifier along with the entropy, skewness and kurtosis for classification.

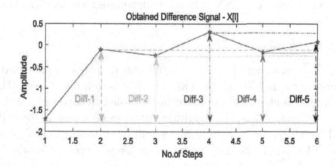

Fig. 2. Difference exemplification of the obtained Fibonacci signal.

3.2 Skewness

In mathematics, a figure is termed as symmetric if it exhibits a point through which a line is drawn perpendicular to x axis, if it divide it into two congruent parts or identical part that can be superimposed. The skewness indicates asymmetry. With respect to statistic, if the mean, median and mode of distribution coincide, then that distribution is termed as symmetric otherwise it is asymmetric. The skewness parameter helps in understanding the direction of frequency distribution (positive or negative) from its symmetry. We use this feature to distinguish between different classes of signal.

3.3 Kurtosis

Kurtosis is used to measure the shape of the distribution. It measures how tails of the distribution differ with respect to normal distribution. It finds out whether the tails of a given distribution contains extreme values.

3.4 Entropy

Entropy is the concept under information theory which is based on information entropy or Shannon entropy. The spectral entropy (SE) of the signal indicates the measure of signals spectral power. In this context, Shannon entropy is the measure of spectral entropy of the signal. It is used as a feature representation in speech recognition and biomedical signal processing applications. The features extraction using SE also employed in fault detection and diagnosis.

4 Results and Discussion

In this work we did vehicle classification using temporal features. Temporal features are extracted using the Fibonacci space based on acoustic signals generated by vehicles. Here four different vehicles are considered for classification like bike, car, van and heavy vehicles. CNN network is developed for classification purpose.

4.1 Database Used

The data (Audio) from which we extracted the features is collected manually by using a mobile phone. Total there are 4 types of vehicle classes (Bikes, Cars, Vans and Heavy Vehicles), that need to be Sampled accordingly and for undergoing feature extraction. We selected different types of Scenario for collecting the Audio data, Like the sounds of the vehicles will be different in different real time scenario. We collected Audio data from the different types of roads, in different traffic situations, in different climate and some audio data separately where we experience less noise. We used these many scenarios for getting better results for the type of vehicle in maximum scenarios. We started recording the public transport Buses (APS RTC) which will be going in separate roads. We recorded the sound of the Public transport buses just a 200 m distance before and after the bus stop, so that we recorded the sound of vehicle when de-accelerating and Accelerating. We even collected the sound recordings of the heavy vehicles (goods carriers and lorry) on the national Highway NH5(because we get the data of vehicles which maintain a constant high speed). We collected the data of small vehicles (cars, bikes and vans) in different traffic modes like it depends on what time (different in morning, afternoon and evening) and what day (varies in weekends and weekdays). We recorded some vehicle sounds (cars and bikes) by taking them to a low noise experience (zero other vehicles and less noise), like we used some college grounds. For betterment we recorded the sounds in the night so that less noise will be experienced. The vehicles sounds are recorded at different speeds and different types of road. All these vehicle sounds are collected from a distance of 1 to 2 m away from the moving vehicle. And a 2 to 3 s recording of each vehicle sound is be collected. Totally a data of 649 recordings in which there are bike sound recordings of 162, car sound recordings of 159, van sound recordings of 168 and heavy vehicle sound recordings of 160 is collected and are being subjected to feature extraction.

4.2 Convolution Neural Network (CNN)

The CNN is one of the widely used Deep Neural Network (DNN) technique in different pattern recognition application such as acoustic signal classification, image classification, music identification. Here, we employ CNN to efficiently compute the deep features for classification of vehicle sounds. In general, CNN take image as an input and apply convolution operations on them using different filter size and different number of filters to extract deep features classification task.

In this work, we used CNN network to classify four vehicle sounds. The considered CNN architecture consists of one convolution layer of 128 convolution filters of filter size (3X3). This convolution layer is followed by the max pooling layer of size (2X2). The output of the pooling layer is connected to the fully connected layer for classification. Here we consider two fully connected layers of both having size 100 neurons. The output layer consists of four units with softmax activation to classify four vehicle sounds (Fig. 3).

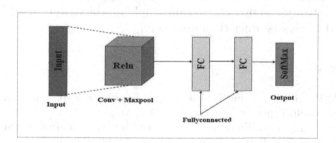

Fig. 3. Difference exemplification of the obtained Fibonacci signal.

4.3 Performance Analysis

The four features such as Fibonacci space area, entropy, kurtosis and skewness is obtained from each frame. The number of frames are truncated to 25 frame to make feature vector static and to feed to CNN. So the dimension of final feature vector is (4X250). The performance analysis is carried on recorded vehicle sound database using CNN network. The Table 1 illustrates the obtained confusion matrix for classification of four vehicle sound. From Table 1, it can be seen that an average recognition rate of 84.47% accuracy is achieved using the temporal features based on Fibonacci space and CNN classifier.

Table 1. Confusion matrix in (%) for vehicle sound recognition

Recognition rate	Bike	Car	Van	Heavy vehicle
Bike	81.25	0	18.75	0
Car	0	90.32	9.68	0
Van	19.35	3.23	77.42	0
Heavy Vehicle	2.78	0	8.33	88.89
Average	84.47			

5 Conclusion

Here we found that 4 vehicle classes can be successfully distinguished using smartphone-quality audio recordings of vehicle passing by. Here we have successfully classified four types of vehicles; cars, vans, heavy vehicle and bikes. This was achieved using careful selection of key temporal features, combined with simple deep learning models. In this work we used CNN network to classify considered vehicle sounds. It is observed that overall 84.47% accuracy can be achieved using CNN network. Further improvement can be done by increasing the feature set, selection of additional features for classification and exploring other combinations of classifications model like Support Vector Machine, Recurrent Neural Network and others. And also applying the current model to classify different kind of classes other than used here.

References

1. Paulraj, M.P., et al.: Moving vehicle recognition and classification based on time domain approach. Procedia Eng. **53**, 405–410 (2013)
2. Nooralahiyan, Y., et al.: Field trial of acoustic signature analysis for vehicle classification. Transp. Res. Part C: Emerg. Technol. **5**, 165–177 (1997)
3. Wu, H., Siegel, M., Khosla, P.: "Vehicle sound signature recognition by frequency vector principal component analysis." In: IMTC/98 Conference Proceedings. IEEE Instrumentation and Measurement Technology Conference, vol. 1, pp. 429–434 (1998)
4. Maciejewski, H., Mazurkiewicz, J., Skowron, K., Walkowiak, T.: "Neural networks for vehicle recognition." In: Proceeding of the 6th International Conference on Microelectronics for Neural Networks, Evolutionary and Fuzzy Systems, vol. 1, p. 5 (1997)

5. Dalir, A., Beheshti, A.A., Masoom, M.H.: "Classification of vehicles based on audio signals using quadratic discriminant analysis and high energy feature vectors." arXiv preprint arXiv 1804.01212 (2018)
6. Lopez, J.E., Chen, H.H., Saulnier, J.: "Target identification using wavelet-based feature extraction and neural network classifiers." CYTEL SYSTEMS INC HUDSON MA (1999)
7. Ankishan, H.: Classification of acoustic signals with new feature: fibonacci space (FSp). Biomed. Signal Process. Control **48**, 221–233 (2019)

An Improved Technique for Preliminary Diagnosis of COVID-19 via Cough Audio Analysis

Tanya Pandhi[1](✉), Teghdeep Kapoor[1](✉), and Bharat Gupta[2](✉)

[1] Department of Computer Science and Engineering,
Jaypee Institute of Information Technology, Noida 201309, Uttar Pradesh, India
pandhitanya@gmail.com, teghdeep@gmail.com
[2] Faculty of Computer Science and Engineering,
Jaypee Institute of Information Technology, Noida 201309, Uttar Pradesh, India
bharat.gupta@jiit.ac.in

Abstract. Humanity has suffered catastrophically due to the COVID-19 pandemic. One of the most reliable diagnoses of COVID-19 is RT-PCR (Reverse-Transcription Polymer Chain Reaction) testing. This method, however, has its limitations. It is time-consuming and requires scalability. This research work carries out a preliminary prognosis of COVID-19, which is scalable and less time-consuming.

The research carried out a competitive analysis of four machine learning models namely, Multilayer Perceptron, Convolutional Neural Networks, Recurrent Neural Networks with Long Short-Term Memory, and VGG-19 with Support Vector Machines. Out of these models, Multilayer Perceptron outperformed with higher specificity of 94.5% and accuracy of 96.8%. The results show that Multilayer Perceptron was able to distinguish between positive and negative COVID-19 coughs by a robust feature embedding technique.

Keywords: Cough diagnosis · Deep learning · Covid-19 · Covid-19 preliminary diagnosis · CNN · MLP · RNN · LSTM · SVM · Machine learning

1 Introduction

Coronavirus is a significant virus that causes illness in both animals and humans. It is a family of RNA viruses that is medium-sized and has a viral RNA genome largest of all known. A new, so far unknown coronavirus, SARS-CoV-2, the cause of COVID-19 disease, belongs to the same subgroup as MERS CoV and SARS-CoV. Coronavirus is known to common people as COVID-19 was declared as a pandemic by WHO(The World Health Organization), on March 11, 2020 [1]. It has forced the world into a mandatory lockdown.

The spread of this virus in the human race has caused 3.35 M deaths in the world as of May 2021 and has brought the economy to a standstill. It has also introduced several challenges worldwide. To date, the mode of transmission of SARS-CoV-2 is unresolved and is a topic of debate among researchers. Most researchers

KC Santosh et al. (Eds.): RTIP2R 2021, CCIS 1576, pp. 346–360, 2022.
https://doi.org/10.1007/978-3-031-07005-1_30

believe that it might be identical to SARS, which transmits through in-person contact or unsanitized surroundings in the form of aerosols and droplets. Studies have accentuated that patients with pulmonary symptoms are at higher risk of transmission [2,3]. However, studies proved that it is also viable from asymptomatic patients [4]. Therefore, concluding that COVID-19 can spread via symptomatic as well as asymptomatic patients. The major task in fighting COVID-19 in most countries is to find asymptomatic patients who might be potential carriers of coronavirus. Currently, widely used methods for the diagnosis of COVID-19 are RT-PCR (Reverse Transcription-Polymerase Chain Reaction) and X-ray or CT scans. Since X-rays require a chest scan at a well-equipped medical facility and are quite expensive, RT-PCR is more widely accepted. However, according to study, this testing is not scalable and sometimes inaccurate [5]. It is also costly, and most countries have faced difficulties buying more test kits. Thus, in near future, there would be a need for an alternate testing method that is simpler, unintrusive, lab-free, and less expensive. Such a method should address all the limitations of current preliminary diagnostic techniques. It must also be based on sound science and identify at-risk individuals effectively.

This research proposes a solution which is a deep neural network that recognizes the differences between COVID-19 positive and negative Coughs using audio classification techniques. It takes input as raw audio files and provides a diagnosis of whether that cough comes from a COVID-infected individual.More precisely the contributions of this research paper are as follows:

- It provides a pre-screening tool for diagnosis of COVID-19 based on deep learning (AI) ubiquitously available to everyone. Its low cost, rapid results and ease of access to everyone makes it a unique solution which can be employed in offices and various institutions as a pre-screening for entry. It can be used as aiding tool to increase the diagnostic capability and devise a treatment plan in areas where adequate supplies, healthcare facilities, and medical professionals are not available.
- We increased our dataset upto 5 times by leveraging data augmentation techniques on the open-source cough audio data set by virufy. Thus, illustrating a potential way to overcome the problem of overfitting in machine learning models due to shortage of dataset.
- The research uses features extracted from samples using sound processing techniques. The research constructed four models by using two main approaches i.e., Time Series waveform approach and Amplitude waveform approach. In the time series waveform approach, we extracted MFCC's which were fed to MLP, CNN and RNN with LSTM. Whereas in amplitude waveform approach we extracted the features from the flatten layer of VGG-19 which were then fed to SVM. Results shows that out of all these four models, MLP was most successful in classifying the COVID-19 positive and negative cough with an accuracy of 96%. Thus, showing that time series waveform approach was able to learn the robust features and was able to generalize classification better in comparison to the Amplitude waveform approach.

- Were able to successfully fine tune multi-layer perceptron to such an extent that it outperformed some of the existing literatures [6, 7].
- Portraying several future directions for our analysis and voice-based diagnosis in the context of COVID-19, which could open the door to pre-screening of COVID-19 and tracking the impact of COVID-19.

2 Background

The primary reason behind the intractability of COVID-19 is that there is a significant delay between infection and diagnosis. Two main types of COVID-19 diagnostic techniques: Laboratory-based testing and Radiography testing.

2.1 Laboratory-Based Testing

Laboratory Testing can further be categorized into two kinds: immunoassays and nucleic acid or molecular tests. Immunoassay tests discern virus-associated proteins whereas Nucleic Acid tests or molecular tests discern the genetic code of the virus. In comparison to Immunoassay tests, Nucleic acid tests are sensitive to early detection and for that reason, they are widely being used during this pandemic. The above tests often depend upon classical technologies one of which is RTPCR(Reverse transcription-polymerase chain reaction) [18]. To perform laboratory-based testing samples were obtained with throat swabs, nasopharyngeal swab, deep airway material, or sputum. Even though this technique is quite sensitive in the early detection of COVID-19, however, there are certain limitations to this technique:

i Geographical and temporal factors limit the availability of testing in various countries.
ii To fulfill the massive time-sensitive demand, it leads to scarcity of clinical testing and increases their cost.
iii The need for a personal visit to the medical facility. Such a visit exposes many segments of the community to coronavirus. This can be a major obstacle, according to the study, the aerosol stability of COVID-19 ranges from three hours up to one week on different planes making it highly stable and hence contagious [8].
iv Many reputed newspapers recently highlighted that the turnaround time stretched to 6–7 working days in a few countries due to laboratories being overflowed with COVID tests. As a result, the virus might have already been transmitted to many, by the time a patient is diagnosed and his treatment starts [9, 10].

v Often medical staff are at higher risk of infection due to these in-person testing techniques. Failure to secure our physicians can further lead to biomedical shortages and increase stress on the already distressed paramedical staff.

vi To protect others from potential exposure, many countries like India have also approved at-home sample collection under the guidelines of ICMR [11]. However, once a patient collects a nasal sample, they need to put it in a saline solution and ship it overnight to a certified lab authorized to run specific tests on the kit. Hence, this approach also introduces delays and could compromise the quality of samples if the sample is stored for too long.

2.2 Radiography Testing

Experts urge that we need more and faster testing to control the coronavirus and many have suggested that Artificial Intelligence (AI) is the solution. According to the study, multiple diagnoses of COVID-19 in development use AI to quickly analyze X-ray or CT scans have shown that in comparison to laboratical tests, radiographic tests provide sharpened sensitivity [12,13]. In order to manage coronavirus, a Thoracic CT scan - an optional imaging modality - can play a crucial role. This type of CT scan is an important aspect of COVID-19 diagnosis as it has higher precision. To produce high-resolution medical images, firstly X-rays from the patient's thorax cavity are picked up by the radiation detection tools, further, the radiographs generated are remodeled to form the medical images. One should look out for certain patterns in the thorax cavity, which might reveal different symptoms. This is examined by a radiographer, or when integrated with the AI-based analysis of the image, may detect COVID-19 with much higher specificity. This might be more efficient than that of a laboratical test such as rRT-PCR. Promising results were shown by study, it was calculated at a 95% confidence interval, having high precision and lower recall of 94% and 37% respectively for a diagnostic test based on radiology [14]. However, these techniques require scanning the chest in a well-equipped and expensive medical laboratory. So, indirectly this method also does not solve the problems faced by office-based tests as accentuated above.

2.3 Cough-Based Testing

Many kinds of research, have been carried out, where various prognostic tools for examination of respiratory infections have been presented which are self-regulating [15–17]. They have used various deep neural networks such as Convolutional Neural Networks (CNNs) to recognize coughs within natural noise and to determine various diseases such as Bronchitis, bronchiolitis, Asthma, COPD, etc. depending on their distinctive cough sound features. Although cough is a frequent medical symptom in many pulmonary diseases, study has demonstrated that depending on different conditions and locations of the underlying irritants, cough from various pulmonary diseases has unique characteristics [7]. Many types of studies have been done, which show that changes in the character of a coughing sound can indicate conditions of lung disease [19,20]. Pathological situations arise as a result of certain conditions such as obstruction, restriction, and integrated patterns. Researchers have made numerous efforts to improve the mechanism of objective classification of coughing, to classify different respiratory infections. Isolation of the cough audio signal helps to distinguish between Covid-19 positive and negative cough based on these features. The analysis of recent neurological symptoms shown by COVID-19 patients developed a link between the brain and COVID-19. This led MIT researchers to evaluate their Alzheimer's biomarkers for COVID-19 diagnosis. To detect Covid-19 coughs, they primarily used vocal cord strength, lung performance, sentiment, and muscular degradation in the human body [21] (Fig. 1).

3   Methodology

3.1   Proposed Architecture

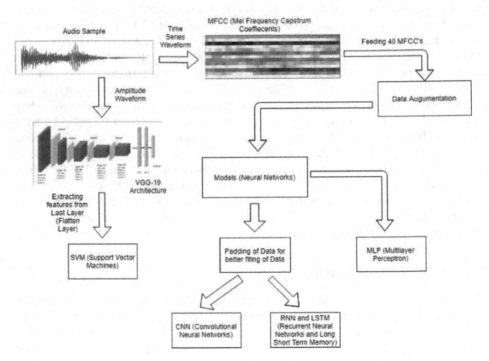

Fig. 1. Proposed architecture

3.2   COVID-19 Cough Dataset

In medical research, finding the right amount and standard data is a difficult task. The dataset used in this study was taken from various sources and combined, COVID 19 cough samples were taken from the virufy open-source audio dataset [22]. The dataset consists of 121 sound segments which are digital audio files in .mp3 format out of which 48 are COVID positive and 73 are negative. Within the dataset, out of three, two relevant discrete attributes for the respective domain were selected as shown in Table 1. The cough audio samples were converted from .mp3 format to .wav format. To ensure consistency all over the dataset, preprocessing of three major sound properties(Audio Channels, Sample Rate, and Bit-depth) was done. The audio channels of the cough samples were integrated into mono channels and the sample rates were modified to the default sample rate of 22.05 kHz. In addition to this, in order to remove the discrepancy in bit depth, the value of each audio file's average amplitude was called down to range between -1 and 1.

Table 1. Selected attribute list from the dataset.

Attributes	Description	Selected
Patient's gender	Male or Female	No
Cough audio sample	Path of the audio file	Yes
COVID status	Positive or Negative	Yes

3.3   Data Augmentation

Some domains have limited access to large data, such as medical image analysis or biomedical audio analysis. As a result, the dataset is not readily available and is quite small in size. This can lead to a problem known as overfitting. Overfitting refers to an event in which a network masters a function with very high variations to the maximum level at which it degrades the performance of the model on unseen data. One of the methods to resolve this problem is data augmentation.

Data Augmentation includes many strategies that improve the diversity and quality of data available for training models so that Deep Learning models can be built on it without facing the problem of overfitting. Audio augmentation algorithms are used to generate synthetic audio data. In this study noise injection, shifting time, changing pitch, and speed were applied to the dataset using librosa (library for Recognition and Organization of Speech and Audio). This provides an easy way to manipulate pitch and speed while a Numpy python package was used to handle noise injection and shifting time. As a result, we were able to increase the dataset by 5 folds.

3.4   Feature Extraction

Past studies have showed that the acoustic of cough sounds may carry important information related to diseases [16]. For extracting these features, in this study two approaches are used. The first one is by extracting MFCC (Mel Frequency Cepstral Coefficient) from Audio Samples. It has been scientifically proven that humans are more efficacious at identifying minute changes in a speech at lower frequencies. Thus, to leverage this property one can use MFCC's i.e., Mel frequency cepstrum coefficients. The MFCC converts the standard frequency to the Mel Scale using Eq. 1. It takes into account the human perceptiveness for sensitivity at appropriate frequencies and is therefore suitable for audio classification and sound processing. Mel scale equation is given below:

$$Mel(f) = 2595log(1 + (f/700)) \tag{1}$$

An audio signal's power spectrum, which is short-term, is represented using the Mel frequency cepstrum (MFC). The first step for obtaining MFC is Fourier transformation. On taking the log of the magnitude of this Fourier spectrum as shown in Fig. 2, and then performing cosine transformation to obtain the spectrum of this log, we observe a crest wherever there is a periodical element in the original time signal [23]. MFCC's are emanated by the cepstrum visualization of sound samples. They are coefficients that altogether form the MFC. The study used the librosa python package to calculate a series of 40 MFCCs for each sample as shown in Fig. 3 and stored it in a pandas data frame.

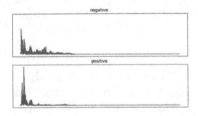

Fig. 2. Fourier transformation of negative and positive cough samples.

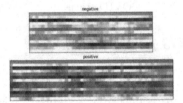

Fig. 3. Mel frequency cepstrum of negative and positive cough samples.

The second approach was extracting important features from the last flatten layer of the VGG-19 model. After that, constructing the VGG-19 model, ImageNet images of size 64 * 64 were fed for pre-training. After this, the NumPy array of pixel values was created by converting the PIL image object. Next, with dimensions of [samples, rows, columns, channels], it was expanded to the 4D array from the same 3D array. According to the VGG19 model, pixel values need to be changed. After this, all we need to do is to extract features.

In the VGG19 model as shown in Fig. 4. The last layer (1000-dimensional) is removed and the flattened layer results in a 4096-dimensional feature vector representation of an input image. After extracting these features, a 60–40 train test split was performed and then fed into the models.

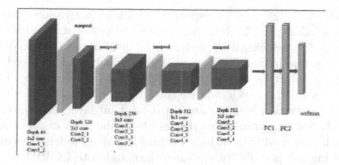

Fig. 4. VGG-19 architecture [24]

4   Model Architecture

Since the introduction of Neural Networks (NN) for pattern recognition, they have outperformed the results obtained with traditional algorithms. For instance, in the system for urban sound classification conducted, the performance of an SVM was compared with different configurations of neural models like a deep neural network (DNN) a recurrent neural network (RNN), and a Convolutional Neural Network (CNN), obtaining better results using a CNN or a DNN than using an SVM or an RNN [25]. Keeping this in mind, this research used 3 different configurations of neural network and SVM. In the end, the results of each model were compared and the best model was chosen.

4.1   Multilayer Perceptron

Multilayer Perceptrons, or MLP for short, is a long-established neural network. A combination of multiple neurons forms a multilayer perceptron. The feeding of data takes place at the input layer which is then processed by the hidden layers. These hidden layers are used to increase the level of abstraction. After the processing of data from the hidden layers, the output layer gives us the final predictions. The study used Data Augmentation (noise, shift, and stretch) to increase the audio dataset in order to overcome overfitting. MLP can be constructed using Keras and Tensorflow backend. The model built in this research was sequential in nature and consisted of four layers to increase the level of abstraction. All the four layers - input layer, two hidden layers, and an output layer are of dense type, which is the standard type in most of the cases. The number of nodes comprised by each of the three layers including input and hidden layers were 256, 128, and 64 respectively with an activation function ReLU and a dropout value of 25%. ReLU has proven to perform extremely well with neural network frameworks, it is explained further more in Appendix A.2. For better generalization in models, dropout is used which randomly excludes nodes from each epoch which in turn decreases the chance of overfitting. Finally, the output layer has 2 nodes which indicate the number of class labels with softmax. Softmax is the activation function used in the output layer, explained further in Appendix A.1. Softmax transforms the results in the form of probabilities, due to which it is highly used with various machine learning models. The model then, based on the highest probability, classifies the cough into COVID-19 positive or negative.

4.2 Convolutional Neural Networks

Another Deep Learning algorithm implemented in this study is Convolutional Neural Network (CNN). It can take an image as input, allot significance to the various elements in the image, and be able to distinguish one from the other. As a precautionary measure, each recording of the input cough, processed with the MFCC package, was divided into 6-second audio clips and was padded as required. The study used the Convolutional Neural Network again with Keras and TensorFlow as a backend. It is a sequential model that comprises of four Conv2D convolution layers out of which two are dense layers. A pooling layer of the MaxPooling2D type is linked with the final convolutional layer. The pooling layer reduces the parameters as well as the requirements for subsequent computation. This in turn reduced the dimensionality of the model. As a result, it shortens the duration of the training and reduces overfitting. The Max Pooling version has taken the greatest size possible of every window. For convolutional layers, the ReLU activation function was used, it is explained further more in Appendix A.2. A dropout value of 50% after the final convolutional layer is applied. The output layer has 2 nodes (number of labels, positive and negative) which are the same as the number of possible classifications. Softmax is the activation function used in the output layer, explained further in Appendix A.1. Softmax transforms the results in the form of probabilities, due to which it is highly used with various machine learning models.The model then, based on the highest probability, classifies the cough into COVID-19 positive or negative.

4.3 Recurrent Neural Networks with Long Short-Term Memory

Recurrent neural network (RNN) is a category of neural networks that help in data sequencing. Based on feedforward networks, RNNs show a similar mechanism of action as in the human brain. To put it simply, there is no alternative algorithm that can produce predictable results in sequential data as accurately as a recurrent neural network can. The model used a sequential model, consisting of two LSTM layers, with four Time distributed layers. All LSTM layers consisted of 128 nodes. After the final LSTM layer, we used a Dropout of the value of 50%. The model has four Time Distributed Layers of dense type with 64, 32,

16, and 8 nodes respectively with an activation function as ReLU (Rectified Linear Activation), it is explained further more in Appendix A.2. The output layer has 2 nodes (number of labels, positive and negative) which are the same as the number of possible classifications. Softmax is the activation function used in the output layer, explained further in Appendix A.1. Softmax transforms the results in the form of probabilities, due to which it is highly used with various machine learning models. The model then, based on the highest probability, classifies the cough into COVID-19 positive or negative.

4.4 Support Vector Machines

Support vector machines or also known as SVM, come under the category of data mining techniques that are used for both classification and prediction. It is able to generalize between two different classes. After providing the SVM model set of labelled training data for every category, it can classify the new text by checking the hyperplane that is able to distinguish between the two classes. After extracting features from the VGG-19 flatten layer as explained in Sect. 3.4. A 70–30 train test split was performed and then fed into a LinearSVM for classification.

5 Results

Predictions generated by models were expected to generalize well and could effectively produce the appropriate category label or data classification of previously unknown data. The effectiveness of the classification model was assessed based on the number of precise and false predictions observed by various models implemented on the unseen database. Accuracy, precision, and recall were the three evaluation metrics used which assess the nature of predictions made by the machine learning models developed in this research.

5.1 Accuracy

Accuracy is a measurement of the approximate level of quantity rather than the actual value of a quantity. It can be computed from the confusion matrix using the equation mentioned below (Table 2).

$$Accuracy = \frac{TruePositives + TrueNegatives}{TruePositives + TrueNegatives + FalsePositives + FalseNegatives} \quad (2)$$

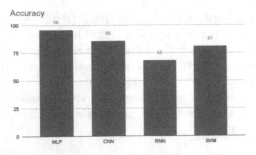

Fig. 5. Overall accuracy is achieved by the models in graphical representation.

Table 2. Overall accuracy is achieved by the models in tabular representation.

Models	Accuracy(in %)
MLP	**96**
CNN	**86**
RNN	**68**
SVM	**81**

The Fig. 5 shows that Multilayer Perceptron and Convolutional Neural Network performed better than the rest of the models with an overall accuracy of 96% and 86% respectively. SVM performed fairly decent with 81% accuracy whereas Recurrent Neural Network was not able to generalize well and had an accuracy of only 68%.

5.2 Precision

In pattern detection, data retrieval, and categorization (machine reading), precision is the ratio of relevant instances among the retrieved instances. Precision is also known as a positive predictive value. In this study, that would be the proportion of patients who were positively identified with COVID-19 in all patients who actually had it. It was computed using the equation given below.

$$Precision = \frac{TruePositives}{TruePositives + FalsePositives} \tag{3}$$

The precision of each model achieved in both negative and positive classes in this study was recorded in Table 3.

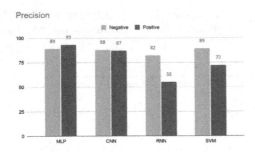

Fig. 6. The precision is achieved by the models in graphical representation.

Table 3. The precision achieved by the models in the tabular representation.

Models	Precision (in %)	
	Postive	Negative
MLP	**93**	**89**
CNN	**87**	**88**
RNN	**55**	**82**
SVM	**72**	**89**

Higher Precision relates to lower false-positive rates. Figure 6 shows that Multilayer Perceptron and Convolutional Neural Networks have lower false-positive rates and are able to classify covid positive patients very well with a precision of 93% and 87% respectively. RNN has a higher false-positive rate and is prone to false alarms. All the models have a lower false-negative rate and are able to classify non-covid patients very well.

5.3 Recall

The recall is the measure of our model that accurately identifies True Positives. It is also known as the sensitivity of the model. Therefore, in all patients with actual COVID-19, recall tells us how many did the model accurately identified as COVID-19 positive. It can be computed using the following equation:

$$Recall = \frac{TruePositives}{TruePositives + FalseNegatives} \tag{4}$$

The recall of each model achieved in both negative and positive classes in this study was recorded in Table 4.

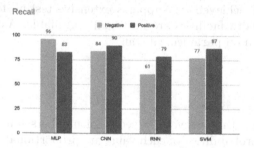

Fig. 7. The recall is achieved by the models in graphical representation.

Table 4. The recall is achieved by the models in tabular representation.

Models	Recall (in %)	
	Postive	Negative
MLP	83	96
CNN	90	84
RNN	79	61
SVM	87	77

Higher Recall relates to higher true positive rates. Figure 7 shows that Convolutional Neural Networks and Support Vector Machines have higher true positive rates for class positive. CNN and SVM correctly identify 90% and 87% of all the positive cases respectively. Multilayer Perceptron and Convolutional Neural Networks have a higher specificity. RNN can only identify 79% of all the positive cases and 61% of all the negative cases.

6 Conclusion

The Trace, Test, and Treat strategy has shown that it is necessary for governments to be able to effectively track the spread of the disease, isolate infected people. This helps in flattening the curve of infection successfully. However, most countries are not able to do enough rapid tests; which is why the alternative proposed can be very helpful. This paper presents an ML model for the initial diagnosis of COVID-19 with cough samples. On the basis of performance evaluation parameters, various models used in this study were analyzed. This analysis revealed that the Multi-Layer Perceptron outperformed with an accuracy of 96%. Convolutional Neural Networks and Support Vector Machines, on the other hand, have performed fairly well in terms of accuracy. Higher precision and lower recall give an extremely accurate result, but it then misses a large number of difficult instances to classify which can't be ignored in COVID-19 diagnosis. Thus, there is a need for models having higher precision and higher recall at the same time for improved generalized classification.

The results show that precision and recall of both Multi-Layer Perceptron and Convolutional Neural Network yielded somewhat comparable results. On the other hand, Recurrent Neural Network and Long Short-Term Memory were not able to generalize well on COVID-19 cough samples due to higher false-positive rates and lower true positive rates.

Overall, Multi-Layer Perceptron was able to generalize well with a higher sensitivity, ensuring low false alarms. These results promise that AI can be used in the clinic and at home as a support system for physicians and the general public in the early detection of COVID-19. It may play an important role in medical diagnosis. This significant achievement supports extensive testing for COVID-19 even in areas where health facilities are not readily available. As a result, it helps to reduce the burden on paramedical staff.

A   Appendix

A.1   Softmax

Softmax is a mathematical function that converts a vector of numbers into a vector of probabilities, where the probabilities of each value are proportional to the relative scale of each value in the vector.

$$\text{Softmax}(x_i) = \frac{\exp(x_i)}{\sum_j \exp(x_j)} \tag{5}$$

where, $\exp(x_i)$ represents standard exponential function for input vector, K represents number of classes in the multi-class classifier, and $\exp(x_j)$ represents standard exponential function for output vector.

A.2   ReLU

The rectified linear activation function or ReLU for short is a piecewise linear function that will output the input directly if it is positive, otherwise, it will output zero. It has become the default activation function for many types of neural networks because a model that uses it is easier to train and often achieves better performance.

$$\text{ReLU}(x) = max(0.0, x) \tag{6}$$

where, x is the input to a neuron.

References

1. Laboratory testing for coronavirus disease (COVID-19) in suspected human cases. https://www.who.int/publications-detail/laboratory-testing-for-2019-novel-coronavirus-in-suspected-human-cases-20200117. Accessed 3 June 2021
2. Guo, G., et al.: New insights of emerging SARS-CoV-2: epidemiology, etiology, clinical features, clinical treatment, and prevention. J. Front Cell Dev. Biol. **8**, 410 (2020). https://doi.org/10.3389/fcell.2020.00410
3. Yu, I.T., et al.: Evidence of airborne transmission of the severe acute respiratory syndrome virus. J. N. Engl. J. Med. **350**(17), 1731–1739 (2004). https://doi.org/10.1056/NEJMoa032867
4. Yang, R., Gui, X., Xiong, Y.: Patients with respiratory symptoms are at greater risk of COVID-19 transmission. J. Respir. Med. **165**, 105935 (2020). https://doi.org/10.1016/j.rmed.2020.105935
5. Kameswari, S., Brundha, M.P., Ezhilarasan, D.: Advantages and disadvantages of RT- PCR in COVID 19. Eur. J. Mol. Clin. Med. **7**(1), 1174–1181 (2020). https://doi.org/10.1016/j.rmed.2020.105935
6. Brown, C., et al.: Exploring automatic diagnosis of covid-19 from crowdsourced respiratory sound data. In: Proceedings of the 26th ACM SIGKDD International Conference on Knowledge Discovery and Data Mining, pp. 3474–3484 (2020). https://arxiv.org/pdf/2006.05919.pdf
7. Imran, A., et al.: AI4COVID-19: AI enabled preliminary diagnosis for COVID-19 from cough samples via an app. J. Inf. Med. Unlocked **20**, 100378 (2020). https://doi.org/10.1016/j.imu.2020.100378
8. Van Doremalen, N., et al.: Aerosol and surface stability of SARS-CoV-2 as compared with SARS-CoV-1. J. N. Engl. J. Med. **382**(16), 1564–7 (2020). https://doi.org/10.1056/NEJMc2004973
9. Delayed RT-PCR reports triggering Covid surge, high transmission rate in Lucknow. The Times of India. https://timesofindia.indiatimes.com/city/lucknow/delayed-rt-pcr-reports-triggering-covid-surge-high-transmission-rate/articleshow/82265365.cms. Accessed 2 June 2021
10. Gujarat: Why RT-PCR test reports 'delayed by 5–7 days'; AG says many undergo tests unnecessarily. The Indian Express. https://indianexpress.com/article/cities/ahmedabad/gujarat-why-rt-pcr-test-reports-delayed-by-5-7-days-ag-says-many-undergo-tests-unnecessarily-7270655. Accessed 2 June 2021
11. Advisory for COVID-19 testing during the second wave of the pandemic. ICMR official advisory. https://www.icmr.gov.in/cteststrat.html. Accessed 2 June 2021
12. Ozsahin, I., Sekeroglu, B., Musa, S.M., Mubarak, T.M., Uzun Ozsahin, D.: Review on diagnosis of COVID-19 from chest CT Images using artificial intelligence. J. Comput. Math. Methods Med. **10** (2020). https://doi.org/10.1155/2020/9756518
13. Fang, Y., Zhang, H., Xie, J.: Sensitivity of chest CT for COVID-19: comparison to RT-PCR. J. Radiol. **296**, 115–117 (2020). https://doi.org/10.1148/radiol.2020200432
14. Adams, H.J., Kwee, T.C., Kwee, R.M.: COVID-19 and chest CT do not put the sensitivity value in the isolation room and look beyond the numbers. Radiology **297**(1), E236–E237 (2020). https://doi.org/10.1148/radiol.2020201709
15. Bales, C., et al.: Can machine learning be used to recognize and diagnose coughs? In: 2020 International Conference on e-Health and Bioengineering (EHB), 29, pp. 1–4 (2020). https://doi.org/10.1109/EHB50910.2020.9280115

16. Amrulloh, Y., Abeyratne, U., Swarnkar, V., Triasih, R.: Cough sound analysis for pneumonia and asthma classification in the pediatric population. In: IEEE 6th International Conference on Intelligent Systems, Modelling, and Simulation, pp.127–131, (2020). https://doi.org/10.1109/ISMS.2015.41

17. Infante, C., Chamberlain, D., Fletcher, R., Thorat, Y., Kodgule, R.: Use of cough sounds for diagnosis and screening of pulmonary disease. In: IEEE global human-itarian technology conference, GHTC, pp. 1–10 (2015). https://doi.org/10.1109/EHB50910.2020.9280115

18. Waltz, E.: How do coronavirus tests work? IEEE Spectr. https://spectrum.ieee.org/the-human-os/biomedical/diagnostics/how-do-coronavirus-tests-work. Accessed 2 June 2021

19. Hirschberg, J., Szende, T.: Pathological cry, stridor and cough in infants, Budapest: Akiademiai Kiado. PMCID: PMC1627937, (1983)

20. Maryam, Z., Fazel, Z.M.H., Mostafa, M.: Application of intelligent systems in asthma disease: designing a fuzzy rule-based system for evaluating the based onlevel of asthma exacerbation. J. J. Med. Syst. **36**, 2071–83 (2012). https://doi.org/10.1007/s10916-011-9671-8

21. Laguarta, J., Hueto, F., Subirana, B.: ACOVID-19 artificial intelligence diagnosis using only cough recordings. IEEE Open J. Eng. Med. Biol. **1**, 275–281 (2020). https://doi.org/10.1109/OJEMB.2020.3026928

22. Khanzada, A., Wilson, T.: Virufy COVID-19 open cough dataset, Github (2020). Accessed 2 Feb 2021

23. Nair, P.: The dummy's guide to MFCC, Medium (2018). https://medium.com/prathena/the-dummys-guide-to-mfcc-aceab2450fd. Accessed 5 June 2021

24. Hewage, R.: Extract features, visualize filters and feature maps in VGG16 and VGG19 CNN models, towards data science (2020). https://towardsdatascience.com/extract-features-visualize-filters-and-feature-maps-in-vgg16-and-vgg19-cnn-models-d2da6333edd0. Accessed 5 June 2021

25. Chang, C., Doran, B.: Urban sound classification: with random forest SVM DNN RNN and CNN classifiers. In: CSCI E-81 Machine Learning and Data Mining Final Project Fall 2016, Harvard University Cambridge (2016)

Satellite Imaging and Remote Sensing

Agricultural Field Analysis Using Satellite Hyperspectral Data and Autoencoder

Pranesh Kulkarni[✉], Medha Wyawahare, Atharva Karwande, Tejas Kolhe,
Soham Kamble, and Akshay Joshi

Department of Electronics and Telecommunication, Vishwakarma Institute of Technology, Pune,
India
kulkarnipranesh1767@gmail.com, {medha.wyawahare,
atharva.karwande18,tejas.kolhe18,soham.kamble18,
akshay.joshi18}@vit.edu

Abstract. In this paper, we have proposed a novel clustering-based approach for the prediction of the quality index of agricultural land. This paper aims to develop a system that can predict the quality index of the land based on the hyperspectral data acquired for the specified region over the period of 6 years. Dataset collected for this research consists of hyperspectral images of agricultural lands belonging to different geographical regions in India. Google earth engine platform has been used to collect the hyperspectral data of the Landsat 8 satellite. Autoencoder and k-means clustering algorithms are used for high-performance dimensionality reduction and clustering of the data respectively. Insurance agencies, NGOs, government bodies can get the benefits from the proposed methodology for client claim verification or for conducting agricultural surveys on large scale. As the data can be collected from a remote location, experts won't need to visit the field each time.

Keywords: Agriculture · Autoencoder · Earth engine · Machine learning · SELU · Spectral indices · Surface reflectance

1 Introduction

Around 45% of the people belong to households where the main source of income is agriculture. In developing nations like India, the primary business of most people is agriculture. After the 19th century lot of research activities are going on to improve the production in this sector. In recent years, many farmers have started practicing precision farming techniques. Precision agriculture is the farming concept that supports the use of high-performance sensors (majorly the sensors used for hyperspectral imaging) and some analytical tools to decide farming strategies and for getting better crop yield [1]. The sensors in recently deployed satellites can capture hyperspectral data very precisely. So the agriculture sector has experienced huge benefits from this highly efficient technology. Scientists and researchers are vigorously working to develop a highly precise system that can supports precision agricultural practices.

KC Santosh et al. (Eds.): RTIP2R 2021, CCIS 1576, pp. 363–375, 2022.
https://doi.org/10.1007/978-3-031-07005-1_31

Satellite images consists of multiple spectral bands. Each band contains various information useful for different applications. With some visible as well as non-visible bands of the satellite, we can analyze the photosynthesis activity, vegetation, or water level in plant bodies. Hyperspectral indices are the mathematical combination of these hyperspectral bands. Researchers have proposed some indices like Normalized Difference Vegetative Index (NDVI), Modified Soil Adjusted Vegetative Index (MSAVI2) and so on which can be useful to analyze plant health and vegetation of the area. The red band and near-infrared band heavily contribute to the estimation of these indices. While short wave infrared band and green band would be useful for estimating NDWI and Green Normalized Difference Vegetation Index (GNDVI). So each band of the satellite contributes towards predicting the quality of agricultural land.

In this research, we have proposed a technique for estimating the quality factor of agricultural land by analyzing the hyperspectral data captured by the satellite over the specific region and artificial intelligence algorithms. By using the google earth engine we have extracted the hyperspectral data for 3000 agricultural fields. Autoencoder is a deep learning network that is used for high-performance compression of the data. For this research, we have deployed this network to extract important features from the data which can be later used for estimating the quality factor of agricultural land. After extracting important features from the data, the k-means clustering method is used for clustering the data in an unsupervised manner. Each cluster will then represent the specific field quality.

Not only farmers but insurance agencies or NGOs working in the agricultural sector also can take benefit of the proposed system. These organizations require a lot of human expertise as well as time for visiting the agricultural sites for their audits or surveys. Also in the covid19 pandemic, it is very difficult for insurance companies for client claim verification. So these tasks can be performed remotely using the proposed methodology of analyzing agricultural sites with hyperspectral data provided by the satellite. Section 2 of the paper explains the work done in this domain by previous researchers. The proposed methodology and experimental results are described in Sect. 3 and Sect. 4.

2   Related Work

Haluk Cetin et al. have proposed a technique to detect nitrogen deficiency in corn using hyperspectral data [2]. They found out that NDVI which is obtained from multispectral analysis of images cannot be used for detecting vegetation stress. They utilized hyperspectral Real-time Dam Acquisition Camera System (RUACS-3) imagery with 120 bands and 2×2 m pixel resolution to examine spectrally sensitive regions for the detection of Nitrogen (N) deficiency. The process involved data pre-processing in which they did rectification and removed sensor noise and different atmospheric effects from images. After pre-processing, they came towards data reduction of huge overwhelming data of hyperspectral imagery. They used a random point sampling approach to achieve this. The final stage was to detect the stress-sensitive spectral, which was accomplished using a quantitative approach like Analysis of Variance (ANOVA), Logistic regression (LR), and Multiple Linear regression (MLR). To visually discriminate stressed regions from healthy vegetation, it was necessary to indicate which spectral regions were particularly sensitive and create a method for displaying these differences. Therefore, crop biophysical variable correlations with wavelength were compared. Detection of early stress in crops is dependent upon accurate spectral data. This research has shown several advantages of hyperspectral imagery over traditional NDVI depictions of crop stress.

Shwetank et al. have used principal component analysis for reducing the dimension of hyperspectral images and further used the compressed data for the classification of rice crop varieties [3]. The author has developed a novel segmented principal component analysis algorithm in which 155 spectral bands of E0-1 satellite are converted into 5 segments based on reflectance properties of these spectral bands. Spectral Angle Mapper (SAM) classification method has been used to classify 16 different land covers along with 5 rice crop varieties. Authors have successfully classified rice crop varieties with 80.2% classification accuracy.

In Northern Italy, Daniela Stroppiana et al. have carried out research for hyperspectral analysis of rice fields [4]. The basic objective of this experimentation was to test the correlation between surface reflectance in spectral bands and the vegetation indices obtained from the multi-spectral sensor. They have chosen, UAV vehicle, DJI S1000 Octocopter with Canon S100 camera, and Tetracam ADCMicro multispectral sensor to capture the images and multispectral data of spatial resolution was about 3 cm by flying it about 70 m above ground. They performed geometric calibration of the sensor using APS. Also, the multispectral data was resampled to a higher value and radiometrically normalized to enhance spectral consistency. Data acquired by the sensor is processed to extract reflectance in the green, red, and NIR channels; RGRI and NDVI vegetation indices and computed and correlated to rice grain yield field measurements. The authors concluded that the UAV systems can be more efficient than satellite remote sensing for crop monitoring.

Jinmika Wijitdechakul et al. have proposed a technique to study the agricultural field and predict its health [5]. To get the aerial images of the fields to study, they mounted 2 multispectral cameras on the Unmanned Aerial Vehicle (UAV). They introduced the SPA concept/framework in their semantic computing solution. They divided SPA as S for the sensing phase, they used UAVs as sensors, which gives out multispectral and IR images as output. P is for the processing phase which is the semantic processing done on those images. A is for the Actuation phase which gives a meaning of the analysis of those multispectral images which they get from the processing phase. They gave simple output as English words, depending on the values of the three indices, namely NDVI, NDWI, and SAVI, they calculated and brightness of the image. As a result, they got to know that, NDVI shows the greenness of plants. Bright area indicates more green area or high NDVI value and dark area indicates no vegetation area. The bright area shows a high NDWI value and indicates high water content. The bright area is shown high soil moisture area. And the final image result is shown a healthy agricultural area which is represented by yellow color and unhealthy is the dark blue area.

Medha Wyawahare et al. have proposed a method to estimate the quality index of agricultural land by using the vegetation indices such as NDVI, MSAVI, and NDWI [6]. The authors claimed that the proposed method predicts the quality index by analyzing the satellite hyperspectral data captured within 6 years. Their proposed method combines the mean of these three vegetation indices estimated at different time instances and precipitation data. K-means clustering algorithm has been used for clustering and support vector machine classifier for the classification task. The research concluded that the MSAVI2 is majorly affecting the index for estimation of agricultural land quality.

We can observe that there are many spectral indices and spectral bands which contributes in prediction of quality of an agricultural land. This paper enlightens the modeling of an agricultural land quality index by effectively combining multiple spectral bands rather than using them separately.

3 Proposed Methodology

The proposed system can efficiently extract the features from hyperspectral data and precisely predicts the quality index of an agricultural field. Autoencoder and K-means clustering methods are used to reduce the dimensionality of the data and to cluster the data. Figure 1 illustrates the method of developing the system for the prediction of the quality index of agricultural land.

3.1 Dataset Preparation

For this research, we have used the USGS Landsat 8 Surface Reflectance Tier 1 data available in the google earth engine dataset [7]. Google earth engine is a cloud-based platform that includes public datasets of geospatial data. Using google earth engine we have developed a web application based on google earth engine datasets, to extract the hyperspectral data captured landsat8 satellite over the specified region of interest. We have identified some agricultural plots in every state of India and by using the web application mentioned before, we have collected the hyperspectral data of 6 years for each agricultural plot. We have identified the spectral bands mentioned in Table 1. The spatial resolution of the images captured by satellite Landsat is 30 m which is quite good for analyzing any field.

Processing the hyperspectral image is a computationally heavy task so we have computed the means of surface reflectance values corresponding to each band to make the system computationally efficient. So one data point in the dataset contains the band means of 7 spectral bands of every surface reflectance record captured by the Landsat 8 satellite at different time instances in the span of 6 years corresponding to one specified agricultural land. We have collected 3000 such data points corresponding to agricultural lands in different regions in India. So, the dataset collected for this research represents the agricultural diversity in India. After collecting the dataset, we have identified and removed the corrupt data points or the datapoints with some error (e.g. negative surface reflectance) to avoid the misclassification errors in machine learning algorithms. We have analyzed the data based on spectral index NDVI [8]. NDVI index can be calculated by the formula:

$$NDVI = \frac{(NIR - RED)}{(NIR + RED)} \tag{1}$$

We have computed the NDVI index corresponding to every record captured by the satellite and after that, we have calculated the average of NDVI indices of the records captured at different time instances corresponding to every agricultural land.

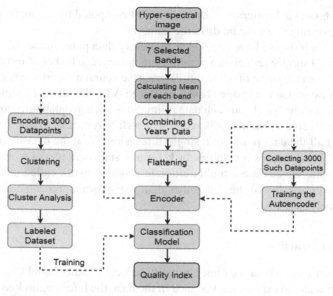

Fig. 1. Block diagram of methodology for training the system to predict the quality factor of an agricultural land.

Table 1. Landsat 8 multispectral bands [7]

Name of the band	Wavelength	Description
B1	0.435–0.451 μm	Band 1 - ultra-blue
B2	0.452–0.512 μm	Band 2 - blue
B3	0.533–0.590 μm	Band 3 - green
B4	0.636–0.673 μm	Band 4 - red
B5	0.851–0.879 μm	Band 5 - near infrared
B6	1.566–1.651 μm	Band 6 - shortwave infrared 1
B7	2.107–2.294 μm	Band 7 - shortwave infrared 2

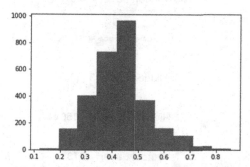

Fig. 2. Histogram of average NDVI calculated for all the agricultural lands (on X-axis) in the dataset.

Figure 2 shows the histogram of average NDVI computed by the method described before corresponding to all the fields in the dataset.

From this analysis, we have concluded that every data point in the dataset consists of a minimum 39 surface reflectance records, and the average NDVI of most of the data points lies between the range of 0.3 to 0.6. To train the neural network we need structural data. So we have sorted the images based on the NDVI index in descending order and selected the first 39 images from each data point. So now each datapoints contains band means of 7 bands corresponding to 39 records of surface reflectance data. After that, we have flattened all the data points to a single dimension. Now the dataset contains 273 features (39*7). It becomes a complex task for any statistical model to fit such high-dimensional data. We can use a highly efficient neural network called autoencoder to reduce the dimensionality of the data rather than a statistical approach called principal component analysis (PCA).

3.2 Feature Extraction

We have chosen autoencoder for dimensionality reduction rather than PCA as the linear map is not sufficient to explain the variance in the data, the information loss is higher in the case of PCA. Autoencoder can efficiently extracts the information with minimal loss of information compared to PCA [9]. Autoencoder is the type of neural network which can compress the data with higher efficiency [10]. This network is divided into three parts. The encoder encodes the data to lower dimensions, latent space contains the extracted features and the decoder tries to retrieve original data from latent space. The objective of the network is to reduce the error between original and reconstructed data. Generally, the mean squared error (MSE) loss function is used to train the network. The network learns to extract the maximum information from the data by reducing the redundant features.

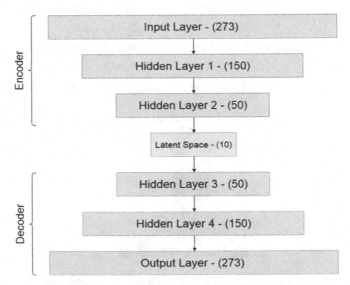

Fig. 3. Proposed network architecture of autoencoder.

So the encoded vector is the general representation of the data. We are only interested in the encoder part which reduces the dimensionality of the data. Figure 3 illustrates the proposed architecture of the neural network. The network reduces the dimensionality from 273 to 10. The activation function for each dense layer is Scaled Exponential Linear Units (SELU) [11]. We have implemented the SELU activation function because of its property of self-normalization and ability to learn faster and better when compared with other activation functions. Table 2 compares the loss of networks trained with different activation functions.

Table 2. Comparison of the performance of the network trained using different activation functions

Activation function	Training loss (MSE)	Validation loss (MSE)
RELU	0.0574	0.0559
TANH	0.0506	0.0518
SELU	0.0447	0.0445

From this comparison, we can conclude that the SELU outperforms other activation functions. So after training the network for 50 epochs, we have fine-tuned the network at an extremely lower learning rate for 200 epochs and extracted the latent vector corresponding to each data point in the dataset.

3.3 Clustering

We have clustered all the agricultural lands based on features extracted by autoencoder from hyperspectral data. K-means clustering algorithm has been used to cluster the data [12]. It is the unsupervised machine learning approach in which 'n' observations or data points are grouped into K clusters where all the data points in the cluster exhibit similar characteristics and each data point belong to only one single cluster or group. This method is useful to classify the data when labels or ground truths are not present. We have clustered all the data points into 10 clusters where each cluster represents the specific type of agricultural land. The value of k = 10 is determined by using the Elbow method [13]. After clustering the data, we have analyzed all the clusters based on the NDVI index. The average NDVI of all the data points belonging to each cluster is computed and quality indices from 0 to 10 are assigned to every cluster based on average NDVI. The low quality index represents unhealthy vegetation or lower land quality while the high quality index represents healthy vegetation or high land quality.

3.4 Classification

Now the dataset is labeled, each agricultural field is associated with a specific quality index. So now it becomes a supervised classification problem where we need to analyze the patterns in the data and based on that pattern the data can be classified i.e. quality index can be predicted. The main purpose of this classification model is for deployment only. When we want to predict the quality of an unknown agricultural plot, this classification model can be used. So to fit the data, we have used an ensemble learning algorithm called the random forest classification algorithm due to its robustness to outliers, ability to tackle the overfitting problem and lower sensitivity to the noise in the data [14]. The base estimator of the random forest classifier is a decision tree. Generally, decision trees are prone to overfitting issues so instead of predicting the output from a single decision tree, the output is decided based on predictions obtained from multiple decision trees where each decision tree is trained with different subsets of the dataset. We have selected the features based on the Pearson correlation coefficient. Features having very less and very high correlation coefficient with dependent variable should be removed in this step. Also, one of the features having high mutual correlation should be removed. We have fed the features extracted from the autoencoder to classifiers as independent variables and quality factors assigned to each data point as dependent features. Hyper parameters of the random forest classifier such as number of base estimators, data splitting ratio, features splitting ratio significantly affect the performance of the model. So we have tuned these hyper parameters one after another. At the first stage, the parameter named as no. of estimators is tuned. Figure 4 illustrates the effect of no. of estimators on the performance of the model. Similarly, the other two parameters such as the ratio of data splitting and the features splitting ratio are tuned. Figure 5 and Fig. 6 explain the effect on accuracy when we change the data splitting ratio and feature splitting ratio correspondingly. 5-fold cross-validation technique used for splitting training and testing set [15]. Generally, this technique is used to obtain less biased results. The performance of the classifier is explained in Sect. 4.

4   Results

We have trained an autoencoder with SELU activation function for 50 epochs and monitored the MSE loss on training and validation data (20% of the total dataset). The whole training dataset is split into 74 batches of batch size 32 and propagated through the network in every epoch.

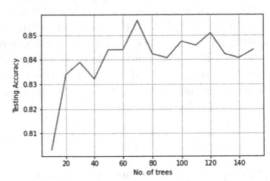

Fig. 4. Plot of No. of estimators Vs testing accuracy. Indicating that the optimum value of No. of estimators is 70

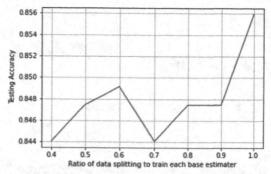

Fig. 5. Plot of data splitting ratio Vs testing accuracy. Indicating that the optimum data splitting ratio is 1.0.

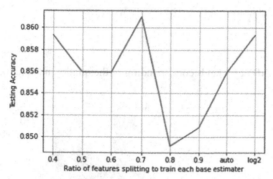

Fig. 6. Plot of Feature splitting ratio Vs testing accuracy. Indicating that the optimum value of features splitting ratio is 0.7

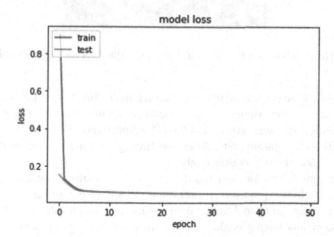

Fig. 7. The change in training and validation loss over the training period.

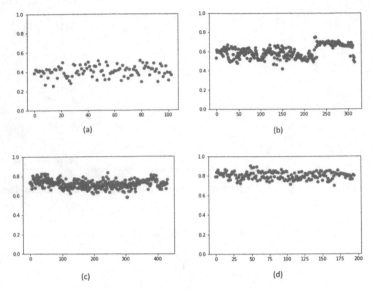

Fig. 8. The average NDVI for lands corresponding to the quality index (a) 0, (b) 4, (c) 7, (d) 9.

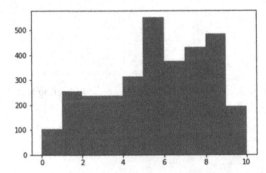

Fig. 9. Histogram of quality index (on X-axis) identified for each agricultural land.

Figure 7 shows the decreasing trend of training and testing loss of the network. After 4 epochs, the rate of decreasing of the error decreases. Finally, after 50 epochs, training loss and validation loss was 0.0447 and 0.0445 respectively. Then we have fine-tuned the model with lower learning rate. After fine-tuning, training loss and validation loss comes out 0.0429 and 0.0428 respectively.

After obtaining labels for clustered data, we have visualized the average NDVI of each data point belonging to every cluster. Figure 8 shows the average NDVI for agricultural land corresponding to different quality indices. The plot shows that the average NDVI of data points having quality index 0 lies between approximately 0.2 to 0.5. Similarly, for the data points with quality index, 9 have an average NDVI greater than approximately 0.8. With this, we can conclude that the higher quality index indicates healthy vegetation. Figure 9 shows the histogram of the quality index determined corresponding to agricultural lands in the dataset. The random forest classification model was

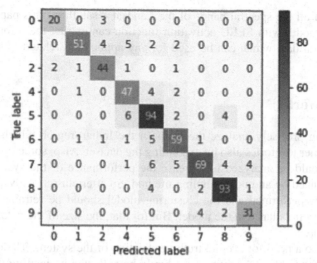

Fig. 10. Confusion matrix created from the results predicted by the model. Indicating the smaller number of false predictions.

trained to fit the labelled data and performance of the model was estimated on testing data (20% of the total data). Table 3 describes the various performance metrics used to analyze the performance of the classification model such as accuracy, precision, recall, F1 score, etc. computed from the confusion matrix shown in Fig. 10. Also the average 5-fold cross validation accuracy was 0.866934. Since the statistical model is deployed for the classification task, the system will require less time to predict the quality index.

Table 3. Performance metrics computed for classification model.

Metric	Score
Accuracy	0.861017
Precision	0.865300
Recall	0.861017
F1 score	0.860990
Cohens kappa score	0.840268

5 Conclusion

The proposed system can efficiently predict the quality index of an agricultural land by analyzing the hyperspectral data of the satellite with 86.6934% accuracy. Farmers, insurance agencies, NGOs or government bodies can take the advantage of the proposed system for their audits and surveys. Basically the proposed quality index is the combination of all the spectral bands of the Landsat 8 satellite. This paper concludes that the autoencoder with SELU activation function can extract the information from the hyperspectral data which can be used for any application related to hyperspectral analysis.

6 Future Work

The system can precisely analyze the lands in the Indian region which can be later modeled for other territories also by expanding the dataset. Also, some other clustering approaches should be analyzed to increase the performance of the system. The data should be balanced by an undersampling method. So after cluster analysis, undersampling should be performed and the clustering model should be retrained in order to remove the class imbalance in the model. But for that, the size of the dataset should be considerably large.

There is also a need for ground truth verification of the system. The data obtained by soil testing or field productivity data should be collected by visiting the site and it should be compared with the quality obtained by the proposed system in order to verify the reliability of the system.

References

1. Singh, P., et al.: Hyperspectral remote sensing in precision agriculture: present status, challenges, and future trends. In: Hyperspectral Remote Sensing, pp. 121–146 (2020)
2. Cetin, H., Pafford, J.T., Mueller, T.G.: Precision agriculture using hyperspectral remote sensing and GIS. In: Proceedings of 2nd International Conference on Recent Advances in Space Technologies, RAST 2005 (2005)
3. Shwetank, J. K., Bhatia, K.: Hyperspectral data compression model using SPCA (segmented principal component analysis) and classification of rice crop varieties. In: Ranka, S., et al. (eds.) IC3 2010. CCIS, vol. 94, pp. 360–372. Springer, Heidelberg (2010). https://doi.org/10.1007/978-3-642-14834-7_34
4. Stroppiana, D., et al.: Rice yield estimation using multispectral data from UAV: A preliminary experiment in northern Italy. In: 2015 IEEE International Geoscience and Remote Sensing Symposium (IGARSS) (2015)
5. Wijitdechakul, J., Sasaki, S., Kiyoki, Y., Koopipat, C.: UAV-based multispectral image analysis system with semantic computing for agricultural health conditions monitoring and real-time management. In: 2016 International Electronics Symposium (IES) (2016)
6. Wyawahare, M., Kulkarni, P., Kulkarni, A., Lad, A., Majji, J., Mehta, A.: Agricultural field analysis using satellite surface reflectance data and machine learning technique. In: Singh, M., Gupta, P.K., Tyagi, V., Flusser, J., Ören, T., Valentino, G. (eds.) ICACDS 2020. CCIS, vol. 1244, pp. 439–448. Springer, Singapore (2020). https://doi.org/10.1007/978-981-15-6634-9_40
7. Gorelick, N., Hancher, M., Dixon, M., Ilyushchenko, S., Thau, D., Moore, R.: Google earth engine: planetary-scale geospatial analysis for everyone. Remote Sens. Environ. **202**, 18–27 (2017)
8. Arabameri, A., Pourghasemi, H.R.: Spatial modeling of gully erosion using linear and quadratic discriminant analyses in GIS and R. In: Spatial Modeling in GIS and R for Earth and Environmental Sciences, pp. 299–321 (2019)

9. Alkhayrat, M., Aljnidi, M., Aljoumaa, K.: A comparative dimensionality reduction study in telecom customer segmentation using deep learning and PCA. Journal of Big Data **7**(1), 1–23 (2020). https://doi.org/10.1186/s40537-020-0286-0

10. Alla, S., Adari, S.K.: Autoencoders. In: Beginning Anomaly Detection Using Python-Based Deep Learning, pp. 123–178 (2019)

11. Sakketou, F., Ampazis, N.: On the invariance of the SELU activation function on algorithm and hyperparameter selection in neural network recommenders. In: MacIntyre, J., Maglogiannis, I., Iliadis, L., Pimenidis, E. (eds.) AIAI 2019. IAICT, vol. 559, pp. 673–685. Springer, Cham (2019). https://doi.org/10.1007/978-3-030-19823-7_56

12. Subasi, A.: Clustering examples. In: Practical Machine Learning for Data Analysis Using Python, pp. 465–511 (2020)

13. Marutho, D., Hendra Handaka, S., Wijaya, E., Muljono: The determination of cluster number at k-mean using elbow method and purity evaluation on headline news. In: International Seminar on Application for Technology of Information and Communication (2018)

14. Breiman, L.: Random forests. Mach. Learn. **45**, 5–32 (2001)

15. Pal, K., Patel, B.V.: Data classification with k-fold cross validation and holdout accuracy estimation methods with 5 different machine learning techniques. In: Fourth International Conference on Computing Methodologies and Communication (ICCMC) (2020)

Development of NDVI Prediction Model Using Artificial Neural Networks

Sandeep V. Gaikwad[1]($\boxtimes$), Amol D. Vibhute[2], and Karbhari V. Kale[1]

[1] Department of Computer Science and IT, Dr. Babasaheb Ambedkar Marathwada
University, Aurangabad 431004, MH, India
sandeep.gaikwad22@gmail.com
[2] School of Computer Science, MIT-World Peace University, Pune 411038, MH, India

Abstract. The use of remotely sensed images in the agriculture sector plays a vital role in knowing crop status on a higher spatial scale.
Researchers have developed various indices for this purpose. The Normalized Difference Vegetation Index (NDVI) is an important indices
that measure the vegetation vigor of crop. The agricultural community
has shown its uses in various applications, viz. crop growth assessment,
crop health monitoring, crop yield estimation, etc. The NDVI forecasting helps to make an educated guess, based on its temporal behavior in
past years, on likely vegetation conditions ahead of time and thus supports decision-makers to formulate mitigation strategies. In this paper,
Moderate-resolution Imaging Spectroradiometer (MODIS) satellite data
has been used to calculate the NDVI, and then NDVI forecasting is
performed based on 2002–2014 NDVI time-series data. The results are
promising and can be used in agricultural applications.

Keywords: Artificial neural network · NDVI · Drought prediction ·
MODIS data · Vegetation cover classification

1 Introduction

The agricultural drought is associated with various subjects like agriculture,
meteorology, hydrology, and plant physiology and is an interaction field for natural and artificial systems [9]. Remote sensing techniques are vital in agricultural
applications for identifying crop stress, crop pigment analysis, and crop disease
analysis [7,13]. Remotely sensed data collected by hyperspectral sensors contain
large continuous narrow wavebands [6,14] that provide essential information
about the crop plants' biochemical and biophysical properties and their different physiological processes [3], which otherwise are unclear in multispectral data.
However, time series gap is more in hyperspectral datasets which is not suitable
for drought prediction. Conversely, the historical time series remote sensing data
and vegetation indices are helpful in drought monitoring, crop yield prediction,

© Springer Nature Switzerland AG 2022
KC Santosh et al. (Eds.): RTIP2R 2021, CCIS 1576, pp. 376–384, 2022.
https://doi.org/10.1007/978-3-031-07005-1_32

detecting weather impacts, and other events relevant to ecology and agriculture [4]. The NDVI, Standard Precipitation Index (SPI), Temperature Condition Index (TCI), and Vegetation Condition Index (VCI) are the most used methods for the analysis of various droughts using time series datasets [7,12]. Furthermore, the artificial neural network-based approach is widely used in developing NDVI-based prediction models to predict and monitor crop status and yield estimation. These methodologies are used in analyzing agricultural droughts.

2   Literature Survey

Several studies have been reported in the literature to predict the drought conditions using spectral indices and machine learning methods. For instance, the authors [4] investigated the study for analyzing the agricultural droughts based on SPI and NDVI relationship to predict wheat production. They developed the NDVI derived prediction models to predict the crop yield with reasonable accuracy [4]. Similarly, the drought prediction model has been developed using SPI, NDVI, TCI, and VCI indices and machine learning algorithms [8]. The developed models were trained using time series data of 30 years and used to predict the drought conditions. The authors [10] have discussed the importance of the spectral properties of crop genotypes, biotic stress, and some physical properties such as chlorophyll, LAI, and soil moisture. In addition, they also have focused on principle component analysis and artificial neural network models for agricultural applications [11]. The authors [15] have focused on seasonal cumulative NDVI based on MODIS data. They have developed a deep learning-based model to predict the drought. Conversely, the monitoring of Rabi crops has been done using NDVI models based on time series MODIS datasets [2]. A similar case study was conducted by [1] to determine the vegetation-precipitation relationship based on NDVI and SPI. The experiment was carried out for the investigation of drought impacts on crops and the environment. However, these studies do not focus on developing time-series NDVI-based models to predict crop health. Therefore, in the present study, we have focused on developing an NDVI-based prediction model using an artificial neural network in the MATLAB platform.

3   Study Area

The study area is located at 20.087 North, 74.683 West latitude, 19.82 South, 74.927 East longitude. Figure 1 shows the study area of the Vaijapur tehsil of Aurangabad district, Maharashtra, India. The region's average rainfall is 520–750 mm, and temperature ranges (34–42 °C) minimum and maximum temperature. The study area comes under the scanty rainfall region; therefore, the region faces drought episodes every 2–3 years.

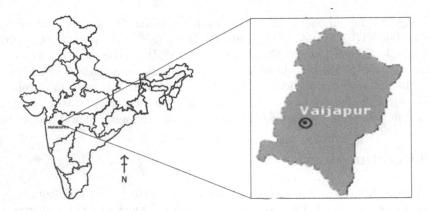

Fig. 1. The study area of the Vaijapur Tehsil of Aurangabad district, Maharashtra, India

4   Dataset

In the present study, MODIS-NDVI datasets were used. The spatial resolution of the MODIS product is 250 m. These datasets were computed from atmospherically corrected bidirectional surface reflectance's masked for water, clouds, aerosols, and cloud shadows. Moreover, the 16-day Maximum Value Composite (MVC) of NDVI product from MODIS-Terra (MOD13A1) was prepared to develop the NDVI prediction model. It provides consistent spatial and temporal information of the vegetation conditions. The dataset information is given in Table 1.

Table 1. Satellite dataset information used for the present study

Dataset	Sensor	Spatial resolution	Interval	Range	Data source
NDVI MOD13Q1	MODIS	250 m	16 day	2002–2014	USGS EarthExplorer

5   Methodology

The methodology has been implemented using Python, MATLAB, and ArcGIS platforms to develop NDVI prediction models and process the satellite images. The workflow of the proposed methodology is demonstrated in Fig. 2 that shows the proposed neural network architectures for predicting drought conditions based on features extracted from MODIS imagery. The significant steps followed in methodology are discussed in detail for the model development.

5.1   Preprocessing

Initially, the preprocessed satellite (MODIS (MOD13Q1) NDVI) time-series datasets were obtained from the USGS earth explorer. The provider has provided

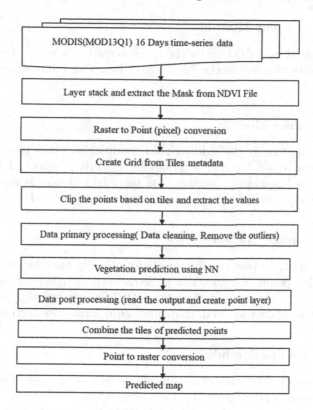

Fig. 2. The workflow of the NDVI prediction model using artificial neural network

atmospheric, geometric, and radiometric corrected datasets. Therefore, we have not done a similar preprocessing. The layer stack utility was used to create a stack of the historical time series of NDVI images. Moreover, the generated and stacked NDVI file was stored in the destination folder. Further, the Area of Interest (AOI) file has been used to mask the non- NDVI images in the destination folder.

5.2 Normalised Difference Vegetation Index (NDVI)

Subsequently, we have used the MODIS NDVI product for vegetation health monitoring. The NDVI (Eq. 1) is based on the difference between the Near Infrared (NIR) and a red visible (RED) band of the electromagnetic spectrum [4,5].

$$NDVI = (\rho NIR - \rho RED)/(\rho NIR + \rho RED) \tag{1}$$

where ρNIR indicates the values of the surface reflectance in a near-infrared region and ρRED indicates the surface reflectance values in a red region of the electromagnetic spectrum.

5.3   Raster to Point Module

The raster to point module converts the masked raster layer into the point value, which is the primary input to the ANN algorithm. This information is stored in CSV format.

5.4   Grid of Tiles Module

The following module is the grid of tiles module, which is used to create a grid using the polygon layer. The grid tiles module is essential for handling the dataset in a low-memory device. The metadata of tiles is stored into the temporary variables that are further used to generate the grid.

5.5   Point Clipping Module

The grid of points and tiles are the inputs for the clip modules, which are used to clip each tile's points. Additionally, it extracts the attribute of the point from the NDVI dataset. The number of inputs NDVI images and clipped points in a file are the same that are saved in shapefile (.shp) format for further processing.

5.6   Data Cleaning Module

It is used to remove the outliers and missing data points from the dataset by iterating the image's pixel-by-pixel value and generating the attribute table. The data cleaning tool transfers the spatial dataset to the suitable data structure for the ANN training and testing in the MATLAB environment.

5.7   Architecture of the ANN

The architecture of the ANN is essential for designing the training, testing, and implementing the network. Every ANN includes several layers and neurons, learning parameters, and input and output functions. The third and fourth sub iteration stores the predicted values and location coordinates in the excel file. The tool stores the Mean Square Error (MSE) of each time series in the georeferenced output raster file. Figure 3 shows the architecture of the ANN.

5.8   Vegetation Cover Prediction Module Using MATLAB

We have provided training data to the ANN algorithm for the prediction of the NDVI values. The entire module is written in a MATLAB script. MATLAB provides convenient functions for designing the ANN models. Firstly, it iterates the shape-files tiles, which consist of the NDVI dataset. Afterward, it constructs the sub iteration from time-series data suitable for ANN training. The sub iteration is used to create the testing data from the time series data set. It also creates the predicted values with an attribute in a CSV file.

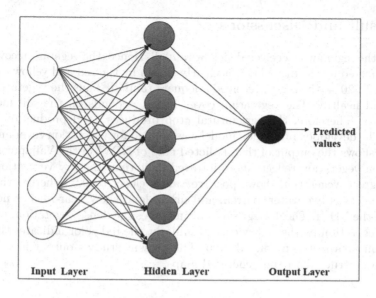

Fig. 3. The architectural details of the neural network

5.9 Data Post-processing Module

This module has used to read the CSV files and generate the point layer of the predicted values. Furthermore, the data point layer is converted as a shapefile in the destination folder.

5.10 Predicted Points Module

This module is used to handle the predicted points, and it merges the point layer into one feature class of predicted values.

5.11 Point of Raster

The point of the raster module is used to perform interpolating raster grid data from grid point and predicted values of the NDVI index. It also creates the metadata file, which includes the information of a coordinate system, height, and width of the NDVI imagery.

5.12 Predicted Map

Finally, the predicted image of NDVI was generated using the ANN algorithm, which is further imported into the ArcGIS software to prepare the prediction map. Moreover, the coordinate grids, true-north direction, scale, and legends were added to the predicted map.

6   Result and Discussions

In 2013, the region was received deficient rainfall. Hence, the vegetation cover was highly affected by the drought. It is clearly shown by the red and yellow color on the map. In 2014, the region received adequate rainfall. Thus the vegetation was dense and healthy. The vegetation cover highly depends on the soil moisture availability. Therefore, the agricultural crop produces good production in the region. The developed prediction model was applied for vegetation cover analysis. Figure 4 shows the output of the predicted map of NDVI of the Vaijapur region. The green vegetation reflects more infrared light than the dry vegetation. The healthy green vegetation shows positive values closer to 0.9, whereas the non-vegetation areas like water, barren, and urban land show near-zero or negative values of the NDVI. The dark green color indicates the dense vegetation, whereas typical vegetation by the yellow color. Similarly, the red color indicates the non-vegetation area in the predicted map. The present study's output is validated with ground truth data and generated maps.

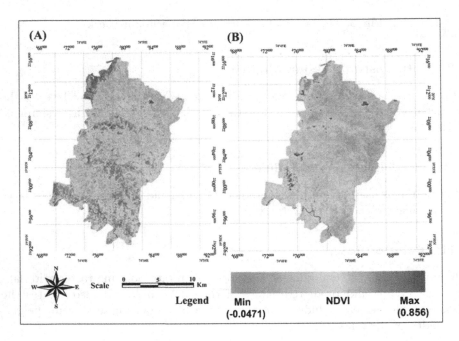

Fig. 4. Predicted map of NDVI of the year (A) 2013 and (B) 2014 (Color figure online)

7   Conclusions

The proposed model was developed using Python, ArcPy, and MATLAB script. MATLAB provides the functions to implement the neural network architecture.

The present research study discusses the development of the model for predicting the vegetation cover using the NDVI time-series dataset and the artificial neural network algorithm. The system requires the historical time series datasets to predict the values of the NDVI of the region. It is significantly used for the vegetation health analysis of the region.

Acknowledgments. The authors are thankful to UGC for providing BSR fellowship and lab facilities under UGC-SAP (II) DRS Phase-I F.No.-3-42/2009, Phase-II 4-15/2015/DRS-II for this study. The authors are also thankful to the Department of Agriculture, Vaijapur Tehsil, for sharing the necessary information for this research study.

References

1. Adede, C., Oboko, R., Wagacha, P.W., Atzberger, C.: A mixed model approach to vegetation condition prediction using artificial neural networks (ANN): case of Kenya's operational drought monitoring. Remote Sens. **11**(9), 1099 (2019)
2. Dempewolf, J., et al.: Wheat yield forecasting for Punjab province from vegetation index time series and historic crop statistics. Remote Sens. **6**(10), 9653–9675 (2014)
3. Dhumal, R.K., et al.: A spatial and spectral feature based approach for classification of crops using techniques based on GLCM and SVM. In: Panda, G., Satapathy, S.C., Biswal, B., Bansal, R. (eds.) Microelectronics, Electromagnetics and Telecommunications. LNEE, vol. 521, pp. 45–53. Springer, Singapore (2019). https://doi.org/10.1007/978-981-13-1906-8_5
4. Dutta, D., Kundu, A., Patel, N.: Predicting agricultural drought in eastern Rajasthan of India using NDVI and standardized precipitation index. Geocarto Int. **28**(3), 192–209 (2013)
5. Gaikwad, S.V., Vibhute, A.D., Kale, K.V.: Design and implementation of a Web-GIS platform for monitoring of vegetation status. ICTACT J. Image Video Process. **11**(3), 2373–2377 (2021)
6. Gaikwad, S.V., et al.: Drought severity identification and classification of the land pattern using Landsat 8 data based on spectral indices and maximum likelihood algorithm. In: Panda, G., Satapathy, S.C., Biswal, B., Bansal, R. (eds.) Microelectronics, Electromagnetics and Telecommunications. LNEE, vol. 521, pp. 517–524. Springer, Singapore (2019). https://doi.org/10.1007/978-981-13-1906-8_53
7. Gaikwad, S.V., et al.: Identification and classification of water stressed crops using hyperspectral data: a case study of Paithan tehsil. In: Krishna, C.R., Dutta, M., Kumar, R. (eds.) Proceedings of 2nd International Conference on Communication, Computing and Networking. LNNS, vol. 46, pp. 911–919. Springer, Singapore (2019). https://doi.org/10.1007/978-981-13-1217-5_89
8. Jalili, M., Gharibshah, J., Ghavami, S.M., Beheshtifar, M., Farshi, R.: Nationwide prediction of drought conditions in Iran based on remote sensing data. IEEE Trans. Comput. **63**(1), 90–101 (2013)
9. Liu, X., Zhu, X., Pan, Y., Li, S., Liu, Y., Ma, Y.: Agricultural drought monitoring: progress, challenges, and prospects. J. Geog. Sci. **26**(6), 750–767 (2016). https://doi.org/10.1007/s11442-016-1297-9
10. Mishra, N., Soni, H.K., Sharma, S., Upadhyay, A.: Development and analysis of artificial neural network models for rainfall prediction by using time-series data. Int. J. Intell. Syst. Appl. **10**(1) (2018)

11. Morid, S., Smakhtin, V., Bagherzadeh, K.: Drought forecasting using artificial neural networks and time series of drought indices. Int. J. Climatol. J. R. Meteorol. Soc. **27**(15), 2103–2111 (2007)
12. Reddy, D.S., Prasad, P.R.C.: Prediction of vegetation dynamics using NDVI time series data and LSTM. Model. Earth Syst. Environ. **4**(1), 409–419 (2018). https://doi.org/10.1007/s40808-018-0431-3
13. Vibhute, A.D., Gawali, B.W.: Analysis and modeling of agricultural land use using remote sensing and geographic information system: a review. Int. J. Eng. Res. Appl. **3**(3), 081–091 (2013)
14. Vibhute, A.D., Kale, K., Dhumal, R.K., Mehrotra, S.: Hyperspectral imaging data atmospheric correction challenges and solutions using QUAC and FLAASH algorithms. In: 2015 International Conference on Man and Machine Interfacing (MAMI), pp. 1–6. IEEE (2015)
15. Zambrano, F., Vrieling, A., Nelson, A., Meroni, M., Tadesse, T.: Prediction of drought-induced reduction of agricultural productivity in Chile from MODIS, rainfall estimates, and climate oscillation indices. Remote Sens. Environ. **219**, 15–30 (2018)

Time Series Forecasting of Soil Moisture Using Satellite Images

K. V. Arya(iD) and Suggula Jagadeesh$^{(\boxtimes)}$

ABV-Indian Institute of Information Technology and Management, Gwalior, India
kvarya@iiitm.ac.in, jagadeeshsuggula23@gmail.com

Abstract. Soil moisture is one of the critical factors in hydrological cycles and agricultural production. Prediction of Soil Moisture content is essential for the rational use and management of water resources. This paper uses measured soil moisture satellite images captured by the SMAP satellite to train the models. Current day time series forecasting approaches are only applicable to tabular data. In this paper, we suggest a pipeline/framework that uses Dimensionality Reduction and Time Series Forecasting techniques for forecasting satellite image time series. Using this pipeline/framework, we can forecast undiscovered soil moisture from past satellite observations. To examine our final pipeline performance, we will conduct experiments for different models to forecast future satellite images from historical satellite images. Finally we can use these predictions to provide strategies for a drought resistant irrigation system.

Keywords: Soil moisture · CNN · PCA · LSTM · Dimensionality reduction · Time series forecasting · SMAP

1 Introduction

Soil Moisture is the amount of water stored in the soil which becomes one of the crucial factors for hydrological cycles and agricultural production, and its precise prediction is essential for the rational use and management of water resources. Soil moisture not only plays a vital role in maintaining plant growth but also is a critical link in the water cycle of soil-plant-atmosphere continuum systems. Soil moisture is a crucial control of evaporation and transpiration at the land atmosphere boundary [11].

Day by Day, due to various human activities, the quality of groundwater resources is deteriorating, and the amount of excavation for the same has significantly risen. The continuous decrease of groundwater levels will lead to a reduction of soil's effective water storage capacity and the soil moisture levels [7].

The growth and decrement of soil moisture directly affect water consumption and the development of crops. Soil Moisture is also an essential indicator of drought resistance, flood control, and precision irrigation decisions in agricultural production. Therefore, Soil Moisture Forecasting is essential for an efficient

© Springer Nature Switzerland AG 2022
KC Santosh et al. (Eds.): RTIP2R 2021, CCIS 1576, pp. 385–397, 2022.
https://doi.org/10.1007/978-3-031-07005-1_33

management of water resources. Most of the current techniques use remote sensors to collect and measure soil moisture which is then used for forecasting. Hence it became usable only for that specific area. Using these remote techniques on a large scale requires more money to purchase that equipment and time to collect data. To overcome this problem we will use satellite images obtained from SMAP satellite to forecast over a large area at once [2]. By using this approach we can save labour cost and time to get the data and for building separate models for each area.

This paper is aimed to integrate Dimensionality Reduction techniques and Time Series Forecasting techniques to make a prediction system that predicts future satellite observations upto next 7 days using forecasting techniques based on past data regular patterns to manage agricultural water resources and promote the increase of crop yield appropriately.

The rest of the paper is organized in the following manner. Sect. 2 discusses the analysis of existing work. The proposed methodology is explained in Sect. 3. The results of the implementation of proposed work is described in Sect. 4. Finally the work is summarized in Sect. 5.

2   Literature Review

Soil moisture is one of the critical factors in hydrological cycles and agricultural production, and its prediction is essential for the rational use and management of water resources. Soil moisture plays a vital role in maintaining plant growth and is a crucial link in the water cycle of soil-plant-atmosphere continuum systems.

Generally, the soil moisture data is collected using remote sensing techniques which are then stored in a specific format. This data is further processed and analyzed by plotting graphs. Later, this data is used to train the forecasting models. Cai et al. (2019) took the Beijing area as the research object, and a model with data fitting capability was proposed to forecast the soil moisture by integrating the dataset and analyzing the time series of the predictive variables [7]. However, this method is only specific to a particular area. Using these remote techniques on a large scale requires more money to purchase that equipment and time to collect data.

All the traditional time series forecasting techniques use statistical methods like ARIMA models [5], or regression methods like Support Vector Regression [15], Polynomial Regression etc. Then Pai et al. (2010) came up with a hybrid approach on combining both statistical models and regression models [15]. But recently, multivariate time series data has been increasing by the day. In many cases, multivariate time series data are having high variables, they are high dimensional and or have noise in data. This type of data, is difficult to forecast using these methods. Another problem with these methods are that they can only predict one step ahead at a time. One step ahead prediction is not useful in all cases, In our case we require a multistep forecast to have an early warning in case of any droughts [8].

With the advantages of recurrent neural networks, a type of neural memory network, many research studies discovered structural separation's effectiveness into discrete encoder and decoder units for both sequenced input and output. This RNN encoder decoder architecture associated with two separated RNNs as an encoder and divaricated decoder parts can be used for multi timestep forecasting [9].

Traditional time series forecasting methods use structured data for forecasts. Here, the data in the form of images (unstructured data). Generally, images are of higher dimensions when compared to tabular data. So we should use dimensionality reduction techniques to reduce the dimensions of images. Wang et al. (2016) tried to investigate the dimensionality reduction ability and see if it has some kind of good property compared with techniques like PCA, LDA, etc. [17].

3   Methodology

3.1   Hardware Setup

In this section, we will see the details of the hardware setup used for this research. We would also thank Google Colab for providing free cloud GPU/CPU services for training the model. The detailed specifications of the setup is shown in Table 1.

Table 1. Hardware setup specifications used in our research

Setup	Specification
Processor (CPU)	Intel Core i7-7700HQ 7th Gen
System memory (RAM) size	8GB DDR4
Graphics (GPU)	Nvidia GeForce GTX 1050
Graphics Memory	4GB GDDR5

3.2   The Proposed Pipeline

In this section, we will see various steps involved in training our pipeline starting from preprocessing of the data, to training the models and comparing their efficiency. All the phases of the project are shown in the work-flow diagram depicted in Fig. 1.

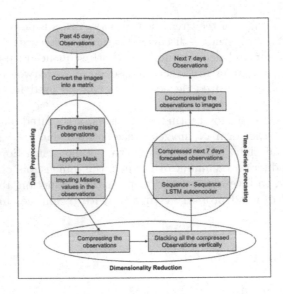

Fig. 1. Workflow diagram

3.3 Dataset Overview

Data is shared publicly by the Meteorological and Oceanographic Satellite Data Archival Centre (MOSDAC). Data is available from MOSDAC in the form of satellite images in gray scale [3]. MOSDAC is an ISRO data portal that provides data through its web-based service. These images are captured by the SMAP spacecraft. The objective of SMAP(Soil Moisture Active/Passive) spacecraft is to monitor soil moisture on a global level and give a mapping with outstanding resolution, area coverage, sensitivity, and revisit times [1,2].

The dataset contains the Indian mosaic of the global soil moisture map. The mosaic consists of a heatmap of the Soil wetness index. The mosaic is standardized to the extreme values of 0 and 1, referring to the dry and saturated soil wetness conditions, respectively. The dimensions of the images are 256 × 272. The portal contains data since 4th April 2015. Figure 2 is the Indian mosaic captured by SMAP spacecraft on date 30–06-2015.

Train/Test Split: When working with time series data, we should also consider the temporal order when splitting the data. The data is split into two parts training set and testing set. The training set consists of data from the period of 4th April 2015 to 29th March 2020. The testing set consists of data from the period of 24th May 2020 to 9th October 2020. The models are fitted on the training set and validated on the testing set.

Fig. 2. The Indian mosaic captured by SMAP satellite on 30–06-2015 [3]

3.4   Data Preprocessing

The images downloaded from the MOSDAC portal are in the Tagged Image File Format (TIFF) format. TIFF format is the most commonly used industry-standard file format. These file formats are usually uncompressed which makes it more suitable for further processing.

The images in the dataset contains Not an Number (NaN) values. After reading the images, we can see that all the background pixels are represented as NaN values. There are also NaN values in the foreground pixels. These NaN values represent missing values. These foreground missing values have occurred due to loss in transmission of data from the SMAP satellite. If we do not remove the missing values, they will cause interference during training process.

To remove these NaN values, a mask had been created using the images in the dataset for separating the foreground and the background pixels and the mask was then used for replacing the background missing values with 0.

To replace the foreground missing values, the temporal order among the images should also be considered while replacing the missing values. Linear interpolation is a technique for fitting a curve using linear polynomials to replace missing values with new data points using the existing data. The missing values are filled with respect to each pixel of the image series by making use of the respective previous year observations. With this we are left with the missing values of the first year of the dataset. We will apply linear interpolation followed by a forward and backward fill to replace the remaining missing values. Figure 3 shows how the raw image captured by satellite on 29th June 2018 is preprocessed. The first image is the original image (We can see the data is missing in the image), the second image is the one after applying the mask on the original image, and the last image depicts the final preprocessed image with the missing values imputed.

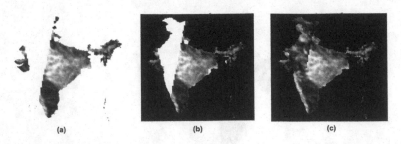

Fig. 3. Data preprocessing on image taken by the SMAP satellite on date 29–06-2018. (a) Raw image (b) Masked image (c) Imputed image

3.5 Dimensionality Reduction

Images are unstructured data with very high dimensions, hence large amount of resources are required to process them and leading the problem of curse of dimensionality. To avoid this problem we use techniques like dimensionality reduction. The images are compressed by reducing the number of dimensions. The transformation is done in a way, such that the low dimensional feature space retains the most important properties of the original data. In this paper we have experimented with Principal Component Analysis and Convolutional AutoEncoders for compressing our satellite image observations.

- *Principal Component Analysis*
  Principal component analysis (PCA) is a linear approach for dimensionality reduction. PCA is a multivariate technique that derives principal components by analysing the data where dependent variables are correlated. The goal of PCA is to extract important information from the data into the principal components. These principal components are uncorrelated with each other, and orthogonal to each other [4].
- *Convolutional AutoEncoders*
  Autoencoders recreate each dimension of the input by passing it through the network. During this process, the input size reduces into a smaller representation across the network. The hidden layers of the Autoencoder have a lesser number of units as compared to that of the input or output layers. Therefore, the middle layers hold the reduced representation of the input, also known as an encoded representation. The output gets reconstructed from this encoded representation of the input [17].

Since our data is in the form of images, we have used convolutional neural networks (CNN) as encoders and decoders. We use a Convolutional Autoencoder for encoding the images. Totally three architectures are designed for the CAE with latent space size of 544 units. These architectures vary in the output layer activation function. Sigmoid, ReLu, and TanH activations are used at the output. Figure 4 shows the encoder architecture used for training in this paper. It is a deep convolutional network used for learning the critical features from an input image. The image goes through multiple convolutions, and the system obtains high-level as well as low-level features. To avoid the problem of vanishing gradients, we added some skip connections to ensure that the gradients propagate through to deeper layers without much diminishing.

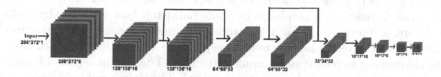

Fig. 4. Encoder architecture of autoencoder with 544 latent space units

Figure 5 shows the decoder architecture used for training in this paper. It is a deep convolutional transpose network used for reconstructing the image from the latent space representation. The network uses high-level features obtained from the latent space representation and tries to reproduce the input image with less reconstruction loss. This network architecture is symmetrically opposite to that of encoder architecture.

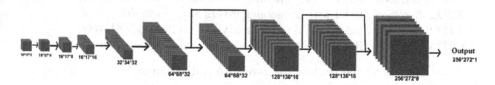

Fig. 5. Decoder architecture of autoencoder with 544 latent space units

3.6   Time Series Forecasting

Time series forecasting is an important technique for analyzing data which have a temporal behavior and forecast future values. It is widely applied in many fields, e.g. power load forecasting, air quality forecasting, medical monitoring, and intrusion detection [6,10].

In this paper, we use Recurrent Neural Networks which uses sequential data or temporal data. These neural networks are generally used for temporal or ordinal problems, such as language translation, sentimental analysis, time series forecasting. In RNN, the output is dependent on the prior sequence of input within the sequence. RNNs have a special memory unit which takes information from previous inputs to influence the current output. But they can not maintain a long-term dependency between different time steps of the data. They also faced the problem of vanishing gradients in the case of long-term dependencies and thus, the weights could not be properly updated during the backpropagation steps. To overcome this problem, Long Short Term Memory Networks (LSTMs) were introduced. In this work, they help in remembering the necessary information and discarding the unnecessary ones. LSTMs have a separate memory cell to remember information unlike regular RNN's [12].

In this paper, we use sequence to sequence learning model of RNN [16] for time series forecasting, which helps to make multistep forecast easily by adding two layers, a repeat vector layer and time distributed dense layer in the architecture. A repeat vector layer is used to repeat the context vector which we get from the encoder to pass it as an input to decoder. The output received from the decoder with respect to each time step is mixed, The timedistributed dense, will apply a fully connected dense layer on each time step and separates the output for each timestep. We also propose stacking additional layers on encoder part and the decoder part of the sequence to sequence model. By stacking LSTM's enables understanding of more complex representation of our time-series data in hidden layers, by capturing information at different levels. We have trained models for 5 different architectures, they vary with respect to the no of stacked layers. Figure 6 shows the representation of the architecture of Seq2Seq Model with 2 encoder layers and 2 decoder layers (E2D2 Model).

- **E1D1**: Seq2Seq Model with 1 encoder layer and 1 decoder layer.
- **E2D1**: Seq2Seq Model with 2 encoder layers and 1 decoder layer.
- **E2D2**: Seq2Seq Model with 2 encoder layers and 2 decoder layers.
- **E3D2**: Seq2Seq Model with 3 encoder layers and 2 decoder layers.
- **E3D3**: Seq2Seq Model with 3 encoder layers and 3 decoder layers.

After training all the models, we have also trained an ensemble model using the predictions from the above models.

4   Results

In this section, we discuss the evaluation metrics used in this work, the results of the techniques used for dimensionality reduction and time series forecasting in the project which are trained on the preprocessed dataset.

4.1   Evaluation Metrics

The evaluation metrics used for comparison in this work are as follows

- *Mean Absolute Error*
  Mean Absolute Error (MAE) is the mean of all absolute differences between the true values and measured values. The formula to calculate mean absolute error between two images f and g is

$$MAE(f,g) = \frac{1}{m \times n} \times \sum_{i=0}^{m} \sum_{j=0}^{n} |f_{ij} - g_{ij}| \tag{1}$$

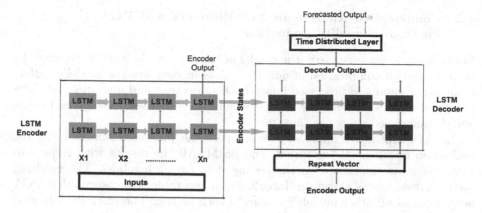

Fig. 6. Architecture of a sequence - sequence LSTM autoencoder (E2D2) [14]

– *Peak Signal to Noise ratio*
PSNR is an image comparison ratio which is calculated with the help of Mean
Square error. It ranges from 0 to *infinity*. The higher the PSNR value, then
the images are more similar[13]. The formula to calculate PSNR is

$$PSNR(f,g) = 10 \times log_{10} \left(\frac{255^2}{MSE(f,g)} \right) \qquad (2)$$

where MSE = Mean Squared Error

$$MSE(f,g) = \frac{1}{m \times n} \times \sum_{i=0}^{m} \sum_{j=0}^{n} (f_{ij} - g_{ij})^2 \qquad (3)$$

– *Structural Similarity Index Measure*
PSNR and MAE gives an estimate of absolute error between two images.
SSIM is a quality metric used to calculate the similarity between two images.
SSIM is calculated as a combination of three factors of image that are loss of
correlation, luminance distortion and contrast distortion[13] The formula to
calculate SSIM is

$$SSIM(f,g) = l(f,g) \times c(f,g) \times s(f,g) \qquad (4)$$

where $l(f,g)$ = luminance comparison, $c(f,g)$ = contrast comparison, $s(f,g)$ =
structure comparison.

$$l(f,g) = \frac{(2\mu_f\mu_g + c_1)}{\mu_f^2 + \mu_g^2 + c_1} \qquad (5)$$

$$c(f,g) = \frac{(2\sigma_f\sigma_g + c_2)}{\sigma_f^2 + \sigma_g^2 + c_2} \qquad (6)$$

$$s(f,g) = \frac{(\sigma_{fg} + c_3)}{\sigma_f + \sigma_g + c_3} \qquad (7)$$

where c_1, c_2, c_3 are positive constants used to avoid null denominator.

4.2 Comparative Analysis of AutoEncoders and PCA for Dimensionality Reduction

In this section, we summarize the results of experiments to analyze the model's performance on compression of our data. We can compare the model's performance of original and processed image both subjective, and quantitatively. The processed images here are the images which are compressed using the models and decompressed using the same model.

In the quantitative approach, we compare the processed images using the evaluation metrics - MAE, PSNR, and SSIM. All the results with respect to each metric are measured on the testing data for each model. The resulting metric values are as shown in Table 2. From the table, we observe that PCA outperformed all other models in terms of each metric. Therefore PCA is used for dimensionality reduction in the project.

Table 2. Comparative analysis of different dimensionality reduction techniques on our dataset

Model	MAE	PSNR	SSIM
PCA	0.00987	32.2307	0.9775
Sigmoid AutoEncoder	0.11955	17.8431	0.2342
Tanh AutoEncoder	0.05517	20.3703	0.46478
Relu AutoEncoder	0.03333	21.3733	0.86290

In the subjective approach, we compare the processed images visually. From Fig. 7, we can say that the output obtained from the model trained using Principal Component Analysis looks a lot similar to the original image. The output obtained from the model trained on the CAE with sigmoid activation function looks blurred when compared to the original image. The output obtained from the model trained on the CAE with Tanh activation function looks oversaturated. The output obtained from the model trained on the CAE with ReLu activation function looks dimmer when compared with original image.

Fig. 7. Outputs of images processed through trained dimensionality reduction models.

4.3 Comparative Analysis of Different LSTM Architectures for Forecasting

In this section, we summarize the results of experiments to evaluate the efficiency of our models in forecasting our results. All models are trained for only 50 epochs due to limited number of resources. Since we are passing the compressed representation of our images, we will get our forecast output in compressed representation. This compressed forecast output is decompressed using the trained PCA model. Now we will have forecast output in form of images, which will be used for calculating the metrics. The metrics used for comparing the forecast images and the actual image on that date. The evaluation metrics used are MAE, PSNR, and SSIM. The results obtained from all the sequence to sequence models trained are evaluated on the basis of the metrics mentioned before and are stored with respect to each time step in Table 3, 4, 5. From the table, we can observe that the outputs obtained from the ensemble model outperformed all other model with respect to all metrics. The Fig. 8 shows the model predictions and the original observation given the input images from 20th July 2020 to 3rd September 2020 to the proposed pipeline. The second row represents the forecast observations of the pipeline. The first row represents the actual observations.

Table 3. Comparative analysis of different encoder decoder models using MAE metric

Model	Day 1	Day 2	Day 3	Day 4	Day 5	Day 6	Day 7
E1D1	0.05531	0.05479	0.05458	0.05454	0.05461	0.05474	0.05491
E2D1	0.05728	0.05539	0.05477	0.05525	0.05621	0.05711	0.05801
E2D2	0.05629	0.05603	0.05578	0.05523	0.05448	0.05384	0.05343
E3D2	0.05273	0.05123	0.05082	0.05093	0.05129	0.05181	0.05239
E3D3	0.05474	0.05404	0.05311	0.05218	0.05131	0.05048	0.04969
Ensemble	0.05007	0.04658	0.04563	0.04488	0.04463	0.04451	0.04450

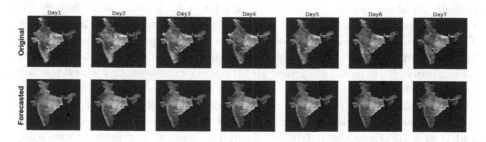

Fig. 8. Forecasted vs Actual images on test data

Table 4. Comparative analysis of different encoder decoder models using PSNR metric

Model	Day 1	Day 2	Day 3	Day 4	Day 5	Day 6	Day 7
E1D1	17.6977	17.7847	17.8206	17.8305	17.8225	17.8121	17.7976
E2D1	17.38692	17.68849	17.78124	17.70986	17.57711	17.44644	17.32045
E2D2	17.58196	17.63901	17.68663	17.77042	17.88177	17.98441	18.06382
E3D2	18.05096	18.26491	18.32834	18.31098	18.26228	18.19406	18.11903
E3D3	17.88011	17.95690	18.07369	18.20166	18.33492	18.46862	18.59368
Ensemble	18.50468	19.19461	19.36398	19.49538	19.5281	19.54068	19.53014

Table 5. Comparative analysis of different encoder decoder models using SSIM metric

Model	Day 1	Day 2	Day 3	Day 4	Day 5	Day 6	Day 7
E1D1	0.85018	0.85116	0.85155	0.85164	0.85161	0.85157	0.85152
E2D1	0.84050	0.84627	0.84896	0.84969	0.84929	0.84838	0.84717
E2D2	0.85083	0.85176	0.85258	0.85388	0.85551	0.85693	0.85784
E3D2	0.85245	0.85546	0.85675	0.85733	0.85761	0.85766	0.85751
E3D3	0.85341	0.85525	0.85722	0.85906	0.86073	0.86233	0.86383
Ensemble	0.86250	0.86995	0.87018	0.87141	0.87149	0.87156	0.87138

5   Conclusions and Future Scope

In this paper, we propose an end-to-end Pipeline for satellite image time series forecasting, which combines the idea of dimensionality reduction and time series forecasting with encoder-decoder learning structure with LSTM. We found by experimenting on autoencoders and PCA that PCA outperforms auto-encoders when dealing with compression of satellite images because in satellite images the structure of the image remains same for all images, like the outline of India in our dataset. There is a high chance of correlation among the pixels of the satellite images, which is captured well by PCA.

In our work, we have experimented different architectures for forecasting the soil moisture. Since Soil Moisture is related to nature many factors like weather affect it. These factors are responsible for the randomness in the series. This randomness decreases the model's performance in predicting accurately. In future the model needs to be trained continuously for identifying new patterns and improving the model efficiency, and the work can be more focused towards improving the forecasting efficiency by using advance techniques like Attention Models, Transformers, etc. which requires more computation power. Interpolating the missing values in a good way requires some domain expertise knowledge and it also increases the reliability of our predictions. For better forecasting, features like weather and factors which affect soil moisture can also be included while training the models.

References

1. Smap - soil moisture active passive – nasa. https://smap.jpl.nasa.gov/mission/description/
2. Smap (soil moisture active/passive) mission. https://directory.eoportal.org/web/eoportal/satellite-missions/s/smap
3. Meteorological oceanographic satellite data archival centre, space applications centre. Isro (2017). https://mosdac.gov.in/soil-moisture-0
4. Abdi, H., Williams, L.J.: Principal component analysis. Wiley Interdisc. Rev.: Comput. Stat. **2**(4), 433–459 (2010)
5. Box, G.E., Pierce, D.A.: Distribution of residual autocorrelations in autoregressive-integrated moving average time series models. J. Am. stat. Assoc. **65**(332), 1509–1526 (1970)
6. Burba, D.: An overview of time series forecasting models (2019). https://towardsdatascience.com/an-overview-of-time-series-forecasting-models-a2fa7a358fcb
7. Cai, Y., Zheng, W., Zhang, X., Zhangzhong, L., Xue, X.: Research on soil moisture prediction model based on deep learning. PLoS One **14**(4), e0214508 (2019)
8. Chang, Y.Y., Sun, F.Y., Wu, Y.H., Lin, S.D.: A memory-network based solution for multivariate time-series forecasting. arXiv preprint. arXiv:1809.02105 (2018)
9. Cho, K., et al.: Learning phrase representations using rnn encoder-decoder for statistical machine translation. arXiv preprint. arXiv:1406.1078 (2014)
10. Du, S., Li, T., Yang, Y., Horng, S.J.: Multivariate time series forecasting via attention-based encoder-decoder framework. Neurocomputing **388**(C), 269–279 (2020)
11. Gill, M.K., Asefa, T., Kemblowski, M.W., McKee, M.: Soil moisture prediction using support vector machines 1. JAWRA J. Am. Water Resour. Assoc. **42**(4), 1033–1046 (2006)
12. Hochreiter, S., Schmidhuber, J.: Long short-term memory. Neural Comput. **9**(8), 1735–1780 (1997)
13. Horé, A., Ziou, D.: Image quality metrics: psnr versus ssim. In: Proceedings of the 2010 IEEE 20th International Conference on Pattern Recognition (2010)
14. Jagadeesh: Multivariate multi-step time series forecasting using stacked lstm sequence to sequence autoencoder in tensorflow 2.0 / keras (2020). https://rb.gy/fdlazo
15. Pai, P.F., Lin, K.P., Lin, C.S., Chang, P.T.: Time series forecasting by a seasonal support vector regression model. Expert Syst. Appl. **37**(6), 4261–4265 (2010)
16. Sutskever, I., Vinyals, O., Le, Q.V.: Sequence to sequence learning with neural networks. In: Advances in Neural Information Processing Systems (2014)
17. Wang, Y., Yao, H., Zhao, S.: Auto-encoder based dimensionality reduction. Neurocomputing **184**, 232–242 (2016)

Author Index

Printed in the United States
by Baker & Taylor Publisher Services